CATHOLIC UNIVERSITY SERIES.

VOL. II.

PROGRESSIVE LESSONS IN HEBREW

PROGRESSIVE
LESSONS IN HEBREW

WITH EXERCISES AND VOCABULARY

BY

REV. ROMAIN BUTIN, S. M., S. T. L., PH. D.
INSTRUCTOR IN SEMITICS, CATHOLIC UNIVERSITY OF AMERICA.

WIPF & STOCK • Eugene, Oregon

Wipf and Stock Publishers
199 W 8th Ave, Suite 3
Eugene, OR 97401

Progressive Lessons in Hebrew
With Exercises and Vocabulary
By Butin, Romain
ISBN 13: 978-1-60608-348-2
Publication date 01/09/2009
Previously published by Catholic Education Press, 1915

TO MY ALMA MATER

THE CATHOLIC UNIVERSITY OF AMERICA

IN HONOR OF

THE TWENTY-FIFTH ANNIVERSARY

OF ITS FOUNDATION

1889 - 1914.

PREFACE.

The Progressive Lessons in Hebrew are intended primarily for beginners, but may be used with equal profit by more advanced students. The aim of the author has been to make it possible for the student to learn the rules by applying them practically, rather than by studying them theoretically. The various signs necessary for reading and writing correctly and some general principles of Hebrew phonology having been summarized in the Introduction, the material of the grammar proper has been arranged in twenty-four lessons, one for each week. The simplest rules of inflection and syntax as well as the elementary structure of a nominal and verbal sentence are explained in the very first lessons, and thus the student is enabled from the beginning to form and translate the sentences given at the end of each lesson in the form of exercises. These exercises are intended as an essential part of the lesson; generally speaking, they contain no form or construction not already explained — which is also true of the examples in the body of the lessons — so that the student can always understand and analyze them without being perplexed by features with which he is not familiar. The sentences given in the exercises are mostly taken or adapted from the Bible and are equivalent to about ten ordinary Chapters of the Text. Besides, three full Chapters (Job, i, ii; Prov. iv) left unpointed are given at the end of the lessons, the pointing, parsing and translating of which will furnish the student the best means to test and improve his proficiency in the mastering of the rules explained in the grammar.

Special attention has been paid to the vocabulary, too often neglected in so-called elementary grammars. A certain number of words are given at the beginning of each lesson and an English-Hebrew vocabulary will be found at the end of the book.

For practical reasons, syntax has been treated along with the morphology, and the writer has often departed from the traditional order in the arrangement of the material. However, a logical index has been added with a view to facilitating a systematic review of the grammar, especially during the second and third readings.

As a complement to the „Progressive Lessons in Hebrew“, a Key is published separately, in which the exercises are translated and the proper method of studying the Lessons is briefly indicated.

We wish to acknowledge our indebtedness to Professors H. Hyvernat and F. Cöln for valuable suggestions and manifold help in the preparation of the work, and also to Dr. A. Vaschalde, who has kindly consented to read the proof-sheets.

Romain Butin.

The Catholic University
of America, April 1915.

TABLE OF CONTENTS.

Page

Preface IX

INTRODUCTION; Orthography and Phonology.

Tables of Consonants and Vowels 1

SECTION I. Elementary Rules for Reading and Writing.

§§

1—7. I. Remarks on the Consonants 3

A. *B·ghadhk·phath.* B. Emphatic Letters. C. *Literae finales.* D. *Literae dilatabiles*, 1. E. Quiescent Letters, 2—5. F. Classification of Consonants, 6. G. Consonants as Numerical Signs, 7.

8—19. II. Remarks on the Vowels 6

A. Full vowels, 8—13. B. Half-vowels, 14—16. C. Syllable-divider, Silent *Sh·wâ*, 17. D. Distinction between Vocal and Silent *Sh·wâ*, 18. E. Classification of vowels, 19.

III. Various Signs of Orthography and Orthoëpy.

20—23. A. *Dâghēsh Forte* 10

24—26. B. *Dâghesh Lene* 11

27. C. *Mappîq* 12

28. D. *Răphè* 12

29. E. *Maqqēph* 12

30—31. F. *Pâsēq* 12

32—36. G. *Méthegh* 12

37—39. IV. Tone or Word-Accent 13

40—42. V. Accents 14

43. VI. *Q·rê* and *K·thîbh* 15

SECTION II. Some Principles of Hebrew Phonology

44—53. A. The Hebrew Syllable 15

54—61. B. Changes in Vowels 17

62—65. C. Modifications of Consonants 19

66—76. D. Peculiarities of Gutturals and of *Rêsh* 19

1. With respect to *Dâghesh Forte*, 66—68. 2. With respect to Vowels, 69—71. 3. With respect to *Sh·wâ*, 72—74. 4. Letter *Rêsh*, 75—76.

77—79. E. Pause 21

LESSONS

LESSON I. Noun (Unchangeable vowels). Article. Nominal Sentence

I. Morphology.

§§

81—85. A. Substantive 24

1. Gender, 81—82. 2. Number, 83—85.

86. B. Adjective 25

87. C. Article 25

88. D. Particle "וְ" 26

II. Syntactical Remarks.

89—90. A. Rules for Article 26

91—92. B. Rules for Adjectives 26

93—95. C. Nominal Sentence 27

LESSON II. The Genitive. The Construct State. Particles בּ, כּ, לְ.

I. Construct State

96. A. Definition and explanation 30

97—99. B. Modification of Endings in Constr. State 30

100—105. C. Use of Constr. State 31

106—107. II. Expression of Genitive by Circumlocution 32

108—111. III. Remarks on the Particles 32

LESSON III. Form of Article before Gutturals. Verbal Sentence.

112—113. I. Article before Gutturals and *Resh* 35

114—117. II. The Verbal Sentence 36

LESSON IV. Gutturals (Review). *Nota Relationis* אֲשֶׁר, (שֶׁ).
The particles, אַ֫יִן, אֵין, יֵשׁ, לֹא.

119—121. I. Some of the Peculiarities of the Gutturals 39

122—123. II. *Nota Relationis* אֲשֶׁר, (שֶׁ) 40

124—126. III. The Particles אַ֫יִן, אֵין, יֵשׁ, לֹא 40

Preliminary Remarks to Hebrew Flection.

127—133. A. Changeable and Unchangeable Vowels 42

134—139. B. Rules for Nominal and Verbal Flection 43

1. Nominal Flection, 134—135. 2. Verbal Flection, 136—139

140. C. Classification of Nouns with regard to Flection 44

LESSON V. I. Nouns, Class I: Nouns with Unchangeable Vowels.

II. Nouns, Class II: *Milra'* Nouns with an Unchangeable Vowel in the Penult. III. Separate Personal Pronouns.

141. I. Nouns, Class I 47

142. II. Nouns, Class II 47

143—149. III. Separate Personal Pronouns 47

A. Form, 143. B. Syntactical Remarks, 144—149.

LESSON VI. Pronominal Suffixes of the Noun.

§§

150—151. A. Form 51

152—156. B. Remarks on the Form 51

157—162. C. Syntactical Remarks 52

163—175. Preliminary Remarks to the Hebrew Verb 54
A. Radicals. 163. B. Classification, 164. C. Modifications of the Root-idea, 165. D. Formations, 166—173. E. Tenses, 173. F. Modes, 174.

LESSON VII. PERFECT: Perfect Indicative of the Strong Verb.

175—179. A. Personal Endings 61

180—181. B. Stem-Formative Prefixes 62

182—188. C. Vowels: 1. First Radical; 2. Second Radical 63

189—192. D. Use of the Perfect 64

LESSON VIII. Infinitive Absolute. IMPERFECT: Infinitive Construct. Imperative (Form).

I. Infinitive Absolute (Infinitive of the Perfect).

193—194. A. Form 67

195—199. B. Use and Syntax 67

200. (IMPERFECT; its various Modes) 68

II. Infinitive Construct (Infinitive of the Imperfect).

201—207. A. Form 69

208—214. B. Use and Syntax 70

215—218. III. Imperative, Form 72

LESSON IX. IMPERFECT (Cont.): Indicative; Cohortative; Jussive; Imperative (Syntax).

I. Indicative.

219—226. A. Form and Flection 76

227—232. B. Use and Syntax 78

II. Cohortative and Jussive.

233—234. A. Form and Flection 80

235—237. B. Use of Imperative, Jussive and Cohortative 81

LESSON X. *Wāw Copulativum. Wāw Consecutivum.* Unclassified Nouns.

238—242. I. *Wāw* Copulative 84

II. *Wāw* Consecutive 85

243—249. A. Form 86

250—259. B. Use and Syntax 87
1. In general, 250. 2. With Imperf. Ind., 251—253. 3. With Perfect, 254—256. 4. Omission, 257—259.

260. III. Unclassified Nouns 89

LESSON XI. Nouns, Class III: Monosylables in *a*, *ē*, *ō*. Nouns, Class IV: Nouns with changeable *Qāmeṣ* and *Ṣērê*.

§§ I. Nouns, Class III.

261—264. A. Origin and Inflection 93

265—266. B. Dissyllabic Nouns following the same analogy 94

II. Nouns, Class IV.

267—271. A. Nouns with *Qāmeṣ* and *Ṣērê*, in general 95

272—275. B. With *Ṣērê* in Ultima and Unchangeable Vowel in Penult 95

LESSON XII. Nouns, Class VI: Segolates. Nouns, Class VI: Nouns in ה ֶ.

I. Nouns, Class V.

276—281. A. Segolates with Ordinary Consonants 99

282—285. B. Segolates with Gutturals 100

286—295. C. Feminine Segolate Endings. D. Mixed Forms. E. Segolates of Stems ע"ו and ע"י. F. Segolates of Stems ל"ה 100

296—297. II. Nouns, Class VI 102

LESSON XIII. Participles.

298—303. A. Origin and Form of Participles 105

304—314. B. Use and Syntax 105

LESSON XIV. Suffixes of the Verb.

I. With Perfect, Imperf. Indic. (Jussive) and Imperative.

315—317. A. Form of Suffixes 111

318—326. B. Union of Suffixes with the Verb 112

1. Perfect, 318—321. 2. Imperf. Indic., Juss., 323—325. 3. Imperat., 326.

327—330. C. Use and Syntax 114

331—334. II. Suffixes with Infin. and Participles 114

LESSON XV. Verbs *Pê-'Aleph*, *Pê-Nûn* and *Pê-Yôdh*.

335—337. I. Weak Verbs in general and Verbs *Pê-'Aleph* 119

338—342. II. Verbs *Pê-Nûn* 120

III. Verbs *Pê-Yôdh*.

343. A. *Pê-Yôdh* following analogy of *Pê-Nûn* 121

344—350. B. *Pê-Yôdh* originally *Pê-Wāw* 121

351. C. *Pê-Yôdh* originally *Pê-Yôdh* 123

LESSON XVI. Direct Subordination of the Noun to the Verb.

352—354. A. Complement of the Verb, Direct Object 126

355—358. B. Double Complement (Double Accusative) 127

359—360. C. Complement of a Passive Verb 129

361—368. D. Adverbial Modifiers 129

LESSON XVII. Prepositions and Adverbs.

§§

369—382. I. Prepositions 134
A. List and Meaning, 369—376. B. Inflection, 377—380.
C. Syntactical Remarks, 381—382.

383—389. II. Adverbs. List 139

LESSON XVIII. Verbs *Lāmedh-Hē*. Demonstrative Pronouns.

390—401. I. Verbs *Lāmedh-Hē* 144
402—408. II. Demonstrative Pronouns 146
A. Form, 402. B. Use and Syntax, 403—408.

LESSON XIX. Verbs *Lāmedh-'Aleph*. Interrogative Particles and Pronouns.

409—412. I. Verbs *Lāmedh-'Aleph* 150
II. Interrogative Sentence.
413—416. A. Morphology. Interrogative Particles and Pronouns . . 151
417—426. B. Use and Syntax 152

LESSON XX. Verbs *'Ayin-'Ayin*. Indefinite Pronouns. Substitutes for Pronouns.

427—440. I. Verbs *'Ayin-'Ayin* 157
441—443. II. Indefinite Pronouns 160
A. Morphology, 441. B. Indefinite Personal Subject, 442.
C. Impersonal Pronoun 'it', 443.
444. III. Pronominal Substitutes 161

LESSON XXI. Verbs *'Ayin-Wāw* and *'Ayin-Yôdh*. Verbal Ideas as Complementary Object of a Verb.

445—455. I. Verbs *'Ayin-Wāw* 165
456. II. Verbs *'Ayin-Yôdh* 167
457—462. III. Verbal Ideas as Complementary Object of a Verb 167

LESSON XXII. Weak Verb (Conclusion). Conjunctions.

463—467. I. Conclusion of Weak Verb 172
A. Doubly Weak Verbs, 463. B. Relation of Weak Verbs to one another, 464. C. Defective Verbs, 465. D. Less common Formations, 466. E. How to find the Root of a Verb, 467.
468—478. II. Principal Conjunctions 174
A. Co-ordinating, 468. B. Subordinating, 469—478.

LESSON XXIII. Apposition. Repetition of Nouns. Comparison of Adjectives. Relative Clause.

479—487. I. Apposition 180
488—493. II. Repetition of Nouns 182

§§
494—496. III. Comparison of Adjectives 182
497—504. IV. Relative Clause 184

LESSON XXIV. Numerals.

505—510. I. Morphology 188
511—529. II. Use and Syntax 189
A. Cardinals, 511—519. B. Ordinals, 520—523. C. Distributives, 524. D. Multiplicatives, 525—528. E. Fractions, 529.

Job, Chapters I and II; Proverbs, Chapter IV 194
Paradigms 198
English-Hebrew Vocabulary 228
Index of Hebrew words 238
Logical Index 244

INTRODUCTION.

ALPHABET.

A. Consonants.

Name	Form	Equivalent	Pronunciation	Numerical Value
'Âleph	א	'	Greek *Spiritus lenis:* h, in hour; often silent	1
Bêth	בּ	b	b, in battle	2
	ב	(ḇ, bh) bḫ	v	
Gímel	גּ	g	g, in give	3
	ג	(ḡ, gh) gḫ	North German g, in Tag	
Dáleth	דּ	d	d	4
	ד	(ḏ, dh) dḫ	th, in though	
Hē	ה	h	h, in hunt; often silent	5
Wāw (Wāu)	ו	w	w, in wagon; often silent	6
Záyin	ז	z	z, in zeal	7
Ḥêth	ח	(ch) ḥ	Guttural sound resembling German ch, in Bach	8
Ṭêth	ט	ṭ	Emphatic t	9
Yôdh	י	y	y, in yonder; often silent	10
Kāph	כּ	k	k, in kill; or c, in catch	20
	כ	(ḵ, kh, [ch]) kḫ	German ch, in Buch	
	ך*			
Lámedh	ל	l	l	30
Mêm	מ	m	m	40
	ם*			
Nûn	נ	n	n	50
	ן*			
Sámekh	ס	s	s, in set	60
'Áyin	ע	'	Peculiar guttural sound to be learned by practice	70

* Form at the end of words.

Name	Form	Equivalent	Pronunciation	Numer-ical Value
Pê	פּ	p	p	
	פ	(p̄, ph, f) p͜h	f, in feel; or ph, in phi-losophy	80
	ף*			
Sādh͜ế	צ	(ç) ṣ	Emphatic s	90
	ץ*			
Qôp͜h	ק	(ḳ) q	Emphatic k or q	100
Rês͜h	ר	r	r	200
Śîn	שׂ	ś	s, in set; (same as *Sāmek͜h*)	300
S͜hîn	שׁ	(š, sh) s͜h	sh, in ship	
Tāw (Tāu)	תּ	t	t, in tell	400
	ת	(ṯ, th) t͜h	th, in thought	

B. Vowels.

1. Full Vowels.

Name	Form	Equivalent	Pronunciation
Pắt͜hah̩	◌ַ	ă	a, in fat
Qā́meṣ	◌ָ	ā or â	a, in father
S·g͜hṓl	◌ֶ	e, when auxiliary vowel;	e, in system
		(é, è) æ in other cases	e, in bed (a in nation)
Ṣērḗ	◌ֵ	ē, sometimes ê	a, in nation
Ḥī́req Qāṭôn	◌ִ	ĭ, sometimes î	i, in pin; some-times i, in machine
Ḥī́req Gādh͜ṓl	◌ִי	î	i, in machine
Qā́mes Ḥātū́p͜h	◌ָ	ŏ	o, in not, pot
Ḥṓlem	◌ֹ	ō, sometimes ô	o, in prone
„ (fully written)	וֹ	ô, rarely ō	
Qĭbbū́ṣ	◌ֻ	ŭ, sometimes û	u, in put; some-times u, in prune
S͜hū́req	וּ	û, rarely ŭ	u, in prune

* Form at the end of words.

2. Half Vowels. *Sh'wâs, Ḥâṭēphs.*

a. Simple	Vocal *Sh·wâ*	ְ	e, in believe
b. Compound	„ „		
	or *Ḥâṭēph*		
	Ḥâṭēph Pâthaḥ	ֲ	very short a
	Ḥâṭēph S·ghôl	ֱ	very short e
	Ḥâṭēph Qâmeṣ	ֳ	very short o

c. Silent *Sh·wâ* syllable-divider, ְ } not transliterated: absence of all vocal sound as t, in booklet.

C. Diphthongs.

ָו	āu	ou, in bough
ָיו	āw	
ַי	ay	i, in pine (but shorter)
ָי	āy	i, in pine
וֹי	ôy	oi, in soil (but o longer)
וּי	ûy	French ouil, in bouillir
ִיו	îu	sound of u, after accented long î.
	îw	

As the signs for quantity often confuse rather than help the beginner, they have been generally omitted in the names of Hebrew consonants, vowels and signs, *v. g. Kaph, Sh·wa, etc.* not *Kâph, Sh·wâ, etc.*

SECTION I. Elementary Rules for READING and WRITING.

Caution. Hebrew is written and read from right to left. Care should be taken to give every letter its proper sound from the beginning. Note carefully the difference between certain letters easily confounded, *v. g.* ב and כ; ג and נ; ד, ר and ך; ה, ח and ת; ו and י; ו, ז and ן; ע and צ; שׁ and שׂ; ם and ס.

I. Remarks on the Consonants.

1. A. Six consonants, בּ, גּ, דּ, כּ, פּ, תּ have two sounds: a harder one indicated by a point (*Daghesh Lene* 24—26) placed in the letter, and a softer one, not indicated in ordinary texts, but in MSS. and in the best editions marked by a line (*Raphe* 28). They are known as the *B·ghadhk·phath.*

In transliteration, the hard sound is rendered by the corresponding English letter; the soft sound, by a dash above or below (*Raphe*) or by adding the letter *h* to the English letter, v. g. בּ = *b*; ב = *ḇ* or *bh*; תּ = *t*, ת = *ṯ* or *th*, etc. To make it clear that *bh*, *gh*, *th*, *dh*, *kh*, *ph* correspond to a single letter in Hebrew, they have, in this grammar, been joined by a curve underneath, *b͡h*, *g͡h*, *t͡h*, etc. The same has been done for *s͡h* = שׁ.

B. The Emphatic consonants ט, ק, צ, ח, are pronounced further back in the mouth or throat than the corresponding sound of *t*, *k*, *s*, *h*. They are transliterated by putting a point under the corresponding English letter: ח = *ḥ*; ט = *ṭ*; ק = *ḳ*; צ = *ṣ*. In this grammar, however, ק is rendered by *q*. *Sāḏḥé* should not be pronounced *ts*.

C. Literae finales. Five letters have special (in reality, older) forms at the end of words, ך, ם, ן, ף, ץ.

D. Literae dilatabiles. As it is forbidden to break up a word at the end of a line, or to leave a blank space not prescribed by the rules, whenever the scribe foresaw that this would happen, he extended, anywhere in the line, certain letters the form of which lent itself to such purpose; this is reproduced in most printed texts. The letters most commonly extended are ם, ח, ל, ה, א.

E. Silent or Quiescent Letters (*Matres Lectionis*).

2. 1. In pointed texts, the four weak consonants א, ה, ו, י, are often found without any vowel-sign (8); in that case, they are not to be pronounced and for that reason are called Silent or Quiescent Letters.

In most cases, these silent letters were originally real consonants; partly on account of their own inherent weakness (especially ה and א) and partly on account of contraction (ו and י), they lost their consonantal value, but still remained as part of the word (etymological orthography; cp. English *sleigh*, *bough*).

The practical loss of the consonant was generally compensated by the lengthening of the preceding vowel. The reader noticed that each one of these silent letters occurred after some definite vocal sounds and hence, the presence of the silent letters became a guide to a correct pronunciation; for this reason, they were called *Matres Lectionis* 'Mothers of the reading'. However, in many cases, especially ה at the end of words, the silent letters were introduced by analogy as pure *Matres Lectionis* to insure a correct pronunciation.

3. 2. Those four consonants are always silent at the end of words, unless they form part of a diphthong (see diagram) or are marked with a point called *Mappîq* (27). Inside a word, they are silent whenever they have no vowel-sign or syllable-divider (8) *v. g.* in מָצָאתָה, א is silent because it has no vowel-sign; ה is also silent because it is final and not marked with a point. In סוּסַי, *susăy*, on the contrary, י forms part of a diphthong and so also ו in סוּסָיו, *sûsāu.*

4. 3. The combination of *Waw* with *a* or *o* and *u* has given rise to a genuine long vowel by contraction (61). With a dot inside, וּ, *Waw* stands for *û* and is called *Shûreq*; with a dot above (and in the best editions slightly to the right, וֹ), it stands for *ô*, and is called *Ḥôlem* (fully written). Both vowels belong to the preceding consonant, which consequently has no other vowel-sign, *v. g.* לוּ = *lû*; לוֹ = *lô*.

The combination of *Yôdh* with the preceding sound of *i* (written with a point under its consonant) forms the long vowel *î* called *Ḥîreq Gādhôl* (fully written), *v. g.* שִׁיר = *Shîr*. *Yôdh* also enters into combination with preceding *Ṣērê* or *S·ghôl* to form the long vowels *ê* and *æ̂*, although no special name is given to these vowels; *v. g.* סוּסֵינוּ, our horses; סוּסֶיךָ, thy horses.

5. 4. When the long vowels *î*, *ê*, *æ̂*, *û*, *ô*, formed, as explained, from the combination of *Waw* and *Yôdh* with a preceding vowel, are written with the silent letter, they are said to be fully written (*Scriptio plena*); at times, however, for calligraphic reasons, the silent letter is left out; then, they are said to be written defectively (*Scriptio defectiva*), *v. g.* קוֹטֵל, *killing* (*Scriptio plena*), קֹטֵל, (*Scriptio defectiva*). When defectively written, they resemble the simple vowels which are not due to any such combination ֹ, ֻ, ִ, ֵ, ֶ; practice and the knowledge of the forms will show whether the simple signs stand for a vowel that should be written fully, or not. In the case of *Qibbûṣ* and *Ḥireq*, however, we may note that they stand for וּ and ִי whenever they are found in an open syllable (52, 53), because short *Qibbûṣ* and *Ḥireq* are found only in a closed, sharpened or half-open syllable (51—53), *v. g.* סֻסִים = סוּסִים, horses; see, however, 67.

The defective spelling is found mostly a) when the letter that would be used as *mater lectionis* appears immediately before, as consonant, *v. g.* מִצְוֹת, *precepts* for מִצְווֹת; b) when there would be two fully written vowels in two successive syllables, *v. g.* נָבִיא, *prophet*, pl. נְבִיאִם, נְבִאִים, or נְבִיאִים.

A vowel that should be fully written, whether it is actually so or not, is marked with a circumflex accent, *ô*, *û*, *î*, *ê*, *æ̂*: see 19.

6. F. Classification of Consonants.

The consonants of the Hebrew alphabet may, for practical purposes, be classified as follows:

Labials	בּ, וּ, מ, פּ
Sibilants	ז, ס, צ, שׂ, שׁ
Dentals	ד, ט, ת,
Linguals	ל, נ
Palatals	ג, י, כ, ק, ר
Gutturals	א, ה, ח, ע.

7. G. Consonants used as numerical signs (see lesson XXIV).

The value of every consonant has been given in the alphabet. The numbers from 500 to 900 are expressed by ת (400) with the addition of the remaining hundreds, *v. g.* תר = 600.

In compound numbers the greater precedes, *v. g.* יא = 11; רלא = 231. 15 is expressed by טו *i. e.* 9 + 6, not by יה; 16 is expressed by טז 9 + 7, not by יו. The reason is that both יה and יו are used as abbreviations of יְהוָה, *Jehovah*.

Thousands are expressed by monads with two points above the letter, *v. g.* א̈ = 1000; ב̈ = 2000.

II. Remarks on the Vowels.

A. Full Vowels.

8. In a vocalized Hebrew text, every consonant, when not final, must be marked with some vocal sign, or, if there is no vocal sound, with syllable-divider or silent *S̱h·wa*. Every letter not marked thus is not to be pronounced; the silent *S̱h·wa*, however, is not written under the last consonant of a word, except in the letter *Kapẖ* (ךְ) and when the word ends in two vowelless consonants, *v. g.* דָּבָר, *word*; but בֵּרֵךְ, *he blessed*; קָטַלְתְּ, *thou (f.) hast killed*.

9. A vowel is always sounded *after* the consonant to which it is affixed; the only exception is the *Paṯhaḥ furtivum* (71) under a final guttural, *v. g.* רוּחַ, *spirit*; hence, two vowels are never pronounced in immediate contact without some consonant between them, the only apparent exception being again *Paṯhaḥ furtivum, v. g.* רוּחַ.

10. All vowel-signs are written under the letter after which they are to be pronounced, except *S̱hureq* and *Ḥolem* fully written, both of which are inserted in their proper place in the consonantal text, and *Ḥolem* defectively written which is placed above the left corner of the letter, coalescing with the diacritical point of שׁ, *v. g.* סוֹס, *horse;* אוֹר, *light;* סֹפֵר, *scribe;* שֹׂנֵא, *enemy.*

11. When followed by שׁ, שׂ, ו, or quiescent א, *Ḥolem* defectively written is placed on the right hand corner of these letters and coalesces with the diacritical point of שׂ, *v. g.* עֹשֶׂה, *doing;* מֹשֶׁה, *Moses;* לֹוֶה, *borrowing;* וַיֹּאמֶר, *and he said.*

From the fact that a) every consonant must have some sign in the body of the word, b) that no syllable begins with a vowel (45) and c) that two vowels are never pronounced in immediate contact, it will be easy to distinguish between שׁ, *sho* or *oś*; ו *ô*, *wo* or *ow*; וּ *û* or *ww* (20—23). For instance, שֹׁמֵר must be pronounced *shômēr*, not *ośmer*, because no word in Hebrew begins with a vowel; עֹשֶׂה must be pronounced *ʿôsæ*, not *osheo*, because two vowels do not come in immediate contact. Similarly אוֹר must be pronounced *ôr*, otherwise א would have no vowel; עָוֹן must be pronounced *ʿāwôn* and לֹוֶה must be pronounced *lôwae*; עִוֵּר must be pronounced *ʿiwwēr*, etc.

12. With final *Kaph* (ך) or *Nûn* (ן), *Qameṣ* and *Sh·wa* are written in the letter on the left of the down stroke, ךָ, ךְ, ןָ. If a point (*Daghesh* 20) must be inserted at the same time, it is placed above the vowel. Ex.: סוּסְךָ, *thy horse;* מֶלֶךְ, *king;* הִנְּךָ, *here thou art.*

13. The same sign ָ stands for both the long vowel *Qameṣ* and the short one *Qameṣ Ḥaṭuph*, the latter, however, only in a closed unaccented syllable (52) or when it is followed by *Ḥaṭeph Qameṣ*, *v. g.* וַיָּקָם, *and he arose*, pron. *wayyāqŏm*; פָּעֳלוֹ *his work*, pron. *pŏʿᵒlô.*

B. Half-Vowels or Vocal *Sh·wâs.*

14. 1. Very often, a consonant is not accompanied by a full vowel but by a weaker sound called half-vowel, Vocal or Moving (less properly Movable) *Sh·wa.* These *Sh·was* are called vocal or moving, to distinguish them from the silent or quiescent *Sh·wa*, or syllable-divider, which indicates the complete absence of any vocalic sound; among Oriental grammarians, 'to move' a consonant is to furnish it with a vocal sound. Vocal *Sh·wa* generally takes the place of an original vowel which in certain cases has a tendency to reappear; cp. 78.

15. 2. Vocal *Sh·was*, graphically considered, may be Simple or Compound. *Sh·wa* is simple when it stands for the sound of a very weak *e* (French mute *e*); its sign is ְ placed under the consonant, *v. g.* קְטֹל, *killing* (pron. *q·ṭōl*).

3. When this half vocal sound tends towards the full vowels *ă, ĕ, ŏ*, the sign for the full vowel is written on the left of the *Sh·wa* sign (ְ); for that reason they are called "compound *Sh·was*," or "*Ḥâṭēphs*". The name of the vowel is added to *Ḥaṭeph* to designate them:

ֲ *Ḥaṭeph Pathaḥ*, *v. g.* עֲמֹד, *to stand*,
ֱ *Ḥaṭeph S·ghol*, *v. g.* אֱלֹהִים, *God*,
ֳ *Ḥaṭeph Qameṣ*, *v. g.* חֳלִי, *sickness.*

16. 4. On account of the weakness of the vocal *Sh·was* (both simple and compound), a consonant thus vocalized does not form a syllable by itself but belongs to the following syllable, *v. g.* גְּבוּל, *border*, *territory* (monos.); בְּרֵאשִׁית, *in the beginning*, *b·rē'|shîth.* Cp. Latin *psalmus;* English *stay.*

In transliteration, *Simple Sh·wa* is marked by a dot (or by *e* written above the line), *Ḥaṭephs* by a small *a, e, o*, written above the line, *v. g.* חֲכָמִים, *ḥ*ᵃ*khāmîm;* פָּעֳלוֹ, *pŏ*ᵒ*lô;* נֶאֱמָן, *næ'*ᵉ*mān.*

C. Syllable-divider, Silent or Quiescent *Sh·wâ.*

17. 1. The absence of any vocal sound, vowel or half-vowel, is indicated by the same sign as Simple Vocal *Sh·wa* (ְ), and is called Silent or Quiescent *Sh·wa* in contradistinction to the Vocal or Moving *Sh·wa*, *v. g.* קָטַלְתָּ (*qāṭaltā*), *thou hast killed.* A consonant with silent *Sh·wa* closes the preceding syllable; hence the name, syllable-divider, *qā-ṭal-tā.*

2. At the end of words, the Silent *Sh·wa* is not written except a) in the letter *Kaph* (ךְ) to distinguish it better from the letter *Nun* (ן) *v. g.* דֶּרֶךְ, *way;* b) when the word ends in two vowelless consonants, *v. g.* קָטַלְתְּ, *thou* (*f.*) *hast killed;* or c) in a few words that end in a consonant with *Daghesh Forte*, *v. g.* אַתְּ, *thou* (*f.*).

From the nature of the case, silent *Sh·wa* is always simple, never compound.

D. Distinction between Simple Vocal *Sh·wa* and Silent *Sh·wa*.

18. 1. Vocal *Sh·wa* occurs at the beginning of a syllable, Silent *Sh·wa* at the end; hence:

a) *Sh·wa* at the beginning of a word is always vocal, *v. g.* קְטֹל, *to kill;* b) *Sh·wa* at the end of a word is always silent, *v. g.* בָּרוּךְ, *blessed*; c) *Sh·wa* after a syllable with a long vowel, if unaccented, is vocal (cp. 52), *v. g.* קָֽטְלוּ, *they killed;* in that case the preceding vowel is generally furnished with *Methegh* (33); d) of two *Sh·was* occurring together, the first is silent and the second vocal, *v. g.* יִקְטְלוּ, (*yiq|ṭ·lû*), *they shall kill;* at the end of words, however, the two *Sh·was* are silent, *v. g.* קָטַלְתְּ, *thou (f.) hast killed;* e) *Sh·wa* under a consonant with *Daghesh forte* (equivalent to two consonants, 20) is vocal, *v. g.* קִטְּלוּ, *they murdered* (*qiṭ|ṭ·lu*); f) *Sh·wa* followed by one of the *B·ghadhk·phath* marked with *Daghesh Lene* (25) is silent, *v. g.* יִכְתֹּב, *he shall write;* g) finally, in certain cases, practice alone will show whether a *Sh·wa* is silent or vocal, *v. g.* קִטְלוּ, *kill ye.*

2. Many grammarians speak of a third kind of *Sh·wa* which they call Medial. This is now given up (See Gesenius, *Grammatik*, § 10d); the peculiarities which led to the admission of such a medial *Sh·wa* are explained differently.

E. Classification of Vowels.

19. 1. According to the organs used in pronouncing them, they are
Gutturals or *a* series: â, ǣ, ā, ă
Palatals or *i* series: ê, î, æ̂, ĕ, ĭ
Labials or *u* series: ô, û, ō, ŏ, ŭ.

2. According to their quantity[1], they are long, short and extra-short (half-vowels).

3. According to their origin, they are:
Naturally or primitively long, â, ê, æ̂, î, ô, û
Tone-long (heightened) { Fully lengthened, ā, ē, ō; half-lengthened ǣ from ă }
Deflected, æ̆ from ĭ; ŏ from ŭ

[1] In classifying vowels according to their quantity, we do so on practical grounds, after a method commonly received; it is probable that the Massorites (authors of the Hebrew vowel-system) were guided more by quality than by quantity.

Pure, ă, ĭ, ŭ
Attenuated, ĭ from ă
Volatilized, various Vocal *S̮h·was.*

4. According to their stability in flection, they are:
Changeable
Unchangeable { by nature, â, ê, ǽ, î, ô, û
by position, short vowels in a closed syllable, provided it be not final (127—133).

In transliteration, the short vowels are generally not marked with any sign, unless attention is to be drawn to the fact that they are short; thus we write: *a, e, i, o, u,* not *ă, ĕ, ĭ, ŏ, ŭ.*

Naturally long (unchangeable) vowels are marked with a circumflex accent: *â, ê, âe, î, ô, û*; tone-long (changeable) vowels are marked with a line *ā, ē, ī, ō, ū.*

III. Various Signs of Orthography and Orthoëpy.

A. Dâg̮hēs̮h Forte.

20. If a consonant coming after a short, rarely after a long, vowel, has a point inside, its pronunciation is to be made sharper, as if it was doubled. This point is called *Dâg̮hēs̮h Forte.*

21. 1. *Dag̮hes̮h Forte* is used:

a) to show that the letter is doubled, either because the identical consonant occurred immediately before without a full vowel, or because a weak letter, generally *Nûn,* has been assimilated to it, *v. g.* חֻקִּי, *my precept,* for חֻקְקִי; יִטַּע, *he shall plant,* for יִנְטַע;

b) as a characteristic sign of certain verbal and nominal intensive forms (171), *v. g.* קִטֵּל, *he murdered;*

c) to maintain short the pronunciation of a vowel which otherwise would become long (§ 52), *v. g.* יָסֹב and יִסֹּב, *he shall surround;*

d) after *Maqqeph* (*Hyphen,* § 29) in the first letter of a monosyllable or dissyllable *Mil̆el* (§ 37) when the preceding word ends in accented ה ָ or ה ֶ, *v. g.* לְכָה־נָּא, *go, I pray;*

e) in general when the pronunciation of a consonant has to be safeguarded, *v. g.* חָדֵלּוּ, *they ceased,* עִקְּבֵי סוּס, *the heels of a horse.*

22. 2. *Dag̮hes̮h Forte* is omitted:

a) always in the case of gutturals, and generally of *Res̮h,* the nature of which does not admit of sharpening or doubling, *v. g.* הָהָר, *the mountain,* for הַהָּר (66);

b) in a final vowelless consonant, (except אַתְּ, *thou, (f.)*, and נָתַתְּ, *thou (f.) hast given*), *v. g.* גַּן, *garden*, for גַּנְן; in this case, the preceding vowel is very often lengthened, *v. g.* רֹב, *multitude* for רֻבְב, (261 ff.);

c) very often in the middle of words when the letter to be *dageshed* has only vocal *Sh·wa* (cp. 87); this applies especially to יְ, וְ, מְ, and sometimes נְ, קְ and sibilants, *v. g.* הַיְאֹר, *the river* for הַיְּאֹר, but הַלְּבוּשׁ, *the garment.*

23. 3. *Daghesh forte* is indicated in transliteration by doubling the *dageshed* letter provided the *Daghesh* is not due to the causes mentioned in 1, d and e; in these latter cases, the *dageshed* letter is written but once.

B. Dâghēsh Lene.

24. A point in one of the *B·ghadhk·phath* (בּ, גּ, דּ, כּ, פּ, תּ) not preceded by a vowel merely indicates that these consonants must be given the hard pronunciation (§ 1), *v. g.* מַלְכִּי, *my king* (*malkî* not *mal·khî*); יִכְתֹּב, *he shall write* (*yikhtōbh*).

The soft sound of a *B·ghadhk·phath* occurs only after a full vowel or a vocal *Sh·wa*; hence, *Daghesh Lene* is used:

25. a) at the beginning of a book, phrase or division of a phrase; hence also after a disjunctive accent (§ 41), *v. g.* בְּרֵאשִׁית, *in the beginning;*

b) when the preceding word ends in a vowelless consonant or when the preceding letter is marked with silent *Sh·wa*, *v. g.* עִם־דָּוִד *with David;* יִכְתֹּב, *he shall write.*

26. Remarks. The letters א, ה, ו, י, when silent (*Matres lectionis*) are not considered as consonants and therefore a *B·ghadhk·phath* does not take *Daghesh Lene* after them, *v. g* אֱלֹהֵי דָוִד, *the God of David*, not דָּוִד.

The presence of a *Daghesh Lene* in the *B·ghadhk·phath* will indicate whether a preceding *Sh·wa* is vocal or silent: if those letters have *Daghesh Lene* the *Sh·wa* is silent, otherwise it is vocal; see however 51.

A point in a *B·ghadhk·phath* after a full vowel cannot be *Daghesh Lene* but must be *Daghesh Forte;* hence, the *dageshed* letter must be sharpened in pronunciation, *v. g.* לִבּוֹ, *his heart* (pron. *libbô*).

C. Mappîq.

27. At the end of words, when one of the four letters, א, ה, ו, י, but more particularly ה, must not be taken as *mater lectionis*, but must be given its consonantal value, it is marked with a point called *Mappîq*, *v. g.* סוּסָהּ, *her horse*, but סוּסָה, *mare.*

In the middle of words, *Mappîq* is not used, for, the ordinary vowel-signs indicate sufficiently whether these letters are quiescent or not (8).

D. Rāphè.

28. *Raphe* is a horizontal stroke over letters; its purpose is the opposite of *Daghesh* and *Mappîq* but more particularly of *Daghesh Lene.* In the more accurate editions of the Bible, every *B·ghadhk·phath* and final *He* is marked with a point or with *Raphe.* In the ordinary printed editions, *Raphe* is used only when the editors want to emphasize the absence of *Daghesh* or *Mappîq*, *v. g.* סוּסָהֿ, *mare*, to distinguish it from סוּסָהּ, *her horse.*

E. Maqqēph.

29. *Maqqeph* is our hyphen; it consists of a horizontal stroke placed towards the top of the letters between two or more words closely connected, to join them under one accent, *v. g.* כָּל־הָאָרֶץ, *the whole earth.* Very commonly, it connects short words and particles with a longer word that precedes or follows, *v. g.* מִן־הָאִישׁ, *from the man;* אֶל־שְׁלֹמֹה, *to Solomon;* וַיְדַבְּרוּ־לוֹ, *and they spoke to him.*

F. Pâsēq.

30. *Pâsēq* is a vertical line placed between two words logically connected, to prevent their being pronounced too quickly as if they formed only one word. It is often used:

31. 1. when the first word ends in the same consonant with which the following word begins, *v. g.* לְדָבָר ׀ רָע, *to an evil thing;* 2. when a word is repeated, *v. g.* יוֹם ׀ יוֹם, *every day;* 3. before the names of the Deity to secure a consciously reverent pronunciation, *v. g.* אַתָּה ׀ אֱלֹהִים, *thou, Elohim.*

G. Méthegh (Bridle).

32. *Méthegh* is a little vertical line placed to the left of a vowel to remind the reader that he ought to give a certain weight to that vowel. Its principal (not exclusive) uses are:

33. 1. With a long vowel, a) in the second open syllable before the main accent, or in the third if the second is closed; b) before vocal *Sh·wa* when it is pretonic. The conjunction וּ does not receive *Methegh*. Ex.: הָֽאָדָם, *the man;* הָֽאַרְבָּעִים, *the forty (men);* קָֽטְלוּ, *they killed:* but וּבָנִים, *and sons,* not וּֽבָנִים; יִקְטְלוּ, *they shall kill,* not יִֽקְטְלוּ, because יִק is a closed syllable; מַלְכֵי, *the kings of,* not מַֽלְכֵי, because מַ has a short vowel.

Two words joined by *Maqqeph* are considered as only one and *Methegh* may be found under the first, *v. g.* לֹֽא־יִצְלָח, *he shall not succeed. Methegh* is also found with a long vowel in a closed syllable before *Maqqeph,* שֶֽׁם־הַנָּהָר, *the name of the river.*

34. 2. With all vowels before compound *Sh·wa,* נַֽעֲרוֹ, *his boy.* This is done even when, for rhythmical reasons, the *Ḥaṭeph* before another *Sh·wa* passes into its corresponding vowel, *v. g.* נַֽעַרְךָ, *thy boy,* for נַעֲרְךָ (74).

From the fact that יְהוָֹה (Yahweh) is pronounced אֲדֹנָי which has a *Ḥaṭeph* under the *Aleph,* any prefix to it is marked with *Methegh,* even when *Yodh* (*Aleph*) becomes silent in pronunciation, *v. g.* לַֽיהוָֹה, *to Jehovah.*

35. 3. In all preformatives of הָיָה, *to be,* and חָיָה, *to live,* when ה and ח have silent *Sh·wa, v. g.* יִֽהְיֶה, *it shall be;* also very often in וַֽיְהִי, *and it was, v. g.* וַֽיְהִי־כֵן, *and it was so.*

36. The presence of *Methegh* will show whether a *Sh·wa* is silent or vocal, and consequently, whether the sign ָ is to be pronounced ā or ŏ (cp. 52) *v. g.* קָֽדְשׁוּ, *they were consecrated* (*qādh·shû*), but קָדְשׁוֹ *his sacredness* (*qŏdhshô*).

IV. Tone or Word-Accent.

37. 1. Every word in Hebrew has its own tone or stress of the voice. The tone usually rests on the ultima and the word is then called *Milraʿ* (מִלְּרַע, *accented below*), *v. g.* דָּבָר, *word;* סוּסִים, *horses.* Less frequently, the tone is on the penult and then the word is called *Milʿēl* (מִלְּעֵיל, *accented above*), *v. g.* מֶ֫לֶךְ, *king;* צֶ֫דֶק, *justice.* Cases of accented antepenult do not occur.

38. 2. A closed penult can have the tone only if the ultima is open. A closed ultima can be without the tone only if the penult is open with a long vowel, *v. g.* קָטַ֫לְתָּ, *thou hast killed;* but, קְטַלְתֶּם, *you have killed.*

39. In a vocalized text, the cantilation-signs or accents are usually placed on the syllable that has the tone. When separate words are quoted, *v. g.* in grammars, dictionaries, etc., the place of the accent is marked by the signs ˂, ˃, ´, but only in a *Mil'êl, v. g.* דָּבָ֫ר, not דָּבָ֑ר (except for emphasis) but מֶ֫לֶךְ.

The term "accent" should be avoided to designate the stress of the voice, because, according to Hebrew usage, this term is applied to the various signs by which the melody is indicated (40—42).

The place of the accent may determine the sense, *v. g.* בָּ֫נוּ, *in us*; בָּנ֫וּ, *they built.*

V. Accents.

40. 1. In a vocalized Biblical text, almost every word is marked with a sign, called accent, corresponding to its relative function in the sentence, and filling the office of our punctuation marks. Almost all those signs are attached to the tone-syllable, either above or below.

Some accents, however, are always written on the first letter of the word, regardless of the tone, they are called prepositive; others are written at the end, and are called postpositive. In some editions both prepositives and postpositives are often repeated on the tone-syllable.

2. The accents are divided into two classes: those which indicate that a word must be separated from the following and are called *dis*junctive, and those which indicate that a word must be joined to the following and are called *con*junctive.

3. Three of the poetical books, Psalms (תְּהִלִּים), Job (אִיּוֹב), and Proverbs (מִשְׁלֵי), known in grammars as תא"ם, from the combination of the first letter of the name of each of these books, have special accents.

41. Out of the numerous Hebrew accents, we give here only the more common disjunctives.

    a) Ordinary books:

        Sillûq (־֑) placed under the last word of the verse and followed by *Sôph Pasûq* (:). Care should be taken not to confound *Sillûq* with *Methegh*.

        '*Athnâḥ* (־֑) separates the principal members of a sentence.
        S·ḡholtâ (־֒) (postpositive) indicates a secondary break.
        Zâqēph Qāṭôn (־֔)
        Zâqēph Gādhôl (־֕) } mark a break less than that of *Athnaḥ*.
        R·bhîa' (־֗) indicates a minor break, sometimes introduces

a quotation. The point of *R·bhîa'* is generally larger than that of *Holem*.

42. b) Poetical books:

Sillûq, as above.

'Olæ W·yôrēdh (◌֫◌֥) indicates the principal members of the verse.

'Athnâh divides the second half of the verse. If the verse is short, *'Athnâh* indicates the end of the first half.

The most common conjunctive accent is *Mûnah* (◌֣); *Methegh* is not written when it would fall on a syllable marked with *Mûnah*.

VI. Q·rê and K·thîbh.

43. In many passages of the Bible, a word is marked with ° or * (*Circellus* or *Asteriscus*). This sign indicates a correction to be made in the text and refers the reader to the margin where the correction is given; there, the reader will find first the wrong reading followed by 'כ = כְּתִיב (Aramaic, *written*) and then the right reading followed by 'ק = קְרֵי (Aramaic, *read*). As a sufficient hint for the experienced reader, the Massorites have placed on the wrong reading of the text or *K·thîbh,* the vowel-signs belonging to the *Q·rê* which must be substituted, *v. g.* 1 K. xii, 33, the text exhibits the wrong reading מִלְּבַד not with its own punctuation מִלְּבַד, but with that of the correct מִלִּבּוֹ. When a word is *always* to be replaced by another, the asterisk is omitted and the marginal correction is not given, only the vowels of the *Q·rê* are written under the *K·thîbh*. The most common *Q·rê perpetuum* is the one having reference to the divine name יהוה. The correct pronunciation is probably יַהְוֶה, *Yahweh,* but it is always pronounced אֲדֹנָי, *'Adonāi,* and therefore is vocalized יְהוָה. When יהוה comes immediately before or after אֲדֹנָי, it is pronounced *'elohim* and vocalized יֱהוִה with the vowels of אֱלֹהִים. In like manner, יְרוּשָׁלֵם, is to be pronounced *Y·rushaláyim* and is vocalized יְרוּשָׁלִַם.

SECTION II. Some principles of Hebrew PHONOLOGY.

A. The Hebrew Syllable.

44. There are as many syllables as there are full vowels; simple vocal *Sh·wa* or *Hateph* does not constitute a syllable but belongs to the following syllable (16).

Pathah Furtivum (71), which is placed under a guttural to help its pronunciation, does not form a new syllable.

45. 1. Beginning of the syllable.

a) Every Hebrew syllable begins with one consonant or at most two; if the latter, the first consonant has vocal *S̲h·wa.* No syllable can begin with a vowel, except וּ (§ 49), *v. g.* תּוֹרָה, *law;* לְבוּשׁ, *garment;* וּלְבוּשׁ, *and a garment.*

46. b) No syllable can begin with three consonants; if through inflection and combination, such a case would arise, an auxiliary vowel is inserted (or rather a primitive vowel reappears in a form more or less pure) after the first consonant, thus giving rise to a new syllable.

α) This auxiliary vowel is regularly *Ḥîreq Qatôn, v. g.* לְבוּשׁ + בְּ becomes בִּלְבוּשׁ not בְּלְבוּשׁ.

47. β) If the second consonant is יְ, the *Yod̲h* coalesces with the preceding *Ḥireq* and becomes *Ḥireq Gād̲hôl; v. g.* יְהוּדָה + בְּ = בִּיְהוּדָה (α) = בִּיהוּדָה, *in Judah;* לִיהוּדָה, *to Judah;* וִיהוּדָה, *and Judah.*

48. γ) If one of the two consonants has a *Ḥaṭeph,* the auxiliary vowel is always the one of the *Ḥaṭeph, v. g.* יַעֲמֹד, *he shall stand,* for יְעֲמֹד; אֱוִיל, *fool,* לֶאֱוִיל, *to a fool.*

49. δ) The conjunction ו before a consonant with *S̲h·wa* becomes וּ, *v. g.* שְׁלֹמֹה + וְ = וּשְׁלֹמֹה, *and Solomon,* except in cases just mentioned, 47, 48; see further § 88.

50. 2. End of the syllable.

a) A syllable may end in a vowel with or without a *mater lectionis,* and is then called OPEN, *v. g.* גָּלָה, *he manifested* = *gā* + *lāh,* i. e. two open syllables.

b) It may end in a consonant, and is called CLOSED, *v. g.* אֶל־, *to.*

c) It may end in two vowelless consonants, and is called DOUBLY CLOSED, *v. g.* קָטַלְתְּ, *thou (f.) hast killed.* This occurs only at the end of words and in that case both letters have silent *S̲h·wa* (§ 17, 2). To avoid harshness in pronunciation, an auxiliary vowel, generally *S·g̲hôl* (or *Pathaḥ* with gutturals, and *Ḥireq* with *Yod̲h*) is often inserted between the two consonants, *v. g.* מֶלֶךְ, *king,* for מַלְךְ; נַעַר, *boy,* for נַעְר; זַיִת, *olive,* for זַיְת.

d) A syllable may end in the same letter with which the following syllable begins; this common letter is written but once and takes *Daghesh Forte:* the syllable that precedes it is called SHARP, ACUTE, SHARPENED, *v. g.* קִטֵּל, *he murdered, Qiṭṭēl.*

51. e) There is another syllable called INTERMEDIATE, HALF-OPEN, LOOSELY CLOSED, WAVERING, OPENED. Although graphically an open syllable, essentially it is closed, and hence, the quantity of vowels follows the rules of a closed syllable. It occurs: α) when an auxiliary vowel is added to prevent a word from beginning with three consonants (46), *v. g.* בִּנְפֹל, *in falling* = *Bi-n·phol.* (Note that פ is without *Daghesh Lene* which it ought to have, if *Sh·wa* was silent); β) when a *Daghesh Forte* should have been placed in a guttural but could not on account of the nature of that letter, (67), *v. g.* נִחַם, *he comforted* for נִחֵּם; γ) before some verbal and nominal suffixes to be learned by practice (see paradigm A).

52. 3. Syllables with regard to quantity.

a) Unaccented syllables.

α) Open syllables have long vowels, *v. g.* קָטַל, *he killed, qā-ṭắl.*

β) Closed, doubly closed and sharpened syllables have short vowels, *v. g.* הִקְטִיל, *he caused to kill, hiq-ṭîl;* קִטֵּל, *he murdered, qit-ṭēl.*

53. b) Accented syllables.

α) Open syllables have long vowels, *v. g.* סוּסֵ֫נוּ, *our horse;* exceptions mostly refer to the intermediate syllables mentioned above.

β) Closed syllables may be short or long; doubly closed and sharpened syllables are generally short, sometimes long (*v. g.* 433). The vowel in a sharpened syllable is, besides, generally one of the shortest vowels ă, ĭ, ŭ. Ex.: קָטַ֫לְתָּ, *thou hast killed;* יִקְטֹל, *he shall kill;* קָטַלְתְּ, *thou* (*f.*) *hast killed;* קִטֵּל, *he murdered;* חֻקִּים, *precepts.*

B. Changes in Vowels.

54. When the word is inflected, the tone may shift forward towards the end of the word, *v. g.* קָטַל, *he killed,* but קָֽטְלוּ, *they killed;* or it may move backward towards the beginning of the word, *v. g.* יָסֹב, *he shall surround,* but וַיָּ֫סָב, *and he surrounded.* This shifting of the tone brings about modifications in the nature

of the syllables, and consequently also in the quantity of the vowels (52, 53), if they are changeable.

Apart from the vowel-changes brought about by the shifting of the tone, vowels may also be modified as a result of the laws of dissimilation, assimilation or analogy. These will be pointed out when they occur in the study of the forms.

In dealing with vowel-changes, however, we do not intend to trace them back to, or to start from, the primitive vowels; we take the language as it is now, and wish merely to call attention to the short vowel which, in given cases, will replace a long one and *vice versa*. As a matter of fact, the primitive vowels were the short vowels *a*, *i*, *u*; all the others are derived from them. Those primitive vowels have been protected against changes in many forms which to the beginner will appear as derived and secondary.

Changeable vowels may undergo the following changes:

1. Going from long to short.

a) They may be shortened.

55. α) *ǣ*, heightened from *ă*, and *ā* are shortened to *ă*, but often *ă* is further attenuated to *ĭ*, *v. g.* דָּבָר, *word;* דָ of דָּבָר becomes דִ in דִּבְרֵיכֶם, *your words.* The syllable בָר of the same דָּבָר becomes בַר in דְּבַר, *the word of . . .;*

56. β) *ē* becomes *ǣ* or *ĭ* in an unaccented closed syllable and almost always *ĭ* in a sharpened syllable, *v. g.* לֵב, *heart* becomes לֶב־, *the heart of . . . .* and לִבּוֹ, *his heart;*

57. γ) *ō* becomes *ŏ* (*Qameṣ Ḥaṭuph*), more rarely *ŭ* (*Qibbuṣ*), in an unaccented closed syllable and regularly *ŭ* in a sharpened syllable, *v. g.* חֹק, *command,* חָק־, *the command of . . . .,* חֻקִּים, *commands.*

58. b) They may be volatilized, *i. e.* a full vowel may pass into a *Sh·wa*, *v. g.* דָ of דָּבָר becomes דְ in דְּבָרִים; אָרוּר, *cursed,* pl. אֲרוּרִים.

59. c) They may be lost entirely and replaced by silent *Sh·wa*, *v. g.* מֶלֶךְ, *king,* but מַלְכִּי, *my king* (Note that the ל has now silent *Sh·wa* as is shown from the fact that *Kaph* has *Daghesh Lene*).

60. 2. Going from short to long. The process is generally reversed, *v. g.* primitive *ŭ*, which has been kept in a sharpened syllable, will be replaced by *ŏ* in an ordinary unaccented closed syllable, and by *ō* in an open syllable or accented closed syllable, *v. g.* חֻקִּים (חֻקְקִים), חָק־, חֹק, etc.

When and how those changes take place will be seen in the sequel.

61. 3. The contraction of a vowel with a silent *Waw* and *Yôdh* gives rise to naturally long (unchangeable) vowels, as will be seen later on. The most common contractions are

$$a + y = \hat{e} \text{ or } \acute{æ};\ a + w = \hat{o};\ a + hu = a(h)u = au = \hat{o};$$

$$i + y = \hat{\imath};\ o + w = \hat{o};\ u + w = \hat{u}.$$

4. Naturally long *Qameṣ* has generally been obscured to *ô;* see however 131.

C. Modifications of Consonants.

Consonants undergo fewer changes than vowels; the principal changes are:

62. 1. Sharpening or Contraction, when a letter with silent *Sh'wa* is followed by the same letter, and is written but once with *Daghesh Forte, v. g.* כָּרַ֫תִּי, *I have cut,* for כָּרַ֫תְתִּי (177).

63. 2. Assimilation, a) complete, when a consonant (*Nûn, Yôdh, Tāw,* rarely *Lāmedh*) with silent *Sh'wa* passes into the consonant of the following syllable and is replaced by *Daghesh Forte* (cp. Latin *affero* for *adfero*), *v. g.* נָתַ֫תִּי, *I have given,* for נָתַ֫נְתִּי;

b) partial, when a consonant is made to pass into the same class as another, *v. g.* הִצְטַדֵּק, *he justified himself,* for הִצְתַּדֵּק (two emphatic consonants), for הִתְצַדֵּק, with transposition (65).

64. 3. Rejection, when the letter is thrown out without leaving any trace in the form of a *Daghesh Forte* or otherwise. This may occur in the beginning of words (*Aphaeresis*), *v. g.* גַּשׁ, *approach,* for נְגַשׁ; in the middle (*Syncope*), *v. g.* וַיֹּ֫סֶף, *and he collected,* for וַיֹּאסֶף, or at the end (*Apocope*), *v. g.* יָ֫גֶל, for יְגַלֶּה, *let him manifest.*

65. 4. Transposition, or *Metathesis,* when a consonant changes place with another, *v. g.* הִשְׁתַּמֵּר, *he kept himself,* for הִתְשַׁמֵּר.

D. Peculiarities of the Gutturals, א, ה, ח, ע and of Rêsh.

He and *Aleph* at the end of words are not gutturals unless they are marked with *Mappiq* (27).

66. 1. Unlike the other letters, gutturals cannot be strengthened or sharpened by *Daghesh Forte,* their peculiar pronunciation not allowing such a strengthening.

a) In the case of א and generally in the case of ע—rarely in the case of ה, and very rarely in the case of ח— as a compensation for the omission of the sharpening, the preceding vowel is lengthened, *v. g.* הָאֶבְיוֹן, *the poor,* for הַאֶבְּיוֹן; הָעוֹלָה, *the sacrifice,* for הַעּוֹלָה.

67. b) In the case of ה and ח—seldom in the case of ע and very seldom in the case of א—the preceding vowel remains short, as if the *Daghesh* was actually written; this is called Implicit *Daghesh Forte,* and the preceding syllable is said to be virtually sharpened, *v. g.* הַהוּא, *this,* for הַהּוּא; שִׂחַק, *he jested,* for שִׂחֵּק.

68. c) When the guttural that should be reinforced has *Qameṣ* or *Ḥateph Qameṣ, Pathaḥ* is often dissimilated to *S·ghol,* especially before הָ and חָ; also before הָ and עָ when they are not accented; if הָ and עָ are accented, *Pathaḥ* is regularly lengthened to *Qameṣ, v. g.* הָהָר, *the mountain,* but הֶהָרִים, *the mountains;* see Lesson III.

2. Gutturals with respect to *Vowels.*

69. a) The gutturals prefer immediately before them the sound of *"a"* which is more akin to their own nature. Hence, *Pathaḥ* takes the place of another short vowel, ĭ, ĕ, ŭ, and also often of a tone-long ē or ō, *v. g.* מֶ֫לֶךְ but זֶ֫בַח; יִקְטֹל but יַחְמֹד; וַיִּסֹּב but וַיָּנַח; קַטֵּל but שַׁלַּח. However, when the following syllable has *a,* the *a* demanded by the guttural is often dissimilated to *S·ghol* at the beginning of a word, *v. g.* יַחְמֹד, *he shall be pleased,* but יֶחְדַּל, *he shall cease.*

70. b) The three strong gutturals ה, ח, ע, show also a preference, although not so systematically, for the sound of *a* in the vowel that *follows, v. g.* נַ֫עַר, *boy,* but מֶ֫לֶךְ, *king. Aleph* has a preference for *S·ghol, v. g.* אֶקְטֹל, *I shall kill.*

71. c) Whenever an unchangeable (sometimes also a simple tone-long) vowel other than â precedes a vowelless guttural at the end of words, a *Pathaḥ* is written under the guttural and pronounced before it. This is done merely to facilitate pronunciation; this *Pathaḥ,* called *furtivum,* does not form a syllable and disappears as soon as any addition is made to the word, *v. g.* רוּחַ, *spirit,* רוּחִי, *my spirit,* רוּחֲכֶם, *your spirit.*

3. Gutturals with respect to *Sh·was.*

72. a) Gutturals do not admit of a simple vocal *Sh·wa* but require a *Ḥateph* or Compound *Sh·wa.* ה, ח, ע show preference for *Ḥateph Pathaḥ, v. g.* עֲמַדְתֶּם, *you stood;* חֲזִיר, *swine; Aleph* in close proximity to the tone prefers *Ḥateph S·ghol, v. g.* אֱוִיל, *fool;* but when removed from the tone, *Aleph* often takes *Ḥateph Pathaḥ, v. g.* אֲרֻבָּה, *window;* אֱלֹהִים, *God.*

73. b) Gutturals sometimes admit of silent *Sh·wa*, especially when they close an accented penult, *v. g.* שָׁלַחְתִּי, *I have sent,* also before תֶּם and תֶּן in verbs, *v. g.* שְׁלַחְתֶּם, *you have sent.* In other cases, when not in an accented syllable, ע generally, ה often, and ח less frequently, replace the syllable-divider by a *Ḥateph* corresponding to the preceding vowel, *v. g.* יַעֲמֹד, *he shall stand.* Cp. יִכְתֹּב, *he shall write.*

74. c) Whenever a guttural with *Ḥateph* is followed by a *Sh·wa*, the *Ḥateph* passes into its full vowel, *v. g.* יֶחֱרַד, *he shall tremble,* but יֶחֶרְדוּ, *they shall tremble.*

This new vowel is preceded by *Methegh* as if it were still a *Ḥateph* (34).

4. The letter *Resh* resembles the gutturals in the following points:

75. a) generally, it does not admit a *Daghesh Forte* and almost always requires the lenghthening of the preceding vowel as compensation, *v. g.* בֵּרַךְ, *he blessed,* for בִּרַּךְ;

76. b) it has a preference for the sound of *a* in the preceding vowel, *v. g.* וַיַּרְא, *and he saw;* cp. however, יִרְאֶה, *he shall see;* besides, when preceded by a long vowel, it takes often a *Ḥateph Pathaḥ* instead of a simple vocal *Sh·wa, v. g.* בֵּרֲכוּ, *they blessed,* for בֵּרְכוּ.

E. Pause.

77. By Pause is meant the greater stress laid on the last word of a sentence or clause. *Sillûq, Athnâḥ, ʿÓlæ w·yôrēd,* are generally found under the pausal word, and also sometimes *S·gholtâ, Zâqeph, R·bhîaʿ.* This stress produces various effects of which the lengthening of the vowel and the shifting of the tone are the most important.

78. 1. Lengthening of the vowel.

a) A short vowel in an accented syllable becomes tone-long in a Pause, *v. g.* קָטַל, P. קָטָל; פַּר, P. פָּר.

b) When the last syllable of the word has the accent and is preceded by a vocal *Sh·wa,* this *Sh·wa* in a pause is changed into a tone-long vowel which receives the accent. The vowel to be chosen depends on the origin of the form; the full vowel that has been volatilized is restored and lengthened according to 55—60. Original *Pathah* is often heightened to *S·ghol* in words ending in ◌ִי and before suffix ךָ, *v. g.* קָטְלָה, from קָטַל + ◌ָה, P. קָטָ֫לָה; שְׁבִי for שֶׁבֶי, P. שֶׁ֫בִי; סוּסְךָ, P. סוּסֶ֫ךָ.

79. 2) The tone, which in the Imperfect Indicative with *Waw Consecutivum* (see lesson X) is often found in the penult, is restored to the ultima with consequent modification of vowels according to 53, 59, *v. g.* וַיָּ֫מָת, *and he died,* P. וַיָּמֹת.

LESSON I.

NOUN (Gender and Number). ARTICLE.

NOMINAL SENTENCE.

Vocabulary.

מֹשֶׁה	*pr. n.*	*Moses*
דָּוִד	*pr. n.*	*David*
שְׁלֹמֹה	*pr. n.*	*Solomon*
יִשְׂרָאֵל	*pr. n.*	*Israel*
מַלְכִּי־צֶדֶק	*pr. n.*	*Melchisedech*
מִצְרַיִם	*pr. n. f.* / *pr. n. m.*	*Egypt* / *the Egyptians*
סוּס	*m.*	*horse*
סוּסָה	*f.*	*mare*
גֵּר	*m.*	*resident stranger, sojourner*
מִזְמוֹר	*m.*	*psalm, melody, hymn*
יְאֹר	*m.*	*stream, canal, river Nile*
כּוֹס	*f.*	*cup*
בִּינָה	*f.*	*understanding*

מִטָּה	*f.*	*bed*
מְנוֹרָה	*f.*	*lampstand*
תּוֹרָה	*f.*	*law*
תְּפִלָּה	*f.*	*prayer*
מִצְוָה	*f.*	*commandment, precept*
גִּבּוֹר	*adj.*	*strong, mighty, warrior*
זָר	*pt.*	*stranger, strange*
טוֹב	*adj.*	*good*
כֵּן	*pt.*	*upright*
מֵת	*pt.*	*dead*
צַדִּיק	*adj.*	*just*
מְאֹד	*adv.*	*much, very*
שָׁם	*adv.*	*there*

80. N. B. 1. In this and following lessons, only nouns with unchangeable vowels are used. Unchangeable vowels are a) generally (not necessarily) vowels that are written fully (5); b) short vowels in a closed syllable provided it be not final. See further 128 ff. Real proper names are not inflected because, being determined by their nature, they can neither take the plural nor be construed with a genitive or suffix.

2. Under the term "noun", in Hebrew grammar, are included not only substantives, but also adjectives and partly participles and infinitives in as much as they are verbal nouns.

Examples.

	Masculine		
	Sing.	Plur.	Dual
Subst. without art.	סוּס	סוּסִים	נַעֲלַ֫יִם (sandals)
Subst. with art.	הַסּוּס	הַסּוּסִים	הַנַּעֲלַ֫יִם
S. and adj. without art.	סוּס טוֹב	סוּסִים טוֹבִים	נַעֲלַ֫יִם טוֹבִים
S. and adj. with art.	הַסּוּס הַטּוֹב	הַסּוּסִים הַטּוֹבִים	הַנַּעֲלַ֫יִם הַטּוֹבִים

	Feminine		
	Sing.	Plur.	Dual
Subst. without art.	סוּסָה	סוּסוֹת	שְׂפָתַ֫יִם (lips)
Subst. with art.	הַסּוּסָה	הַסּוּסוֹת	הַשְּׂפָתַ֫יִם
S. and adj. without art.	סוּסָה טוֹבָה	סוּסוֹת טוֹבוֹת	שְׂפָתַ֫יִם טוֹבוֹת
S. and adj. with art.	הַסּוּסָה הַטּוֹבָה	הַסּוּסוֹת הַטּוֹבוֹת	הַשְּׂפָתַ֫יִם הַטּוֹבוֹת

הַסּוּס הַטּוֹב, *the good horse;* הַסּוּס טוֹב, *the horse is good;* תְּפִלָּה וּמִזְמוֹר, *a prayer and a psalm;* מֹשֶׁה וְדָוִד וּשְׁלֹמֹה צַדִּיקִים מְאֹד, *Moses and David and Solomon [were] very just.*

I. Morphology.

A. Substantive.

81. 1. Gender. In Hebrew there are two genders: masculine and feminine. Instead of our neuter, Hebrew uses masc. or fem. which may be singular ŏr plural.

82. a) The masculine has no special ending.

b) The feminine α) may have no special ending; the gender must then be judged from the nature of the noun.

Names of females, countries, instruments, utensils, abstract notions, are feminine, *v. g.* אֵם, *mother;* כּוֹס, *cup.*

β) The great majority of fem. nouns end in an accented ה ָ (originally ת ַ), *v. g.* סוּסָה, *mare;* תּוֹרָה, *law.*

γ) A certain number of fem. nouns end in ת ֶ ֶ which is unaccented; this ending occurs especially with participles and generally as parallel to the regular ending ה ָ (see Lesson IX); Ex., מְדַבֶּ֫רֶת, *speaking.*

δ) Other fem. endings which occur but rarely are: primitive ת or simply ת; nouns in וּת and ית are often abstract; Ex., צָרְפַת, *Sārephath;* מַלְכוּת, *sovereignty, royal power.*

83. 2. Number. Hebrew has singular, plural and a few cases of dual.

a) Plural. α) Masc. nouns regularly form their plural by adding ים (ם) to the singular; this ending takes the accent, *v. g.* סוּס, *horse,* סוּסִים.

β) Fem. nouns regularly form their plural by adding וֹת, if they have no special ending, *v. g.* כּוֹס, *cup,* כּוֹסוֹת; or by changing the fem. ending of the singular into וֹת (ת), *v. g.* תּוֹרָה, *law,* תּוֹרוֹת; the ending וֹת is also accented.

Some masc. nouns form their plural in וֹת and some fem. nouns in ים without thereby changing their gender.

84. The plural form is often used not merely to designate several individuals of a class, but also to designate a certain space, a certain intensity of the idea, abstract and universal notions, and finally a high dignity (plural of majesty). This latter is found especially with the names of the Divinity, *v. g.* אֱלֹהִים, *God.*

85. b) Dual. Masc. nouns form their dual by adding ַיִם, *v. g.* נַעַל, *sandal;* נַעֲלַיִם, *a pair of sandals.* Fem. nouns form their dual by adding the same ending ַיִם to the old fem. ת (instead of ה) which however appears as ת (134), *v. g.* שָׂפָה, *lip;* שְׂפָתַיִם, *lips.*

The dual is almost entirely lost; it has been preserved mostly for objects that go in pairs, *v. g. eyes, ears, lips,* etc.

B. Adjective and Participle.

86. Adjectives and participles are treated like substantives: The fem. sing. is always ה or ת; the plur. is always ים for masc. and וֹת for fem., *v. g.* טוֹב, *good,* fem. טוֹבָה; plur. טוֹבִים and טוֹבוֹת. Instead of the dual, the plur. is used in adjectives and participles, *v. g.* שְׂפָתַיִם טוֹבוֹת, *good lips.*

C. Article.

87. 1. There is no indefinite article in Hebrew.

2. The definite article, which is invariable for all genders and numbers, is הַ prefixed to the noun which it determines, and

followed by *Daghesh Forte* in the first letter of the noun. This form is always found except before a guttural or *Resh*, see Lesson III.

3. When the first letter of the noun has a *Sh·wa*, the *Daghesh* is sometimes omitted, especially with יְ and also occasionally with מְ, נְ, and לְ. Ex.: סוּס, *horse*, הַסּוּס, *the horse;* מְנוֹרָה *a lampstand*, הַמְּנוֹרָה; but יְאֹר, *a stream*, הַיְאֹר, *the stream.*

D. The Particle "ו".

88. The most commonly used conjunction in Hebrew is וְ prefixed to the second word. It has many meanings the most common of which are conjunctive *"and"* and disjunctive *"but"*. It assumes the form וּ when the first letter of the word has *Sh·wa* (49), or is one of the four labials ב, ו, מ, פ (בּוּמַף), *v. g.* מִטָּה וּמְנוֹרָה, *a bed and a lampstand;* תְּפִלָּה וּמִזְמוֹר, *a prayer and a psalm;* but מִצְוָה וְתוֹרָה, *a command and a law.*

II. Syntactical Remarks.

A. Rules for the Article.

89. 1. In general, the article is used when it is used in English.

2. When the article is taken by the substantive, or when the substantive is determined in any way (*v. g.* proper name, noun in the construct state, see 104, 117), it is also taken by all modifying adjectives, *v. g.* הַסּוּס הַטּוֹב, *the good horse;* דָּוִד הַצַּדִּיק, *David the just.* Predicate adjectives do not take the article, *v. g.* הַסּוּס טוֹב, *the horse is good;* צַדִּיק דָּוִד, *David was just.*

90. 3. The article is often used before nouns in the vocative, and before nouns designating the class or species, *v. g.* הַזָּר, *O stranger!* הַסּוּס, *the horse* (in general).

B. Rules for Adjectives.

91. 1. Agreement. a) Regularly, the adjective, both as modifier and as predicate, agrees with the substantive in gender and number, *v. g.* זָר כֵּן, *an upright stranger;* תּוֹרוֹת טוֹבוֹת, *good laws*; טוֹבוֹת הַתּוֹרוֹת, *the laws are good.* b) An adjective qualifying two singular substantives is in the plural, *v. g.* דָּוִד וּשְׁלֹמֹה צַדִּיקִים, *David and Solomon* *were just.* c) **An** adjective qualifying several substantives of different genders is in the **masculine**, *v. g.* הַסּוּסוֹת וְהַסּוּסִים הַטּוֹבִים, *the good mares and horses.* d) Commonly enough, especially when predicate, the adjective agrees with the meaning **rather** than with the grammatical form of the substantive. Thus a collective sing. sometimes has a plur. adjective. Plural of majesty has its adjectives in the singular, *v. g.* גִּבּוֹר אֱלֹהִים, *God is strong.*

92. 2. Place. A modifying adjective is generally placed after the substantive, *v. g.* הַסּוּס הַמֵּת, *the dead horse.*

C. Nominal Sentence.

93. 1. Definition. Every sentence, the predicate of which is a noun (subst., adj., partic., pron., numerals) or its equivalent, is called a nominal sentence, *v. g.* זָרִים מִצְרַיִם *the Egyptians are foreigners.*

94. 2. Copula. Generally, in a nominal sentence, the syntactical relation between subject and predicate is expressed by mere juxtaposition without the copula; in this case, time is not expressed but must be judged from the context. If time must be emphasized, a suitable form of the verb הָיָה *(to be)* is used: טוֹבוֹת הַכּוֹסוֹת, *the cups are (were, shall be) good;* הַכּוֹסוֹת הָיוּ טוֹבוֹת, *the cups were good.*

95. 3. Order and Arrangement. It is a general rule in Hebrew that the first word of a sentence or clause is the more emphatic. In a nominal sentence the most common order is *SUBJECT-PREDICATE* as in English. If emphasis is laid on the predicate, or when the sentence is interrogative, the order is *PREDICATE-SUBJECT;* thus an adjective as predicate often precedes, *v. g.* גִּבּוֹר דָּוִד, *strong was David;* הַתְּפִלָּה טוֹבָה מְאֹד, *the prayer was very good.*

EXERCISES.

I. 1) Give masc. pl. of the following: *horse, upright, just, strong, dead.*

2) Give fem. pl. of *bed, law, cup, prayer, good, upright.*

3) Form fem. sing. of *just, horse, honest, strong, dead.*

4) Place article before the following: בִּינָה, יְאֹר, מְנוֹרָה, זָר, טוֹב, מִזְמוֹר, גֵּר.

5) Connect the following by the conjunction וְ, remembering the rules for *Daghesh Lene*, 24—26 תְּפִלָּה מִזְמוֹר; כֵּן גִּבּוֹר׃ שְׁלֹמֹה דָּוִד; טוֹב צַדִּיק.

II. 1 מֹשֶׁה צַדִּיק׃ — 2 דָּוִד גִּבּוֹר וְכֵן׃ — 3 צַדִּיק הַגֵּר׃ — 4 תְּפִלָּה וּמִזְמוֹר טוֹבִים׃ — 5 מַלְכִּי־צֶ֫דֶק וּמֹשֶׁה צַדִּיקִים מְאֹד׃ — 6 מֵת הַסּוּס הַגִּבּוֹר׃ — 7 מִצְוֹת וְתוֹרוֹת טוֹבוֹת׃ — 8 כֵּן וְצַדִּיק הַגֵּר׃ — 9 מִצְרַ֫יִם זָרִים׃ — 10 דָּוִד גִּבּוֹר וְטוֹב מְאֹד׃

III. 1 The good bed. — 2 The bed is good. — 3 Solomon was a warrior. — 4 David the just was dead. — 5 The psalm and the prayer are very good. — 6 The horses and the mares are dead. — 7 The cup, the bed and the lampstand are there. — 8 Melchisedech and Moses were good and just. — 9 The resident strangers are upright. — 10 The understanding is good. — 11 The good understanding.

LESSON II.

GENITIVE, CONSTRUCT STATE.

PARTICLES לְ, בְּ, כְּ, and וְ.

(Nouns with unchangeable vowels)

Vocabulary.

לְ	*prep.*	*to, for*	לְבוּשׁ	*m.*	*garment, clothing*
בְּ	*prep.*	*in, by, with, by means of (instr.)*	בְּכוֹר	*m.*	*first-born*
כְּ	*prep.*	*as, like*	תְּחִלָּה	*f.*	*beginning*
מִן		*from, out of (material)* *(latin ab, ex)*	יִרְאָה	*f.*	*fear*
אֲשֶׁר	*rel.*	*who, which, that*	בְּרִית	*f.*	*covenant*
אַבְרָהָם	*pr. n.*	*Abraham*	מִכְשׁוֹל	*m.*	*stumbling-block*
יִצְחָק	*pr. n.*	*Isaac*	בְּדִיל	*m.*	*tin, lead*
יַעֲקֹב	*pr. n.*	*Jacob*	כְּסִיל	*m.*	*fool*
יוֹסֵף	*pr. n.*	*Joseph*	סֻכָּה	*f.*	*booth*
יְהוּדָה	*pr. n.*	*Juda*	נְתִיבָה	*f.*	*way, path*
רְאוּבֵן	*pr. n.*	*Reuben*	זֵד	*adj.*	*presumptuous, insolent*
גְּבוּל	*m.*	*border, territory, boundary*	תִּירוֹשׁ	*m.*	*new wine, must*
			פִּקּוּדִים	*m.*	*precepts, orders, commands.*

	Sing.		Plural		Dual	
	Masc. (Fem.)	Fem.	Masc.	Fem.	Masc.	Fem.
Absol. St.		ֶת ; ָה	ִים	...וֹת	ַיִם	...תַיִם
Constr. St.		ֶת ; ַת	ֵי	...וֹת	ֵי	...תֵי
Subst. Constr.	סוּס	סוּסַת	סוּסֵי	סוּסוֹת	עֵינֵי (*eyes*)	שִׂפְתֵי (*lips*)
Adject. „	מֵת	מֵתַת	מֵתֵי	מֵתוֹת		

Examples.

כּוֹס הַזָּר	*the cup of the stranger*	סוּס הַזָּר	*the horse of the stranger*
יִרְאַת אַבְרָהָם	*the fear of Abraham*	סוּס זָר	*a stranger's horse*
סוּסֵי יוֹסֵף	*the horses of Joseph*	סוּס לְזָר	*a horse of the stranger*
כּוֹסוֹת תִּירוֹשׁ	*cups of new wine*	הַסּוּס לַזָּר	*the horse of the stranger*
סֻכּוֹת יִשְׂרָאֵל	*the booths of Israel*	הַסּוּס אֲשֶׁר לַזָּר	*the horse of the stranger*

I. The Construct State.

A. Definition.

96. The forms given in the preceding lesson are the forms used when a noun stands alone or in apposition to another noun (absolute state). There is, besides, another form, generally with shorter endings. This shorter form is taken by a noun when it is immediately followed by another with which it unites to denote an object or idea made up of the combination of both. Hence the noun is said to be in construction or in the CONSTRUCT STATE.

The noun in the construct state (*nomen regens*) forms with the following (*nomen rectum*) a kind of compound word, often joined by *Maqqeph* (cp. *landlord, Lord's prayer*, etc.). The two words must be pronounced together and the stress is laid on the *nomen rectum* which has the principal accent. The effort made in uniting them in pronunciation results in the shortening of the vowels of the first, if these vowels are changeable. Here we shall examine only the changes in the endings, since most of the nouns used have unchangeable vowels.

B. Modifications of endings in the Construct State.

97. 1. Singular. a) Words without special ending in the absolute state suffer no change in the construct, *v. g.* סוּס הַזָּר, *the horse of the stranger.*

b) Feminine nouns in ָה have the older ending ַת; fem. nouns in ֶת, וּת, ִית, do not change, *v. g.* בִּינָה, constr. בִּינַת; בְּרִית, constr. בְּרִית.

98. 2. Plural. a) Masc. nouns change ִים to ֵי, *v. g.* סוּסִים, *horses*, but סוּסֵי דָוִד, *the horses of David.*

b) Fem. nouns do not change their ending in the constr. *v. g.* מִטּוֹת, *beds*, מִטּוֹת הַזָּרִים, *the beds of the strangers.*

99. 3. Dual. Both masc. and fem. change ־ַיִם into ־ֵי, *v. g.* עֵינֵי הַגֵּר, *the eyes of the sojourner;* שִׂפְתֵי הַצַּדִּיק, *the lips of the just man.*

C. Use of the Construct State.

100. 1. In general, the constr. state can be used in Hebrew when a compound word or possessive case are used in English, or when the relation between two words is expressed by the prep. *of.* The most common use is to express a GENITIVE, *v. g.* תְּחִלַּת הַתְּפִלָּה, *the beginning of the prayer.* Apart from the genitive proper, the constr. state can be used when the *nomen rectum* gives a closer definition of the *nomen regens,* whether it be genus, species, measure, material or quality, *v. g.*, מְנוֹרַת בְּדִיל, *a lampstand of tin;* טוֹבַת בִּינָה, (*a female*) *good of understanding, i. e. of good understanding;* but see Lesson XXIII.

101. 2. Only one *nomen regens* can be joined to a *nomen rectum* by means of the construct state. If there are several, another construction must be used. A phrase like "*the horse and the mare of the foreigner*" should be rendered "*the horse of the foreigner and his mare*", or we should adopt one of the ways mentioned in 106, 107.

102. 3. One *nomen regens,* however, can have several genitives. Yet this construction is avoided, and Hebrew prefers to repeat the *regens, v. g.* סוּסֵי דָוִד וּשְׁלֹמֹה, *the horses of David and Solomon,* but better סוּסֵי דָוִד וְסוּסֵי שְׁלֹמֹה.

103. 4. A series of genitives may be formed by a *nomen rectum* serving at the same time as *regens* to a genitive depending on it, *v. g.* תְּחִלַּת תְּפִלַּת דָּוִד *the beginning of David's prayer.* See also § 106.

104. 5. A noun in the constr. state never takes the article and is never determined by itself; if it has to be determined, this is done by determining the following genitive which takes the article, or which is determined by its own nature (see 117), *v. g.* proper names. Ex.: מִטַּת גֵּר, *a bed of a sojourner;* מִטַּת הַגֵּר, *the bed of the sojourner;* סוּסֵי דָוִד, *the horses of David.*

The undetermined Hebrew *regens* must often be rendered in English with the definite article. Yet strictly speaking, the compound itself is undetermined, *v. g. the owner of a land=an owner of land=a landowner.*

105. 6. Nothing should come between the constr. state and the *nomen rectum.* All modifiers qualifying the *nomen regens* must be placed after the *nomen rectum,* because, strictly speaking, all those modifiers qualify the whole compound, *v. g.* סֻכַּת אַבְרָהָם הַטּוֹבָה, *the good booth of Abraham.*

In some cases, it may be difficult to know whether a modifier belongs to the whole compound or only to the *nomen rectum, v. g.* סוּס יוֹסֵף הַטּוֹב may mean: *the good horse of Joseph,* or *the horse of the good Joseph.* To avoid amphibology, use may be made of the other ways for expressing a genitive, mentioned in the following section.

II. Expression of the Genitive by Circumlocution.

106. 1. The genitive relation between two nouns may also be indicated by means of the preposition לְ (*to*) prefixed to the second noun, the first remaining in the absolute state. This method is used:

a) to prevent too long a series of subordinate nouns in the constr. state (103), *v. g.*. תְּחִלַּת הַתְּפִלָּה לְדָוִד, *the beginning of David's prayer;*

b) to prevent a noun from being determined by a following determinate genitive, as would be the case according to 104, and to avoid the amphibology mentioned in 105 (note), *v. g.* סוּס הַגֵּר, *the horse of the resident stranger;* סוּס לַגֵּר, *a horse belonging to the resident stranger;* הַסּוּס הַטּוֹב לְגֵר, *the good horse of a resident stranger.*

107. 2. The genitive relation may also be indicated by a kind of relative clause אֲשֶׁר לְ, *which (belongs) to.* This expression denotes the real possessor, and is commonly used when a genitive depends on more than one subst., *v. g.* הַמְּנוֹרָה וְהַמִּטָּה וְהַסֻּכָּה אֲשֶׁר לְאַבְרָהָם, *the lampstand, the bed and the booth of Abraham.*

III. Remarks on the Particles.

108. 1. When followed by a consonant with a simple *Sh·wa,* the three particles, בּ, כּ, ל, are sounded with *Ḥireq* (46), *v. g.* בִּנְתִיבָה, *on a path;* לִכְסִיל, *to a fool;* כִּבְרִית מֹשֶׁה, *according to the covenant of Moses.*

109. 2. When they are followed by the article, the ה of the latter is elided and its vowel goes over to the particle, *v. g.* לַגֵּר, *to the stranger,* for לְהַגֵּר; בַּסֻּכָּה, *in the booth,* for בְּהַסֻּכָּה; כַּסּוּס, *like the horse,* for כְּהַסּוּס.

110. 3. The preposition מִן (*from, out, out of*) may be kept as an independent word, united to the following by *Maqqeph;* thus usually before the article, *v. g.* מִן־הַנְּתִיבָה, *away from the path.* Commonly, however, it is prefixed to the following word and its *Nun* is assimilated to the first letter which consequently takes *Daghesh Forte* (21). The *Daghesh* is sometimes omitted when the letter has *Sh·wa;* Ex.: מִמִּכְשׁוֹל, *away from a stumbling-block;* מִכְּסִיל, *from a fool;* מִבְצִיר, *from the vintage of* (בָּצִיר).

111. 4. When a word begins with a *Yodh* marked with *Sh·wa,* the *Yodh* coalesces with the *Hireq* of the particles (also after ו 47, 49, and מִ), *v. g.* מִיאֹר, *from a stream,* for מִיְאֹר; בִּיהוּדָה *in Judah;* וִיהוּדָה, *and Judah;* מִיהוּדָה, *from Judah.*

(On the particles before gutturals, see Lesson IV).

EXERCISES.

I. 1) Review forms of fem. sing. and of masc. and fem. plural.

2) Give the constr. state sing. of the following: *law, stumbling-block, bed, booth, lampstand, cup, covenant.*

3) Can a proper name be in the constr. state? (104).

4) Give constr. state plur. of *cups, prayers, warriors, just men, commands, orders, laws, fools, insolent.*

5) Translate into Hebrew: *to the stranger*; *to a first-born; to a fool; in the path; in the beginning; like the warrior; from the psalm; from the path; as Reuben*; *in Egypt; according to the covenant.*

II. 1. לִרְאוּבֵן, בְּכוֹר יַעֲקֹב׃ – 2. כּוֹסוֹת תִּירוֹשׁ׃ – 3. יִרְאַת יְהוָה׃
– 4. לַגֵּרִים אֲשֶׁר בִּגְבוּל יִשְׂרָאֵל׃ – 5. מִזְמוֹר לְדָוִד׃ – 6. מְתִים הַסּוּסִים
אֲשֶׁר לְמִצְרָיִם׃ – 7. מִצְרַיִם זָרִים בְּיִשְׂרָאֵל וּבִיהוּדָה׃ – 8. לְיוֹסֵף מִטָּה
וּמְנוֹרַת בְּדִיל׃ – 9. כּוֹס תִּירוֹשׁ מִכְשׁוֹל בִּנְתִיבַת הַכְּסִיל׃

III. 1. The covenant is very good. – 2. The fear of the strangers. – 3. At (in) the beginning of the prayer. – 4. From the river of Egypt. – 5. Cups of must. – 6. The insolent strangers are like stumbling-blocks for the just sojourners. – 7. The horses of the warriors of Israel. – 8. Reuben, the first-born of Israel, was of good understanding. – 9. According to the covenant of Melchisedech, the just. – 10. In a psalm of David. – 11. In the psalm of David. – 12. A good law is a stumbling-block on the path of the fool.

LESSON III.

GUTTURALS. FORM of the ARTICLE BEFORE GUTTURALS. VERBAL SENTENCE.

Vocabulary. Nouns.

אֵל	*m.*	*hero, god, God*
אֱלֹהַ	*m.*	*god, God*
אֱלֹהִים	*m.*	*gods, God*
יְהוָה	*pr. n.*	*Yahweh, Jehovah, the Lord*
אֲדֹנָי	*m.*	*the Master, the Lord, Lord*
עֶלְיוֹן	*a.*	*high, Most High*
שְׁמוּאֵל	*pr. n.*	*Samuel*
שָׁאוּל	*pr. n.*	*Saul*
עֹלָה	*f.*	*burnt-offering*
רוּחַ	*f.*	*(m.) spirit, wind*
רָם	*pt.*	*high (Ramah), exalted*
חָרָבָה	*f.*	*dry land*
עָרִיץ	*a.*	*terrible, awe-inspiring*
אֶבְיוֹן	*a.*	*poor (Ebionite)*
אוֹר	*m.*	*light*
חֲזִיר	*m.*	*swine*
חֻקָּה	*f.*	*order, precept*
הוֹד	*m.*	*splendor, majesty*
גּוֹי	*m.*	*people (non-Jews)*
עָב	*m. and f.*	*cloud*
עֵד	*m.*	*witness*
עֵדוֹת	*f. pl.*	*testimonies (precepts)*
רֵאשִׁית	*f.*	*beginning*
אֶת־,אֵת		*(sign of accusative)*
אֶת־,אֵת	*pr.*	*with*
אֶל־	*pr.*	*towards, to, after verbs of motion*

Verbs.

לָקַח	*he took*	שָׁלַח	*he sent*	נָתַן	*he gave*
לָקְחָה	*she took*	שָׁלְחָה	*she sent*	נָתְנָה	*she gave*
לָקְחוּ	*they took*	שָׁלְחוּ	*they sent*	נָתְנוּ	*they gave*

שָׁמַר	*he kept*	מָשַׁח	*he anointed*
שָׁמְרָה	*she kept*	מָשְׁחָה	*she anointed*
שָׁמְרוּ	*they kept*	מָשְׁחוּ	*they anointed*

Examples.

הָֽאֶבְיוֹן	*the poor man*	הַֽחֲזִיר	*the swine*	הָרוּחַ	*the spirit*
הָעֵד	*the witness*	הֶֽעָרִיץ	*the terrible one*	הֶחָרָבָה	*the dry land*
הָֽאֱלֹהִים[1]	*the (true) God*	הָֽעֶלְיוֹן	*the Most High*	הָרֵאשִׁית	*the beginning.*

לָקַח דָּוִד אֶת־הַסּוּס, *David took the horse;* מָשַׁח שְׁמוּאֵל אֵת שָׁאוּל, *Samuel anointed Saul;* נָֽתְנוּ דָוִד וּשְׁלֹמֹה כּוֹס תִּירוֹשׁ לָֽאֶבְיוֹנִים, *David and Solomon gave a cup of new wine to the poor.*

I. Article before Gutturals and Resh.

112. 1. If the noun to which the article is to be prefixed begins with a guttural or *Resh*, attention must be paid:

a) to the guttural itself, inasmuch as a guttural does not take *Daghesh* (66, 121);

b) to the vowel of the article:

Pathah may be retained (Implicit *Daghesh Forte*)
Pathah may be heightened or dissimilated to *S·ghol*
Pathah may be lengthened to *Qameṣ*.

113. 2. Before the gutturals the article will have the following forms:

Article	Gutturals
הַ[1] before	*He* and *Heth* (ה and ח) with any vowel but *Qameṣ* or *Hateph Qameṣ*
הֶ before	*Heth* with *Qameṣ* or *Hateph Qameṣ* (◌ָ, ◌ֳ); unaccented הָ and עָ or עֳ
הָ[2] before	accented הָ and עָ; *'Ayin* (ע) with any vowel but unaccented ◌ָ or ◌ֳ; *'Aleph* and *Resh* always.

[1] The appellative names of God sometimes take the article; generally, however, they do not, *v. g.* אֱלֹהִים or הָאֱלֹהִים; עֶלְיוֹן or הָעֶלְיוֹן. יְהוָה of course, being essentially a proper name determined by itself, never takes the article. For the same reason, יְהוָה cannot be in the constr. state; the common phrase יְהוָה צְבָאוֹת is probably only an abbreviation for יְהוָה (אֱלֹהֵי) צְבָאוֹת, Jehovah (God) of hosts.

3. Therefore, the various gutturals will take the article as follows:

Gutturals	Article		Examples
א and ר	always	הָ	הָאֵל *the god (God)*
			הָרוּחַ *the spirit*
ע	unaccented עָ or עֻ . . .	הֶ	הֶעָבִים *the clouds*
	in all other cases	הָ[1]	הָעָב *the cloud*
ח	חָ or חֳ.	הֶ	הֶחָרָבָה *the dry land*
	in all other cases	הַ[2]	הַחֲזִיר *the swine*
ה	accented הָ	הָ	הָהָר *the mountain*
	unaccented הָ	הֶ	הֶהָרִים *the mountains*
	in all other cases	הַ[2]	הַהוֹד *the majesty, splendor*

II. Verbal Sentence.

114. 1. Definition. Every sentence the predicate of which is a finite verb is a verbal sentence.

115. 2. Order and Arrangement. In a verbal sentence the predicate verb ordinarily precedes the subject, and the subject precedes the object, hence: *VERB-SUBJECT-OBJECT*; *v. g.* שָׁלַח דָּוִד כּוֹס, *David sent a cup.*

We find also other arrangements according to the desired emphasis or simple rhythm; thus, the subject often precedes the verb in secondary, explanatory, or circumstantial clauses, *v. g.*, מָשַׁח שְׁמוּאֵל אֶת־שָׁאוּל וְקִישׁ שָׁלַח אֶת־שָׁאוּל . . ., *Samuel anointed Saul; now Qish had sent Saul . . .*

116. 3. Agreement. A predicate verb generally agrees with the subject in number and gender, *v. g.* שָׁמַר מֹשֶׁה, *Moses kept;* נָתְנוּ הַגֵּרִים, *the strangers gave.* As remarked for adjective (§ 91d), the agreement may be one of meaning, not of grammatical form; thus plurals of majesty take the verb in the singular, *v. g.* שָׁלַח אֱלֹהִים, *God sent.*

When the predicate verb precedes the subject, very often it remains in the 3 m. sing. even when it refers to a plural subject, or to several subjects, or even to a feminine subject, *v. g.* שָׁמַר מֹשֶׁה וְאַהֲרֹן, *Moses and Aaron kept.*

---

[1] The article is rarely הַ before ע, *v. g.* הַעִוְּרִים, *the blind ones.*

[2] The article is very rarely הָ before ה and ח, *v. g.* הָחַי, *the living creature*; always however before הֵמָּה, הֵם, הֵנָּה, *v. g.* הָהֵם, הָהֵמָּה, *those* (masc.); הָהֵנָּה *those* (fem.) see 149.

117. 4. Direct Object. The direct object is known from the context. When the direct object is determined, it is often preceded by the particle אֵת or אֶת־.

A noun is determined by its nature, (*v. g.* proper names); by the article; by a pronominal suffix; in the case of a construct state, by a following determinate genitive.

The particle אֵת merely indicates the direct object and should not be translated in English, nor should it be confounded with the preposition אֵת, אֶת־ which means *with, together with* (see Paradigm H).

EXERCISES.

I. The light. The splendor. The burnt-offering. The dry land. The spirit. The swine. The cloud. The clouds. The horse. The gods. The Most High. The booth. The canal. The covenant.

The precepts of the law. The laws of Israel. The laws, the precepts, the commands, the orders and the testimonies which Jehovah gave. The swines of the Egyptians. The majesty of Solomon. A psalm of David. The light of the nations.

He gave. He sent. They kept. She took. They anointed. She kept. They took. He anointed.

II. 1. נָתַן שְׁלֹמֹה סוּסִים טוֹבִים לְגִבּוֹרֵי יִשְׂרָאֵל׃ – 2. שָׁלַח דָּוִד אֶת־הַזָּרִים מִגְּבוּל יִשְׂרָאֵל׃ – 3. שָֽׁמְרוּ אַבְרָהָם וְיִצְחָק וְיַֽעֲקֹב אֶת־בְּרִית יְהוָֹה אֱלֹהֵי יִשְׂרָאֵל׃ – 4. תְּפִלַּת הַצַּדִּיק כְּעוֹלָה טוֹבָה לְאֵל עֶלְיוֹן׃ – 5. יְהוָֹה אֱלֹהִים רָם וְגִבּוֹר מְאֹד׃ – 6. מָשַׁח שְׁמוּאֵל אֶת־שָׁאוּל וְאֶת־דָּוִד׃ – 7. שָֽׁמְרוּ גִּבּוֹרֵי יְהוּדָה אֶת־עֵדוֹת יְהוָֹה׃ – 8. מֵתִים הַסּוּסִים אֲשֶׁר נָתַן דָּוִד לִשְׁלֹמֹה׃

III. 1. The terrible nation sent horses to Solomon. – 2. The precepts of the Most High God are good. – 3. Solomon took the cups of new wine. – 4. David gave a horse to the stranger. – 5. Samuel anointed Saul. – 6. A good law is a light. – 7. The spirit of Jehovah sent Samuel to Israel. – 8. The precepts of the law are a stumbling-block to the fool. – 9. Israel kept the dry land; they gave the (Nile-) canals to the Egyptians.

LESSON IV.

GUTTURALS (continued). NOTA RELATIONIS אֲשֶׁר. THE PARTICLES לֹא, יֵשׁ, אֵין, אַ֫יִן.

Vocabulary. Nouns.

לוּחַ (pl. וֹת)	*m.*	*tablet*
עֵדוּת	*f.*	*testimony*
אֱוִיל	*a.*	*fool, foolish.*
בְּרִית	*f.*	*covenant*
כָּרַת בְּרִית		*made a covenant*
אֶ֫רֶץ (הָאָ֫רֶץ)	*f.*	*earth*
הַר (הָהָר)	*m.*	*mountain*
אֲרוֹן (הָאָרוֹן)	*m.*	*ark, chest*
חַג (הֶחָג)	*m.*	*feast*
פַּר (הַפָּר)	*m.*	*bull*
עַם (הָעָם)	*m.*	*people*
רֵאשִׁית	*f.*	*beginning*
צֹאן	*f.&m.*	*coll., small cattle, sheep, flock*
נוֹרָא	*pt.*	*terrible, awe-inspiring*
	(*pl.f.*)	*wonderful things (terribilia)*

שָׁם	*adv.*	*there,* אֲשֶׁר שָׁם, *where*
מִשָּׁם	*adv.*	*thence,* אֲשֶׁר מִשָּׁם, *whence*
לֹא (לוֹא)	*adv.*	*not*
עִם־	*prep.*	*with (often in the sense of dealing with)*
עַל־	*prep.*	*upon, over*
אַ֫יִן	*cst.*	אֵין *(non existence) sometimes mere negation 'not'; often 'there (is) not'*
יֵשׁ, יֶשׁ־		*(existence) used as verb 'there is, . . . are'*
שֶׁ·		*which*

Verbs.

כָּרַת	*he cut off, made (a covenant)*	שָׁחַט	*he slaughtered, offered (sacrifice)*	אָמַר	*he said*
				אָמְרָה	*she said*
כָּֽרְתָה	*she " "*	שָֽׁחֲטָה	*she " "*	אָמְרוּ	*they said*
כָּֽרְתוּ	*they " "*	שָֽׁחֲטוּ	*they " "*	לֵאמֹר	*to wit, saying*
הָלַךְ	*he went*				

Examples.

אֶרֶץ יִשְׂרָאֵל, *the land of Israel;* בָּאָרֶץ, *in the land;* לֶאֱוִיל, *to a fool;* לָאֱוִיל, *to the fool;* לֵאלֹהִים, *to God;* מֵהַר, *from a mountain;* מִן־הָהָר, *from the mountain;* מֵיְהוָה, *from Jehovah;* לֹא כָּרְתוּ בְרִית עִם־יְהוָה, *they did not make a covenant with Jehovah;* וְאֵין אַבְרָהָם שָׁם, *and Abraham was not there;* יֵשׁ סוּסִים עַל־הֶהָרִים, *there are horses on the mountains.*

118. Six words in the singular have always *Qameṣ* in the syllable that follows the article; they are: אֶרֶץ, הַר, אֲרוֹן, חַג, פַּר, עַם: הָאָרֶץ, הָהָר *etc.*

I. Some Peculiarities of the gutturals.

(Review; see 66—76).

119. 1. The gutturals do not admit of simple vocal *S̱h·wa,* but require a *Ḥaṭeph* or compound *S̱h·wa* (72).

This *Ḥaṭeph* is commonly *Ḥaṭeph Paṯhaḥ, v. g.* חֲזִיר, *swine;* שָׁחֲטוּ, *they slaughtered.* In close proximity to the tone, *Aleph* shows preference for *Ḥaṭeph S·g̱hol, v. g.* אֱוִיל, *fool;* but when removed from the tone, *Aleph* often takes *Ḥaṭeph Paṯhaḥ:* אֲרוּבָּה, *window,* but not always: אֱלֹהִים, *God.*

120. 2. When a vowelless consonant, more particularly the particles ב, כ, ל, ו, is prefixed to a guttural with *Ḥaṭeph* this consonant is sounded with the vowel of the *Ḥaṭeph* (48), *v. g.* לֶאֱוִיל, *to a fool;* לַחֲזִיר, *to a swine.*

The two words אֱלֹהִים, *God* and אֱמֹר, *to say, saying,* do not follow that rule: after the particles ב, כ, ל, ו, *Aleph* becomes silent and the particles are sounded with *Ṣere, v. g.* לֵאמֹר, *saying* (*dicendo*), for לֶאֱמֹר; וֵאלֹהִים, *and God,* for וֶאֱלֹהִים.

In אֲדֹנִי, *my master,* and אֲדֹנָי, *the Lord, Aleph* loses its consonantal value after the particles ב, כ, ל, ו, which are sounded with *Paṯhaḥ, v. g.* כַּאדֹנִי, לַאדֹנִי; יְהוָה, pronounced אֲדֹנָי, is treated exactly like אֲדֹנָי, *v. g.* לַיהוָה, בַּיהוָה (34).

121. 3. The gutturals and also the letter *Reṣ̌h* do not admit of *Dag̱heṣ̌h Forte* (66); the preceding vowel is either lengthened as compensation (mostly before א, ר, ע) or remains short and is treated as if the *Dag̱heṣ̌h* was actually written (implicit *Dag̱heṣ̌h,* virtual strengthening), mostly before ה and ח). In the preceding lesson we have seen the application of this rule to the article.

The preposition ·מִ (מִן) (110) before a guttural (even before ה and ח, except very few cases) becomes מֵ, *v. g.* מֵהַר, *from a mountain;* מֵיְהוָה, *from Jehovah*, not מִיהוָה (111), because it is pronounced as if written מֵאֲדֹנָי.

II. Nota Relationis, אֲשֶׁר.

122. 1. The particle אֲשֶׁר, mentioned § 107, is not a relative in our sense of the term. It is a particle that connects a word to be explained with an explanatory clause. In English, such a connection is indicated either by mere juxtaposition, *v. g. the horse I saw*, or by a relative pronoun, *the horse which I saw.* Of itself, אֲשֶׁר indicates merely that there is such a relation, but does not show whether the relation is one of time, place or person. Consequently, the kind of relation that is intended is often indicated by a suitable adverb or pronoun (497 ff.), *v. g.* הָאָרֶץ אֲשֶׁר הָלַךְ מִשָּׁם אַבְרָהָם, *the land whence went Abraham.*

123. 2. Instead of אֲשֶׁר, a proclitic שֶׁ, the origin of which is different from אֲשֶׁר, is sometimes used, and is generally followed by a *Dag̱hes̱h Forte* in the next letter; before gutturals, *Dag̱hes̱h* is of course omitted, but *S·g̱hol* is generally (it is rarely שַׁ or שָׁ) kept, although this seems to go against the rules for gutturals, *v. g.* הַגֵּר שֶׁלֹּא הָלַךְ, *the stranger who did not go;* יְהוָה שֶׁאֵל יִשְׂרָאֵל, *Jehovah, who is the God of Israel.*

III. The Particles אַיִן, אֵין, יֵשׁ, לֹא (see Paradigm H).

124. A. אַיִן and אֵין (constr. state of אַיִן) are really substantives denoting non-existence; but their substantival nature has been lost, so that practically they are used either as mere negative particles, *no, without*, or as negative verbs, *there (is) not, there (are) not.*

1. As a negative particle, אֵין is generally used (אַיִן, more seldom) and is always placed before the substantive, *v. g.* אֵין בְּרִית, *without a covenant.*

2. As negative verbs, both can be used in a nominal sentence; אַיִן stands always after the subject and אֵין mostly before, *v. g.* וְאֵין יַעֲקֹב עַל־הָהָר, *and Jacob was not on the mountain.*

125. B. Similarly יֵשׁ, יֶשׁ־, originally a substantive meaning *existence*, is practically always used as a verb in a nominal sentence, *there is, there are.* Generally, it is placed before the substantive the existence of which is asserted, *v. g.* יֵשׁ אֱלֹהִים בְּיִשְׂרָאֵל, *there is a God in Israel.*

126. 3. The particle לֹא (לוֹא) is used to negative a verbal clause, and in certain cases, a nominal sentence (145) or individual words; ordinarily, it is placed immediately before the negatived word. Ex.: לֹא הָלַךְ דָּוִד, *David did not go;* לֹא־זָר הוּא, *he is not a stranger;* לֹא־כֵן, *unrighteous.*

EXERCISES.

I. 1) Review. Usual endings of feminine nouns in singular and plural. Plural endings of masc. nouns. Form of the article before ordinary consonants; . . . before consonant with *Shwa*; . . . before gutturals. Form of the construct state. Use of the construct state. Place of the adjective qualifying a constr. state. Other ways of expressing a genitive besides the constr. state. When does the adjective take the article?

2) The earth. The people. With the Lord (Yahweh). To the feast. To a swine. With a fool. On the mountain. They did not go. He did not give. She did not say. Abraham was not there.

II. 1. אֵין זָר בָּאָרֶץ׃ – 2. לֹא שָׁחֲטוּ צֹאן׃ – 3. יֵשׁ מִכְשׁוֹל בַּנְּתִיבָה׃ – 4. נָתַן דָּוִד כּוֹס תִּירוֹשׁ לִשְׁלֹמֹה׃ – 5. לֹא כָּרְתוּ בְּרִית הַגּוֹיִם הֶעָרִיצִים עִם־יְהֹוָה אֱלֹהֵי יִשְׂרָאֵל׃ – 6. לָקְחוּ אֶת־אֲרוֹן בְּרִית וְאֶת־לוּחֹת הָעֵדוּת׃ – 7. הָלַךְ אַבְרָהָם מִשָּׁם אֶל־הָהָר אֲשֶׁר אָמַר יְהֹוָה וְאֵין צֹאן לָעֹלָה׃ – 8. יֵשׁ אֵל גִּבּוֹר בְּיִשְׂרָאֵל וּבִיהוּדָה, יְהֹוָה אֱלֹהִים אֲשֶׁר רָם וְצַדִּיק וְנוֹרָא מְאֹד׃ – 9. כָּרְתוּ עָרִיצֵי הַגּוֹיִם אֶת־הָאֶבְיוֹנִים מִן־הָאָרֶץ וְאֵין גִּבּוֹרֵי יִשְׂרָאֵל שָׁם׃ – 10. אֵין בִּינָה לַכְּסִיל׃

III. 1. The Lord (Yahweh) God made a covenant with the people of Israel. – 2. The people slaughtered small cattle (as) a sacrifice to God. – 3. The mountain of David which is in the land of Israel. – 4. The just ones of the land went to the feast of the Tabernacles (booths) according to the precepts of the Lord. – 5. The fierce nations sent horses to Abraham, but Abraham was not there. – 6. There are good sojourners in the land of Egypt. – 7. They kept the tables of the testimony in the ark of the covenant. – 8. The fear of the Lord was upon the Egyptians. – 9. Samuel anointed David and the fear of God was upon the people. – 10. God gave laws, and statutes, and commandments, and precepts, and testimonies to the people of the land.

* * *

PRELIMINARY REMARKS ON HEBREW FLECTION.

A. Changeable and Unchangeable Vowels.

B. Rules that govern changes of vowels in the inflection of Nouns and Verbs.

C. Various Classes of Nouns grouped according to the vocal variations which they undergo.

A. Changeable and Unchangeable Vowels.

127. Unchangeable vowels are those which do not change or disappear in the course of inflection. Which vowels are unchangeable will be learned by practice and by the study of the forms. Generally speaking, the following vowels are unchangeable:

128. 1. regularly, all long vowels fully written (unchangeable by nature), *v. g.* סוּס, *horse;* צַדִּיק, *just.*

This applies also to cases in which a vowel, which should be fully written, has the defective spelling (5), especially to *Ḥolem* when *Ṣere* follows in the next syllable, *v. g.* קֹטֵל, *killing*, for קוֹטֵל.

129. 2. a short vowel in a closed or sharpened syllable provided it be not final (unchangeable by position), *v. g.* מִכְשׁוֹל, *stumbling-block;* גַּנָּב, *thief.*

This rule applies to the simple form without any addition (as would be the personal suffixes or the feminine ending), *v. g.* in מַלְכִּי, *my king*, the syllable מַל is not unchangeable because the simple masculine form is מֶלֶךְ; so also מַלְכָּה, *queen.*

130. 3. a long vowel that has arisen as a compensation for the omission of a *Dag̱hesẖ Forte* in the case of a guttural (66), *v. g.* חָרָשׁ, *artificer,* for חַרָּשׁ.

131. 4. Special rules for *Qameṣ*.

Generally speaking, *Qameṣ* is only tone-long and changeable, for primitively long *Qameṣ* has usually been obscured to *ô* (וֹ), 61. *Qameṣ* is naturally long and unchangeable: a) in a biliteral or after a vocal *S̱h·wa*, in a triliteral monosyllable, *v. g.* עָב, *cloud* (261), כְּתָב, *writing;*

132. b) in a final closed syllable following a sharpened syllable, *v. g.* גַּנָּב, *thief*, or after a guttural or *Reš̱h* the sharpening of which has been omitted and the preceding vowel lengthened as compensation (66, 130), *v. g.* חָרָשׁ, *artificer.* In those nouns, however, *Qameṣ* (by exception) is shortened to *Paṯhaḥ* in the constr. state of the singular, *v. g.* constr. גַּנַּב, חָרַשׁ;

133. c) before quiescent *Alepẖ*, *v. g.* מִקְרָא, *assembly.*

B. General rules for nominal and verbal flection.

1. Nominal Flection.

134. Rule I. In Hebrew, there is a tendency to have an open pretone syllable, *i. e.* an open syllable immediately before the tone, with a long vowel, and an unaccented closed syllable with a short vowel (52). The vowel of the antepretone, if changeable, is volatilized, *v. g.* דָּבָר, *word*, pl. דְּבָרִים; חֻקָּה, *precept*, pl. חֻקּוֹת.

135. Rule II. When the tone moves forward, Hebrew flection requires that we should shorten all vowels as much as possible, beginning from the place of the tone and going backward, observing Rule I, and the laws of Hebrew syllable-formation (45 ff.).

1st. application: דָּבָר pl. דְּבָרִים; the syllable רִים has the tone; בָ is pretonic and, consequently, retains *Qameṣ* בָ; דּ is antepretonic and its vowel volatilized, hence דְּבָרִים; so also דְּבָרִי, *my word.*

2d. application: דִּבְרֵי חֲכָמִים, *words of wise men*, from uninflected דָּבָר חָכָם. דִּבְרֵי, being in the constr. state, has no primary accent (96); the main accent is on the last syllable of חֲכָמִים, and the two words are considered as only one. Applying the rules just given, we have מִים with the tone; כָ remains pretone-long; חָ, not being pretonic is volatilized, חֲ (72); רֵי is unchangeable; *Qameṣ* of בָ is volatilized, בְ, and so should be *Qameṣ* under דּ (rule II); but because it is forbidden to have two vocal *S̱h·was* in the beginning of a word (46), *Ḥireq* (attenuated from original *Paṯhaḥ*) is inserted, hence דִּבְרֵי חֲכָמִים. So also דִּבְרֵיכֶם, *your words, etc.*

3d. application: דְּבַר דָּוִד, *the word of David.* In the constr. state of the singular, the original closed ultima of דָּבָר, having lost its accent, becomes short (52) *Qameṣ* to *Pathaḥ* (55); דָ not being pretonic, since the tone has shifted to the last syllable of דָּוִד, becomes דְ with *Sh·wa.* The same takes place before suffixes which begin with a consonant except ְךָ which is everywhere treated as a light suffix; see later, 150.

2. Verbal Flection.

136. a) In general, the verb follows the same rules as the noun, *v. g.* קְטָלוֹ, *he killed him;* קְטַלְתֶּם, *you killed,* from קָטַל; יִשְׁלָחֵנִי, *he will send me,* from שָׁלַח, *to send, etc.*

137. b) Differences. *α*) Probably to differentiate between verbal and nominal forms, before the ending ָה of the 3 f. s. and וּ of the 3 pl. (not before pronominal suffixes beginning with a vowel, see Paradigm A), the vowel of the antepretone (first radical) is kept and that of the would-be pretone, if changeable, volatilized, *v. g.* קָטַל, *he killed,* but קָטְלָה, *she killed,* not קְטָלָה; קָטְלוּ, *they killed,* not קְטָלוּ. On the other hand, קְטָלוֹ, *he killed him,* not קָטְלוֹ, because וֹ is a pronominal suffix (see Lesson xiv, 315—317).

138. β) When the vowel of the second radical is ō or ē in conjunction with an unchangeable vowel in the preceding syllable, it is volatilized before all additions (including suffixes) beginning with a vowel, *v. g.* יִקְטֹל, *he shall kill;* but יִקְטְלֵנִי, *he shall kill me;* תִּקְטְלִי, *thou (fem.) shalt kill;* יִקְטְלוּ *they shall kill.*

139. These two peculiarities (137, 138) do not apply to verbal Pause; there, the vowel of the second radical is regularly kept as tone-long (78, 79), *v. g.* קָטְלָה P. קָטָלָה; יִקְטְלוּ P. יִקְטֹלוּ.

C. Various classes of nouns.

140. For greater facility, Hebrew nouns can be reduced to certain groups or classes according to the changes which they undergo in their flection. Leaving aside a few irregular nouns not easily classified (260), the others can be grouped in six classes:

I. Class. Nouns with unchangeable vowels, among which are also included those explained in § 132, *v. g.* סוּס, *horse;* זָר, *stranger;* בְּרִית, *covenant;* גַּנָּב, *thief, etc.*

II. Class. *Milra'* Nouns, *i. e.* with the tone on the ultima, having a changeable vowel in the penult and an unchangeable vowel in the ultima, *v. g.* גָּדוֹל, *great.*

III. Class. Monosyllabic Nouns in ă, ē, ō, and a few dissyllabic Nouns following their analogy, *v. g.* כַּף, *palm (of the hand); לֵב, heart;* חֹק, *precept;* קָטָן, *small.*

IV. Class. *Milra'* Nouns with changeable *Qameṣ* or *Ṣere, v. g.* דָּבָר, *word;* זָקֵן, *old.*

V. Class. Segolate Nouns, generally accented on the penult (*Mil'el*), *v. g.* מֶ֫לֶךְ, *king;* נַעַר, *boy;* מָ֫וֶת, *death* or exceptionally on the last, *v. g.* פְּרִי, *fruit.*

VI. Class. *Milra'* Nouns ending in ה ֶ, *v. g.* שָׂדֶה, *field.*

These classes have been arranged according to the simple form of the masculine. The feminines are classed and inflected according to their corresponding masculine form, real or supposed, *v. g.* מַלְכָּה, *queen* from מֶ֫לֶךְ, *king,* belongs to Class V; צְדָקָה, *righteousness* from (supposed) צָדָק, belongs to Class IV.

LESSON V.

I. NOUNS, CLASS I: Nouns with unchangeable vowels.

II. NOUNS, CLASS II: *Milra'* Nouns with changeable vowel in penult.

III. SEPARATE PERSONAL PRONOUNS.

Vocabulary. Nouns.

אֶפְרַיִם	*p. n.*	*Ephraim*	חֲמוֹר	*m.*	*donkey, ass*
בִּלְעָם	*p. n.*	*Balaam*	אָתוֹן	*f.*	*she-ass*
קִישׁ	*p. n.*	*Qish (Cis)*	נָבִיא	*m.*	*prophet*
פַּרְעֹה	*p. n.*	*Pharaoh*	מָקוֹם	*m.*	*place*
בָּרוּךְ	*p. n.* / *pt.*	*Baruch* / *blessed*	קָדוֹשׁ	*a.*	*holy*
			חָסִיד	*a.*	*pious, kind*
כָּבוֹד	*m. and f.*	*glory*	גַּם	*adv.*	*also*
אָדוֹן	*m.*	*master (said of God and man)*	בְּתוּלָה	*f.*	*girl, virgin*
			אָרוּר	*pt.*	*cursed*
אֲדֹנָי	*p.n.*	*Adonai (divine name) my Master*	בָּחוּר	*pt.*	*chosen*
אָסִיר	*m.*	*prisoner*	בָּחוּר, pl. בַּחוּרִים	*m.*	*young man*
גָּדוֹל	*a.*	*great, large*	כִּי	*conj.*	*that, because, but*

Verbs.

דִּבֵּר	*he spoke*	מִלֵּט	*he delivered*	מָלַךְ	*he reigned*
דִּבְּרָה	*she spoke*	מִלְּטָה	*she delivered*	מָלְכָה	*she reigned*
דִּבְּרוּ	*they spoke*	מִלְּטוּ	*they delivered*	מָלְכוּ	*they reigned*

בִּקֵּשׁ, *he sought, etc.;* קָדַשׁ, *he was holy;* הִקְדִּישׁ, *he sanctified;* הִתְקַדֵּשׁ, *he sanctified himself;* חָמַל, *he had pity* (עַל).

Examples.

כּוֹס גְּדוֹלָה, *a large cup;* כְּבוֹד אֱלֹהֵי יִשְׂרָאֵל, *the glory of the God of Israel;* דִּבְּרוּ הַנְּבִאִים, *the prophets spoke;* הֵמָּה דִבְּרוּ, *they themselves spoke;* אֲנַחְנוּ צַדִּיקִים, *we are just.*

I. Nouns, Class i (Paradigm B).

141. These nouns, having unchangeable vowels, suffer no changes; they merely receive the sign of the plural, construct, *etc.*, as explained in the preceding lessons. The nominal suffixes (150) are also added to them without occasioning any modification in the vowels, *v. g.* סוּס, *horse,* pl. סוּסִים; constr. pl. סוּסֵי; סוּסָה *mare,* pl. סוּסוֹת, *etc.*

As noted above (132), words like גַּנָּב, *thief,* חָרָשׁ, *artificer,* shorten *Qameṣ* to *Pat͟hah͟* in the construct state of the singular, *v. g.* גַּנָּב, constr. st. sing. גַּנַּב; pl. גַּנָּבִים, constr. pl. גַּנָּבֵי, *etc.*

II. Nouns, Class ii (Paradigm C).

142. In these nouns, the only vowel to suffer changes is the penult since the ultima is unchangeable: it becomes *S͟h·wa* whenever it is not pretonic (134). This occurs 1. before all accented additions, *v. g.* גָּדוֹל, *great,* pl. m. גְּדוֹלִים; fem. גְּדוֹלָה, pl. גְּדוֹלוֹת; 2. in the construct state masc. sing. (96, 135), *v. g.* גְּדוֹל.

III. Separate personal pronouns (Paradigm A).

A. Form.

143. The personal pronouns in Hebrew occur: 1. as a separate word and 2. in abbreviated forms, as personal preformatives (221) or afformatives (177), pronominal suffixes of the noun (150) and of the verb (316). The form of the separate personal pronouns is given in Paradigm A.

B. Syntactical Remarks.

144. The separate pronoun is unchangeable and indeclinable; it occurs in the nominative and can be coupled only with וְ and הֲ interrogative.

145. The separate pronouns are used: 1. as subject in a nominal sentence, *v. g.* אֲנִי יוֹסֵף, *I am Joseph;* צַדִּיק אַתָּה יְהוָה, *righteous art Thou, O Lord.* With a separate pronoun as subject, a substantive predicate is negatived by לֹא not by אֵין, *v. g.* לֹא־זָר הוּא, *he is not a stranger* (cp. 126, 124).

146. 2. Frequently, the pronoun of the third person takes the place of the copula. In reality, the subject, noun or phrase, is placed at the beginning of the sentence (*casus pendens*, 487) for the sake of emphasis or rhythm, and is resumed by the pronoun, *v. g.* וְחַנָּה הִיא מְדַבֶּ֫רֶת, *and Hannah was speaking*, lit.: (*As to*) *Hannah, she was speaking* (cp. same usage in French, *Pierre, est-il venu?*).

147. 3. In a verbal sentence, the separate pronoun placed before the verb gives greater emphasis to the subject, *v. g.* הוּא מָלַךְ, *he* (*himself*) *reigned.* Sometimes, however, it is used merely to give more fullness to a clause.

148. 4. The separate personal pronoun is used to emphasize the pronominal suffix that precedes and sometimes that follows; see 162.

149. 5. Separate Personal Pronouns as Demonstratives. The separate pronouns of the third person are often used with the article; in that case they are not personal pronouns but are used as demontratives הַהוּא, הַהִיא, *that, that one;* הָהֵ֫מָּה, הָהֵם, *those* (m); הָהֵ֫נָּה *those* (f.).

EXERCISES.

I. The glory of the Lord. The she-asses of Qish. The great prophets. The chosen people. Blessed (are) the pious. I am Balaam. Thou art Samuel. They are prophets. You are prisoners. Thou art not the master of the land. There are no prophets there. There is a stumbling-block on the path.

II. 1. שָׁחֲטוּ צאן בִּמְקוֹם הָעֹלָה׃ – 2. קָדוֹשׁ קָדוֹשׁ יְהוָה צְבָאוֹת׃ – 3. בִּקֵּשׁ שָׁאוּל אֶת־הָאֲתוֹנוֹת לְקִישׁ בְּהַר אֶפְרַ֫יִם וְגַם בְּאֶ֫רֶץ צוּף (Suph) וְאֵין הָאֲתוֹנוֹת שָׁם׃ – 4. הָלַךְ שְׁמוּאֵל אֶל־עֵלִי (Eli)׃ – 5. שָׁלְחוּ אֲרוֹן בְּרִית יְהוָה אֱלֹהֵי יִשְׂרָאֵל׃ – 6. תְּפִלַּת הַחֲסִידִים כְּעֹלַת פָּרִים לַיהוָה׃ – 7. וּבְיִשְׂרָאֵל נְבִיאִים גְּדוֹלִים וְהֵ֫מָּה הָלְכוּ אֶל־הַמָּקוֹם אֲשֶׁר אֲרוֹן בְּרִית וְלוּחוֹת הָעֵדוּת שָׁם׃ – 8. בָּרוּךְ אַבְרָהָם לְאֵל עֶלְיוֹן׃ – 9. קָדוֹשׁ וְגָדוֹל יְהוָה,

הוּא מִלֵּט אֶת־עַם יִשְׂרָאֵל מִגּוֹי לֹא חָסִיד׃ – 10. נוֹרָא וְגָדוֹל הוּא׃ – 11. יְהוָֹה
אֱלֹהֵי יִשְׂרָאֵל עָשָׂה (made) נוֹרָאוֹת וּגְדוֹלֹת׃ – 12. וְלֹא חָמַל נְבוּכַדְנֶאצַּר
(Nabuchodonosor) עַל בָּחוּר וּבְתוּלָה׃

III. 1. Saul offered a sacrifice in the place where Samuel was. – 3. Blessed is the Lord who sent great prophets to the people of the land of Israel. – 3. The prisoners spoke, saying: great is the glory of Solomon. – 4. Joseph said, I am not a stranger. – 5. Saul reigned in Israel; (it was) he (who) delivered the people from the terrible nations. – 6. Abraham and Melchisedech gave glory to the Lord, because they were just and pious. – 7. Israel is a chosen people, the blessed one of Jehovah. – 8. Cursed be the fools who have said: "There is no God in Israel, because He has not delivered the people from the Egyptians." – 9. Pharaoh reigned over Egypt.

LESSON VI.

PRONOMINAL SUFFIXES OF THE NOUN.

Vocabulary. Nouns.

בְּאֵר[1] (I)	f.	well, pit
בָּמָה (I)	f.	{high place, place of worship}
גְּבוּרָה (II)	f.	strength, valor, exploits
קוֹל (ות) (I)	m.	voice, sound
מְלוּכָה (II)	f.	royalty, sovereignty
מַלְכוּת (I)	f.	royal power, kingdom

נֵר (ות) (I)	m.	lamp
רִאשׁוֹן (I)	a.	first, former
יְשׁוּעָה (II)	f.	salvation
יְהוֹשֻׁעַ, יְהוֹשֻׁעַ	pr. n.	{Josue, Joshua, Jesus}
צוּר (I)	m.	rock, cliff, support
פֶּה	m. constr. פִּי	mouth
אוֹתוֹ, אֹתוֹ		him (acc.)
אִתּוֹ		with him

Verbs.

דָּרַשׁ	he had recourse to, consulted		זָכַר	he remembered
בִּקֵּשׁ	he sought, looked for		הִזְכִּיר	he reminded, he mentioned (caused to remember)
כָּתַב	he wrote, noted down			
שָׁמַע	he heard		שָׁפַט	he judged

Examples.

יְהוָה צוּרֵנוּ, *the Lord is our support;* גְּבוּרָתָם הָרִאשׁוֹנָה, *their former strength;* גְּדוֹלָה גְּבוּרָתָם, *their strength is great;* לְבוּשׁ מַלְכוּתוֹ, *the apparel of his royal power = his royal apparel.*

---

[1] The Roman figures between curved lines indicate the Class to which the noun belongs, according to §§ 140, 141.

A. Form (Paradigm *A*).

150. If the personal pronouns must be in an oblique case, instead of the separate pronouns, a modified and shorter form is used. The pronouns in that shorter form are attached as suffixes to the noun by which they are governed.

	With a noun in the sing. the construct state of which ends in					With a noun in the plural.	
	a Vowel v. g. פֶּה *mouth, constr.* פִּי			*a Consonant* v. g. סוּס *horse;* סוּסָה *mare, constr.* סוּסַת		v. g. סוּסִים, סוּסֵי, *horses;* סוּסוֹת, *mares.*	
1 c.	י	*my*	פִּי (*for* פִּיי)	–ִי	סוּסִי / סוּסָתִי	–ַי P. –ָי	סוּסַי / סוּסוֹתַי
2 m.	ךָ[1]	*thy*	פִּיךָ	–ְךָ P. –ֶךָ[4]	סוּסְךָ	–ֶיךָ	סוּסֶיךָ / סוּסוֹתֶיךָ
2 f.	ךְ[1]	*thy*	(פִּיךְ)	–ֵךְ P. –ָךְ	סוּסֵךְ	–ַיִךְ[4] P. –ָיִךְ	סוּסַיִךְ
3 m.	ו, הוּ	*his*	פִּיו, פִּיהוּ	ו (ה) (–ֵהוּ)[3]	סוּסוֹ	–ָיו *–ֵיהוּ	סוּסָיו
3 f.	הָ	*her*	פִּיהָ	–ָהּ[2] (–ֶהָ)[3]	סוּסָהּ	–ֶיהָ	סוּסֶיהָ
1 c.	נוּ	*our*	פִּינוּ	–ֵנוּ (–ָנוּ)	סוּסֵנוּ	–ֵינוּ	סוּסֵינוּ
2 m.	כֶם[1]	*your*	פִּיכֶם	–ְכֶם	סוּסְכֶם	–ֵיכֶם	סוּסֵיכֶם
2 f.	כֶן[1]	*your*	פִּיכֶן	–ְכֶן	סוּסְכֶן	–ֵיכֶן	סוּסֵיכֶן
3 m.	הֶם, מוֹ	*their*	פִּיהֶם, *פִּימוֹ[5]	–ָם (*–ָמוֹ)	סוּסָם	–ֵיהֶם *–ֵימוֹ	סוּסֵיהֶם
3 f.	הֶן	*their*	פִּיהֶן	–ָן	סוּסָן	–ֵיהֶן	סוּסֵיהֶן

151. N. B. [1] A phenomenon common to all Semitic languages is the interchange of ת and כ, *v. g.* אַתָּה, suff. ךָ; אַתֶּם, suff. כֶם.

[2] When –ָהּ follows a noun ending in a consonant it takes the *Mappiq* and is thus distinguished from the ordinary fem. ending, *v. g.* סוּסָה, *mare*, סוּסָהּ, *her horse.*

[3] The forms –ֵהוּ and –ֶהָ are used only with nouns in –ֶה 296.

[4] Note that instead of *Ṣere* in the penult, we have *S'ghol* when the pronoun suffix ends in *Qameṣ*, *v. g.* –ֶךָ, –ֶהָ, –ֶיךָ, –ֶיהָ, but –ֵנוּ, –ֵינוּ, etc.

[5] Poetical forms.

B. Remarks.

152. 1. Although the pronominal suffixes of the noun are rendered by our possessive adjectives, strictly speaking they are real personal pronouns, *v. g.* סוּסֵי + נוּ = *the horses of us.* The noun therefore is really in the constr. state, and the suffixes are added as genitives. This explains why the noun is generally in the form of a constr. state before suffixes.

153. 2. The suffixes should regularly be added directly to the fem. plur. of the constr. state (83b); but, by analogy with masc. nouns, they generally take ֵי֫ (ending of the constr. state masc. plur.) between the ending וֹת and the suffixes, *v. g.* בָּמוֹתֵיכֶם, *your high places.* There are, however, instances in which the pronouns are added directly to the fem. ending, more particularly ־ָם and ־ָן 3 f. pl.; this is the rule with שֵׁמוֹת, *names;* דֹּרוֹת, *generations* and, in some books, also with אָבוֹת, *fathers, v. g.* שְׁמוֹתָם, דֹּרוֹתָם, אֲבוֹתָם and אֲבוֹתֵיהֶם, but דֹּרוֹתֵיכֶם, etc.

154. 3. The four suffixes which by themselves form a closed syllable, כֶם, כֶן, הֶם, הֶן, are always accented, and are called grave or heavy. Of the others (light suffixes), those which form by themselves a separate syllable immediately following a full vowel are not accented; those in which one of these conditions is lacking are accented, *v. g.* סוּסֵ֫ינוּ, סוּסֶ֫יהָ, פִּיהוּ, סוּסֶ֫יךָ, *etc.* but סוּסִי, סוּסָם, סוּסוֹ, סוּסָךְ, סוּסְכֶם, סוּסֵיהֶם, *etc.* Note, however, סוּסַ֫יִךְ, with *Ḥireq* as helping vowel, for סוּסָיִךְ (50).

155. 4. The pronominal suffixes are also added to prepositions in the same way as to the noun (Paradigm H), *v. g.* לִי, *to me,* לוֹ, *to him;* בּוֹ, *through him, etc.*

The prepositions לְ and בְּ before plur. suffixes are sounded with *Qameṣ v. g.* לָהֶם, *to them;* בָּהֶם, *in them;* לָכֶם, *to you* (378).

The particle of direction אֵת, אֶת־ regularly becomes אוֹת (אֵת) with suffixes (except אֶתְכֶם, *you,* אֶתְהֶן, *them, illas*), *v. g.* אוֹתִי, *me,* אוֹתוֹ, *him.*

The preposition אֵת, אֶת־ becomes regularly אִתּ, *v. g.* אִתִּי, *with me,* אִתְּכֶם, *with you.*

Many prepositions, besides, change their form before suffixes and look like a noun in the constr. state plur. The most commonly used of these are אֶל־, *to,* and עַל־, *upon, v. g.* אֵלָיו, *to him,* עֲלֵיכֶם, *upon you.*

156. 5. The suffixes after a consonant are only apparently different from the suffixes after a vowel: in reality they are identical. Originally, Hebrew nouns as well as Semitic nouns in general ended in a vowel, *a, i, u*, which has been dropped. Some traces of this vowel are still found. This explains why we have '*a*' before some suffixes, and '*e*' before others, and also why כֶם, כֶן, have no *Daghesh Lene* although they follow a syllable essentially closed.

C. Syntactical Remarks.

157. 1. After a noun the suffix corresponds to our possessive adjective; after a preposition, to our personal pronoun. In both cases, the suffix can have an objective (demonstrative) or a subjective (reflexive) meaning; the context will show which one is meant, *v. g.* עִמָּהּ may mean *with her* or *with herself;* סוּסוֹ may mean *his horse* (*equus eius*), and *his own horse* (*equus suus*).

158. 2. Since the relation between a noun and a suffix is that of a construct state to its *nomen rectum,* the rules given §§ 100—105 apply here also:

a) The suffix must be repeated after each noun, *v. g.* נָתַן יְהוָה אֶת־תּוֹרֹתָיו וְאֶת־חֻקּוֹתָיו וְאֶת־מִצְוֹתָיו לְיִשְׂרָאֵל׃, *the Lord gave Israel His laws, precepts and commandments.*

159. b) A noun with a pronominal suffix never takes the article, because it is already determined by the suffix; but, all modifying adjectives of a noun with suffixes must have the article (104, 105), *v. g.* גְּבוּרָתָם הָרִאשׁוֹנָה, *their former strength* (but גְּדוֹלָה גְבוּרָתָם, *their strength is great*).

160. c) Very often the suffix is placed after a genitive although it refers to the whole compound (cp. article before genitive, 104), *v. g.* לְבוּשׁ מַלְכוּתוֹ, *the apparel of his royalty,* instead of *his apparel of royalty* = *his royal apparel;* יְהוָה צוּר יְשׁוּעָתוֹ, *the Lord is the rock of his salvation,* instead of *his rock of salvation* = *his saving help.*

161. d) Instead of a suffix to indicate possession, a circumlocution may be used, *v. g.* הַסּוּס אֲשֶׁר לִי, for סוּסִי, *my horse* (cp. 107).

162. 3. As noted in the preceding lesson (148), the pronominal suffix is often emphasized by the separate pronoun which may precede but generally follows, *v. g.* כְּבוֹד יְהוָה כְּבוֹדֵנוּ גַּם אֲנַחְנוּ, *the glory of the Lord is our glory also* (cp. French: *est notre gloire, nous aussi*). *"In the place where dogs licked the blood of Naboth, shall dogs lick thy blood,* גַּם אַתָּה, *even thine"* 1 K. XXI, 19 ..... *ton sang, toi aussi.*

EXERCISES.

I. 1) Review vocabulary.

2) My voice. Our salvation. Your booth. To their horses. My master. Your warriors. In their high places. In his cup. His large horses. The place of their sacrifices. His former strength. Her garments. Our good lamps. In his light. Our support. His commands. Their prisoners. Thy prisoners. The

beds of their great men. Our good prophets. To me. To them. In them. To us. To thee. In him. Me (dir. obj.), you, them. With them. With him.

II. 1. מִצְוֹת יְהוָה נֵר לַצַּדִּיק וְתוֹרָתוֹ אוֹר לֶחָסִיד׃ – 2. כְּבוֹד יְהוָה
כְּבוֹדֵנוּ גַּם אֲנַחְנוּ׃ – 3. נְבִאִים גְּדוֹלִים הֵמָּה וְרוּחַ יְהוָה בָּהֶם׃ 4. לָקַח דָּוִד
אֶת־צִיּוֹן (Zion) וְאֶת־גְּבוּלָהּ וְאֶת־הָעָם אֲשֶׁר בָּהּ׃ – 5. זָכַר יְהוָה אֶת־דָּוִד,
אוֹתוֹ וְאֶת־הָעָם אֲשֶׁר אִתּוֹ׃ – 6. שָׁמַר שְׁלֹמֹה חֻקּוֹת אֱלֹהִים וְתוֹרָתוֹ וּמִצְוֹתָיו
וְעֵדוֹתָיו וּפִקּוּדָיו׃ – 7. שָׁמְעוּ גּוֹיֵי הָאָרֶץ אֶת־הוֹד שְׁלֹמֹה וְאֶת־כְּבוֹד יְהוָה
אֱלֹהָיו׃ – 8. נָתַן יְהוָה הוֹד מַלְכוּת לִשְׁלֹמֹה׃ – 9. בָּרוּךְ יְהוָה צוּרִי׃ – 10. אָמַר
מֹשֶׁה לִיהוֹשֻׁעַ׃

III. 1. God is our support, for great is His strength. – 2. The horse and mare of the stranger. – 3. The Lord heard our prayer, but we (emphatic) have not kept his precepts. – 4. Our God is strong and terrible and His glory is great among (ב) the nations. – 5. Saul, David and Solomon reigned in Israel, because God gave them sovereignty over its territory. – 6. The prophets went to the place of their sacrifices. – 7. The nations heard of the great and wonderful things of the God of Israel.

* * *

PRELIMINARY REMARKS ON THE VERB.

A. Radicals.

163. Although originally there were many biliteral roots, and perhaps most roots were such, in the course of time the majority of them became triliteral. On these three letters the fundamental meaning depends. Each one of the three consonants that constitute the word is called a Radical. To designate them two methods are used: either they are called simply, 'first', 'second', ,third', radical, or, according to the Jewish usage adopted commonly in modern grammars, each one of the radicals of the old Jewish paradigm פָּעַל, *to make,* is used to designate the corresponding radical in any verb. *Pe* (פ) will mean the first radical in general, because it is the first radical in פָּעַל; '*Ayin* (ע) will designate the second radical, and *Lamedh* (ל) the third, *v. g.* ירה, *he threw,* is a verb *Pe-Yodh* (פ"י), '*Ayin-Resh* (ע"ר) and *Lamedh- He* (ל"ה).

B. Classification.

164. Hebrew verbs are grouped into two classes, according to the nature of their radicals. 1. Strong verbs are those the three radicals of which are strong letters, *i. e.* are maintained throughout the inflection. 2. Weak verbs are those, one or more radicals of which undergo changes in the inflection, and occasionally may be even left out.

C. Modifications of the Fundamental Idea of the Root.

165. By means of internal modifications or external additions (prefixes), Hebrew is able to express corresponding modifications of meaning which in our languages would often have to be expressed by a special verb or phrase.

1. By means of internal modifications, the idea of the simple form is presented with some additional shades of meaning based on the special activity of the subject while doing the action itself. Thus the idea of the simple form may be further qualified as intensive, extensive, iterative, productive, conative, etc., *v. g.* (*to kill*), *to murder*, *to kill many*, *kill often*, *try to kill*, *etc.* Those shades of meaning were probably at one time expressed by as many different internal modifications, but, generally speaking, one single form now expresses them all (see, however, 171). It consists in strengthening the middle radical by means of *Daghesh Forte*, *v. g.* קָטַל, *he killed*, קַטֵּל (now קִטֵּל or קַטֵּל), *he murdered.* This form is called reinforced.

2. The prefixing of הַ to the simple form indicates that the subject is not doing the action himself, but causes another agency to act, the subject here not being the immediate agent of the action, *v. g.* הַקְטַל, (now הִקְטִיל), *he caused .... to kill.* This form is called causative.

3. The action may be performed by the agent and revert to him, or it may be performed by two agents on each other, the verbal idea is then reflexive or reciprocal. This is obtained by prefixing נְ (now נִ, הִנ) to the simple form, and הִת to the reinforced form, *v. g.* נִקְטַל, *he killed himself* (*also was killed*, 170); הִתְקַטֵּל, *he murdered himself;* הִתְלַכֵּד, *to grasp each other.* Theoretically the causative also

could have a reflexive, *he forced himself to kill*, but it has not been preserved in Hebrew.

4. By changing the first vowel into *ŭ* (*ŏ*) (not, however, in the reflexive forms) the subject is made the recipient of the action done by another agent, passive, *v. g.* קִטֵּל, *he murdered*, קֻטַּל, *he was murdered;* הִקְטִיל, *he caused . . . to kill*, הָקְטַל, הֻקְטַל, *he was made to kill.* The passive of the simple form has been lost in Hebrew (170).

D. Formations or Stems.

166. 1. The form which a verb assumes to express the fundamental idea and its modifications, is called a Stem or Formation (improperly Conjugation). From what has been said (165) it is seen that there are in Hebrew seven formations commonly used, *qāṭal, niqṭal, qiṭṭēl, quṭṭal, hiṯhqaṭṭēl, hiqṭîl, hoqṭal;* it does not mean however that they all occur in every verb; out of about 1400 verbs, only seven have the seven Formations.

167. a) The simple idea of the verb is expressed by the simplest Stem. This stem is called the **Fundamental Stem** (Grundstamm) or more commonly *Qal (light)* from the fact that it receives no modifications, except personal afformatives or preformatives. All the others are called **Derived, Derivative Stems,** or according to Jewish usage, **Heavy Formations.**

168. b) In each Formation, the 3 m. s. of the Perfect (175 ff.) is the simplest form relatively to the rest of the inflection. With the exception of the simple stem which retains the name *Qal,* it is by the 3 m. s. that each one of the Derivative Stems is designated individually. The name, however, does not vary with each verb, but is taken from the same verb פָּעַל, already mentioned (163). The form that this verb has in the 3 m. s. of the various formations gives the name to that formation, regardless of the verb to which it is applied, see Diagram.

The 3 m. s. of *Qal* is the simplest of all verbal forms, and is generally considered as 'the root' of the verb itself. Hence it is that in the Dictionaries the verb is given under that form and not under the infinitive as in our modern languages (see however, 445); hence it is also that many lexicographers group under the 3 m. s. of *Qal* all the words (verbs, nouns, prepositions, etc.) composed of the same essential radical letters.

169. DIAGRAM.

	Fundamental Stem	Derivative Stems					
Name	*Qal*	*Niph'al*	*Pi'el*	*Pu'al*	*Hithpa'el*	*Hiph'il*	*Hoph'al*
Older Form	Qaṭála	Naqṭála Hinqatála	Qaṭṭála	Quṭṭála	Taqaṭṭála Hithqaṭṭála	Haqṭála	Huqṭála
Present Form	קָטַל	נִקְטַל	קִטֵּל, קִטַּל	קֻטַּל	הִתְקַטֵּל	הִקְטִיל	הָקְטַל, הֻקְטַל
Meaning	*he killed*	*he killed himself; was killed*	*murdered*	*was murdered*	*murdered himself*	*he caused to kill*	*was made to kill*

2. Remarks on the Various Stems.

170. a) Remarks on *Niph'al*. *Niph'al* is mostly used as a substitute for the primitive passive of *Qal* which has been apparently lost; often, however, it retains its primitive reflexive or even reciprocal meaning, *v. g.* לָכַד, *he captured,* נִלְכַּד, *he was captured;* (דִּבֶּר), *he spoke,* נִדְבַּר, *he conversed, (talk together)*; שָׁמַר, *he kept, guarded,* נִשְׁמַר, *he guarded himself.*

Note that in many modern languages also, a passive idea is often expressed by a reflexive verb, *v. g.* French: *cela s'appelle;* German: *es nennt sich* = it is called.

171. b) Remarks on the Reinforced Stems (*Pi'el, Pu'al, Hithpa'el*).
In the reinforced stems, the intensity or repetition is represented by a strengthening of the middle radical, or by some substitute and equivalent formations.

Among these substitute formations may be mentioned: 1) a form obtained by lengthening the vowel of the first radical instead of sharpening the middle radical, קוֹטֵל (for older קָטַל). This was used to express the Conative implying a protracted effort to reach a certain aim. Its passive is קוֹטַל and its reflexive הִתְקוֹטֵל; they are called *Pô'el, Pô'al, Hithpô'el* and are often used, instead of the form *Pi'el*, in verbs ע״ע (428). 2) a form apparently derived from biliteral roots by repeating the last radical and lengthening the vowel, and thus resembling exactly the forms just mentioned under 1.: קוֹמֵם, קוֹמַם, הִתְקוֹמֵם. They are called *Pôlel, Pôlal, Hithpôlel* and are regularly used instead of *Pi'el, etc.* in the so-called verbs ע״ו and ע״י (455 ff.).

On other substitutes, see 466.

α) *Pi'el.* In *Pi'el*, the form *Qiṭṭal* is more common than the form *Qiṭṭel*. *Pi'el* is used to express Intensity, *v. g.* שִׁבֵּר, *he broke,* שִׁבֵּר, *he broke to pieces;* Extension, *v. g.* קָבַר, *he buried,* קִבֵּר, *he buried many;* Repetition, *v. g.* כָּתַב, *he wrote,* כִּתֵּב, *he wrote often, made it a business to write;* Production (similar to *Hiph'il*) more particularly with intransitive verbs (factitive), *v. g.* לָמַד, *he learned,* לִמֵּד, *he taught;* כָּבֵד, *he was heavy,* כִּבֵּד, *he made heavy, honourable;* Denomination, *i. e.* verbal derivation from nouns, numerals, *etc. Pi'el* then indicates that the subject busies himself with the idea expressed by the word from which the verb is derived, *v. g.* שָׁלֹשׁ *three,* denom. *Pi'el,* שִׁלֵּשׁ, *he divided in three parts; he did for the third time;* קֵן, *nest,* קִנֵּן, *made a nest.*

β) *Pu'al. Pu'al* is the passive of *Pi'el,* and sometimes is used as the passive of *Qal, v. g.* קִדֵּשׁ, *he consecrated,* קֻדַּשׁ, *he was consecrated.*

γ) *Hithpa'el. Hithpa'el* is primarily a reflexive of *Pi'el* but is often reciprocal and sometimes passive, *v. g.* לָכַד, *he captured,* הִתְלַכֵּד, *to grasp each other;* גִּדֵּל, *he rendered powerful,* הִתְגַּדֵּל, *he magnified himself.*

172. c) Remarks on the Causative Stems (*Hiph'il* and *Hoph'al*).

α) *Hiph'il* indicates that the subject causes another agency to act and produce the action. It is regularly the Causative of *Qal, v. g.* קָדַשׁ, *he was holy,* הִקְדִּישׁ, *he caused to be holy, he sanctified.*

β) *Hoph'al* is the passive of *Hiph'il* and sometimes is used as passive of *Qal, v. g.* הִשְׁכִּיב, *he laid,* הָשְׁכַּב, *he was laid.* The form הֻקְטַל, instead of הָקְטַל, is also common, and is even prevalent in the participle, מֻקְטָל.

E. Tenses.

173. Strictly speaking, there are no tenses in Hebrew. The fundamental idea that causes differences in the verbal flection is that of completed or not completed action. The complete action or state is expressed by the Perfect and the incomplete action by the Imperfect. The terms 'Perfect' and 'Imperfect' must be taken here in their etymological sense and not in the sense which they have in our modern languages.

That *completeness* or *incompleteness* must be judged not merely from the point of view of the writer or reader but also and mostly from the relation that one action has to another, and from the nature of the action or state, thus: The Perfect denotes what is concluded, or what is represented as concluded, although it may be present or even future (see 190, 191).

The Imperfect denotes the beginning, the unfinished, the continuing, the habitual, the often repeated, or that which is considered in the process of becoming.

Hence, it would be better to speak of a Perfect and Imperfect **state** than of a Perfect and Imperfect **tense** = time from *tempus*.

F. Modes.

174. These fundamental ideas are capable of modal differences. The idea of the Perfect offers little opportunity for variations and is consequently Indicative; the only other variation being a Verbal Noun or Infinitive Absolute.

The idea of the Imperfect is more apt to have modifications. To that series belong the Infinitive Construct, Imperative, Indicative, Jussive, Cohortative and Participles.

The Perfect and Imperfect are distinguished by their characteristic vowels and also by the way in which the personal pronouns and other formative additions are added to the Stem. In the Perfect, all these additions are placed after the Stem; in the Imperfect, they are placed before or partly before and partly after, but never after only. See Lessons vii, viii, xi.

LESSON VII.

PERFECT:

Perfect of the Strong Verb.[1]

Vocabulary.

Qal	*Niph'al*	*Pi'el*	*Pu'al*	*Hithpa'el*	*Hiph'il*	*Hoph'al*
פָּקַד	נִפְקַד	(פִּקֵּד)[3]	(פֻּקַּד)	הִתְפַּקֵּד	הִפְקִיד	הָפְקַד
to visit,[2] seek, muster,	be visited, be sought, be missed	muster	be passed in review	be mustered	set over, make overseer	be visited, be made overseer.
(דָּבַר)	(נִדְבַּר)	דִּבֵּר	(דֻּבַּר)	הִדַּבֵּר	הִדְבִּיר	—
to speak	converse	speak	be spoken	converse	cause to flee.	
שָׁמַר	נִשְׁמַר	(שִׁמֵּר)	—	הִשְׁתַּמֵּר	—	—
to keep, watch	be on one's guard	pay regards to		keep oneself.		
קָדַשׁ*[4]	נִקְדַּשׁ	קִדֵּשׁ	קֻדַּשׁ	הִתְקַדֵּשׁ	הִקְדִּישׁ	—
to be consecrated[5], be set apart, be hallowed	show oneself sacred	consecrate, observe as holy, sanctify	be consecrated	keep oneself apart, sanctify oneself	consecrate, set apart, sanctify.	

---

[1] In arranging the list of verbs, the first meaning given is always that of *Qal*, without further indication. If, however, *Qal* does not occur, the *Qal* form is inclosed between square brackets and followed generally by one of the active Stems; *v. g.* [שָׁחַת] *Pi.* (Lesson viii).

[2] The meaning is generally given in the infinitive, but for brevity's sake 'to' is often omitted.

[3] Formations or Stems that are rare have been placed between curved brackets, *v. g.* צָדַק . . . (*Niph.* be justified); when *Qal* itself is rare, the meaning alone is inclosed between curved brackets, *v. g.* בָּרַךְ (to bless).

[4] Verbs marked with an asterisk have the Imperfect in '*a*'; as a rule, however, verbs with 2d. or 3d. guttural, which always have '*a*', are not marked thus.

[5] Verbs which in *Qal* are translated by 'to be' should not be mistaken for passive verbs. They are really 'stative' *i. e.* indicate the state in which the subject is found, *v. g. to be consecrated = to be in a state of consecration, to be holy, etc.*

*צָדֵק to be just, righteous; (*Niph.* be justified); *Pi.* justify; *Hithp.* justify oneself; *Hiph.* justify.

עָמַד to stand; *Hiph.* station; set up, confirm; (*Hoph.* be caused to stand.

*שָׁלַח to send; (*Niph.* be sent); *Pi.* send off; *Pu.* be sent off; (*Hiph.* send).

מָלַךְ to reign; *Hiph.* make king, cause to reign; (*Hoph.* be made king).

שָׁפַט to judge, govern; *Niph.* enter into a controversy, plead.

*שָׁכַב to lie down, lodge; (*Hiph.* lay); *Hoph.* be laid down in death.

*לָבֵשׁ to wear, be clothed; (*Pu.* be clothed); *Hiph.* clothe, deck.

בָּרַךְ (to bless, kneel); (*Niph.* bless oneself); *Pi.* bless; *Pu.* be blessed; *Hithp.* bless oneself; (*Hiph.* cause to kneel).

†שָׁבַת[1] to cease, rest; *Niph.* cease; *Hiph.* cause to cease, exterminate.

זָכַר to remember; (*Niph.* be thought of); *Hiph.* remind, mention.

*כָּבֵד to be heavy; (*Niph.* be honoured); *Pi.* to honour; (*Pu.* be honoured); (*Hithp.* make oneself heavy); *Hiph.* cause to be honoured.

*קָטֹן to be small; (*Hiph.* cause to be small).

*גָּדַל to grow up, become great; *Pi.* make powerful; (*Pu.* be made powerful); *Hithp.* magnify oneself; *Hiph.* make great, do great things.

*בָּחַר to choose; *Niph.* be chosen; *Pu.* be selected (object often with בְּ).

*שָׁמַע to hear; *Niph.* be heard; (*Pi.* cause to hear); *Hiph.* cause to hear, proclaim.

(Paradigms I to L).

A. Personal Endings.

175. 1. The flection begins with the 3 m. s. which may be considered as a participle or verbal adjective (*Nomen agentis*); its fem. is indicated by the usual fem. ending ־ָה (for ־ַת), and the plural for both genders of the 3 person by וּ. Hence קָטַל means: *one who has killed, i. e. a killer;* קָטְלָה means: *a female killer;* הִקְטִיל means: *one who has caused to kill, etc.*

176. 2. In order to develop the *Nomen agentis* into a finite verb, Hebrew adds to it the personal pronouns; so that every form of the finite verb is a nominal sentence with the pronoun as subject and the verbal noun as predicate. Those pronouns are the common personal pronouns (143), but in a shorter form, as follows: תָּ for אַתָּה

---

[1] Verbs marked with a cross have their Imperfect both in '*o*' and '*a*'.

(אַתָּ); תְּ for אַתְּ (אַתִּי); תִּי for אָנֹכִי (with change of כ to ת [151]); תֶּם for אַתֶּם; תֶּן for אַתֵּן; נוּ for אֲנַחְנוּ or אֲנוּ. In the third person, however, no pronouns are used, because the subject is very often a substantive, or in any case is easily supplied from the context.

Thus the endings of the Perfect are as follows:

	3 m.	3 f.	2 m.	2 f.	1 c.
Sing.		***ָה	***תָּ	***תְּ	***תִּי
Plur.	***וּ	***וּ	***תֶּם	***תֶּן	***נוּ

177. 3. When the last Radical of the verb is identical with the first letter of the personal afformatives, a contraction often takes place, *i. e.* the letter is written but once with *Daghesh Forte, v. g.* כָּרַתִּי, *I have cut off*, for כָּרַתְתִּי; נָתַנּוּ, *we gave*, for נָתַנְנוּ.

178. 4. Tone. The endings of the 3 p. ָה and וּ, being regular nominal endings, are accented except in *Hiph'il, v. g.* קָֽטְלָה, קָֽטְלוּ, but הִקְטִ֫ילָה. The pronouns of the second and first persons are unaccented, except תֶּם and תֶּן which have always the tone (cp. nominal suffixes כֶם and כֶן, 154).

B. Stem-formative Prefixes.

179. 1. *Qal, Pi'el* and *Pu'al* have no stem-formative prefixes. In the other stems, the prefix is indicated in the name of the stem. In *Niph'al, Hiph'il* and *Hoph'al*, the prefix forms a closed syllable with the first consonant of the verb, and consequently, the second radical, if *B·ghadhk·phath*, takes *Daghesh Lene* (25), *v. g.* נִשְׁפַּט, *he pleaded.*

180. 2. *Hithpa'el.* The prefix הִתְ of *Hithpa'el* forms by itself a closed syllable and therefore, the first radical, if *B·ghadhk·phath*, has *Daghesh Lene, v. g.* הִתְגַּדֵּל, *he magnified himself.*

b) The ת of the preformative is assimilated to a following ט, ד, ת, which consequently have *Daghesh Forte, v. g.* הִדַּבֵּר, *he conversed*, for הִתְדַּבֵּר.

c) The ת of the preformative is always transposed, when followed by ס, שׂ, שׁ, *v. g.* שָׁמַר *he kept*, הִשְׁתַּמֵּר, *he kept himself*, for הִתְשַׁמֵּר.

d) The ת is changed to ט and transposed in a verb beginning with צ, *v. g.*, צָדַק, *he was righteous*, הִצְטַדֵּק, *he justified himself*, for הִתְצַדֵּק.

181. 3. With a first guttural verb (cp. 151,4), when second radical has *a*, the preceding syllable has *S·ghol* instead of *Ḥireq* or *Pathaḥ:* thus in *Niph'al* and *Hiph'il* (formerly *Haph'al*), נֶעֱמַד, הֶעֱמִיד.

C. Vowels.

1. Vowel under the first radical.

182. a) Whether the first radical has a vowel and which vowel should be used, is indicated in the name of the Stem.

It is to be remembered that a verb first guttural, instead of a Syllable-divider, takes regularly a *Ḥateph* corresponding to the vowel of the Stem-formative prefix (73), *v. g.* נֶעֱמַד, הֶעֱמִיד. If the *Ḥateph* is followed by a *Sh·wa*, it passes into its corresponding full vowel, but is still preceded by *Methegh* (74), *v. g.* נֶֽעֶמְדוּ for נֶעֱמְדוּ.

183. b) In *Pi'el, Pu'al* and *Hithpa'el*, the vowel being in an acute syllable is unchangeable (129).

With a middle guttural, *Daghesh Forte* is omitted and the preceding vowel of the first radical is lengthened as compensation before א and ר, but remains short before ה, ח, ע (66, 67).

184. c) For the vowel of the first radical in *Qal*, see 134, 135, 137: pretone long, 134; volatilized, 135; kept in third persons, 137. See Paradigms I—L.

2. Vowel of the second radical.

185. a) The vowel of the second radical is the characteristic vowel. Generally speaking, the idea of a concrete action is expressed by the vowel *a*, *v. g.* קָטַל, *he killed;* שָׁמַר, *he kept.* The idea of a state or quality is expressed by *ē* or *ō* (primitively *ĭ* and *ŭ*) *v. g.* כָּבֵד, *he was heavy;* קָטֹן, *he was small.*

There are about 50 verbs in *ē* called 'verbs middle *ē*' and 10 in *ō* 'verbs middle *ō*'. This distinction, however, between active and stative verbs is preserved only in *Qal* but does not exist in the Derivative Stems.

186. b) In *Qal* the vowel of the second radical is kept before the pronouns (2 and 1 persons), *v. g.* קָטַלְנוּ, *we killed;* קָטֹנְתִּי, *I was small.* In verbs middle ē, however, the *e* is changed to *Pat̲haḥ* before the pronouns, *v. g.* כָּבֵד, *he was heavy;* כָּבַדְתָּ, *thou wast heavy,* not כָּבֵדְתָּ.

187. c) In the Derivative Stems, the vowel of the second radical is regularly *Pat̲haḥ* before the pronouns, *i. e.* the primitive vowel has been retained (169), *v. g.* דִּבֶּר, *he spoke;* דִּבַּרְתֶּם, *you spoke;* הִקְדִּישׁ, *he sanctified;* הִקְדַּשְׁתִּי, *I sanctified.*

188. d) Before the monosyllabic accented endings ◌ָה and וּ the vowel of the second radical is volatilized (137), *v. g.* קָטְלוּ, *they killed.* Middle guttural of course has *Ḥaṭep̲h̲*, *v. g.* בָּחֲרָה, *she chose.*

(On the influence of the Pause, see 77 ff.)

D. Use of the Perfect.

189. The Perfect in Hebrew, as noted above (173), serves to express actions, events or states which the writer wishes to represent from the standpoint of completion, whether they be past, present or future.

According to the requirements of sense and context, the Hebrew Perfect may be rendered by various Tenses and Modes in English:

190. 1. By the English Perfect or Complete Tenses: Present Perfect, Past Perfect (Pluperfect), Future Perfect, *v. g.* שָׁמַרְתִּי, *I have kept;* כַּאֲשֶׁר דִּבֶּר לוֹ אֱלֹהִים, *according to what God had told him (David).*

191. 2. By the English Simple or Primary Tenses, especially Past (Preterite, Aorist) but also Present or Future; *v. g.* Past, הָלַךְ, *he went;* Present, זָכַרְנוּ, *we remember, i. e. we have called to mind* (thus, often verbs expressing moral or physical states or conditions, cp. Latin: *odi eum, I hate him);* Future, when the action is conceived by the writer or speaker as certainly to be fulfilled, such as prophecies, *etc., v. g.* עַד־יַהַץ נִשְׁמַע קוֹלָם, *their voice shall be heard unto Yahaṣ,* Is. xv, 4.

192. 3. By the various tenses of the Potential Mode, *v. g. if the God of my father had not been with me,* שִׁלַּחְתָּ אוֹתִי, *thou wouldst have sent me away.* Note that even in English we might say: *"thou hadst sent me away."*

EXERCISES.

I. He spoke; they made king; you remember; you have consecrated; he lay down; he entered into a controversy; thou shalt (surely) keep; you have kept; we shall have consecrated; we are righteous; you spoke; you (f.) conversed; thou rememberest; we grew up; I clothed; thou didst magnify thyself; we magnified ourselves; thou wast visited; they justified; you were small; she caused to be honoured; she chose; I heard; they were clothed; etc. P. she chose; they heard.

II. 1. דִּבֵּר יְהוָה אֶל־הַנָּבִיא לֵאמֹר זָכַרְתִּי אֶת־הַחֲסִידִים וְאֶת־הַצַּדִּיקִים: –
2. אֲנִי הִכְבַּדְתִּי אֶת־יִשְׂרָאֵל בְּגוֹיֵי הָאָרֶץ: – 3. אֲנִי יוֹסֵף אֲשֶׁר בָּחַר אֱלֹהִים
בִּי: – 4. הִמְלִיךְ יְהוָה אֶת־דָּוִד עַל־יִשְׂרָאֵל: – 5. נִשְׁמְרוּ לוּחוֹת הָעֵדוּת בַּאֲרוֹן
הַבְּרִית: – 6. וְהוּא הִצְטַדֵּק בְּעֵינֵי (in the eyes) הָעָם: – 7. בִּקַּשְׁתֶּם
אֶת־יְהוָה: – 8. קוֹל אֱלֹהִים לֹא שֻׁמְּעוּ וְיִרְאַת יְהוָה לֹא בָּחֲרוּ: – 9. בִּקֵּשׁ
שָׁאוּל אֲתֹנוֹת קִישׁ בִּגְבוּל יִשְׂרָאֵל: – 10. זָכַרְנוּ, גַּם אֲנַחְנוּ, אֶת־מִצְוֹת יְהוָה
וְאֶת־תּוֹרֹתָיו: – 11. הָשְׁכַּב הָאֶבְיוֹן עַל־הַמִּטָּה: – 12. פָּקַדְתִּי עַל־מִצְרַיִם
כַּאֲשֶׁר פָּקַדְתִּי עַל־יְהוּדָה: – 13. הִשְׁמִיעַ יְהוָה אֶת־הוֹד קוֹלוֹ: – 14. פָּקַד
שָׁאוּל אֶת־הָעָם אֲשֶׁר עִמּוֹ: – 15. כִּבַּדְתֶּם אֶת־נְבִיאֵי יִשְׂרָאֵל:

III. 1. Samuel grew up among the people. – 2. The pious were on their guard against (מִן) the terrible strangers. – 3. Saul sought the she-asses of Qish; Samuel spoke with him, made him king and also caused him to be honoured among the nations. – 4. The prophets sanctified themselves and also sanctified the people. – 5. Isaac entered into a controversy with Abimelech concerning (עַל) the wells. – 6. The warriors honoured the prophets that were in the land. – 7. We remember the precepts and the laws of the Lord. – 8. The people of Israel was passed in review on the mountain of David. – 9. Jehovah blessed Abraham and in Abraham all (כָּל־) the peoples of the earth were blessed.

LESSON VIII.

PERFECT (Contin.): Infinitive absolute.

IMPERFECT:

Infinitive construct; Imperative.

Vocabulary.

כָּתַב to write, enroll, describe, note down; *Niph.* be written; *Pi.* make a business of writing.

לָחַם* (to fight); *Niph.* wage war, fight.

סָגַר to close, shut; *Niph.* be shut up; *Pi.* deliver up to; *Pu.* be shut; *Hiph.* deliver up.

שָׁכַן to dwell, settle down; *Pi.* establish; *Hiph.* to lay.

כָּבַשׁ to bring into bondage, subdue; *Niph.* be brought into bondage; *Pi.* conquer.

בָּגַד† to deal treacherously.

[קָטַר] *Pi.* to make sacrifice smoke; *Pu.* be fumigated; *Hiph.* make sacrifice smoke, burn incense; *Hoph.* be made to smoke.

שָׁאַל* to ask, inquire; (*Niph.* ask for leave of absence); *Pi.* beg, practice beggary; *Hiph.* grant, give.

מָשַׁח* to anoint; (*Niph.* be anointed).

חָבַשׁ to bind, harness; (*Pi.* bind); (*Pu.* be bound).

סָפַר to count; *Niph.* be numbered; *Pi.* recount; *Pu.* be related.

לָמַד* to learn; *Pi.* teach; *Pu.* be taught.

גָּנַב to steal; (*Niph.* be stolen; *Pi.* steal away; *Pu.* be stolen away; *Hithp.* go by stealth).

עָזַב to leave, forsake; *Niph.* be left, forsaken; *Pu.* be deserted.

כָּרַת to cut off, hew, make a covenant; *Niph.* fail, be cut off; (*Pu.* cut off); *Hiph.* destroy; (*Hoph.* be destroyed).

בָּטַח* to trust; *Hiph.* make secure, cause to trust.

שָׁכַח* to forget; *Niph.* be forgotten; *Pi.* cause to forget; *Hithpa.* be forgotten.

מָאַס* to reject; (*Niph.* be rejected.)

[מָהַר] *Pi.* to hasten (*Niph.* be hurried).

שָׁחַט* to slaughter, to sacrifice; (*Niph.* be slaughtered).

[שָׁחַת] *Pi.* to ruin, spoil; *Niph.* be spoiled; *Hiph.* to ruin, to destroy.

Vocabulary.

אָסַף to gather, collect; *Niph.* be gathered; *Pi.* gather harvest; *Pu.* be gathered; *Hithp.* gather themselves.

*זָבַח to slaughter for sacrifice; *Pi.* id.

בְּתוֹךְ in the middle of.

נְאֻם *m.* utterance, divine message.

Infinitive Absolute (Paradigms I to L).

A. Form.

The Infinitive is represented in Hebrew by two forms. Strictly speaking, both are verbal Nouns (*Nomen actionis*). The one with longer vowels never enters in combination or construction, and hence, is called Infinitive Absolute; the other on the contrary readily enters into construction, and is called Infinitive Construct. These two forms must be kept clearly apart and are distinct in formation, meaning and use.

193. The Infinitive Absolute is derived from the Perfect but has as characteristic vowel *ô* (often defectively written), originally *â*, under the second radical in *Qal*, *Niph.*, *Pu.*, and sometimes *Pi.*; it has *ê* in *Pi.*, *Hithp.*, *Hiph.* and *Hoph.* No special forms for Stative verbs occur.

Third guttural verbs take *Pathaḥ Furtivum* after *ô* and *ê* (§ 71).

194. Besides the Stem-formative prefix *Ni*, *Niph'al* also uses *Hin*, the *Nun* of which is always assimilated to the first radical of the Stem, *v. g.* הִקָּטֵל for הִנְקָטֵל.

With a first guttural, the *Daghesh* is omitted and *Hireq* lengthened to *Ṣere* (66), *v. g.* הֵאָסֵף for הִנְאָסֵף.

B. Use and Syntax.

Examples:

1. a) פָּקוֹד פָּקַדְתִּי, *I have surely visited;* שָׂרוֹף יִשָּׂרֵפוּ, *they shall be utterly burned;* b) הָלְכוּ הָלוֹךְ, *they kept on going;* c) שָׁמוֹעַ לֹא־שְׁמַעְתֶּם, *you have refused to hear.* 2. זָכוֹר אֶת־יוֹם הַשַּׁבָּת, *remember the Sabbath day.*

1. In connection with a finite verb, the Infinit. Abs. is used:

195. a) before and sometimes after a finite verb of the same stem to emphasize the actual occurrence, energy or intensity of the idea of the stem; or, in the case of a conditional sentence, the importance of a condition, *v. g.* פָּקוֹד פָּקַדְתִּי אֶתְכֶם, *I have surely visited you* (Ex. III, 16); אִם שָׁפוֹט תִּשְׁפֹּט, *if thou will indeed judge.*

With Derivative Stems, especially *Niph'al*, the Infin. *Qal* is often used, *v. g.* שָׁאוֹל יִשָּׁאֲלוּ, *they will surely ask;* שָׂרוֹף יִשָּׂרְפוּ, *they shall be utterly burned.*

The Infin. Abs. is often best rendered in English by means of an adverb, or by one of the Emphatic or Progressive Modes: *he did go, he was going.*

196. b) after its finite verb, especially in the case of הָלַךְ, *to go,* the Infin. Abs. sometimes implies continuance, *v. g.* הָלְכוּ הָלוֹךְ, *they kept on going.* Occasionally, two Infinitives are thus joined in the same sense of continuance; the first of these Infinitives is generally הָלוֹךְ or some kindred verb indicating motion, *v. g.* הָלַךְ הָלוֹךְ וּבָכֹה, *he went, weeping as he went* (2 Sam. III, 16).

On the use of the participle in the same sense as the Infin. Abs., see 311.

197. Sometimes, the Infin. Abs., especially *Hiph'il*, is used with a finite verb with which it has no relation in etymology or meaning; in that case, it describes the circumstances of an action and is often treated as an adverb, *v. g.* דַּבֵּר הֵיטֵב, *he spoke well;* כַּבֵּד הַרְבֵּה, *he honoured much.*

198. c) The negative particle generally precedes the finite verb, *v. g.* שָׁמוֹעַ לֹא־שְׁמַעְתֶּם, *you have refused to hear.*

199. 2. The Infin. Abs. is used as a substitute for a finite verb, when, the sense being otherwise clear, the writer wishes to give more alertness to the sentence. Thus, often in the beginning of a sentence, in various meanings to be determined from the context, more particularly as an invitation or command, *v. g.* זָכוֹר אֶת־יוֹם הַשַּׁבָּת, *remember the Sabbath day.* Cp. French: *voir page . . . . i. e. see page . . . .;* *se rappeler, i. e. il faut se rappeler;* cp. also German *Einsteigen! all aboard.*

IMPERFECT.

200. Unlike the Perfect which is generally Indicative, the Imperfect has several Modes.

1. The Infinitive Construct or Verbal Noun, merely pointing out to the action or state in the process of becoming, without any determination of person, time, *etc., v. g.* קְטֹל, *killing, to kill.*

2. The Imperative, expressing a command or wish that an action be done or a state entered into by the person spoken to, *v. g.* קְטֹל *kill.*

3. The Indicative, stating the fact that a certain subject is connected with an action or state which in some way is considered as incomplete, *v. g.* יִקְטֹל, *he shall kill.*

4. The Cohortative, implying self-encouragement to do an action, *v. g.* אֶקְטְלָה, *let me kill.*

5. The Jussive, akin to the Imperative in meaning, but where the command is given in the form of a personal statement, *v. g.* יַקְטֵל, *let him cause to kill.*

6. To those should be added the Participles which in meaning and generally also in form resemble closely the other Modes of the Imperfect, *v. g.* מְקַטֵּל, *murdering.*

II. Infinitive Construct.

A. Form.

1. Vowel of the Second Radical (characteristic vowel).

201. a) In *Qal.* The Infin. Constr. of *Qal* has ō under the 2d. radical in the majority of active and even of stative verbs, *v. g.* קְטֹל, שְׁמֹר, לְבֹשׁ, *etc.* It has ă in a certain number of stative verbs and a few active (intransitive) verbs, *v. g.* שְׁכַב, *to lie down.*

202. b) Derivative Stems. The Derivative Stems have generally ē (î in *Hiph'il*), *v. g.* קַטֵּל, הִקָּטֵל, הַקְטִיל.

The vowels ō and ē before *Maqqeph*, before a word accented on the first syllable and (ō only occasionally, 331) before the consonantal suffixes ךָ, כֶם, כֶן, are shortened to ŏ and ĕ respectively, *v. g.* בַּקֶּשׁ־דַּעַת, *to seek knowledge.*

203. With verbs third guttural, the ō of Inf. *Qal* is followed by *Pathah Furtivum* (71). *Sere* of the Derivative Stems is regularly replaced by *Pathah* except in a Pause, *v. g.* שְׁלֹחַ, *to send*; *Pi.* שַׁלַּח, *to send off*, P. שַׁלֵּחַ.

2. Vowel of the First Radical.

204. a) In *Qal.* Originally, the vowel of the first radical in *Qal* was *u* or *i* for active verbs and *a* for stative verbs; this vowel has been regularly volatilized. The proclitic particle לְ (rarely בְּ) forms a closed syllable with the first radical, *v. g.* לִנְפֹּל, לִכְתֹּב, but בִּנְפֹל, בִּכְתֹב, rarely בְּכְתֹב, *etc.*

Gutturals, of course, have a *Hateph* in every case, *v. g.* עֲמֹד, לַעֲמֹד, בַּעֲמֹד.

205. b) Derivative Stems.

Niph'al has *Qameṣ, v. g.* הִקָּטֵל.
Pi'el and *Hithpa'el* have unchangeable *Pathah,* קַטֵּל, הִתְקַטֵּל.
Hiph'il has *Sh·wa,* but with first gutt. *Ḥateph,* הַקְטִיל, הַעֲמִיד.

206. 3. Stem-formative Prefixes.

These prefixes are the same as in the Perfect, except *Hiph'il* where the primitive *Ha* has been preserved and *Niph'al* which has the prefix *Hin* (see Infin. Abs., 194), *v. g.* הַקְטִיל, הִקָּטֵל, הֵעָמֵד.

207. 4. When an accented addition is made to the infinitive, the change in the accent causes the fall of the vowel under the second radical. The form in *Qal* would then begin with three consonants, which is not allowed (46). In that case, a short vowel is placed under the first radical: this vowel is regularly *ŏ* or *ŭ*, קָטְלְ, קֻטְלְ, and is a remnant of the older form *qŭtŭl;* verbs in *a*, have often *a* or *i*, קַטְלְ, קִטְלְ.

This applies to the cases in which the Infin. takes the feminine ending ה ָ (constr. ת ַ), *v. g.* קָרְבָה, *to approach;* אַהֲבָה, *to love;* שִׂנְאָה, *to hate;* מָשְׁחָה, *to anoint, etc.*

On the Infin. Constr. with suff. see 331, 332.

B. Use and Syntax.

Examples:

1. לָנוּ הַסְגִּיר אותו, *it is for us to deliver him up.* 2. וַיְהִי כִּשְׁמֹעַ דָּוִד, *and it came to pass that when David had heard;* וַיְהִי בְּהַקְטִיר הָעָם, *and it came to pass that while the people were burning incense;* מִשְּׁמֹר יְהוָה אֶתְכֶם, *because the Lord kept you;* לִכְרֹת עֵצִים, *in order to cut down trees;* לִשְׁאֹל מֶלֶךְ, *in asking for a king;* הוסִיף לָהֲלֹךְ, *he went again;* לְבִלְתִּי שַׁלַּח, *in not sending.* 3. לִפְנֵי שַׁחֵת יְהוָה אֶת־סְדֹם, *before the Lord had destroyed Sodom.*

208. In general, the Hebrew Inf. Constr. can be used when in English we use the Infinitive.

1. Without Prepositions. It may be in the nominative, genitive or accusative, *v. g.* לָנוּ הַסְגִּיר אותו, *it is for us to deliver him up.*

209. 2. With Prepositions. The meaning of the Inf. Constr. with prepositions is generally clearly indicated by the preposition itself.

a) With בְּ and כְּ, the Inf. Constr. is used in temporal clauses especially after וַיְהִי, *and it came to pass*, and וְהָיָה, *it shall come to pass.*

With בְּ, the Inf. generally indicates an action which occurs at the same time as that of the principal verb (English: *while, during*); with כְּ, it indicates an action of prior occurrence (English: *when, after*), *v. g.* וַיְהִי כִּשְׁמֹעַ דָּוִד, *and it came to pass that when David had heard;* וַיְהִי בְּהַקְטִיר הָעָם, *and it came to pass that while the people were burning incense.*

210. c) The preposition מִן, מִ, מֵ often means *because, so that, since, on account of*, but is still oftener used negatively, *so that not*, especially after verbs implying restraint, cessation (cp. 494), *v. g.* מִשְּׁמֹר יְהוָה אֶתְכֶם, *because the Lord kept you;* אֹתִי מָאֲסוּ מִמְּלֹךְ עֲלֵיהֶם, *they have rejected me so that I should not reign over them*, 1 Sam. VIII, 7.

211. d) With the preposition לְ, the Infinitive Constr. expresses various ideas:

α) aim and purpose, *v. g.* שָׁלַח שְׁלֹמֹה עֲבָדִים לִכְרֹת עֵצִים, *Solomon sent (his) servants to cut down trees;*

β) motive, attending circumstance, explanation or amplification of preceding statement, *v. g.* (*the wickedness that you have done*) לִשְׁאֹל לָכֶם מֶלֶךְ, *in asking for yourselves a king*, 1 Sam. XII, 17;

γ) very often, the Infin. Constr. expresses the verbal complement of a finite verb or of a verbal equivalent, thus: after verbs or phrases indicating command, permission or propriety, such as צִוָּה, *to command* (Lesson XVIII); . . . הָיָה לְ, *he was to . . .;* . . . עָלַי לְ, *I have to . . .;* . . . יֵשׁ לְ, *it is proper to . . .;* . . . אֵין לְ . . . לֹא לְ, *it is not possible, not permissible to . . . etc., v. g.* צִוָּה לִכְתֹּב, *he commanded to write;* אֵין לְהַזְכִּיר, *it must not be mentioned;*

δ) thus also after verbs of *repeating, finishing, beginning* (see 457). In such cases, English will often render the Hebrew Infinitive by the corresponding finite verb and the Hebrew finite verb by an adverb. Ex.: הוֹסִיף לָלֶכֶת, *he went again*, lit. *he added to going.* Sometimes the preposition לְ is omitted.

212. e) The Infinitive Constr. is negatived by לְבִלְתִּי, not by לֹא; the preposition לְ is not repeated before the verb, *v. g.* (*Pharaoh acted treacherously*) לְבִלְתִּי שַׁלַּח אֶת־הָעָם לִזְבֹּחַ לַיהוָה, *in not sending the* *people to sacrifice to the Lord* (cp. Exod. viii, 25). See also 210 and 211 γ.

213. f) When the Infin. Constr. is used with prepositions, it is not customary to have other Infinitives co-ordinated with the first in the same construction; the discourse usually proceeds by means of a finite verb, *v. g.* עַל עָזְבָם הָעָם אֶת־תּוֹרָתִי וְלֹא שָׁמְעוּ בְּקוֹלִי, *because the people have forsaken my law and have not hearkened unto my voice,* lit. *because of the forsaking of the people my law and* (*because*) *they have not hearkened* . . . . (Cp. Jer. ix, 12).

214. 3. The Infinitive Constr. partakes of the nature both of the noun and of the verb. As a noun, it can be put in the nominative (cp. 208), in the genitive, in the accusative and in the construct state before a following genitive; as a verb, it can govern the same cases as a finite verb; it can also, at least apparently, have a subject in the nominative. In fact, the same infinitive may at the same time play the part of a verb and that of a noun. When both object and subject are expressed, the usual order is *Inf.-subj.-obj.;* more rarely *Inf.-obj.-subj.* The following examples will illustrate those various points: בִּשְׁלֹחַ יְהֹוָה אֶתְכֶם, *in the Lord's sending you = when the Lord sent you,* Deut. ix, 23; לִפְנֵי שַׁחֵת יְהוָֹה אֶת־סְדֹם וְאֶת־עֲמֹרָה, *before the Lord had destroyed Sodom and Gomorrah,* Gen. xiii, 10; בִּשְׁלֹחַ אתו סַרְגוֹן, *when Sargon sent him;* cp. ex. in 213.

III. Imperative. **Form** (Paradigm I-L).

215. 1. Characteristic Vowel.

Generally, the Imperative has the same vowel as the Infinitive Construct; the following point of difference must however be noted, viz. that the stative verbs as well as verbs 2d. or 3d. gutt. have regularly *ă* instead of *ō* as characteristic vowel under the second radical, *v. g. Inf.* לְבֹשׁ, *Imp.* לְבַשׁ; *Inf.* שְׁחֹט, *Imp.* שְׁחַט; *Inf.* שְׁלֹחַ, *Imp.* שְׁלַח.

216. 2. Afformatives. As in most languages, the personal pronoun, always 2 p., is not expressed in the Imperative. To indicate the gender and number, afformatives are used: 2 f. s. has accented ִי; 2 m. pl. has accented וּ; 2 f. pl. has unaccented נָה. Besides, the

2 m. s. has often the emphatic accented ending ָה for the explanation of which see Cohortative, 233.

217. As in the Inf. Constr. (207), when the accented afformatives are added, a change takes place in the tone, which causes the vowel to be volatilized. To prevent the word from beginning with two Vocal *Sh·was*, a short vowel, generally *Ḥireq*, (even with gutturals) sometimes *Qameṣ Ḥaṭuph* (207) and with first guttural occasionally *S·ghol*, is inserted after the first radical, *v. g.* קִטְלוּ, קִטְלִי. In a Pause, however, קְטֹלוּ, קְטֹלִי.

218. If followed by *Maqqeph*, by a word accented on the first syllable or by a consonantal suffix (202), ō and ē are shortened to ŏ and ĕ respectively, *v. g.* שְׁמָר־לְךָ, *observe.*

EXERCISES.

I. 1) Give the Infinitive Absolute of the following verbs: to write; to keep; to settle down; to hear; to gather; to hasten; to teach; to deliver up (Hiph.); to recount; to offer incense; to reign; to close; to anoint; to seek; to destroy; to lie down; to fight; to send; to deal treacherously; to trust; to put on; to stand; to be gathered.

2) Give the Infinitive Construct of the same verbs.

3) Give the Imperative of the same (the first in 2 m. s.; the second, in 2 f. s.; the third, in 2 pl. m.; the fourth, in 2 pl. f.; the fifth, in 2 m. s., etc.).

4) Translate: You have surely heard; he kept on going; he went to teach; they hastened to write down and to recount; while David lay down; after David had heard; when Israel had settled down; etc.

II. 1. גֻּנֹּב גֻּנַּבְתִּי מֵאֶרֶץ הָעִבְרִים׃ – 2. כִּי בָגוֹד בָּֽגְדוּ בִּי בֵּית (house)
יִשְׂרָאֵל וּבֵית יְהוּדָה נְאֻם־יְהוָה׃ – 3. שָׁמוֹר אֶת־יוֹם (day) הַשַּׁבָּת לְקַדֵּשׁ
אֹתוֹ׃ – 4. צִוָּה (commanded) יְהוֹשֻׁעַ לִכְתֹּב אֶת־הָאָרֶץ׃ – 5. גַּם אֹתָם הִקְדִּישׁ
דָּוִד לַיהוָה עִם־הַכֶּסֶף (silver) וְהַזָּהָב (gold) אֲשֶׁר הִקְדִּישׁ מִכָּל־הַגּוֹיִם אֲשֶׁר
כִּבֵּשׁ׃ – 6. וַיְהִי בִּשְׁכֹּן יִשְׂרָאֵל בָּאָרֶץ הַהִיא׃ – 7. אָמַר יְהוָה עַל־עֲזֹב יִשְׂרָאֵל
אֶת־תּוֹרָתִי וְלֹא שָׁמְעוּ בְקוֹלִי וְלֹא הָלְכוּ בָהּ׃ – 8. וַיְהִי בְּהַכְרִית אִיזֶבֶל
(Jezabel) אֵת נְבִיאֵי יְהוָה׃

III. 1. There shall be an altar (יִֽהְיֶה מִזְבֵּחַ) to Jehovah in the midst of the land of Egypt. – 2. Pharaoh acted treacherously in not sending away the people to sacrifice to Jehovah. – 3. Thou didst forget Jehovah, thy God, by not observing his statutes and his precepts. – 4. And it came to pass that when the people had heard the sound of the trumpet (הַשּׁוֹפָר) . . . – 5. Thou hast not hearkened unto the voice of Jehovah, thy God, to keep his commandments and his statutes. – 6. Zadok (צָדוֹק) and Nathan (נָתָן) went to anoint Solomon. – 7. Now the Philistines had gathered to fight against Israel. – 8. Israel and Judaḥ have dealt very treacherously against me, saith the Lord.

LESSON IX.

IMPERF. (Contin.): INDICATIVE; COHORTATIVE; JUSSIVE; IMPERATIVE.

Vocabulary. Verbs.

פָּתַח, to open; *Niph.* to be open; *Pi.* free, loosen; *Hithp.* loosen for oneself

*חָזַק, to be strong; *Pi.* strengthen, make strong; *Hithp.* strengthen oneself, take courage; *Hiph.* make strong, strengthen.

*חָרֵשׁ, to be silent, deaf; *Hiph.* show deafness, keep silence.

*קָשַׁב, (to be attentive); *Hiph.* listen, give attention.

עָבַד, to work, till, serve; *Niph.* be tilled; (*Pu.* be worked); *Hiph.* compel to labor, . . . to serve; (*Hoph.* be enticed to serve).

[מָאֵן], *Pi.* מֵאֵן to refuse.

גָּזַל, to tear away, rob, plunder; *Niph.* be taken away).

דָּרַשׁ, to consult, seek, study, practice; *Niph.* let oneself be consulted.

קָבַר, to bury; *Niph.* be buried; (*Pi.* bury many); (*Pu.* be buried).

[שָׁלַךְ], *Hiph.* to throw, cast; *Hoph.* be cast.

דָּרַךְ, to tread, to march; *Hiph.* tread down, lead.

שָׁבַר, to break; *Niph.* be broken; *Pi.* shatter; (*Hiph.* cause to break); (*Hoph.* be shattered).

*דָּבַק, to cling; *Pu.* be joined together; *Hiph.* cause to cling; *Hoph.* be made to cling.

*שָׁלֵם, (to be complete); *Pi.* complete, recompense; *Pu.* be repaid; *Hiph.* complete, perform.

*שָׁלַם, to be at peace; *Pu.* *id.* *Hiph.* make peace; *Hoph.* live in peace

*רָכַב, to mount, ride; *Hiph.* cause to ride.

הָרַג, to kill, slay, destroy; (*Niph.* & *Pu.* be slain).

אָמַן, to support (only participle); *Niph.* make firm, be made firm; *Hiph.* believe, stand firm.

עָשַׁק, to oppress; (*Pu.* be crushed).

עָזַר, to help; (*Niph.* be helped).

Nouns.

עַתָּה, *adv.* now,
אַף, *conj.* also,
זְרוֹעַ, (I)(*m.*) arm, strength,
יַחַד, *adv.* together,
עָשִׁיר, (ii) *adj.* rich,
טוֹבָה, (i) *f.* goodness, prosperity,
יָתוֹם, (ii) *m.* orphan,
שָׁלוֹם, (ii) *m.* peace, soundness, completeness,
הֲ, (הָ, הֶ) sign of interrogation (Latin *ne*, *num*, see 413).

Diagram of Preformatives and Afformatives in Imperf. INDIC.

1

	Sing.	*Plur.*
3 *m.*	יִ***	יִ****וּ
3 *f.*	תִּ***	תִּ***נָה
2 *m.*	תִּ***	תִּ***וּ
2 *f.*	תִּ***י	תִּ***נָה
1 *c.*	אֶ***	נִ***

2

	3 *m.*	3 *f.*	2 *m.*	2 *f.*	1 *c.*
Sing.	יִ***	תִּ***	תִּ***	תִּ***י	אֶ***
Plur.	יִ****וּ	תִּ***נָה	תִּ***וּ	תִּ***נָה	נִ***

I. Indicative. See Paradigms I-L.

From the fact that the Indicative is the most commonly used of all the Modes of the Imperfect, it is generally called simply 'Imperfect'. To avoid all possible confusion, we give it its full name 'Imperf. Indicative'.

A. **Form and Inflection.**

219. 1. Formative vowels and afformatives. — The formative vowels of the Indicative as well as the afformatives for gender and number are the same as those of the Imperative (215, 216, 218). In the singular there are no afformatives except 2 f. which has the sign of the feminine ִי. In the plural, the 1 p. has no afformative; the other persons have וּ (in the older books often וּן) for the masculine, and נָה for the feminine. The afformatives וּ and ִי, being accented (except in *Hiph'il*), occasion vowel-modifications in the same manner and in the same cases as in the Imperative (217). A guttural takes *Ḥateph* instead of simple vocal *Sh'wa* (72), and often also instead of syllable-divider (73); this *Ḥateph* is changed to the corresponding vowel when followed by another *Sh'wa*, but this new vowel is still preceded by *Methegh* (74). In the Pause, the characteristic vowel is kept, accented, and lengthened, if not already long. Ex.: יִקְטֹל, יִשְׁלַח, יַעֲמֹד; יִקְטְלוּ, יִשְׁלְחוּ, יַעַמְדוּ; P. יִקְטֹ֫לוּ, יַעֲמֹ֫דוּ, יִשְׁלָ֫חוּ.

220. Whatever be the origin of those afformatives, it will help the student to remember, 1) that the ending ִי of the 2 f. s. was also at one time the ending of the separate pronoun of the corresponding person, אַתִּי; 2) that וּ (וּן) is the sign of the plural in verbs, *v. g.* יִקְטֹל, יִקְטְלוּ; תִּקְטֹל, תִּקְטְלוּ; 3) that נָה in the fem. pl. is also found in the separate pronouns for the fem. pl. אַתֵּנָה, הֵנָּה (Paradigm A).

On changes of afformatives before object-suffixes, see Lesson XIV.

221. 2. Preformatives. — a) In the Perfect, we considered the verbal forms with personal pronouns as nominal sentences, 175, 176; here also, for practical purposes, we may consider the Imperf. Ind. as a kind of nominal sentence (93) in which we connect a certain person with the idea expressed by the Infinitive or *Nomen actionis*, in any sense except that of a perfected action. Thus, תִּקְטֹל is for אַתָּה + קְטֹל, *thou killing, thou (for a) killing.*

222. In the Imperfect Ind. the personal pronouns are prefixed instead of being suffixed as in the Perfect. The reason for the difference comes from the fact that Hebrew wants the more emphatic word in the beginning (95); now, in the completed action, the fact that the action has been completed is, generally speaking, more important than the subject, while in an action not yet completed, we pay more attention to the person of the agent, which alone has a full concrete reality.

223. b) Form of the personal Preformatives. Persons are indicated by Preformatives derived, like the personal afformatives of the Perfect, from the separate pronouns, but in a still more modified form. All the second persons both sing. and plur. have ת prefixed. This ת is nothing else than the characteristic consonant of the separate pronouns of the second person, *v. g.* אַתָּה, אַתְּ, אַתֶּם, אַתֶּן or אַתֵּנָה.

The 1 p. s. has א a remnant of אֲנִי; the 1 p. pl. has נ from אֲנַחְנוּ or נַחְנוּ, *v. g.* אֶקְטֹל, *I shall kill;* נִקְטֹל, *we shall kill.*

The third persons have י and ת (f.) the origin of which is not clear, יִקְטֹל, תִּקְטֹל.

224. c) Vowel of the Preformatives. The original vowel of the personal Preformatives was *Paṯhaḥ*, which has been modified as follows:

α) In *Qal, Paṯhaḥ* is attenuated to *Ḥireq* (cp. *Niph'al, Hiph'il, etc.* 165, 169), יִקְטֹל, תִּקְטֹל, *Aleph* (70) prefers *S'ghol,* אֶקְטֹל.

With a verb first gutt. the personal Preformatives take either *Paṯhaḥ* or *S'ghol;* generally, they take *Paṯhaḥ* when the characteristic vowel is *o*, and

S·ghol, when it is *a* (69) or when the first radical is *Aleph*, *v. g.* יַעֲמֹד, יֶחֱזַק, יֶאֱסֹף. The guttural then receives a *Ḥaṭeph* corresponding to the vowel of the Preformatives.

β) In *Pi'el* and *Pu'al*, original *Pathaḥ* is volatilized according to 134, 136; *Aleph*, of course, takes a *Ḥaṭeph* (72), יְקַטֵּל, יְקֻטַּל, אֲקַטֵּל.

γ) In *Niph'al*, *Hithpa'el*, *Hiph'il* and *Hoph'al*, *Pathaḥ* was for the same reason first volatilized, then the *He* (ה) of the stem-formative prefix was elided and its vowel sounded with the personal Preformatives, 224, 206, 179—181; *S·ghol*, however, is generally found under *Aleph* instead of *Ḥireq*. Ex.: יִקָּטֵל for יְהִנָּקֵטֵל; יִתְקַטֵּל for יְהִתְקַטֵּל; יַקְטִיל for יְהַקְטִיל; יָקְטַל for יְהָקְטַל; with gutt. *Niph.* יֵעָמֵד for יְהִנָּעֵמֵד; אֶתְקַטֵּל. *Niph'al* has often *Ḥireq* instead of *S·ghol* under *Aleph*, *v. g.* אֶקָּטֵל and אִקָּטֵל.

In *Qal* the Preformatives form a closed syllable with the first radical, *v. g.* יִכְתֹּב, *he shall write;* in the other stems the syllable of the Preformatives is that of the Stem-formative prefixes, after the elision of the *He*, יְשַׁכֵּב, יַשְׁכִּיב, יִתְכַּבֵּד.

B. Use of the Imperfect Indicative.

Examples:

225. 1. עַל־גְּבוּל יִשְׂרָאֵל אֶשְׁפּוֹט אֶתְכֶם, *I will judge you in the border of Israel*; לֹא תִגְנֹב, *thou shalt not steal*; אִם־שָׁמוֹעַ תִּשְׁמְעוּ בְּקוֹלִי, *if indeed you obey my voice.* — 2. טֶרֶם יִשְׁכָּבוּ, *before they lay down*; הִשָּׁמֶר לְךָ פֶּן תִּדְרֹשׁ, *take heed to thyself that thou inquire not.* — 3. תִּשָּׁחֵת הָאָרֶץ, *the land was being destroyed*; יָתוֹם לֹא יִשְׁפֹּטוּ, *they judge not the fatherless.*

226. In general, the Imperfect Indicative is used to denote actions still unfinished from any standpoint, *v. g.* 1) from the standpoint of the speaker; 2) from the standpoint of another action; 3) or from the nature of the action to be expressed. Thus the Imperf. Indic. is used:

227. 1. to state an action still future from the point of view of the speaker; either of the speaker proper, *v. g.* in quotations, or of the author in his own narrative:

a) in the sense of our future, *v. g. Thus saith the Lord* . . . עַל־גְּבוּל יִשְׂרָאֵל אֶשְׁפּוֹט אֶתְכֶם. *I will judge you in the border of Israel*, Ezech. xi, 10; יִשְׁמֹר יְהוָה, *Jehovah will keep*;

b) to express a wish or threat, a command or prohibition, a permission or refusal, because the action commanded, *etc.*, is necessarily incomplete when the speaker gives the order or permission, *v. g.* לֹא תִּגְנֹב, *thou shalt not steal,* Ex. xx, 13; *when thou shalt besiege a city . . . thou shalt not destroy,* לֹא־תַשְׁחִית, *the trees thereof . . . .; only the trees which thou knowest that they are not trees for food, thou shalt destroy* תַּשְׁחִית, Deut. xx, 19, 20;

However, to express command, wish, etc., Imperative, Jussive, Cohortative are mostly used (235).

c) often in interrogative and exclamatory clauses, *v. g.* וְאֵיךְ נִגְנֹב *how then should we steal?* Gen. xliv, 8;

d) often in conditional sentences, because the verification of the condition is still contingent, *v. g.* אִם־שָׁמוֹעַ תִּשְׁמְעוּ בְּקֹלִי, *now therefore if indeed you obey my voice,* Ex. xix, 5;

228. 2. to denote an action following another in point of time or logical dependence, and consequently considered as not yet completed when this other action takes place; thus:

a) often after the particles, אָז, *then;* טֶרֶם, *not yet*; בְּטֶרֶם, *before; v. g.* טֶרֶם יִשְׁכָּבוּ, *before they lay down,* Gen. xix, 4;

b) to express aim and purpose, especially after the telic or final conjunctions, אֲשֶׁר, *that;* בַּעֲבוּר, יַעַן, לְמַעַן, לְמַעַן אֲשֶׁר, *in order that;* לְבִלְתִּי, *that . . . not;* פֶּן־, *lest, that . . . not, v. g.* הִשָּׁמֶר לְךָ . . . פֶּן תִּדְרשׁ לֵאלֹהֵיהֶם, *take heed to thyself that thou inquire not after their gods,* Deut. xii, 30;

229. 3. to indicate an action which, from its nature, is viewed as unfinished; thus:

a) to indicate an action that lasted, progressed, evolved in the past or is still doing so in the present. Mere duration is expressed by the participle (see lesson xiii). Ex.: תִּשָּׁחֵת הָאָרֶץ, *the land was destroyed, i. e. was being destroyed*; Ex., viii, 20 [24]; מַה־תְּבַקֵּשׁ, *what seekest thou?* Gen. xxxvii, 15. The Perfect Indic. often alternates with the Imperf. Indic.;

230. b) to denote an action frequently repeated, customary, habitual. Such actions are conceived as forming part of a series not yet closed or completed. This use of the Imperf. Ind. is common in proverbs, etc., *v. g.* יָתוֹם לֹא יִשְׁפֹּטוּ, *they judge not the fatherless,* Is., i, 23; *(now Hannah spoke in her heart; only her lips moved)* וְקוֹלָהּ לֹא יִשָּׁמֵעַ, *and her voice was not heard,* 1 Sam. i, 13;

231.   c) to form descriptive adjectival clauses by mere juxtaposition without the relative particle אֲשֶׁר, v. g. בִּנְיָמִין זְאֵב יִטְרָף, *Benjamin is a ravenous wolf*, Gen. XLIX, 27 (503).

N. B. From the above use of the Imperf. Indic. we see that it occurs when in English we would have a great variety of modes and tenses, such as *Past, Present, Future; Indicative, Subjunctive, Potential, Progressive, etc.* Besides, in many cases, the Perfect might be used; the choice depends on the view-point of the author and on the effect which he wishes to produce.

II. COHORTATIVE and JUSSIVE.

A. Form and Inflection.

232.   1. Cohortative. The Cohortative is the Mode of self encouragement and is therefore used only in the first person. Its characteristic is an accented ־ָה added to the corresponding persons of the Indicative. The change in the place of the accent brings about a modification of the vowels exactly similar to that of the Indicative with the endings וּ and ־ִי, v. g. אֶקְטְלָה, *let me kill*.

In a Pause the vowel is kept, lengthened if not long, and retains the tone, v. g. אֶקְטְלָה, P. אֶקְטֹלָה.

The ending ־ָה is also added to the 2. m. Imp. (216), קָטְלָה, *do kill*. Probably the ־ָה of the Cohortative and of the Imperative is a remnant of a *Modus Energicus* still preserved in some of the Semitic languages.

233.   2. Jussive. a) The Jussive naturally does not occur in the first person.

b) The Jussive is externally the same as the Indicative, but if the characteristic vowel is ־ִי or וּ, these two vowels are changed to ē and ō, yet, only in persons that have no afformatives, *i. e.* 3 s. (m. and f.) and 2 m. s., v. g. יִקְטֹל, J. יִקְטֵל; יַקְטִיל, J. יַקְטֵל; יִקְטְלוּ, J. יַקְטִילוּ.

234.   Apart from these cases, whether a form is a Jussive or an Indicative can be known α) from the context; β) from the vocalization of a prefixed *Waw* (see following lesson, 238); γ) from the fact that the Jussive is negatived by אַל and not by לֹא as the Indicative.

B. Use of the Imperative, Cohortative and Jussive.

Examples:

1. אַל־תִּקְטֹל, *do not kill.* — 2. נַֽעַבְדָה, *let us serve.* — 3. שְׁאַל־נָא בֵּֽאלֹהִים, *ask, I pray, of God.*

235. 1. Those three Modes are very much allied in meaning and usage. The Imperative is always affirmative and is used only for the second persons. The first person is supplied by the Cohortative, and the third, by the Jussive. Even the second pers. in a negative sentence must be supplied by the Jussive. As noted above (227 b), the Indicative may sometimes be used instead of an Imperative, Cohortative or Jussive. The Indicative is weaker in an affirmative sentence, but is stronger in a negative sentence, *v. g.* קְטֹל, *kill;* אֶקְטְלָה, *let me kill;* אַל־תִּקְטֹל, *do not kill;* לֹא־תִקְטֹל, *thou shalt not kill.*

As noted in 234, it is sometimes impossible to tell whether a form is a Jussive or an Indicative, except from the context.

236. 2. Construed independently or in real co-ordination (*Waw copulativum, 238*) those three Modes are used to express commands, wishes, requests; to ask permission (Cohort.), or to grant it (Juss., Imper.) When negative, they express prohibition, imprecation, *etc.*, *v. g.* נַֽעַבְדָה, *let us serve;* הַקְשִׁ֫יבָה, *listen;* זְכֹר אַל־תִּשְׁכַּח, *remember, forget not.*

237. 3. When a command is given in a more courteous manner, these Modes are followed by the particle ־נָא, *please, I pray,* (French: *donc;* German: *doch*). With the Cohortative, this particle frequently implies a strengthening of the self-determination. In negative sentences, נָא comes between the negative particle and the verb. Ex.: שְׁאַל־נָא בֵּֽאלֹהִים, *ask, I pray, of God,* Jud. xviii, 5; יִזְכָּר־נָא הַמֶּ֫לֶךְ, *let the king remember, I pray,* 2 Sam. xiv, 11; אַל־נָא תַּעֲזֹב אֹתָנוּ, *leave us not, I pray thee,* Num. x, 31.

Often, especially in the later books and in the beginning of a sentence, the Jussive seems to have lost much of its original meaning, and apparently has the sense of an ordinary Imperfect Indicative.

(On Jussive, Cohortative and Imperative with *waw*, see next Lesson).

EXERCISES.

I. He shall open; you shall listen; they have served; let them serve; they shall not refuse; let them not refuse; they shall be broken; thou shalt bury; he shall consult; do not (thou) break; do not (thou) break, I pray; they shall be strong; let me ask, I pray; they shall plunder: do not (thou) oppress; let them reject; let them not reject, I pray; let us not forsake; they [always] speak.

II. 1. בַּיּוֹם הַהוּא, נְאֻם יְהוָה צְבָאוֹת, אֶשְׁבֹּר אֶת־הַזָּרִים וְלֹא יַעַבְדוּ יַעֲקֹב עוֹד אוֹתָם׃ – 2. הֲגוֹי גַּם־צַדִּיק תַּהֲרֹג׃ – 3. גֵּר וְיָתוֹם לֹא תַעֲשֹׁקוּ׃ – 4. אֲדַבְּרָה־נָּא שָׁלוֹם בָּךְ . . . ׃ – 5. דָּבַק בַּיהוָה אֱלֹהֵי יִשְׂרָאֵל׃ – 6. לֹא־תִדְרְשׁוּ שְׁלוֹם הַגּוֹיִם וְטוֹבָתָם לְמַעַן תֶּחֶזְקוּ׃ – 7. וְלֹא יִשְׁכְּבוּ אֶת־גִּבּוֹרִים׃ – 8. יְהוָה יִלָּחֵם לָכֶם, וְאַתֶּם תַּחֲרִשׁוּן׃ – 9. אַל־תְּמָאֵן לַעֲזֹר אֶת־הָאֶבְיוֹן׃ – 10. הִשָּׁמֶר לְךָ פֶּן־תִּדְרֹשׁ לֵאלֹהֵיהֶם לֵאמֹר אֵיכָה יַעַבְדוּ הַגּוֹיִם אֶת־אֱלֹהֵיהֶם וְאֶעֶבְדָה גַּם אָנִי׃

III. 1. Moses said to God, The people of Israel will not believe me nor hearken unto my voice. – 2. Listen, Job (אִיּוֹב), hear me; be silent and I will speak. – 3. You shall not oppress and you shall not despoil. 4. – The Lord, thy God, shalt thou hear, and Him shalt thou serve, and to Him shalt thou cling. – 5. If you do not hearken unto me . . . and if you reject my statutes, I too shall reject you. – 6. To thee is an arm with strength. - 7. Observe and seek out the precepts of Yahweh, your God. – 8. [As to] you, do not make a covenant with the nations of the land.

LESSON X.

WAW COPULATIVUM. WAW CONSECUTIVUM. UNCLASSIFIED NOUNS.

Vocabulary. Verbs.

עָבַר to pass over, cross; pass beyond, through, along; go on, emigrate; transgress; (*Niph.* be forded; *Pi.* to lead across); *Hiph.* bring, dedicate, *etc.*, causative of *Qal* in its various meanings. *Hithp.* be arrogant.

[בָּקַשׁ] *Pi.* to seek; (*Pu.* be sought).

קָבַץ to gather, collect; *Niph.* gather, intr.; *Pi.* gather together; (*Hithp.* gather together, intr.).

חָדַל* to cease; with מִן, let alone.

רָחַץ to wash, wash away, bathe; (*Pu.* be washed); (*Hithp.* wash oneself).

טָהֵר to be clean, pure; *Pi.* cleanse, purify; (*Pu.* be cleansed); *Hithp.* purify oneself.

כָּזַב (to be a liar); (*Niph.* to be proven a liar); *Pi.* lie, tell a lie; (*Hiph.* prove some one to be a liar).

צָעַק / זָעַק } to cry out; (*Niph.* be summoned; *Pi.* cry aloud; *Hiph.* call together).

שָׂמַח to rejoice, be glad; *Pi.* and (*Hiph.*) gladden.

בָּעַר to burn, consume; *Pi.* kindle, consume; (*Pu.* be burnt); *Hiph.* to kindle.

לָכַד to capture, seize; *Niph.* be captured; (*Hithp.* grasp each other).

סָמַךְ to support, place hands on (victim); *Niph.* support oneself; (*Pi.* revive).

תָּמַךְ to grasp, support; (*Niph.* be seized).

שָׁכַר* to be or become drunken; *Pi.* and *Hiph.* make drunken; (*Hithp.* show oneself drunken, act as a drunken person).

[שָׁבַע] *Niph.* to swear, take an oath; *Hiph.* cause to take an oath, adjure.

חָשַׁב to think, account; *Niph.* be thought, esteemed; *Pi.* consider, devise, plan; (*Hithp.* reckon oneself).

[מָלַט] *Niph.* to slip away, escape; *Pi.* let escape; *Hithp.* escape; (*Hiph.* give birth).

פָּלַט (to escape); *Pi.* and (*Hiph.*) bring into security.

שָׂרַף to burn; *Niph.* be burned *Pi.* burn; *Pu.* be burned (cp. *Seraphim*).

Vocabulary. Verbs.

קָרַב (קָרֵב) to come near; (*Niph.* be brought); *Pi.* cause to approach; *Hiph.* bring, present.

רָחַק to be or become remote; (*Pi.* send away); *Hiph*, remove, create a distance between.

כָּשַׁל to stumble, totter; *Niph. id.*; *Hiph.* cause to stumble; *Hoph.* be overthrown.

[שָׁרַת] *Pi.* to minister, to serve.

סָלַח to forgive; (*Niph.* bè forgiven).

Nouns.

בָּבֶל *p. n. Babylon,*
נְבוּכַדְנֶאצַּר *p. n. Nabuchodonosor*
גְּדַלְיָהוּ *p. n. Godolias*
פֹּה *adv. here,*
חוֹמָה (*I*) *f. wall*

מְצוּדָה (*I*) *f. siege-works, rampart*
גְּמוּל (*I*) *m. action, retribution*
גְּמוּלָה (*I*) *f. retribution*
נָשִׂיא (*II*) *m. prince, chief*
חִירָם *p. n. Hiram.*

Examples:

I. A. זִבְחוּ . . . וּבִטְחוּ אֶל־יְהוָֹה, *offer sacrifices and trust in the Lord.* B. רְחַץ וּטְהַר, *wash in order to be clean;* לֹא אִישׁ אֵל וִיכַזֵּב, *God is not a man that He should lie;* עִבְדוּ אֶת־יְהוָֹה וְלֹא תִשָּׁבְרוּ, *serve the Lord that you may not be broken.* II. B. 2. וְלֹא זָכַר אֶת יוֹסֵף וַיִּשְׁכָּחֵ אתו, *and he remembered not Joseph and forgot him;* וַיְהִי כִּשְׁמֹעַ חִירָם וַיִּשְׂמַח מְאֹד, *and it came to pass, when Hiram had heard, that he rejoiced greatly.* 3. שְׁמַע בְּקוֹלָם וְהִמְלַכְתָּ, *hear their voice and cause (a king) to reign;* כִּי יִצְעַק וְשָׁמַעְתִּי, *when he crieth, I will indeed hear;* לְמַעַן שִׁמְךָ וְסָלַחְתָּ, *for thy name's sake, forgive.* 4. וְהוּא שָׁפַט . . . . אֶת־יִשְׂרָאֵל, *now he had judged Israel.*

In this lesson, a distinction is made between the syntactical force of the conjunction וְ when prefixed to an Imperative, Jussive or Cohortative, and the same conjunction when prefixed to the Indicative both of the Perfect and of the Imperfect. The former is called *Waw* copulative, the latter, *Waw* consecutive.

I. Waw Copulative.

238. The conjunction וְ (וּ, וִי, וַ, 45 ff.; 88, 120) when immediately prefixed to an Imperative, Jussive or Cohortative, co-ordinates these Modes to what precedes; a distinction must however be made between the various ideas that such a co-ordination implies.

239. A. It may imply mere co-ordination in meaning as well as in form, *v. g.* זִבְחוּ . . . וּבִטְחוּ אֶל־יְהוָֹה, *offer sacrifices . . . and trust in the Lord.*

240. B. Although co-ordinated in form with what precedes, in meaning and connotation those Modes are often used to express the purpose aim or consequence of the action that precedes; the use of those Modes in the above cases is due to the fact that the purpose, aim or consequence is desired and willed by the speaker; (cp. the English sentence *"come and see,"* in which the speaker desires that the person spoken to should both come and see, the second act being in reality the aim of the first: *„come in order to see"*). Often, however, such a Hebrew construction is best rendered in English by a conditional, causal, temporal or concessive clause, the protasis (antecedent) of which is expressed in what precedes, and the apodosis (consequent) by the Imperative, Jussive or Cohortative.

241. 1. This occurs mostly when the Imperative, Jussive or Cohortative with וְ are preceded by a clause in which is found another one of these Modes (cp. Latin *divide et impera*, or English *bring it and let him see it*); *v. g.* רְחַץ וּטְהָר, *wash and be clean, i. e. wash in order to be clean;* יְבַעֶר אִישׁ אֶת־בֵּית הָאֶבְיוֹן וִישַׁלֶּם־לוֹ, *if a man burns the house of the poor he shall compensate him*, lit. *let a man burn the house of the poor and let him compensate him.*

2. It occurs also after interrogative and negative clauses, *v. g.* הַאֵין פֹּה נָבִיא לַיהוָה וְנִדְרְשָׁה מֵאֹתוֹ, *is there not here a prophet of Jehovah, that we may inquire of him?* 1 K. xxii, 7; lit. *is there . . . . and (if there is) let us inquire of him;* לֹא אִישׁ אֵל וִיכַזֵּב, *God is not a man that he should lie,* Num. xxiii, 19 (cp. Latin Vulgate, *non est Deus quasi homo, ut mentiatur*).

242. 3. The second verb expressing a consequence of the action of the first is negatived by the Indicative with לֹא, instead of the Jussive with אַל; as a rule, וְאַל really co-ordinates its clause to a preceding one, *v. g.* עִבְדוּ אֶת־יְהוָה וְלֹא תִשָּׁבֵרוּ, *serve the Lord that you may not be broken;* זְכֹר וְאַל תִּשְׁכַּח, *remember and do not forget.*

II. Waw Consecutive.

When the conjunction ו is prefixed to the **Indicative** of the Perfect or of the Imperfect, it indicates a certain dependence of that verb on what precedes, and hence is called 'Consecutive'.

A. Form.

1. Prefixed to the Indicative of the Perfect.

243. a) The *Waw* itself in no way differs from the *Waw* copulative (238);

244. b) the accent, however, generally goes over to the personal afformatives of the 1 and 2 p. s. (not 1 p. pl.) unless the Perfect to which *Waw* is prefixed is in a Pause or (although less regularly) is before a word accented on the first syllable, *v. g.* קָטַ֫לְתָּ but וְקָטַלְתָּ֫; הִקְטַ֫לְתִּי but וְהִקְטַלְתִּ֫י; in a Pause: וְקָטָ֫לְתָּ, וְהִקְטַ֫לְתִּי.

In all the other persons, the tone generally retains its place, *v. g.* וְקָטַ֫לְנוּ, וְהִקְטִ֫ילוּ.

245. c) The shifting of the tone does not affect the quantity of the vowels, except in the few verbs with middle ō in which the vowel ō is shortened to *Qameṣ Ḥaṭuph*, *v. g.* קָטֹ֫לְתָּ, וְקָטָלְתָּ; יָכֹ֫לְתָּ, *thou wast able* but וְיָכָלְתָּ; in a Pause, however, וְיָכֹ֫לְתָּ.

246. 2. Prefixed to the Indicative of the Imperfect, a) *Waw* is vocalized with *Pathaḥ* followed by *Daghesh Forte, Pathaḥ* undergoing the same modifications as the article (87, 113), viz. before *Yodh* with *Sh·wa*, the *Daghesh* is omitted (87); before א, *Pathaḥ* is lengthened to *Qameṣ* and *Daghesh Forte* omitted (113), *v. g.* יִקְטֹל but וַיִּקְטֹל; אֶקְטֹל but וָאֶקְטֹל; יְקַטֵּל but וַיְקַטֵּל.

247. b) In direct contrast to the Perfect, the *Waw consecutive* of the Imperf. Ind. draws the tone backward on the penult, if the nature of the syllable allows it (38); from the principles given § 38, this can occur in the strong verb only in *Niph.*, and in the Intensive Stems with middle א or ר when the vowel of the first radical is lengthened by compensation, 183. Even there, the retraction of the tone is rare with the 1 p. s. and in the Pause. Ex.: וַיִּלָּ֫חֶם, *and he fought;* וַיְבָ֫רֶךְ, *and he blessed,* but וַיִּקְטֹל, וַיְקַטֵּל, וָאֲבָרֵךְ, *etc.* When the penult has *î* or *û*, the retraction of the tone does not usually take place, cp. 350, *v. g.* וַיֵּיטֵב, וַיּוֹשֵׁב..

248. c) When the retraction of the tone occurs, the ultima being unaccented, takes a shorter vowel, *v.g.* וַיִּלָּ֫חֶם, וַיְבָ֫רֶךְ. In *Hiph.*, although the retraction of the tone does not take place, still ִי is shortened to *Ṣere, v. g.* יַקְטִיל, וַיַּקְטֵל. Cp. Jussive, 233.

d) Very often 1 p. s. and 1 p. pl. have the accented ending ָה after *Waw* consecutive, *v. g.* וָאֶקְטְלָה; (Cohortative would be וְאֶקְטְלָה, with copulative Waw).

B. Use of Waw Consecutive.

1. In general.

249. The fundamental distinction between the Indicative of the Perfect and that of the Imperf. given in Lessons vii and ix does not seem to hold, whenever the *Waw* consecutive is prefixed to either of them. Formerly, it was thought that the presence of the *Waw* was actually changing an Imperf. into a Perfect and *vice versa;* hence this *Waw* was called '*Waw* conversive'. This view is now abandoned; both Perfect and Imperfect are considered as retaining their proper meaning. The phenomenon is rather a psychological one; the *Waw*, immediately prefixed to the Indicative both of the Perf. and of the Imperf., implies, in the mind of the writer, not the mere co-ordination of two or more verbs, but the logical or, at least, temporal dependence of the second on the first, on a preceding clause, or on a whole context. All the verbs thus connected form in the mind of the author one chain or series linked together, in which the verbs with *Waw* consecutive, are judged from the point of view of the first verb, and from **that point of view** are considered as expressing a completed or not completed action. If, however, the conjunction is separated from the verb by any word or particle, the series is broken and a new series is begun.

2. Imperfect Indicative with *Waw* consecutive.

When the first verb of the series is a Perfect, all the verbs connected with it by *Waw* consecutive are in the Imperf. Ind. Hence, the Imperf. Indic. with *Waw* consecutive is used:

250. a) as the historical tense α) to continue a narrative begun with a Perfect, *v. g.* שָׁלַח וַיִּלְכֹּר, *he sent and he captured* (when he sent he had not yet captured); לֹא זָכַר אֶת־יוֹסֵף וַיִּשְׁכָּחֵ אתו, *he remembered not Joseph and forgot him.*

251. β) Often we find an Imperf. Ind. with *Waw* consecutive at the beginning of a sentence, chapter or book; in that case, the missing Perfect is understood in the mind of the writer, who sums up the whole preceding narrative as equivalent to a Perfect, *v. g.* וַיְדַבֵּר אֱלֹהִים אֶל־מֹשֶׁה, *and God spoke to Moses* (passim) *i. e.* all that has been narrated took place and then God spoke, *etc.*

252. γ) At the beginning of a new sentence or section, we find frequently the narrative resumed by the impersonal וַיְהִי, *and it came to pass* (Imperf. of הָיָה) followed by another Imperf. Indic. with *Waw* consecutive, *v. g.* וַיְהִי כִּשְׁמֹעַ חִירָם וַיִּשְׂמַח מְאֹד, *and it came to pass, when Hiram had heard that he rejoiced greatly,* 1 K. v, 21 (7), *i. e.* . . .

"[all that precedes took place] and it happened that Hiram heard, and he rejoiced." Thus it is seen that clauses introduced by וַיְהִי often correspond to temporal or circumstantial clauses in English. However, וַיְהִי must always be separated from the following Imperf. by some word or phrase, as in the above example: כִּשְׁמֹעַ חִירָם;

253. b) in conditional (temporal, causal, concessive, etc.) sentences, when the protasis is expressed by the Perfect, *v. g.* יַעַן מָאַסְתָּ אֶת־יְהוָה וַיִּמְאָסְךָ, *because thou hast rejected the Lord, he will reject thee*, cp. 1 Sam. xv, 23.

3. Indicative Perfect with *Waw* consecutive.

Conversely, when the first verb of the series is an Imperfect the following verbs are joined to it by means of *Waw* consecutive with the Perfect. Thus the Perfect with *Waw* consecutive is used:

a) to continue the discourse.

254. α) in a narrative begun with one of the Modes of the Imperfect, *v. g.* שְׁמַע בְּקוֹלָם וְהִמְלַכְתָּ לָהֶם מֶלֶךְ, *hearken unto their voice, and make them a king*, 1 Sam. viii, 22 (here the Perfect is supposed to carry into completion the idea expressed by the initial Imperative); יִשְׁכַּח הַדָּבָר הַזֶּה וְשִׁלַּחְתִּי אֹתְךָ, *he shall forget this thing and I will send thee*;

255. β) without a preceding Imperfect, in which case, what precedes must be considered as the equivalent of an Imperfect (cp. 251), *v. g.* אֵין־יִרְאַת אֱלֹהִים בַּמָּקוֹם הַזֶּה וַהֲרָגוּנִי, *the fear of God is not in this place, and they will slay me*, cp. Gen. xx, 11; לְמַעַן שִׁמְךָ יְהוָה וְסָלַחְתָּ, *for thy name's sake, o Lord, forgive*, Ps. xxv, 11.

256. The narrative is often resumed with הִנֵּה, *behold* followed by a substantive or participle, or by וְהָיָה, *and it will come to pass, and it happened usually* (frequentative Perfect with *Waw* consecutive instead of an Imperfect, 230) used as a parallel to וַיְהִי with the same construction, *v. g.* וְהָיָה בִּקְרָב־אִישׁ וְשָׁלַח אֶת־יָדוֹ וְהֶחֱזִיק בּוֹ, [and all that precedes was going on] *and it happened that, when any man came nigh, he would put forth his hand and take hold of him*, cp. 2 Sam. xv, 5.

257. b) in the apodosis of conditional (temporal, causal, etc.) sentences, the protasis or antecedent of which is expressed by one of the Modes of the Imperfect, *v. g.* כִּי־יִצְעַק אֵלַי וְשָׁמַעְתִּי, *when he crieth to me, I will hear,* Ex. xxii, 26.

4. Circumstantial Clauses.

258. Circumstantial clauses, which by their nature break the continuity of a narrative by giving some attendant circumstance, do not admit of *Waw* consecutive. In such clauses, if a finite verb is used with the conjunction *'and'*, the conjunction must be separated from the verb; generally the subject precedes the verb (115); a participial construction is very common in such clauses (Lesson xiii, 310). Ex.: וַיִּקְבְּרוּ אֶחָיו אוֹתוֹ וְהוּא שָׁפַט אֶת־יִשְׂרָאֵל, *and his brethren buried him; now he had judged Israel* . . . cp. Judges, xvi, 31.

259. Remarks. 1. It must be remembered that, from our point of view, the Imperf. Indicative with *Waw* consecutive belongs to the same period of time as the Perfect that precedes; and *vice versa* the Perfect consecutive, to the same period as the preceding Imperfect. The consequence is that all the verbs forming one series, whether Perfect with Imperfect consecutive, or Imperf. with Perf. consecutive, ought to be rendered by the same English tense.

2. As appears from the above examples, *Waw* is used much more frequently than the English *'and'*. Not only does it correspond to English *'and'* but it can be used practically for all co-ordinating conjunctions. Besides, many clauses which in English are introduced by subordinating conjunctions are in Hebrew merely co-ordinated by means of *Waw* (cp. 469).

260. III. Unclassified Nouns.

	Sing.				Plur.			
	abs.	const.	light suff.	grave suff.	abs.	const.	light suff.	grave suff.
1	אָב father,	אֲבִי	אָבִי	אֲבִיכֶם	אָבוֹת	אֲבוֹת	אֲבוֹתַי	אֲבֹותֵיכֶם
2	אָח brother,	אֲחִי	אָחִי	אֲחִיכֶם	אַחִים	אֲחֵי	אַחַי (אֶחָי) אֶחָיו	אֲחֵיכֶם
3	אָחוֹת sister,	אֲחוֹת	אֲחֹתִי	אֲחֹתָם	—	—	אַחְיוֹתָיו	אַחְיֹתֵיהֶם
4	(חָם) husband's father,		חָמִיךְ	—	—	—	—	—
5	חָמוֹת husband's mother,		חֲמוֹתֵךְ					
6	אִישׁ man,	אִישׁ	אִישִׁי		אֲנָשִׁים	אַנְשֵׁי	אֲנָשָׁיו	אַנְשֵׁיהֶם
7	אִשָּׁה f. { woman, wife,	אֵשֶׁת	אִשְׁתִּי		נָשִׁים	נְשֵׁי	נָשָׁיו	נְשֵׁיהֶם

	Sing.					Plur.			
	abs.		const.	light suff.	grave suff.	abs.	const.	light suff.	grave suff.
8	יוֹם	m. day,	יוֹם	יוֹמוֹ	יוֹמָם	יָמִים	יְמֵי	יָמָיו	יְמֵיהֶם
9	עִיר	f. city,	עִיר	עִירִי	עִירָם	עָרִים	עָרֵי	עָרָיו	עָרֵיהֶם
10	רֹאשׁ	m. head,	רֹאשׁ	רֹאשִׁי	רָאשְׁכֶם	רָאשִׁים	רָאשֵׁי	רָאשָׁיו	רָאשֵׁיהֶם
11	בַּ֫יִת	m. house,	בֵּית	בֵּיתִי	בֵּיתְכֶם	בָּ֫תִּים	בָּתֵּי	בָּתֶּ֫יךָ	בָּתֵּיהֶם
12	שֵׁם	m. name,	שֶׁם־ שֵׁם	שְׁמִי	שִׁמְכֶם	שֵׁמוֹת	שְׁמוֹת		שְׁמוֹתָם
13	בֵּן	m. son,	בֶּן־, בֵּן	בְּנִי		בָּנִים	בְּנֵי	בָּנַי	בְּנֵיהֶם
14	בַּת	f. daughter,	בַּת	בִּתִּי	בִּתְּכֶם	בָּנוֹת	בְּנוֹת	בְּנֹתַי	בְּנֹתֵיכֶם
15	אָמָה	f. handmaid,		אֲמָתִי		אֲמָהוֹת	אַמְהוֹת	אַמְהֹתַי	אַמְהֹתֵיכֶם
16	(מַי)	m. water,				מַ֫יִם	מֵי, מֵימֵי	מֵימָיו	מֵימֵיהֶם
17	(שָׁמַי)	m. heaven,				שָׁמַ֫יִם	שְׁמֵי	שָׁמָיו	שְׁמֵיכֶם
18	אֶחָד	m. one, certain (one),	אַחַד						
19	אַחַת	P. אֶחָת f. id.,	אַחַת						
20	הַר	P. הָר (118) m. mountain,	הַר	הֲרָרִי הַרֲרִי	הַרְכֶם	הָרִים	הָרֵי (הַרֲרֵי)	הָרַי	הֲרָרֶ֫יהָ
21	אֱמֶת	(for אֱמֶ֫נֶת) f. truth, firmness, faithfulness,	אֱמֶת	אֲמִתּוֹ	אֲמִתְּךָ				
22	כְּלִי	P. כֶּ֫לִי m. utensil, vessel,	כְּלִי		כֶּלְיְךָ	כֵּלִים	כְּלֵי	כֵּלֶ֫יךָ	כְּלֵיכֶם
23	בְּהֵמָה	animal, cattle,	בֶּהֱמַת	בְּהֶמְתְּךָ	בְּהֶמְתְּכֶם	בְּהֵמוֹת	בַּהֲמוֹת		
24	עַד	P. [וָ]עֶד m. perpetuity,							
25	שֶׂה	m. & f. one of a flock, sheep, ewe.	שֵׂה	שֵׂיוֹ					

EXERCISES.

I. 1. My father; our father; your brother; your names; their names; our cities; the houses of Israel; his days; their sons and their daughters; the men and women of Judah; the heavens of the Lord; the waters of Egypt; the mountains of Israel; your mountains; the faithfulness of God; my faithfulness; your cattle; the animals of Jacob; the names of your fathers; their fathers; the days of Josue; their sisters and your handmaids.

2. He stole and he captured; he made them drunk and they stumbled; thou hast sworn; and thou hast sworn; and he clung; and they asked; and she wrote; and I shall send; and you shall hear; and they passed over.

II. 1. וְאֶקְבְּצָה אֶל־אֲדֹנִי אֶת־כָּל־יִשְׂרָאֵל וְיִכְרְתוּ אִתְּךָ בְּרִית וּמָלַכְתָּ עַל־כָּל־הָעָם׃ — 2. שִׁמְעוּ אֶת־קוֹלִי וְדִבַּרְתֶּם אֶל־אִישׁ יְהוּדָה׃ — 3. וַיַּעַבְדוּ הָעָם אֶת־יְהוָה כֹּל יְמֵי יְהוֹשֻׁעַ׃ — 4. אָמַרְתִּי אֲדֹנָי יֱהוִה אַל־תַּשְׁחֵת אֶת־הָעָם וּזְכֹר לְאַבְרָהָם לְיִצְחָק וּלְיַעֲקֹב׃ — 5. וַיִּלְכְּדוּ אֶת־עָרֵי הַמְּצֻרוֹת אֲשֶׁר לִיהוּדָה׃ — 6. וְנִלְכְּדוּ גִּבּוֹרֵי בָבֶל כִּי אֵל גְּמֻלוֹת יְהוָה שַׁלֵּם יְשַׁלֵּם׃ — 7. וַיִּקְרְבוּ רָאשֵׁי הָאָבוֹת לִבְנֵי גִלְעָד, וַיְדַבְּרוּ לִפְנֵי מֹשֶׁה וְלִפְנֵי רָאשֵׁי אָבוֹת לִבְנֵי יִשְׂרָאֵל׃ — 8. וַיִּשְׁמְעוּ, הֵמָּה וְהָאֲנָשִׁים, כִּי הִפְקִיד נְבוּכַדְנֶאצַּר אֶת־גְּדַלְיָהוּ׃ וַיִּשָּׁבַע לָהֶם גְּדַלְיָהוּ וּלְאַנְשֵׁיהֶם לֵאמֹר ..׃ — 9. חֲדַל מִן־הָעָם וְנַעַבְדָה אֶת־מִצְרָיִם׃ — 10. אֲקַבֵּץ אֹתָם אֶל־הַמָּקוֹם אֲשֶׁר בָּחַרְתִּי לְשַׁכֵּן אֶת־שְׁמִי שָׁם׃ — 11. וַתַּשְׁכִּבֵהוּ אֶת־בְּנָהּ עַל־מִטַּת אִישׁ הָאֱלֹהִים׃

III. 1. And Cain (קַיִן) killed Abel (הֶבֶל) his brother. — 2. We are brothers, sons of one man. — 3. And he spoke, saying: I am thy son, thy first born, Esau (עֵשָׂו). — 4. And Israel served the Lord all the days of Josue. — 5. Thy brethren also, bring with thee, that they may minister unto thee. — 6. They took the heads of the men, the sons of their master. — 7. Do not oppress and do not slaughter. — 8. Trust in the Lord and do not make a covenant with the gods of the nations. — 9. If thou hear me and observe my covenant. — 10. Let them take courage so that they serve not the Egyptians.

LESSON XI.

NOUNS, CLASS III: Monosyllables in *ă, ē, ō.* Other nouns following the same analogy; *Paradigm* D.

NOUNS, CLASS IV: Nouns with Changeable *Qameṣ* and *Ṣere; Paradigm* E.

Vocabulary. Nouns.

Learn the nouns given in Paradigms D and E and add the following:

Class III.

לֵב, (וֹת), *m. heart*

רַב, *a. many, numerous*

עֵת, *m. time*

בַּד, *m.* 1) *linen,* 2) *separation, part*

לְבַדּוֹ, *he alone*

לְבַדִּי, *I alone*

כֹּל, *m. entirety, all*

קָטוֹן, (II) *a. small, little*

קָטָן, *a. small, little*

מְעַט, *m. (fewness) few, a little*

נָקִי, *a. innocent*

עָנִי, *a. poor*

עָמֹק, *a. deep*

נָקֹד, *a. speckled*

Class IV.

אָדָם, *m. man*

יָשָׁר, *a. just, upright*

צָבָא (וֹת) *m. army, host*

כָּבֵד, *a. heavy*

מַלְאָךְ, *m. messenger, angel*

מַלְאָכִי, *pr. n. Malachias*

מוּסָר, *m. correction, instruction*

מִסְפָּר, *m. number*

נִשְׁאָר, *pt. that which remains, remnant*

בְּרָכָה, *f. blessing*

בְּרֵכָה, *f. pool*

מִזְבֵּחַ, *m. altar*

עֵץ, *m. tree, wood*

טָמֵא, *a. unclean*

אַלְמָנָה, *f. widow*

כִּסֵּא, *m.* (כִּסְאִי, כִּסְאוֹת, 22) *throne*

[תּוֹלְדוֹת], *f. pl. generations*

אוֹצָר, *m. store, treasury*

יֹצֵר, *pt. maker*

גֹּאֵל, *pt. redeemer, avenger*

מָשָׁל, *m. proverb, parable*

תּוֹעֵבָה, *f. abomination, hateful thing*

תּוּגָה, (I) *f. grief*

שָׂרִיד, (II) *m. survivor.*

Verbs.

*כָּעַס to be vexed; (*Pi.*) and *Hiph.* provoke to anger.

[שָׁאַר], נִשְׁאַר, *Niph.* to remain, be left over; *Hiph.* to leave, to spare.

NOUNS, CLASS III: Monosyllables in *ă, ē, ō;* other nouns following the same analogy.

A. Monosyllables.

1. Origin and Formation.

261. It may be of some help to the student to know that the monosyllables of this class are derived from stems ע״ע (Lesson XX) and belong to the same formation as the nouns known as *Segolates* (Lesson XII). These stems, although originally biliteral, became triliteral in the course of time through the repetition of their last radical. When the nominal formation called for a strong full vowel between the last two identical radicals, they were kept separate, *v. g.* לֵבָב, *heart;* but when (as in the *Segolate* formation) these letters were not separated by a full vowel, they were contracted, *v. g.* לֵב, *heart,* for לִבְבְ. A few nouns of this class are derived from roots Middle *Nun* in which the vowelless *Nun* has been assimilated (63), *v. g.* אַף, *nose, anger,* for אַנְף. In all those nouns the last radical should have a *Dagheṣh Forte,* but *Dagheṣh* cannot be written in a final vowelless consonant (22); hence they appear as pure monosyllables. However, under the influence of the tone, the vowel of the first radical has been lengthened, *i* to *ē, u* to *ō*; *Pathaḥ* has been retained, but in a Pause becomes regularly *Qameṣ.* Only half a dozen words of this class appear with *Qameṣ* outside of a Pause, *v. g.* יָם, *sea;* מָן, *manna.* Monosyllables with *Qameṣ,* as a rule, belong to a different formation; they are mostly participial forms from stems ע״ו (Lesson XXI), and their *Qameṣ* is unchangeable (131). The same may be said of participles and adjectives — not substantives — with *Ṣere*: the great majority of them are from stems ע״י and their *Ṣere* is unchangeable. Finally, in a few monosyllables with *Ṣere, Ṣere* is volatilized whenever it is not pretonic and consequently those nouns belong to Class IV, *v. g.* עֵץ, *tree.*

2. Inflection.

262. a) Since in all those nouns the *Dagheṣh Forte* has been omitted only because it cannot be placed in a final vowelless consonant, it reappears as soon as the consonant is no longer final, and the preceding vowel reverts to its original shortness; henceforth, it may be considered as unchangeable (cp. English "stop" but "stopping".) This law will be verified with all inflectional additions, *v. g.* כַּף, *palm of the hand,* כַּפִּי, כַּפְּכֶם; אֵם, *mother,* אִמִּי, אִמְּכֶם; חֹק, *precept,* חֻקִּים.

263. b) The constr. sing. is generally the same as the absolute. When followed by *Maqqeph, Ḥolem* and sometimes *Ṣere* are shortened to *Qameṣ Ḥaṭuph* and *S·ghol* respectively, *v. g.* חֹק constr. חָק, but

חָק־; לֵב, לֵב, לֶב־. The same occurs sometimes before suffixes beginning with a consonant; in that case, the *Daghesh Forte* is omitted, *v. g.* חָקְכֶם, *your precept.*

264. c) Remarks. α) In the plural and before suffixes beginning with a vowel, *Pathah* is sometimes attenuated to *Hireq, v. g.* פַּת, *fragment,* pl. פִּתִּים.

β) When the last letter is א, ר or ע, which do not take *Daghesh Forte* (66), the preceding vowel is lengthened as compensation, *v. g.* פַּר, פָּרִים, for פַּרִּים. *Heth* takes implicit *Daghesh Forte* (67).

γ) Some nouns appear also occasionally with a triliteral form, *v. g.* הָרֵי and הַרְרֵי, *the mountains of . . .*

δ) The few nouns with *Qameṣ*, which belong to this formation, are treated exactly like those with *Pathah*, except that in the constr. sing. they retain *Qameṣ, v. g.* יָם, constr. יָם, יַמִּים.

ε) אִי, *island*; עִי, *heap of ruins;* צִי, *ship* are treated like אֵם, *v. g.* אִיִּים, עִיִּים, צִיִּים.

B. **Dissyllabic Nouns** following the same analogy.

265. 1. About twenty nouns with *Qameṣ* or *Pathah* in the ultima and almost all the nouns having changeable *Holem* in the ultima with a changeable vowel in the penult follow the inflection of the monosyllables in *a* and *ō* respectively: before all additions, the vowel of the penult is volatilized (135), and the last consonant receives *Daghesh Forte, v. g.* נָקֹד, *speckled,* pl. נְקֻדִּים; גָּמָל, *camel,* גְּמַלִּים.

קָטֹן, *small,* is used only in the absolute, and constr. sing.; all the other forms are derived from the parallel adjective קָטָן, *v. g.* קָטֹן pl. קְטַנִּים.

The few nouns in *ō* with an unchangeable vowel in the penult either are altogether unchangeable or are treated like those with *Ṣere* (272, 273), *v. g.* קָדְקֹד, *crown of the head,* pl. קָדְקֳדִים.

נָקִי, *innocent* and עָנִי, *poor* also double the *Yodh* before additions, the *Qameṣ* of the penult being volatilized, *v. g.* נְקִיִּים (cp. 264, ε). Thus also the fem. of some of the gentilic adjectives in ־ִי, *v. g.* עִבְרִי, *Hebrew,* f. עִבְרִיָּה.

266. 2. The feminine nouns appear as קְטַנָּה, פְּקֻדָּה and their vowel is unchangeable, *v. g.* פְּקֻדָּה, *office, visitation,* פְּקֻדַּת, פְּקֻדָּתִי.

II. NOUNS, CLASS IV: Nouns with changeable *Qameṣ* and *Ṣere* (Paradigm E).

A. **General Rules** (cp. 134, 135).

267. 1. Masculine Nouns. a) *Qameṣ* and *Ṣere* are kept as often as they are prètonic, *v. g.* מַלְאָכִים, *messengers, angels;* דְּבָרִים, *words;* זְקֵנִים, *old.*

268. b) *Qameṣ* and *Ṣere* are shortened to *Pathaḥ* whenever they are in an unaccented closed syllable: thus, in the constr. sing. and before grave suffixes of the singular, *v. g.* עוֹלָם, *eternity,* constr. עוֹלַם; זָקֵן, *old,* constr. זְקַן; דָּבָר, דְּבַרְכֶם, *your word.* However, when the last radical is א, *Ṣere* is kept in the constr. state, *v. g.* טָמֵא, *unclean,* טְמֵא.

269. c) *Qameṣ* and *Ṣere* are volatilized — or sometimes thrown out — as often as they cease or fail to be in an open pretonic syllable, *v. g.* דָּבָר, pl. דְּבָרִים; לֵבָב, לְבָבִי, *my heart;* מִשְׁפָּט, מִשְׁפְּטֵיהֶם *their judgments.*

270. d) If, in applying the preceding rule, two vocal *Sh·was* would occur at the beginning of the word, a helping vowel, generally *Ḥireq* (*Pathaḥ* with a guttural) is placed under the first consonant (46—48), *v. g.* דָּבָר, דִּבְרֵיהֶם, *their words;* חָכָם, *wise,* חַכְמֵי הַגּוֹיִם, *the wise ones of the nations.*

271. 2. Feminine Nouns. The feminine nouns appear with ָה added to their real or supposed masc. form and with the changes necessitated by the shifting of the tone to that ending, *v. g.* אַלְמָנָה, *widow;* צְדָקָה, *justice;* זָקֵן, *old,* fem. זְקֵנָה; יָשָׁר, *upright,* fem. יְשָׁרָה; constr. צִדְקַת; with suff. צִדְקָתוֹ, צִדְקַתְכֶם.

Often, however, *Ṣere* preceded by *Aleph* is unchangeable, *v. g.* שְׁאֵלָה, *request,* constr. שְׁאֵלַת not שֶׁאֱלַת; טְמֵאָה, *unclean,* constr. טְמֵאַת; *Ṣere* is unchangeable also in some other nouns, *v. g.* בְּרֵכָה, *pool,* constr. בְּרֵכַת not בִּרְכַּת (בִּרְכַּת is the constr. of בְּרָכָה, *blessing*).

B. **Special Rules** for *Ṣere* in the **ultima** with an **unchangeable** vowel in the **penult.**

272. 1. Masculine Nouns. a) *Ṣere,* instead of being kept in an open syllable as pretone-long (134), is volatilized before additions beginning with a vowel (138), *v. g.* שֹׁפֵט, (*judging*) *judge*, pl. שֹׁפְטִים, not שֹׁפֵטִים; מִזְבֵּחַ, *altar*, constr. מִזְבַּח, מִזְבְּחִי, *etc.;* כִּסֵּא, *throne*, כִּסְאִי.

273. b) Before suffixes beginning with a consonant (כֶם, כֶן, and also ךָ) *Ṣere* reverts to original *Ḥireq*; often, however, it is shortened to *S·ghol* (or to *Pathah* with a guttural as second or third radical), *v. g.* אֹיִבְכֶם, *your enemy;* שֹׁפֶטְךָ; *your judge;* גֹּאַלְךָ, *thy redeemer;* מִזְבַּחֲךָ, *thy altar.*

274. 2. F e m i n i n e N o u n s. a) Participles in the feminine follow the same rules as the masculine nouns, *i. e.* lose *Ṣere* before the tone, *v. g.* מְדַבֵּר, fem. מְדַבְּרָה, fem. plur. מְדַבְּרוֹת; it is to be noted that in the sing. (not in the plural), along with the ordinary fem. in ־ָה, participles have very often the fem. in ־ֶ־ֶת or, with a final *Aleph*, often ־ֵאת, *v. g.* מְדַבֶּרֶת, מוֹצֵאת, cp. following Lesson 286, 287.

275. b) Substantives are treated like ordinary feminine nouns with changeable *Qameṣ* and *Ṣere, v. g.* תּוֹעֵבָה, *abomination*, constr. תּוֹעֲבַת; תּוֹלֵדוֹת, *generations* (*genealogy*) constr. תּוֹלְדוֹת.

EXERCISES.

I. His people; my hand; the hands of the man; the judge alone; our mother; their camels; the bulls; the heifers; the bulls and the heifers of the enemies of Solomon; the innocent ones; their priests and their levites; the pool of Siloah (שִׁלֹחַ); the blessing of Abraham; the corpse of an unclean animal; fools are wise in their own heart; old men (were) the judges of the people; the words of David; great peoples are small in the sight (לִפְנֵי) of the Lord; the deep seas of Israel; the justice of God; his teeth; the request of his mother; the abominations of the nations; the proverbs of Solomon; the angels of God; his angels; thy messengers; the statutes of God; their statutes.

II. 1. וְהִכְעַסְתִּי לֵב עַמִּים רַבִּים׃ — 2. וְעָבַדְתָּ יְהוָה אֱלֹהֶיךָ, לִשְׁמֹר חֻקֹּתָיו, מִצְוֺתָיו וּמִשְׁפָּטָיו׃ — 3. הָיוּ לְאִיּוֹב (Job had) סוּסִים וּפָרִים וּפָרוֹת וַחֲמֹרִים רַבִּים וְגַם גְּמַלִּים אֵין מִסְפָּר׃ — 4. חֲכָמִים אֲנַחְנוּ וְתוֹרַת יְהוָה אִתָּנוּ׃ — 5. וְנִשְׁלְחָה מַלְאָכִים בְּכָל גְּבוּל יִשְׂרָאֵל׃ — 6. מַיִם עֲמֻקִּים דִּבְרֵי פִי־אִישׁ׃ — 7. וְעָמְדוּ הָאֲנָשִׁים לִפְנֵי הַכֹּהֲנִים וְהַשֹּׁפְטִים׃ —

XI.

8. וַיְבָ֣רֶךְ שְׁמוּאֵ֗ל אֶת־הָעָם֙ בְּשֵׁ֖ם יְהוָ֥ה צְבָאֽוֹת׃ — 9. בְּנִ֣י אִם־חָכַ֣ם לִבֶּ֑ךָ יִשְׂמַ֖ח לִבִּ֣י גַם־אָֽנִי׃ — 10. וְעַתָּ֞ה אֶשָּֽׁפְטָ֤ה אִתְּכֶם֙ לִפְנֵ֣י יְהוָ֔ה אֵ֥ת כָּל־צִדְק֖וֹת יְהוָ֑ה אֲשֶׁ֥ר עָשָׂ֛ה (he did) אִתְּכֶ֖ם וְאֶת־אֲבוֹתֵיכֶֽם׃

III. 1. And the Lord God said: it is not good for man to be alone (lit. not good the being, הֱיוֹת, of a man alone). — 2. And the prophet took the body (corpse) of the man of God, in order to bury him. — 3. Come near, (ye) nations, to hear, and hearken, (ye) peoples; let the earth hear. — 4. Write upon the tablet of thy heart. — 5. And Saul sent messengers, and the Spirit of God came (was וַתְּהִי) upon the messengers of Saul, and they too prophesied (וַיִּתְנַבְּאוּ). — 6. The levites were (more) upright of heart in sanctifying themselves than (מִן) the priests. — 7. A wise son gladdens a father; but a foolish son is the grief of his mother. — 8. And Jehu (יֵהוּא) destroyed all those that remained of the house of Aḥab (אַחְאָב) and all his great men, and all his priests until he left to him no survivor.

LESSON XII.

I. NOUNS, CLASS V: Segolates.

II. NOUNS, CLASS VI: Nouns in ־ֶה.

Vocabulary.

הֶ֫בֶל	*m.* *vapor, breath, vanity*	בֹּ֫קֶר	*m. morning*
אֶ֫רֶץ	*f. earth*	חָכְמָה	*f. wisdom*
בֶּ֫גֶד	*m. garment*	קְטֹ֫רֶת	*f. smoke of sacrifice, incense*
לֶ֫חֶם	*m. bread*	מְלָאכָה	*f. work, occupation*
רַ֫חַם, רֶ֫חֶם	*m. womb*	מַמְלָכָה	*f. kingdom*
רַחֲמִים	*m. pl. compassion*	מִשְׁפָּחָה	*f. family, clan*
נַ֫עַל	*m. shoe, sandal*	תָּ֫וֶךְ	*m. middle*
זֶ֫רַע	*m. seed, posterity*	שׁוֹר	*m. head of cattle, bullock*
נֵ֫צַח, נֶ֫צַח	*m. perpetuity*	חַ֫יִל	*m. strength, army*
קֶ֫בֶר	*m. grave, sepulchre*	יַ֫יִן	*m. wine*
עֵ֫זֶר	*m. help*	חֵיק	*m. bosom*
חֶ֫רֶב	*f. sword*	דִּין	*m. judgment*
חֹ֫רֶב	*f. dryness, desolation*	רֹאֶה	*pt. seeing, seer*
חֹרֵב	*pr. n. Horeb*	מִקְנֶה	*m.* *possession, cattle*
חֹ֫דֶשׁ	*m. month, new moon*		

Add to these the words given in Paradigm F.

I. Segolates (Class V).

276. These nouns are really monosyllables with the vowel under the first radical, thus forming a doubly closed syllable. This vowel may be any of the three primitive short vowels *a, i, u,* (qaṭl, qiṭl, quṭl). To facilitate prononciation (50) an unaccented auxiliary vowel was added under the second radical. This helping vowel is generally ***S·gḫol*** (50). Under the influence of the tone the primitive vowel has been lengthened, ***Paṯhaḥ*** to ***S·gḫol, Ḥireq*** to ***Ṣere, Qibbuṣ*** to ***Ḥolem,*** *v. g.* מֶ֫לֶךְ for מַלְךְ; סֵ֫פֶר for סִפְר; בֹּ֫קֶר for בֻּקְר. On account of the prevalence of ***S·gḫol,*** this class has been called the Class of Segolates.

A. Segolates with ordinary Consonants.

1. Masculine Nouns (Paradigm F, 1, 2, 4, 5).

277. a) Singular. α) The construct state of the singular is the same as the absolute, *v. g.* מֶ֫לֶךְ, *king,* מֶ֫לֶךְ יִשְׂרָאֵל, *the king of Israel;* סֵ֫פֶר, *book,* סֵפֶר תּוֹלְדוֹת נֹחַ, *the book of the genealogies of Noah.*

278. β) In the singular, all additions are made to the primitive form, *v. g.* מַלְכִּי, *my king,* מַלְכָּה, *queen,* סִפְרִי, *my book,* from original מַלְךְ, סִפְר. Primitive *Qibbuṣ* is generally deflected to *Qameṣ Ḥaṭuph,* because *Qameṣ Ḥaṭuph* usually takes the place of *Qibbuṣ* in an ordinary closed syllable. Primitive *Ḥireq* is also sometimes lengthened to *S·ghol,* while *Pathaḥ* is sometimes attenuated to *Ḥireq.* With all additions, in the singular, the first syllable is closed, *v. g.* מַלְכִּי *my king,* not מַלְכִי; קָדְשִׁי, *(qodhshi) my sanctuary;* סִפְרִי, *my book;* עֶזְרוֹ *his help.*

279. b) Dual. The ending ־ַ֫יִם of the absolute state is added to the primitive form according to the rules just given for the singular, *v. g.* רַגְלַ֫יִם, *feet;* אָזְנַ֫יִם, *ears.* In the constr. and before suffixes, the dual follows the analogy of the plural.

280. c) Plural. α) In the plural, Segolates follow the analogy of Class IV (lesson XI): the first (original) vowel is volatilized in the absolute state and before light suffixes, while the second (auxiliary) vowel becomes pretone-long *Qameṣ, v. g.* מְלָכִים, *kings;* בְּקָרִים, *mornings;* סְפָרִים, *books;* סְפָרֶ֫יךָ, *thy books.* Sometimes, however, primitive *Qibbuṣ* becomes *Ḥateph Qameṣ, v. g.* חֳדָשִׁים, *months.* In קֹ֫דֶשׁ, *sanctuary, sacred things,* and שֹׁ֫רֶשׁ, *root, Qibbuṣ* becomes *Qameṣ* according to the Massora, קָדָשִׁים, שָׁרָשִׁים, but analogy both Hebrew and Semitic bids us pronounce *Shorāshim, Qodhāshim* with *Qameṣ Ḥaṭuph.*

281. β) In the constr. state and with grave suffixes, the primitive form reappears, but the first syllable is half open, instead of being closed as in the singular, *v. g.* מַלְכֵי יִשְׂרָאֵל, *the kings of Israel,* not מַלְכֵּי; contrast מַלְכִּי, *my king.*

2. Feminine Nouns (Paradigm F, 7, 8, 9).

282. The feminine in the singular is derived from the primitive form by adding ־ָה, *v. g.* מַלְכָּה, *queen;* סִפְרָה, *book, letter.* In the plural, feminine nouns follow the analogy of the masc., *v. g.* מְלָכוֹת, *queens,* מַלְכוֹת, *the queens of ...*

B. Segolates with Gutturals (Paradigm F, 3, 6).

They follow exactly the same inflection as above, the ordinary peculiarities of gutturals being taken into account (66ff).

283. a) With first guttural, the primitive vowels are lengthened in the usual way (276), *v. g.* אֶרֶץ *earth;* חֹדֶשׁ, *new moon.*

Before additions, primitive *Ḥireq* (or *Ḥireq* derived from *Pathaḥ* by attenuation) is often replaced by *S·ghol, v. g.* עֶזְרוֹ, *his help* from עֵזֶר; עֶזְרָה, *help.*

284. b) With second guttural, primitive *Pathaḥ* is kept; primitive *Ḥireq* and *Qibbuṣ*, however, appear regularly as *Ṣere* and *Ḥolem, v. g.* נַעַר, *boy;* פֹּעַל, *work.*

Silent *Sh·wa* is often replaced by *Ḥateph,* which causes the first syllable to be half open, *v. g.* נַעֲרוֹ, *his boy,* not נַעְרוֹ. When this *Ḥateph* is followed by another *Sh·wa*, it passes into its corresponding full vowel which is still preceded, by *Methegh*, *v. g.* נַעַרְכֶם, *your boy;* נַעַלְךָ, *thy sandal* (cp. 74).

285. c) Nouns with second or third guttural have almost invariably *Pathaḥ* as auxiliary vowel, except a few nouns with middle ה and middle ח, *v. g.* זֶרַע, *seed, posterity;* נַעַר, *boy;* but אֹהֶל, *tent;* לֶחֶם, *bread;* רֶחֶם or רַחַם, *womb.* With final *'Aleph, S·ghol* is regularly found, *v. g.* פֶּרֶא, *wild ass.*

The plural is regularly נְעָרִים, אֲרָצוֹת, זְרָעִים, נַעֲרֵי: note, however, אֹהָלִים (אָהֳלֵי).

C. Feminine Segolate Endings (Paradigm F, 10, 11).

286. 1. Singular. Some few substantives and many participles have a feminine in ◌ֶ◌ֶת, ◌ֵ◌ֶת, ◌ִ◌ֶת. The last two syllables of these nouns are treated as Segolates, according to the corresponding form of the masc., *v. g.* קְטֹרֶת, *incense,* with suff. קְטָרְתִּי, cp. קָדְשִׁי; גְּבֶרֶת, *lady,* גְּבִרְתִּי; יוֹנֶקֶת, *twig,* יוֹנַקְתּוֹ.

287. 2. In the plural, we must distinguish: when there is no masculine corresponding to the feminine, they are treated as pure Segolates, *v. g.* יֹונְקוֹת, *twigs.* When there is a masc. form, as in participles, the fem. is modeled after it, *i. e.* is derived from the form in ◌ָה, *v. g.* מְדַבֶּרֶת, fem. of מְדַבֵּר, *speaking,* pl. m. מְדַבְּרִים, pl. f. מְדַבְּרוֹת (274).

D. Mixed Forms (Paradigm F, 12).

288. Some fem. nouns, the absolute state of which ends in הָ‑ָ, have a segolate form in the constr. and before suff. This occurs especially in fem. nouns beginning with *Mem*, *v. g.* מִלְחָמָה, *war, battle*, constr. מִלְחֶמֶת; מִשְׁפָּחָה, *family*, constr. מִשְׁפַּחַת; מְלָאכָה, *occupation, work*, (with quiescent *'Aleph*, 2), constr. מְלֶאכֶת; thus also מַמְלָכָה, *kindgom, reign, etc.*

E. Segolates of Stems ע"ו and ע"י (Paradigm F, 13, 14, 15).

289. 1. Most nouns of a segolate formation belonging to stems ע"ו and ע"י appear already in the absolute state with the contracted form, *v. g.* שׁוֹר, *head of cattle,* for original שַׁוְר *(qatl)*; צוּר, *rock*, for צֻוְר *(qutl)*; דִּין, *judgment*, for דִּיְן *(qitl)*. Thus also the fem., *v. g.* שֵׂיבָה *grey hair, old age*; בִּינָה, *understanding.* All those vowels are unchangeable.

290. 2. A limited number of nouns, however, remain uncontracted in the absolute state of the singular and rarely of the plural. Nouns with middle *Waw* have *S·ghol* as auxiliary vowel with original *Pathah* in the first syllable lengthened to *Qameṣ, v. g.* מָוֶת, *death*; תָּוֶךְ, *middle.* Nouns with middle *Yodh* have *Ḥireq* as helping vowel, with *Pathah* retained in the first syllable, *v. g.* זַיִת, *olive, olive tree*, pl. זֵיתִים; חַיִל, *strength, army*, pl. חֲיָלִים; עַיִן, *eye.*

291. 3. In the constr. st. and before all additions, a contraction takes place, $a+y=\hat{e}$; $a+w=\hat{o}$. Henceforth, the vowels are unchangeable, *v. g.* זַיִת, constr. זֵית, זֵיתִי, pl. זֵיתִים; חַיִל, constr. חֵיל, (pl. חֲיָלִים), חֵילֵיהֶם; מָוֶת, constr. מוֹת, מוֹתִי.

F. Segolates of Stems ל"ה (Paradigm F, 16, 17, 18).

1. Masculine. a) Singular.

292. α) These generally appear with *Sh·wa* under the first radical and ‑ִי under the second. They are derived from roots originally ל"י or ל"ו (see Lesson XVIII). On account of the presence of the *Yodh*, the auxiliary vowel was generally *Ḥireq,* which coalesced with *Yodh* into an accented *Ḥireq Gadhol*, thus causing the volatilization of the primitive vowel under the first radical, *v. g.* פְּרִי, *fruit,* for פַּרְיְ; in the case of primitive *Qibbuṣ*, a *Ḥateph Qameṣ* is frequently found instead of a simple *Sh·wa*, especially with a guttural, *v. g.* חֳלִי, *sickness* for חֻלְיִ, but also דְּמִי, *quiet, rest.* In a Pause, the primitive vowel is retained and lengthened: *Pathaḥ* to *S·ghol* (or sometimes *Qameṣ*); *Ḥireq* to *Ṣere; Qibbuṣ* to *Ḥolem, v. g.* P. פֶּרִי; חֲצִי, *half,* P. חֵצִי; P. חֹלִי.

β) The constr. st. is the same as the absolute.

293. γ) Before additions in the singular, the primitive vowel reappears under the first radical, *Pathaḥ* and *Ḥireq* generally in the form of *Ḥireq* or *S·ghol* and primitive *Qibbuṣ* in the form of *Qameṣ Ḥatuph, v. g.* פִּרְיוֹ, *his fruit;* פֶּרְיְךָ, *thy fruit;* חֶצְיוֹ, *his half;* חָלְיוֹ, *his sickness.*

294. b) Plural. The plural is formed exactly as that of the ordinary Segolates, *v. g.* גְּדָיִים, *kids;* חֳלָיִים, *sicknesses.* The constr. st. in most of those nouns has the same vowels as the absolute and merely changes ִים to ֵי, *v. g.* גְּדָיֵי, *the kids of . . .;* חֳלָיֵי, *etc.*

295. 2. Feminine. These are generally formed like other feminine Segolates from the primitive form, but often by simply adding ָה to the masculine and doubling the *Yodh, v. g.* אַלְיָה, *fat tail;* שְׁבִיָּה, *captivity;* גְּדִיָּה. In the plural, they follow the analogy of the masc., *v. g.* גְּדָיִים, fem. גְּדִיּוֹת.

II. Nouns, Class VI:

Milra' Nouns ending in ֶה, from stems ל"ה (Paradigm G).

296. A. Masculine.

1. In the constr., ֶה is anomalously changed to ֵה, *v. g.* שָׂדֶה *field,* constr. שְׂדֵה.

2. Before all additions, ֶה is thrown out and the vowel of the penult, if changeable, follows the rules of nouns class IV (267 ff.).

N. B. With those nouns, the sing. suffixes of the third pers. are ֵהוּ and ֶ ָה (151). To this class belong probably יָד, *hand,* דָּם, *blood,* רֵעַ, *friend,* with ֶה already elided in the absolute.

297. B. Feminine. The feminine appears with the ending ָה instead of ֶה; they follow the rules of class IV (267 ff.).

EXERCISES.

I. Your garments; their bread; our shoes; thy shoe; my help; the swords of the warriors of Israel; the new moons; the wisdom of Solomon; the kings of (the) nations; the feet of the prophet; the letters of the kings; our kings; your work; the shoes of your feet; the lion of the land of Judah; the desolation of the earth; your posterity; his death; their eyes; the shepherds; your families; his occupation; their olive trees; his sword; his great sword; the fruit of the fields; the years of the reign of David; the words of thy lips; their armies; the bosom of his mother; the throne of judgment; in the middle of Egypt.

II. 1. וְאַתֶּם מַמְלֶכֶת כֹּהֲנִים וְגוֹי קָדוֹשׁ׃ — 2. כֹּה אָמַר יְהוָה אֱלֹהֵי
יִשְׂרָאֵל עַל־בָּתֵּי הָעִיר וְעַל־מַלְכֵי יְהוּדָה׃ — 3. וַיִּשְׁלַח אֶת־נַעֲרֵי בְּנֵי
יִשְׂרָאֵל׃ — 4. אוֹי (woe!) לִי, כִּי אִישׁ טְמֵא־שְׂפָתַיִם אָנֹכִי וּבְתוֹךְ עַם
טְמֵא־שְׂפָתַיִם אָנֹכִי עֹמֵד (am staying)׃ — 5. וַיִּשְׁלַח יַעֲקֹב גְּדָיִים
לְאִמּוֹ׃ — 6. וְהִלְבַּשְׁתָּ אֶת־אַהֲרֹן (Aaron) אֵת בִּגְדֵי הַקֹּדֶשׁ וּמָשַׁחְתָּ
אֹתוֹ וְקִדַּשְׁתָּ אֹתוֹ׃ — 7. הָרַג מֶלֶךְ אֶת־אוּרִיָּהוּ (Urias) בְּחֶרֶב וַיַּשְׁלֵךְ
אֶת־נִבְלָתוֹ אֶל־קִבְרֵי בְּנֵי הָעָם׃ — 8. אֲשֶׁר לֹא־הִקְשִׁיב אֶל־דְּבַר יְהוָה
וַיַּעֲזֹב אֶת־עֲבָדָיו וְאֶת־מִקְנֵהוּ בַּשָּׂדֶה׃

III. 1. His blood (shall be) upon his head and we (shall be) innocent. — 2. And the rest of the deeds of Joachim (יְהוֹיָקִים) and his abominations are written in the book of the kings of Israel and of Judah. — 3. Vanity of vanities, and all is vanity. — 4. Let the Lord send thee help from the sanctuary. — 5. The Proverbs of Solomon, son of David, king of Israel. — 6. After (אַחֲרֵי) the death of Abraham, they buried him in the field of Ephron (עֶפְרֹן). — 7. And the head of Dagon and the palms of his hands were broken. — 8. The fear of the Lord is the beginning of wisdom. — 9. All the shepherds are an abomination to the Egyptians.

LESSON XIII.

PARTICIPLES.

Vocabulary. Verbs.

מָשַׁךְ to draw, drag; *Niph.* & (*Pu.*) be postponed.

מָשַׁל (I) to rule; *Hiph.* cause to rule.

מָשַׁל (II) to use a proverb, speak in parables; *Niph.* & (*Hithp.*) to be similar; (*Hiph.* compare).

שָׁפַךְ to pour; *Niph.* & (*Pu.*) be poured out; (*Hithp.* pour itself).

שָׂבַע to be sated, satisfied; (*Niph.* id.); (*Pi.*) & *Hiph.* satisfy.

שָׂכַל (to be prudent); *Hiph.* consider, teach, act prudently, prosper.

הָרַס to throw down, tear down; *Niph.* be thrown down; *Pi.* overthrow.

צָלֵחַ & צָלַח to advance, prosper; *Hiph.* make prosperous, show prosperity.

זָרַע to sow, scatter seed; *Niph.* be sown, fructified; (*Hiph.* produce seed).

קָצַר (I) to reap, harvest.

*קָצַר (II) to be short; (*Pi.* & *Hiph.* shorten).

קָרַע to tear, rend; (*Niph.* be rent).

†חָפֵץ to delight in.

חָמַד to desire, take pleasure in; *Niph.* be desirable; (*Pi.* desire greatly).

Nouns.

לֶקַח (V) *m. instruction, teaching*

חֵפֶץ (V) *m. delight*

יָחִיד (II) *a. solitary, only one*

(פָּנֶה) פָּנִים (VI) *m. & f. pl. face, faces*

נְעוּרִים (II) *m. pl. youth, early life*

אֵשׁ (III) *f. (m.) fire*

נֶאֱמָן (IV) *pt. faithful*

חָזֵק (IV) *a becoming strong*

דָּם (VI) *m. blood*

דֶּרֶךְ (V) *m. (f.) way, journey, manner*

אַלּוּף (I) *a. & m. docile; friend*

אָדָם (IV) *m. man*

אֲדָמָה (IV) *f. earth, ground*

עֶבֶד (V) *m. servant*

שָׂמֵחַ (IV) *a. glad*

שִׂמְחָה (V) *f. joy*

דַּל (III) *a. low, weak, poor*

גָּדֵל (IV) *pt. growing, becoming large*

סָרִיס (I) *m. eunuch, officer, chamberlain*

רִנָּה (V) *f. ringing cry* generally of joy

דּוֹר —וֹת, —ִים (I) *m. generation*

דִּמְעָה (V) *f. tears (coll)*

עַמּוּד (I) *m. pillar, column*

לָבֶטַח *in security*

לָנֶצַח *forever*

לְעוֹלָם וָעֶד *forever and ever*

298. The Participle is the *nomen agentis* as the Infinitive is the *nomen actionis.* The Participle does not indicate a transitory action but always implies a certain duration and permanency in some activity or state, and can best be understood as a kind of "permansive", or qualitative. The stative verbs have no real participles but have a verbal adjective indicating an inherent quality or state.

A. **Form of the Participles** (Paradigms I—L).

299. 1. In the reinforced and causative stems, the Participle is the same as the Indicative Imperfect with מ prefixed instead of the personal Preformatives and with *Qameṣ* in the last syllable instead of *Pat͟haḥ* in *Pu'al* and *Hop͟h'al, v. g.* יְקַטֵּל, part. מְקַטֵּל; יְקַטֵּל, part. מְקֻטָּל; יִתְקַטֵּל, part. מִתְקַטֵּל; יָקְטַל (יֻקְטַל), part. מָקְטָל and oftener מֻקְטָל (172); יַקְטִיל, part. מַקְטִיל.

300. 2. In *Nip͟h'al,* the Part. is the same as the Perfect with *Pat͟haḥ* lengthened to *Qameṣ, v. g.* נִקְטַל, part. נִקְטָל.

301. In *Qal,* act. verbs have two participles, one active and the other passive, קֹטֵל, קוֹטֵל (originally קָטִל), *killing* and קָטוּל, *killed.* Stative verbs have a verbal adjective resembling the Perfect, *v. g.* קָטֹן, כָּבֵד.

302. 3. With gutturals, the regular vowels *Ṣere* and *Shureq* are uniformly kept, *v. g.* שֹׁחֵט, שָׁחוּט. With third guttural, *Pat͟haḥ furtivum* is inserted, *v. g.* שֹׁלֵחַ, שָׁלוּחַ. However, if the third guttural is ע, *Pat͟haḥ* is often found instead of *Ṣere, v. g.* נֹטַע, *planting.*

303. 4. Inflection. Participles are inflected like substantives: those in *a* (*Nip͟h., Pu., Hop͟h.*) and verbal adjectives of stative verbs are inflected like Nouns, Class IV, 267—271; those in *ē*, like Nouns, Class IV, 272—274; feminines in ת◌ֶ◌ֶ like Segolates, 286, 287. Passive participles *Qal* are inflected like Nouns, Class II, 142. Participles *Hip͟h.* have unchangeable vowels, 128.

B. **Syntax.**

Examples:

1. שֹׁמֵר אֱלֹהִים, *God always keeps.* 2. נֶחְמָד, *desirable.* 3. לָבוּשׁ בַּדִּים or לְבוּשׁ בַּדִּים, *clothed in linen.* 4. שֹׁפֵךְ דַּם הָאָדָם, *whosoever sheddeth man's blood;* דּוֹר הֹלֵךְ וְדוֹר בָּא וְהָאָרֶץ לְעוֹלָם עֹמָדֶת, *one generation passeth away and one generation cometh but the earth abideth for ever;*

וְאַבְרָהָם עוֹדֶנּוּ עֹמֵד לִפְנֵי־יְהוָה, *and Abraham was still standing before the Lord;* כָּל־אִישׁ זֹבֵחַ זֶבַח וְקָרֵב נַעַר הַכֹּהֵן, *when any man offered a sacrifice, the priest's servant would approach;* וְהַנַּעַר הוֹלֵךְ וְגָדֵל, *and the boy was growing larger.* 5. הַעֹזֶבֶת אַלּוּף וּבְרִית שָׁכֵחָה, *she who forsakes a friend and forgets a covenant.* 6. אֵינֶנִּי עֹבֵר אֶת־הַיַּרְדֵּן, *I am not going over the Jordan.*

304. 1. In general, the Participle indicates the continuous exercise (298) of a certain activity (active) or a state more or less permanent resulting from the action of some external agency (passive), *v. g.* שֹׁמֵר אֱלֹהִים, *God always keeps.* The participle, of itself, has no reference to time; which tense should be used in rendering it into English, must be inferred from the context (94). If the writer wishes to represent explicitly the action as completed from some standpoint (173), he uses הָיָה, וַיְהִי (189); if on the contrary he wishes to represent the action as incomplete (226 ff), he uses יִהְיֶה, וְהָיָה, *v. g.* וְהַנַּעַר הָיָה מְשָׁרֵת, *and the boy was ministering continually,* 1 Sam. ii, 11.

305. 2. The passive Participle corresponds to our past Part. in *-ed*; often, however, especially in *Niph'al,* it corresponds to our adjectives in *-able, -ible, -worthy, v. g.* נֶחְמָד, *desirable.*

306. 3. Participles, both active and passive, and verbal adjectives of stative verbs are construed either a) as verbs with object (with or without preposition) and remain in the absolute state, *v. g.* לָבוּשׁ בַּדִּים, *clothed in linen;* אֹיֵב אֶת־דָּוִד, *hating David;* or b) they may be construed as nouns in the const. state with their object in the genitive, *v. g.* לְבוּשׁ בַּדִּים, *clothed in linen;* בְּרוּךְ יְהוָה, *the blessed one of Jehovah;* עָרֵיכֶם שְׂרֻפוֹת אֵשׁ, *your cities burned with fire.*

Generally the agent of a passive verb is introduced by לְ; see Lesson XV, 359.

4. As noun, the Participle both active and passive may be employed as substantive and as adjective.

307. a) As substantive, the Participle can be used both as subject or as object of a finite verb; it has often the meaning of *whosoever, any one who* (independent relative clause, 491) and frequently expresses a condition, more particularly when preceded by כֹּל, כָּל־, *all, v. g.* שֹׁפֵךְ דַּם הָאָדָם בָּאָדָם דָּמוֹ יִשָּׁפֵךְ, *whosoever sheddeth man's blood, by man shall his blood be shed,* Gen. IX, 6.; cp. *casus pendens,* 487.

308. b) As adjective modifying a determinate substantive, *α*) the Part. has often the force of a dependent (adjectival) relative clause, *v. g.* מִזְבַּח יְהוָה הֶהָרוּס, *the altar of the Lord that had been broken down,* lit.: *the broken down one,* 1 K. xviii, 30;

309. β) it is often used as predicate in a nominal sentence with substantive or pronoun subject. The pronoun of the 3 p. s., הוּא, *he,* may be omitted when the context precludes all possibility of a mistake. Ex.: דּוֹר הוֹלֵךְ וְדוֹר בָּא וְהָאָרֶץ לְעוֹלָם עֹמָדֶת, *one generation passeth away and one generation cometh but the earth abideth for ever,* Ec. i, 4; וְהוּא עוֹמֵד עֲלֵיהֶם, *and he was standing by them,* Gen. xviii, 8; וְהִנֵּה עֹמֵד עַל־הַגְּמַלִּים, *behold, he was standing by the camels,* Gen. xxiv, 10;

310. γ) it occurs as predicate, especially in circumstantial clauses, often with conditional, temporal, concessive or similar meaning (generally *subj. pred.*) to indicate an action occurring at the same time as the one of the main verb. The participial clause may either precede or follow the main clause, and is often introduced by עוֹד, *still (while)* or הִנֵּה, *behold,* to which a pronominal subject is mostly added in the form of a verbal suffix (see Paradigm H). Besides, generally, the second clause (participle or main verb) is introduced by וְ, *v. g.* הָלְכוּ מִשָּׁם הָאֲנָשִׁים וְאַבְרָהָם עוֹדֶנּוּ עֹמֵד לִפְנֵי־יְהוָה, *the men went away from there, while Abraham was still standing before the Lord;* עוֹדָם מְדַבְּרִים עִמּוֹ וְסָרִיסֵי הַמֶּלֶךְ הִגִּיעוּ, *while they were yet talking with him, the king's chamberlains came,* Esth. vi, 14; כָּל־אִישׁ זֹבֵחַ זֶבַח וְקָרֵב נַעַר הַכֹּהֵן, *when any man offered a sacrifice, the priest's servant would approach,* cp. 1 Sam. ii, 13; see 258.

311. δ) The participle הֹלֵךְ, הוֹלֵךְ, *going,* often precedes other participles or adjectives to denote continuous increase in the activity expressed by them, *v. g.* וְהַנַּעַר הוֹלֵךְ וְגָדֵל, *and the boy was growing larger,* 1 Sam. i, 26 (cp. French: *allait grandissant*). In English, such constructions are often best rendered by an adjective or adverb in the comparative, sometimes repeated, *v. g.* בֵּית דָּוִד הֹלֵךְ וְחָזֵק, *the house of David waxed stronger and stronger,* cp. 2 Sam. iii, 1; see 196.

312. ε) The Participle used adjectively agrees with the substantive or pronoun in gender, number and, if not predicate, also in determination (91), *v. g.* הָאָרֶץ לְעוֹלָם עוֹמֶדֶת, *the earth abideth forever;* מִזְבַּח יְהוָה הֶהָרוּס, *the altar of the Lord that had been broken down,* 1 K. xviii, 30.

313. 5. The participial construction is generally continued by means of a finite verb often preceded by וְ (cp. Infin. 213), *v. g.* הָעֹזֶבֶת אַלּוּף נְעוּרֶיהָ וְאֶת־בְּרִית אֱלֹהֶיהָ שָׁכֵחָה, (*the woman*) *that forsaketh the friend of her youth and forgetteth the covenant of her God,* Prov. II, 17.

314. 6. The Participle is negatived by אֵין or אֵין (124); the pronoun subject is generally suffixed to אֵין in the form or a verbal suffix (see Paradigm H), *v. g.* אֵינֶנִּי עֹבֵר אֶת־הַיַּרְדֵּן, *I am not going over the Jordan,* Deut. IV, 22.

EXERCISES.

I. He is collecting; they are rejoicing; a man is thinking; men are delighting; the servants are writing; you are trusting; they (fem.) are asking; the kings are ruling; the just are serving; he is tearing his garments; they are delighting; while he was sowing; while they were standing; whoever remembers; she who forsakes; they are pouring; the faithful ones of the earth; the pious dwell in the land in security; God is faithful; the fruit is desirable; I am teaching a good doctrine.

II. 1. שֹׁמְרִים הֵם אֶת־דֶּרֶךְ יְהוָה כַּאֲשֶׁר שָׁמְרוּ אֲבוֹתָם׃ — 2. דְּבוֹרָה שֹׁפְטָה אֶת־יִשְׂרָאֵל בָּעֵת הַהִיא׃ — 3. הַזֹּרְעִים בְּדִמְעָה בְּרִנָּה יִקְצֹרוּ׃ — 4. מְקַבֵּץ אָנֹכִי אֶת־בְּנֵי יִשְׂרָאֵל מִכָּל־הָאֲרָצוֹת׃ — 5. וְהַסְּפַרְוִים (the Sepharvites) שֹׂרְפִים אֶת־בְּנֵיהֶם בָּאֵשׁ׃ — 6. וְיִשְׂמְחוּ חֲפֵצֵי צִדְקִי׃ — 7. וְנֶחְמָד הָעֵץ לְהַשְׂכִּיל׃ — 8. הָלְכוּ מִשָּׁם הָאֲנָשִׁים וְאַבְרָהָם עוֹדֶנּוּ עֹמֵד לִפְנֵי יְהוָה׃ — 9. וַתִּשְׁמַע עֲתַלְיָה (Athaliah) אֶת־קוֹל הָעָם וַתִּקְרַב וְהִנֵּה הַמֶּלֶךְ עֹמֵד עַל־הָעַמּוּד כַּמִּשְׁפָּט וְכָל־עַם הָאָרֶץ שָׂמֵחַ וַתִּקְרַע עֲתַלְיָה אֶת־בְּגָדֶיהָ׃ — 10. וְהִנֵּה עוֹדֶנָּה מְדַבֶּרֶת עִם־הַמֶּלֶךְ וְנָתָן (Nathan) הַנָּבִיא קָרֵב׃

III. 1. Jehovah, thy God, is a faithful God, who keepeth His covenant with them that keep His commandments. — 2. And Jehovah spoke unto you out of the midst of the fire, you heard the voice of words, but you did not see His face. — 3. And Samuel reported all the words of the Lord to the people, who were asking him for a king. — 4. God is ruling with His strength for ever; His eyes observe (תִּצְפֶּינָה) the nations. — 5. And the boy Samuel was growing on, and becoming better with God and with men. — 6. And there was (וַתְּהִי) war between the house of Saul and the house of David; and David waxed stronger and stronger and the house of Saul waxed weaker and weaker. — 7. Thy brother's blood crieth unto me from the ground. — 8. And behold, Sarah (שָׂרָה) thy wife shall have a son; now, Sarah was hearing at the door of the tent. — 9. Do not approach hither (הֲלֹם); put off (שַׁל) thy shoes from thy feet, for the place whereon thou art standing is holy ground.

LESSON XIV.

SUFFIXES OF THE VERB. (Paradigms A and M).

Verbs.

רָשַׁע to be wicked, act wickedly; *Hiph.* to condemn.

[שָׁכַם] *Hiph.* to start, rise early.

צָחַק
שָׂחַק to laugh; *Pi.* to jest.

צָעַד to step, march; (*Hiph.* cause to march).

גָּמַל to deal out to, recompense, wean, ripen; (*Niph.* become ripe).

חָלַק to divide, share; *Niph.* be divided; *Pi.* divide, apportion; (*Pu.* be divided; *Hithp.* divide among themselves; *Hiph.* receive a portion).

גָּאַל to redeem, act as kinsman; (*Niph.* be redeemed).

בָּלַע *Qal* & *Pi.* to swallow down, engulf; (*Niph.*, *Pu.* & *Hithp.* be swallowed).

[כָּפַר] *Pi.* to cover up, pacify, atone; *Pu.* be covered, atoned for; (*Hithp.*; *Niph.*)

הָפַךְ to turn, overthrow; *Niph.* turn oneself, change; (*Hithp.* turn every way; *Hoph.* be turned).

חָלַץ to equip for war; *Niph.* be equipped; (*Hiph.* invigorate).

חָלַץ (to draw off, withdraw; *Niph.* be delivered); *Pi.* rescue.

חָבַר to unite, be joined, tie a magic knot; *Pi.* make an ally of; *Pu.* be allied with; (*Hithp.* make an alliance; *Hiph.* join).

חָבַשׁ to bind; (*Pi.* restrain; *Pu.* be bound).

תָּפַשׂ to lay hold, wield; *Niph.* be seized; (*Pi.* grasp).

[זָהַר] *Hiph.* (to be light) instruct, warn; *Niph.* be instructed, warned.

Nouns.

רָשָׁע (iv) *a. wicked*

רֶשַׁע (v) *m. wickedness*

רִשְׁעָה (v) *f. wickedness*

רַע (iii) *m. evil, distress. a. evil, bad*

זֶבַח (v) *m. sacrifice*

נֶפֶשׁ (v) *f. soul, man*

כֶּסֶף (v) *m. silver, money*

זָהָב (iv) *m. gold*

מִשְׁתֶּה (iv) *m. feast, drink*

מִקְנֶה (vi) *m. cattle, possession*

מַחֲנֶה (vi) *m. & f. camp, encampment*

Nouns.

רָעָה (iii) f. evil, injury
גּוֹרָל (iv) m. & f. lot, portion
מִקְדָּשׁ (iv) m. sacred place, sanctuary
מוֹעֵד (iv) m. appointed time or place, meeting

עָוֺן (ii) m. guilt
בָּקָר (iv) m. (coll.) ox, cattle
צַעַד (v) m. step, course of life
מַשְׁקֶה (vi) m. butler, drink

חֵלֶק (v) m. portion, territory
אֱנוֹשׁ (i) m. man
רְכוּשׁ (i) m. possession
עַל־פִּי according to.

I. Perfect; Imperf. Indic. Juss. and Imperative.

315. The personal pronouns as objects of a verb can be expressed by the directive particle אֵת [אוֹת] with the suffixes of the noun (117, 155), v. g. קָטַל אוֹתוֹ, *he killed him;* or they may be added directly to the verb, v. g. קְטָלוֹ, *he killed him.* The object pronouns of 2 p. pl. are almost universally introduced by אֵת, v. g. שָׁמַע אֶתְכֶם, *he heard you.*

In connection with verbal suffixes, two things must be considered: A. the form of the verbal suffixes themselves, and B. the modifications which they bring about in the verb when they are united with it.

A. Form of the Verbal Suffixes.

316. 1. The verbal suffixes are essentially the same as those of the noun (Paradigm A). The 1 p. s., however, is נִי instead of ־ִי.

As in the noun, contractions and elisions take place: הוּ־ֵ֫ often becomes וֹ or (rarely) הֹ; הָ־ֵ֫ become ה־ָ֫; יהוּ־ֵ֫ generally becomes יו־ָ֫, with elision of ה; תהוּ־ֵ֫ sometimes becomes תוֹ־ֵ֫ with elision of ה and sharpening of ת; תָה־ֵ֫ always becomes תָּה־ֵ֫; the ה of the 3 p. pl. הֶם and הֶן is elided together with its vowel after a long vowel, v. g. קְטָלוּם for קְטָלוּהֶם; הֶם־ and הֶן־ become ם־ָ֫, ן־ָ֫; the combination תְךָ־ֵ֫ has always a helping vowel, תֶ֫ךָ־ֵ֫.

317. 2. Tone. The rule given for the nominal suffixes in 154 applies also to the verbal suffixes. The grave suffixes are accented; the light suffixes, which form by themselves a separate syllable following a full vowel, are not accented, and so also all suffixes after the

3 p. f. s. (320); the heavy suffixes as well as the light suffixes in which one of the two conditions is lacking, are accented, except after 3 f. s. *v. g.* קְטָלַנִי, קְטָלוּךָ, קְטַלְתְּהוּ, קְטָלָם, קְטָלוֹ, קְטָלְךָ.

B. Union of Suffixes with the Verb.

1. Perfect.

318. a) *Endings of the verb.* In the Perfect, old endings have been preserved (169), bringing about vowel-changes in the other syllables (321), *v. g.* 3 m. s. [*qaṭala*] *q·ṭāla,* for *qāṭal* (קָטַל); 3 f. s. [*qaṭalat*] *q·ṭālát,* for *qāṭ·lah* (קָטְלָה); 2 f. s. *q·ṭalti* (176), for *qāṭalt* (קְטַלְתִּי); 2 pl. *q·ṭaltû,* for *q·ṭaltem* or *q·ṭalten* (קְטַלְתּוּ). The 2 pl., however, seldom occurs with suffixes.

The vowel *a* under the final consonant of the 3 m. s. is generally but improperly called a connective vowel as it is really part of the verbal form; for the sake of convenience, however, it has been given with the suffix in Paradigm A. This *Pathaḥ* is generally lengthened to *Qameṣ* (tone-long) before light suffixes except before נִי (sometimes written נִּי) where the primitive *Pathaḥ* remains pure even in the 2 m. s. The contact of this *Pathaḥ* with certain suffixes gives rise to the contractions mentioned in 316.

319. The final *Pathaḥ* of the verbal form is volatilized before ךָ‎ְ, but in a pause is lengthened to *S·ghol* (ךָ‎ֶ) and sometimes fully lengthened to *Qameṣ,* in which case the *Qameṣ* of the suffix is dropped. Before ךְ, *Pathaḥ* is changed to *Ṣere,* קְטָלֵךְ.

320. The third person feminine sing. has this peculiarity that the syllable that precedes ת is always accented and this causes the suffix of 3 pl. to be sounded with a short vowel, although this vowel arises from contraction, *v. g.* קְטָלָתַם.

321. b) *Vocalic Changes within the verb.* The changes, that take place in the verbal forms when suffixes are added, are those given in 134—139. The vowel of the first radical, being no longer pretonic (317), is regularly volatilized; the vowel of the second radical, on the contrary, is retained and becomes pretone-long in an open syllable and short in a closed syllable. Verbs *middle ē* retain *Ṣere.* With an unchangeable vowel in the first syllable *ē* and *ō* are volatilized when they would be in an open pretone-syllable and are shortened to *S·ghol* and *Qameṣ Ḥaṭuph* respectively in a closed or half-open syllable, *i. e.* before ךָ, כֶם, *v. g.* קְטָלַנִי, שְׁכֵחַנִי, קְטָלַתְּה, קִטְּלַנִי, קִטֶּלְךָ.

2. Imperfect Indicative.

322. a) *Ordinary Suffixes.* α) The suffixes, except ךָ and כֶם (כֶן does not occur), are added to verbal forms ending in a consonant by means of an accented connective *Ṣere* (or *S·ghol* when the suffix has the *a* sound, 151, 4). The shifting of the tone causes the volatilization of ō and ē (138) of the second radical, *v. g.* יִקְטְלֵנִי, יִקְטְלֶהָ, יְקַטְּלֵנִי. Verbs with Imperf. in *a* retain the *Pathaḥ* which is lengthened to *Qameṣ* (138), *v. g.* יִלְבָּשֵׁהוּ, *etc.* With first gutt. we have יַעַבְדֵנִי, according to 74.

323. β) Before ךָ and כֶם, ō and ē are shortened to *Qameṣ Ḥaṭuph* and *S·ghol*, but are retained in a pause; the verbal form has no connective vowel. *Ṣere* of the second syllable is retained with a verb 3 gutt., *v. g.* יִקְטָלְךָ, קְטָלְךָ, יִקְטָלְכֶם; אֲשַׁלֵּחֲךָ (*Pi'el*), *I shall send thee.*

324. γ) Suffixes are added to forms ending in a vowel without any further changes, *v. g.* יִקְטְלוּנִי, יִקְטְלוּךָ, *etc.* Verbs with Imperf. in *a,* however, have *Qameṣ* under the second radical (322), *v. g.* יִלְבָּשׁוּנִי, תִּלְבָּשִׁינִי. Instead of the afformative נָה of 2 and 3 f. pl., we have the ordinary form of the plural in verbs, viz. וּ; this form is then treated as those which end in a vowel, *v. g.* תִּקְטְלוּנִי, תִּלְבָּשׁוּנִי.

325. b) *Suffixes with Nun Energicum.* The *Nun Energicum* is an accented ֶ֫ן (originally ַ֫ן, still found occasionally in ַ֫נִי of the Perfect) which in the various modes of the Imperf. often precedes the suffixes נִי, ךָ, הוּ, הָ, נוּ, especially in a pause. The *Nun* is assimilated to a following *Nun* or *Kaph*, *v. g.* ֶ֫נִּי; ֶ֫ךָּ, for ֶנְנִי and ֶנְךָ. The *He* of הוּ and הָ is absorbed by *Nun Energicum* which is consequently reinforced, יִקְטְלֶ֫נּוּ, יִקְטְלֶ֫נָּה, for יִקְטְלֶנְהוּ, יִקְטְלֶנְהָ.

This *Nun Energicum* is a remnant of an old *Modus Energicus* still preserved in Arabic.

3. Imperative with Suffixes.

326. Suffixes are added to the Imper. as to the Imperf. Indicative, נָה being replaced by וּ. In 2 m. s., the Imper. with ō becomes קָטְלְ (217) (sometimes קִטְלְ) with a half-open syllable; Imper. with *Pathaḥ* retains ă under the second radical and lengthens it to *Qameṣ* as in the Indicative. Ex.: כָּתְבֵם, (*kothbhem*, not *kothbem*); שְׁלָחֵנִי; שִׁמְעוּנִי.

C. Syntax.

327. 1. The pronominal object of a verb must be expressed by אֵת (אֶת, אוֹת, את) with the ordinary suffix of the noun and not by the verbal suffix in the following cases:

a) when, for the sake of emphasis, the pronoun precedes the verb, *v. g.* שָׁמַע כִּי אֹתוֹ מָשְׁחוּ לְמֶלֶךְ, *he had heard that they had anointed him king,* 1 K. v, 15 (1);

b) when a suffix is already attached to the verb, *v. g.* הִשְׁמִיעַנִי אֹתָהּ, *he made me hear it;*

c) generally when a second accusative follows with אֶת, *v. g.* וַתִּבְלַע אֹתָם וְאֶת־בָּתֵּיהֶם, *and it swallowed them and their households,* Num. xvi, 32;

d) almost without exception with כֶם, and always with כֶן (315, 322; see further, 331—334).

328. 2. The neuter obj. *"it"* is mostly expressed by the 3 f. s. and sometimes by the 3 f. pl. in the form of a verbal suffix, or in the form of a nominal suffix with a suitable particle, הֶאֱמִן בַּיהוָה וַיַּחְשְׁבֶהָ לּוֹ צְדָקָה, *he believed in the Lord and He reckoned it to him for righteousness,* Gen. xv, 6. Very often, however, the neuter pronoun is not expressed.

329. 3. Sometimes the pronoun suffix agrees in gender or number with the logical rather than with the grammatical subject, *v. g.* יִהְיֶה זַרְעֲךָ בְּאֶרֶץ לֹא לָהֶם וַעֲבָדוּם, *thy posterity shall sojourn in a land not theirs and they shall serve them,* Gen. xv, 13.

330. 4. The suffix is very rarely added to a verb in a reflexive sense, except when it is strongly emphatic. The reflexive idea is expressed by one of the reflexive stems; cp. 444.

II. Suffixes with Verbal Nouns.

A. Infinitive Construct (Paradigm M).

331. 1. With suffixes (also before ךָ, כֶם, כֶן, cp. Segolates, 278) the usual form is קָטְלִ, but with verbs 2 or 3 gutt., often קְטָלִ or קִטְלִ. Generally, the first syllable is half-open, but sometimes simply closed; the latter is the rule with ךָ, כֶם, כֶן, *v. g.* בְּכָתְבוֹ *while he was writing;* בְּאָסְפְּךָ, *while thou wast collecting;* פִּתְחִי, *my opening.*

With ךָ (כֶם, כֶן), forms like קָטְלְךָ also occur, *v. g.* עָמְדְךָ, *thy standing.*

332. 2. As noted above (214), the Inf. Constr. can be construed as a noun and as a verb. As a verb, it takes the verbal suffix to designate the object; this occurs mostly with the pronouns of the 1 p. נִי and נוּ. In the other cases, the pronoun, both object and subject, is in the form of a nominal suffix and the context alone will show which is meant, *v. g.* דָּרְשׁוֹ may mean *his inquiring* or *the inquiring of (from) him.* If there is danger of confusion or if the Inf. is accompanied by its subject (214), the object suffix is introduced by אֵת, *v. g.* כִּשְׁמֹעַ שְׁלֹמֹה אתו, *when Solomon had heard him.*

B. **Participle** (Paradigms E and M).

333. The form of the Part. with suffixes has already been explained (142, 267—274). To indicate the verbal object, only the verbal suffix of 1 p. s. occurs. In the other persons, the nominal suffix is regularly used. To know whether the suffix is object or subject the context must be examined; the presence of the article will indicate that the Part. is taken as a verb and not as a noun, and that the suffix is objective and not subjective, because a noun with suffixes does not take the article (159).

334. Certain particles like אֵין, הִנֵּה, *behold,* עוֹד, *(there is) still,* etc., which connote a verbal idea, often take verbal suffixes like the Imperf., even with *Nun Energicum;* see Paradigm H.

EXERCISES.

A. Perfect. 1. *Hiph'il*: I consecrated thee; he destroyed them; thou hast reminded me; I have made thee king; he has condemned me; thou didst warn him; he adjured me; they made him ride; he provoked him.

2. *Qal*: He has forsaken us; he divided them; you preserved me; he has gathered us; we remembered him; she forgot them; he has redeemed thee; he overthrew them.

3. *Pi'el*: He sought thee; I sought him; he delivered us; the earth swallowed her up; he narrated it; thou didst pacify him.

B. Imperfect Indicative. 1. *Hiph'il*: He will remove me; he will compel us to serve; he will remind thee; . . . them; . . . her; . . . him; do not warn him; do not condemn me.

2. *Qal* with *a*: He shall hear us; you shall send me; he shall anoint thee; thou wilt hear her; you will ask me; you will redeem them; we will swallow them.

3. *Qal* with *ō*: He will visit you; he will write them; he will overthrow him; thou shalt remember me; . . . him; . . . her; I will keep thee; . . . thee (fem.); . . . you; you will judge them; I shall not forsake them.

C. Imperative: Hear us; . . . me; . . . them; bury her; send them; keep us; destroy it (fem.); help (ye) me; send us; inform (ye) us (make us hear).

Practice some of those forms in a Pause, and with *Nun Energicum*.

D. Infinitive Construct: His sending; sending him; in his sending him; my consulting; consulting me; while they kept; my choosing; while we remember.

E. Participles: My judge; judging me; . . . thee; our redeemer; the one hating you; redeeming me; . . . thee; collecting them.

II. 1. אָמַר יוֹסֵף אֶל־הַמַּשְׁקֶה אִם יִזְכֹּר פַּרְעֹה אֹתְךָ וְהִזְכַּרְתַּ֫נִי אֶל־פַּרְעֹה׃ — 2. יְהוָה הִסְגִּירָם בְּיַד אֹיְבֵיהֶם׃ — 3. אִם יִפְקֹד יְהוָה עַל־רְשָׁעִים עֲוֹנָם וּדְרָשׁ֫וּהוּ בְּכָל־לֵב וְכַפֵּר עָוֹן וְלֹא־יַשְׁחִיתָם׃ — 4. יִזְכֹּר יְהוָה אוֹתְךָ וְקִבֶּצְךָ מִכָּל־הָעַמִּים׃ — 5. כֹּה אָמַר יְהוָה גֹּאַלְכֶם׃ — 6. לְמַד בִּינָה, אַל תַּעַזְבֶהָ וְתִשְׁמְרֶ֫ךָּ׃ — 7. מָה־אֱנוֹשׁ כִּי־תִזְכְּרֶנּוּ וּבֶן־אָדָם כִּי־תִפְקְדֶנּוּ׃ — 8. בְּךָ בָּטְחוּ אֲבוֹתֵינוּ בָּטְחוּ וַתְּפַלְּטֵ֫מוֹ׃ — 9. וַיֹּ֫אמֶר שְׁמוּאֵל אֶל־עֵלִי הִנֵּ֫נִי׃ — 10. וָאֶתְפֹּשׂ בַּלֻּחֹת וָאַשְׁלִיכֵם מֵעַל יָדָי וָאֲשַׁבְּרֵם לְעֵינֵיכֶם׃

III. 1. He spoke against us and against our judges that judge us. — 2. The hand of God is upon all those that seek Him for good, but His power is against those who forsake Him. — 3. All my days, I shall remember thee, Jerusalem. — 4. The arms of the wicked shall be broken; Jehovah upholds the just. — 5. Thus shall ye speak to the king of Judah that sent you unto me to consult me. — 6. And the earth opened its mouth, and swallowed them up, and their households, and all the men that belonged to Qoraḥ, and all (their) possession. — 7. Hiram, king of Tyre (צוֹר), sent his servants unto Solomon; for he had heard that they had anointed him (emphatic) king in place of his father. — 8. When I speak to the wicked, and thou dost not give him warning, nor speakest to warn the wicked from his wicked way, his blood shall I require from thy hand.

LESSON XV.*

WEAK VERBS: *PE-ALEPH; PE-NUN; PE-YODH.*

Vocabulary. Verbs.

אָבַד to go astray, perish; *Pi.* & *Hiph.* destroy.

אָכַל to eat; *Niph.*; (*Pu.*); *Hiph.*

אָמַר to say; *Niph.*; (*Hithp.* boast); (*Hiph.* avow).

אָחַז to grasp, lay hold of; *Niph.*; (*Pi. Hoph.*).

נָתַן to give, put, set; *Niph.*; *Hoph.*

* נָגַשׁ to approach, draw near; *Niph.*; (*Hithp.*); *Hiph.*; (*Hoph.*).

נָגַשׂ to press, oppress; *Niph.*

נָטַע to plant, sow; (*Niph.*).

נָגַע to touch, strike; *Niph.*; *Pi.*; (*Pu.*); *Hiph.*

[נָצַב] *Niph.* to take on'es stand; *Hiph.*; *Hoph.*

יָדַע to know; *Niph.*; (*Pi.* make known; *Pu.*; *Hithp.*); *Hiph.*; (*Hoph.*).

יָלַךְ } הָלַךְ } to go, (*Niph.*); *Pi.*, walk; *Hithp.*, walk about; *Hiph.*

[יָאַל] *Hiph.* to show willingness, be willing, consent.

יָשַׁב to dwell, remain; (*Niph.* be inhabited); *Hiph.* (*Hoph.*).

יָכֹל Perf. to be able, prevail; *Hoph.* Imperf. *id.*

יָעֵף to be weary; (*Hoph.*).

יָסַר *Qal* & *Pi.* to chastise, admonish; (*Niph.*; *Hiph.*).

יָסַף to add; (*Niph.*); *Hiph.* add, do again.

יָגַע to toil, grow weary; *Pi.* & *Hiph.* cause to toil.

[יָכַח] *Hiph.* to decide, correct, rebuke; (*Hoph.*; *Niph.*; *Hithp.*).

יָעַץ to advise; *Niph.* consult together; *Hithp.* conspire.

יָרַד to descend; *Hiph.* bring down; *Hoph.*

* Henceforth we shall give only the meaning of *Qal;* as to the Derivative Stems, we shall mention which of them occur, but will give the meaning only when it cannot be inferred safely from the simple idea.

Vocabulary. Verbs.

[יָצַב] *Hithp.* to set or station oneself.

[נָבַט] (*Pi.*) & *Hiph.* to look.

נָבַל (to be foolish); *Pi.* treat as foolish.

נָבֵל to sink, languish.

לָקַח to take; *Niph.*; *Pu.*; (*Hithp.*; *Hoph.*).

נָפַל to fall; (*Hithp.*); *Hiph.*

נָצַר to watch, keep.

יָצַר to form, fashion; (*Niph.*; *Pu.*; *Hoph.*)

* יָרַשׁ to inherit, take possession of; (*Niph.*; *Pi.*); *Hiph.*

[יָשַׁע] *Hiph.* to save; *Niph.*

* יָבֵשׁ to be dried, withered; (*Pi.*); *Hiph.*

* יָטַב to be good, well, glad; *Hiph.*

* יָקַץ to awake.

* יָשַׁר to be smooth, right; *Pi.* & (*Hiph.*) make straight; (*Pu.*).

* יָשֵׁן to sleep; *Niph.* be inactive; *Pi.* make sleep.

[סָתַר] *Niph.* to hide, conceal oneself; (*Pi.*) & *Hiph.* hide, conceal (*Pu.*; *Hithp.*

[אָפַק] *Hithp.* to force oneself, restrain oneself.

אָהַב to love.

Nouns.

לֵץ (i) *pt. scorner*

קוֹמָה (i) *f. stature, height*

מָרוֹם (ii) *m. height, high location*

תְּאֵנָה (i) *f. fig, fig-tree*

מַדָּע (i) *m. thought, knowledge*

הַיַּרְדֵּן (יַרְדֵּן) *pr. n. Jordan*

עֹשֶׁר (v) *m. riches*

אִמְרָה (v) *speech, utterance*

אֹמֶר (v) *m. speech (without suff.)*

(אֵמֶר) (v) *m. utterance (with suffix.)*

שְׂמֹאל / שְׂמֹאול (i) *m. left hand*

מַר (iii) *a bitter, m. bitterness*

יָמִין (ii) *f. right hand*

אַיִל (v) *m. ram, leader*

עַתּוּד (i) *m. he-goat, leader*

תָּמִים (ii) *a. complete, sound, perfect*

בָּדָד (ii) *m. solitude,* לְבָדָד, *alone*

335. Weak Verbs in general. Weak verbs are those one or more radicals of which are lost or modified in the course of the inflection. The classes of weak verbs are: פ״א; פ״ן; פ״י; ע״ע; ע״ו; ע״י; ל״ה; ל״א. Some verbs are doubly weak, such as יָרָה, נָכָה, נָטָה, אָפָה, *etc.;* see Lesson XXII.

With regard to verbs which have a weak first radical (א, נ, י), it must be remembered that originally the stem-formative prefixes as well as the personal preformatives were sounded with *Pathah* (169, 224): *Naktala, Haktala* or with *Qibbuṣ, Huqṭala.* Many of the so-called irregularities of these verbs are due to the contraction of the vowel of the preformative with their initial weak consonant; cp. 4, 61, 63.

I. Verbs *Pê-Aleph* (Paradigm R).

336. Most of the verbs beginning with *Aleph* are inflected in all stems as a first gutt. verb; only five verbs, properly called *Pe-Aleph,* exhibit some differences, and that, only in the Imperfect Indic. *Qal;* they are: אָכַל, *to eat;* אָמַר, *to say;* אָבַד, *to perish, to go astray;* אָבָה, *to be willing;* אָפָה, *to bake.* The two verbs אָחַז, *to seize* and אָסַף, *to collect,* occasionally follow their analogy.

In the Imperf., Indic., Juss. and Cohort. of *Qal,* the initial *Aleph* of those verbs coalesced with the *Pathah* of the preformative (2) which was lengthened to *â* and is now further obscured to *ô* (61), *v. g.* יֹאכַל, for יָאכַל, for יַאְכַל.

337. These verbs have *ă* or *ē* in the second syllable; in a Pause, the vowel is almost invariably *Ṣere, v. g.* יֹאכֵל. This *Ṣere* is generally shortend to *S·ghol* in an unaccented closed syllable after *Waw Consecutivum, v. g.* וַיֹּאמֶר (247).

Aleph, being quiescent, is often omitted in the spelling, *v. g.* אֹמַר for אֹאמַר; thus also תֹּסֶף, וַיֹּסֶף from the verb אָסַף, *to collect;* care must be taken not to confound those forms with the *Hiph'il* of יָסַף, *to add* (345), וַיּוֹסֶף.

II. Verbs *Pê-Nûn* (Paradigm N).

A. In General.

338. Most of the differences between the *Pe-Nun* verbs and the regular strong verbs are to be explained according to 63: whenever the *Nun* would form a closed syllable with a preformative, it is assimilated to the second radical; cp. מִשָּׁם for מִן־שָׁם. This occurs 1) in Imperf. *Qal* (Indic. Juss. Cohort.), *v. g.* יִפֹּל, for יִנְפֹּל; יִגַּשׁ, for יִנְגַּשׁ; 2) in Perf. *Niph.*, *v. g.* נִגַּשׁ, for נִנְגַּשׁ; 3) in *Hiph.*, *v. g.* הִגִּישׁ, for הִנְגִּישׁ; 4) in *Hoph.*, *v. g.* הֻגַּשׁ, for הֻנְגַּשׁ.

B. Inf. Constr. and Imper. *Qal.*

339. 1. When the characteristic vowel of the Imperfect is *a* (*e,* only in נָתַן *to give*), the *Nun* is elided in the Inf. Constr. and Imper., *v. g.* גַּשׁ, תֵּן. Besides, the Inf. Constr. generally takes the feminine ending (207), not in the form of ה ָ, but in the form of the original ת ְ; then with the addition of a helping vowel, it is treated exactly as a Segolate (Lesson XII), *v. g.* גֶּשֶׁת, for גַּשְׁתְּ; גַּעַת; with suffixes, גִּשְׁתִּי (278 ff). On בּ, כּ, לְ, before such Infinitives, see Lesson XVII, לָגֶשֶׁת.

340. 2. Verbs which have *o* in the Imperf. are regular in Inf. Constr. and Imperative, *v. g.* נָפַל, Imperfect Indic. יִפֹּל, Inf. נְפֹל, Imper. נְפֹל.

Nûn is sometimes kept in a Pause, *v. g.* יִנְצֹרוּ, *they shall watch.*

Nûn is not assimilated or elided in verbs that are at the same time middle gutt. except in נָחַם, *to console oneself*, and נָחַת, *to go down*, *v. g.* יִנְהַג, not יִהַג, *he shall lead*, but *Niph.* נִחַם with implicit *Daghesh Forte*, not נִנְחַם.

341. C. In *Qal* and *Hoph'al*, the verb לָקַח, *to take*, is treated like a *Pe-Nun* verb, and its *Lamedh* assimilated or elided accordingly, *v. g.* יִקַּח; תִּקְחִי; יִקְחוּ; קַח; קַחַת; הֻקַּח. Note that *Qôph* with *Sh·wa* does not take *Daghesh Forte*, 22.

342. D. The verb נָתַן, besides the assimilation of the first *Nun*, also assimilates the last *Nun* to a following consonantal afformative, *v. g.* נָתַתִּי, for נָתַנְתִּי; Inf. Constr. תֵּת, for תִּנְתְּ, and with suff. תִּתִּי, *etc.*

III. VERBS *PÊ-YÔDH.*

A. **Verbs *Pê-Yôdh* and *'Ayin-Ṣādhê*,**

commonly called פ״י 3 Class (Paradigm Q).

343. Verbs with *Yodh* as first, and *Sadhe* as second radical follow the analogy of the verbs *Pe-Nun*: the *Yodh* is assimilated like the *Nun* in the above class. Such are: יָצַק, *to pour;* יָצַע, *to spread under;* יָצַג, *to place;* יָצַת, *to set on fire, to burn.* The verb יָצַר, *to fashion,* may be inflected according to this or the following class. Ex.: יִצֹּק: *Niph.* נִצַּת; *Hiph.* הִצִּיג *etc.*

B. **Verbs *Pê-Yôdh*,** originally ***Pê-Wāw*,**

commonly called *Pe-Yodh* 1 Class (Paradigm O).

344. To this class belong the great majority of the verbs *Pe-Yodh.* The peculiarities of these verbs arise from the fact that they were originally *Pe-Waw* and that, in many forms, *Waw* has been kept in some way or other.

1. *Yodh* is found in all stems in which it is initial (*Qal*, *Pi.*, *Pu.*) and regularly also in *Hithpa'el*, *v. g.* יָשַׁב; יִשֵּׁב; יֻשַּׁב; (הִתְיַשֵּׁב).

345. 2. The original *Waw* reappears in all stems where there is a stem prefix (*Niph.*, *Hiph.*, *Hoph.*), and sometimes in *Hithpa'el*. The *Waw* undergoes the following modifications: in *Niph.* and *Hiph.*, it contracts to ô with the original *Pathah* of the preformatives, and in *Hoph.* it contracts to û with preceding *Qibbuṣ* (4, 61, 169), *v. g.* *Niph.* נוֹשַׁב, for נַוְשַׁב; *Hiph.* הוֹשִׁיב, for הַוְשִׁיב; *Hoph.* הוּשַׁב, for הֻוְשַׁב.

3. Imperfect *Qal.* a) Indic. Juss. Cohort.

346. α) Verbs (mostly transitive), which have ē (gutt. *a*) as characteristic vowel, lose *Yodh* and take ê under the preformatives. This ê, although defectively written, is unchangeable and may be due to the contraction of the primitive *Pathah* of the preformative with the *Yodh* (for *Waw*) of the verb: $a + y = ê$ (61), *v. g.* יֵשֵׁב, יֵדַע: the verb הָלַךְ (יָלַךְ, see 348) belongs to this class.

β) Verbs (mostly intransitive), which have *a* as characteristic vowel, retain *Yodh* which coalesces with the preformative in יִי (4, 61), *v. g.* יִירַשׁ for יִיְרַשׁ.

347. b) Inf. Constr., Imperative.

Eight verbs, mostly of class α, follow the analogy of *Pe-Nun* verbs, *i. e.* appear with the elision of the *Yodh* and the femin. ending for the Infin. Constr.; besides, the Imper. has often the form with ָה (216, 233). They are: יָלַד, *to bring forth;* יָשַׁב; יָרַד; הָלַךְ, (יָלַךְ); יָצָא, *to go out* (Lesson xxii); יָדַע; יָחַד, *to be united;* יָקַע, *to be dislocated*, *v. g.* Infin. Constr. שֶׁבֶת, דַּעַת; Imper. שֵׁב and שְׁבָה; דַּע; רְדָה, P. רֵדָה.

All the others retain the *Yodh*, *v. g.* יָרַשׁ; יָסַד.

348. 4. The verb הָלַךְ (יָלַךְ) partly belongs to the class *Pe-Yodh*: the form הָלַךְ is used in all formations where *Pe-Yodh* is regular; a supposed form יָלַךְ is used in all formations where *Pe-Yodh* is irregular, *v. g.* Perf. *Qal* הָלַךְ, *Pi.* הִלֵּךְ but *Hiph.* הוֹלִיךְ; *Qal* Imperf. Indic. יֵלֵךְ; Inf. לֶכֶת; Imper. לֵךְ, לְכָה.

349. 5. The verb יָכֹל, *to be able*, is somewhat defective inasmuch as the only Imperf. used is יוּכַל which is a *Hoph.* form with the meaning of *Qal.*

350. 6. In all the verbs of class α (346), the accent is drawn backward and the final vowel shortened after *Waw Consecutivum* (247, 38), *v. g.* יֵשֵׁב, but וַיֵּ֫שֶׁב; commonly, when the penult has *î* (class β) or *û* (*Hoph*.), especially when the ultima has *Pathaḥ*, the retraction of the tone does not take place (247), *v. g.* וַיִּישַׁן, וַיֵּיטַב; וַיּוּשַׁב, *etc.*; with a vowel other than *Pathaḥ* in the ultima, וַיִּ֫יצֶר, *and he fashioned.*

C. Verbs *Pê-Yôdh* originally *Pê-Yôdh*,
commonly called *Pe-Yodh* 2 Class (Paradigm P).

351. Only seven verbs belong to this class: יָשַׁר, *to be straight, level, right;* יָטַב, *to be good;* יָקַץ, *to awake* (cp. קוּץ); (יָלַל) *Hiph.* הֵילִיל, *to cry, howl;* יָשֵׁן, *to sleep;* (יָמַן) *Hiph.* הֵימִין, *to go to the right;* יָנַק, *to suck.*

In *Qal*, they are treated like the preceding class with Imperf. in *a* (346), *v. g.* יִיטַב, but in *Hiph.* the contraction is $a + y = ê$, *v. g.* הֵיטִיב (not הוֹטִיב). None of them occur in *Hoph'al* and only יָשֵׁן has the *Niph'al* form נוֹשַׁן.

EXERCISES.

I. And he said; he shall eat; you shall seize; they (fem.) shall perish; they shall eat (pause); they shall grasp.

I gave; I shall draw near; you shall take your stand; thou shalt not touch; to come near (Inf. Const.); to fall; she shall watch; take (Imper.); you were taken.

He was willing; he shall go; go; to go; he went; he made them go; he caused to dwell; they shall be weary; go down and take possession of the land; he shall deliver you; I shall be able; I shall be able to go; he shall save; he shall save us; they shall touch; he went again; you descended; and he brought them down; he shall chastise them; he willingly dwelt in the land; and it shall be good; and he slept; I shall not be able to go.

II. 1. נֹצֵר תְּאֵנָה יֹאכַל פִּרְיָהּ׃ — 2. אַל־תֹּאמַר נִסְתְּרָה דַרְכִּי מֵיְהֹוָה וּמֵאֱלֹהַי מִשְׁפָּטִי יַעֲבוֹר׃ — 3. וַתֹּאבַ֫דְנָה הָאֲתֹנוֹת לְקִישׁ אֲבִי שָׁאוּל׃ — 4. וַיֹּ֫אמֶר יוֹסֵף אֶל־אֶחָיו גְּשׁוּ־נָא אֵלַי וַיִּגָּ֫שׁוּ׃ — 5. הַחָכְמָה וְהַמַּדָּע נָתוּן

לָךְ (Par. H) וְעֹשֶׁר וְכָבוֹד אֶתֶּן־לָךְ׃ — 6. עֵת לָטַעַת וְעֵת לַעֲקֹר (uproot)
נָטוּעַ׃ — 7. אֶת־חֻקֹּתַי תִּשְׁמְרוּ לָלֶכֶת בָּהֶם׃ — 8. וַיּוֹאֶל הַלֵּוִי לָשֶׁבֶת
אֶת־הָאִישׁ׃ — 9. בְּשָׁלוֹם יַחְדָּו אֶשְׁכְּבָה וְאִישָׁן כִּי אַתָּה יְהוָה לְבָדָד
לָבֶטַח תּוֹשִׁיבֵנִי׃ — 10. וַיִּיטְבוּ דִבְרֵיהֶם בְּעֵינֵי חֲמוֹר (Hamor)׃ —
11. וַיִּיקֶץ נֹחַ מִיֵּינוֹ וַיֵּדַע אֵת אֲשֶׁר־עָשָׂה (had done) לוֹ חָם בְּנוֹ
הַקָּטָן׃ — 12. וְלֹא יָכֹל יוֹסֵף לְהִתְאַפֵּק לְכֹל הַנִּצָּבִים עָלָיו׃ — 13. וַיַּצְמַח
יְהוָה עֵץ הַחַיִּים בְּתוֹךְ הַגָּן וְעֵץ הַדַּעַת טוֹב וָרָע׃ — 14. וְיִעֲפוּ נְעָרִים
וְיִגָּעוּ וְהַבֹּטְחִים בַּיהוָה יֵלְכוּ וְלֹא יִיעָפוּ׃

III. 1. Rebuke not a scorner, lest (פֶּן־יִשְׂנָאֶךָּ) he hate thee; rebuke a wise man and he will love thee. — 2. The righteousness of the perfect shall make straight his way; but the wicked shall fall by his own wickedness. — 3. And the king put forth his hand, saying: lay hold on him, and his hand dried up. — 4. When (כִּי) your children shall ask their fathers (153), then ye shall inform (let know) your children, saying: Israel came over this (הַזֶּה) Jordan on dry land: for (אֲשֶׁר) the Lord, your God, dried up the waters of Jordan from before you until ye were passed over (Inf. const.). — 5. Hear, [my] sons, the instruction of a father, and attend to know understanding, because I will certainly give you a good doctrine; forsake not my law. — 6. The land which Jehovah swore to your fathers to give them. — 7. For, you are going over the Jordan to possess the land which Jehovah, your God, giveth you and you shall possess it and dwell therein. — 8. Hasten ye to my father and say unto him, Thus saith thy son Joseph, come down unto me, do not tarry.

LESSON XVI.

DIRECT SUBORDINATION OF THE NOUN TO THE VERB.

Vocabulary. Verbs.

יָלַד to bring forth, beget; *Niph.* and *Pu.* be born; *Pi.* act as midwife; *Hiph.* beget; (*Hoph.*).

רָגַם to stone.

סָקַל *Qal* and *Pi.* to stone; (*Niph.*; *Pu.*).

[נָגַד] *Hiph.* to tell, declare; *Hoph.*

שָׂבַע, שָׂבֵעַ to be satisfied; (*Niph.*; *Pi.*); *Hiph.*

נָסַע to break camp, set out, journey; (*Niph.*); *Hiph.*

[נָצַל] *Niph.*, to save oneself, escape; (*Pi.* spoil); *Hiph.* rescue; (*Hoph.*; *Hithp.*).

שָׁכַל, שָׁכֹל* to be bereaved; *Pi.* make childless; (*Hiph.*).

חָסֵר* to lack, be wanting; (*Pi.*; *Hiph.*).

צָרַח to cry, roar.

פָּגַע to meet, encounter, entreat; *Hiph.* make entreaties.

קָשַׁר to bind, league together, conspire; *Niph.*; (*Pi.*; *Pu.*; *Hithp.*).

צָעַק, זָעַק to cry, cry out; *Niph.* be summoned; *Hiph.* call together.

חָלַם to dream.

[פָּאַר] *Pi.* to beautify; *Hithp.*

[מָגַן] *Pi.* to deliver up, give.

כָּעַס (to be vexed); (*Pi.*) and *Hiph.* provoke to anger.

Nouns.

יֶ֫לֶד (v) *m. child*

אֶ֫בֶן (ـִים) (v) *f.* (*m.*) *stone*

קֶ֫שֶׁר (v) *m. conspiracy*

נֶ֫גַע (v) *m. plague, strike*

שַׁ֫עַר (v) *m. gate*

אֹ֫הֶל (v) *m. tent*

תִּפְאָרָה (v) (286—287) *f. beauty*

עֲטָרָה, constr. עֲטֶ֫רֶת (v) (286) *f. crown*

עָקֵב (iv) *m. heel, footprint*

חַי (iii) *a. living*

חַיִּים (iii) *m. pl. life*

קָהָל (iv) *m. assembly*

Nouns.

קָצִיר (ii) *m. harvest, branches*
עָפָר (iv) *m. dust*
חֲלוֹם (i) *m. dream*
שֵׁשׁ (iii) *m. byssus, fine linen*
שְׂעֹרָה (שְׂעֹרִים) (i) *f. barley*
כַּעַס (v) *m. vexation, anger*
שֶׁקֶר (v) *m. falsehood*
פֶּתַח (v) *m. opening*
צְעָקָה, זְעָקָה (iv) *f. cry, outcry*
צַר (iii) *m. adversary*
צָרָה (iii) *f.* "
מִדְבָּר (iv) *m. wilderness*
מֵישָׁרִים (iv) *m. pl. evenness, equity*
מִישׁוֹר (i) *m. level place, uprightness*
נֶגֶב (v) *m. Negeb, south*
נְעוּרִים (ii) *m. pl. youth, early life*

נֵכָר (iv) *m. foreigner, that which is foreign*
נָכְרִי, נָכְרִיָּה (iii) *a. alien, foreign*
עֵצָה (iv) *f. advice, counsel*
סָרִיס (iv) *eunuch, officer*
שָׁלֵם (iv) *a. whole, complete*
חֵלֶב (v) *fat*
מְרִיא (ii) *m. fatling*
כֶּבֶשׂ (v) *m. lamb*
קִנְיָן (i) *m. acquisition, thing acquired*
טַבָּח (i) *m. cook, guard*
הָמוֹן (ii) *m. (f.) murmur, multitude*
נֶגֶד, (נֶגְדִּי) *prep. and adv. in front of, opposite to*
נָגִיד (iv) *m. leader, ruler.*

A. Complement of the Verb. Direct Object.

Examples:

1. יַעֲזָב אֶת־אָבִיו וְאֶת־אִמּוֹ, *he shall leave his father and mother.* — 2. שָׂבַעְתִּי עֹלוֹת אֵילִים, *I have had enough of the burnt-offerings of rams;* וְאַתָּה לְבַשׁ בְּגָדֶיךָ, *but thou, put on thy clothes.* — 3. קָשְׁרוּ קֶשֶׁר, *they formed a conspiracy.*

352. 1. The direct object of a trans. verb or of an intrans. verb in the causative stems, (*Hiph.* and sometimes *Pi.,* 171) is merely added to the verb. When the object is determined (117), it is often introduced by the directive particle אֵת (אֶת־, אוֹת, אֹת), in ordinary prose books, seldom in poetry, *v. g.* יַעֲזָב אֶת־אָבִיו וְאֶת־אִמּוֹ, *he shall leave his father and mother,* Gen. ii, 24.

Some substantives used commonly with certain verbs are sometimes omitted elliptically after those verbs: *v. g.* כָּרַת, for כָּרַת בְּרִית, *make a covenant;* שָׁחַט and זָבַח *slaughter*, with the object understood.

353. 2. Many verbs, which in our languages are intransitive and which are occasionally intransitive in Hebrew, can also be construed as transitive verbs, thus: a) verbs denoting fullness or want, such as מָלֵא, *to be full of;* שָׂבַע, *to have enough of;* חָסֵר, *to be wanting, to lack;* שָׁכֹל, *to be bereaved, etc., v. g.,* שָׂבַעְתִּי עֹלוֹת אֵילִים, *I have had enough of the burnt-offerings of rams,* Is. I, 11.

b) verbs of putting on, putting off clothes, such as לָבַשׁ, *put on, be clad;* פָּשַׁט, *to be stripped, to strip, etc., v. g.* וְאַתָּה לְבַשׁ בְּגָדֶיךָ, *and thou, put on thy clothes,* 1 K. XXII, 30; cp. latin, *induere.*

c) Thus also verbs of coming in, going out; inhabiting, dwelling; speaking, *etc.* Generally, however, the intransitive construction with a suitable preposition is preferred (see Lesson XVII).

354. 3. Cognate object (internal or absolute object).

The verb frequently receives an object in the form of an undetermined noun derived from the same stem and very often accompanied by an intensifying adjective or by a genitive. The function of this cognate object is similar to that of the Inf. absolute (195, 196) and generally emphasises the verbal idea; sometimes, however, it expresses a concrete example of the effect or product of the action. Ex.: וְכִעֲסַתָּה צָרָתָהּ גַּם־כַּעַס, *her adversary continually oppressed her, i. e. provoked her sore;* 1 Sam. I, 6; וַיִּקְשְׁרוּ עָלָיו קֶשֶׁר בִּירוּשָׁלַםִ, *and they formed a conspiracy against him in Jerusalem,* 2 K. XIV, 19; קְבוּרַת חֲמוֹר יִקָּבֵר, *he shall be buried with the burial of an ass,* Jer. XXII, 19.

B. Double Complement (Principal and Secondary Object; Objective Complement).

Examples:

1. וַיַּלְבֵּשׁ אוֹתוֹ בִּגְדֵי־שֵׁשׁ, *and he arrayed him in garments of fine linen.* — 2. הַיְלָדִים אֲשֶׁר חָנַן אֱלֹהִים אֶת־עַבְדֶּךָ, (*they are*) *the children whom God has graciously given thy servant;* אַב־הֲמוֹן גּוֹיִם נְתַתִּיךָ, *I have made thee the father of a multitude of nations;* וַיִּיצֶר אֶת־הָאָדָם עָפָר, *and he made man out of the dust.* — 3. הוּא יְשׁוּפְךָ רֹאשׁ, *he shall bruise thee on the head.* — 4. וַיִּשְׁמַע מֹשֶׁה אֶת־הָעָם בֹּכֶה, *and Moses heard the people weeping.*

Two complements are added to the verb without the help of prepositions:

355. 1. After the causative stems (*Hiph.*, *Pi.*) of verbs which in *Qal* take their object in the accusative, *v. g.* וַיַּלְבֵּשׁ אותו בִּגְדֵי־שֵׁשׁ, *and he arrayed him in garments of fine linen,* Gen. XLI, 42.

To understand this construction better, we may consider the principal object (person) as the object of the causative idea, and the secondary object or objective complement as the direct object of the simple idea contained in the verb, *v. g.* in the clause: *he arrayed him in garments of fine linen* the double accusative may easily be understood by rendering it thus: *he caused HIM to put on GARMENTS of fine linen.*

356. 2. After *Qal*-Stems which have a meaning akin to that of the causative stems, i. e. which express an influence upon the object through some external means, such as

a) verbs of covering, giving, asking, *etc., v. g.* הַיְלָדִים אֲשֶׁר־חָנַן אֱלֹהִים אֶת־עַבְדֶּךָ, (*they are*) *the children whom God has graciously given thy servant,* Gen. XXXIII, 5;

b) verbs of making, preparing, forming into something:

α) to designate the product or office, *v. g. he built* אֶת־הָאֲבָנִים מִזְבֵּחַ, *the stones into an altar,* 1 K. XVIII, 32; אַב־הֲמוֹן גּוֹיִם נְתַתִּיךָ, *I have made thee the father of a multitude of nations,* Gen. XVII, 5. As a rule, however, the office is expressed by לְ, and so also frequently the product of the action (cp. 372, 3). β) to indicate the material out of which a thing is made, *v. g.* וַיִּיצֶר יְהוָה אֱלֹהִים אֶת־הָאָדָם עָפָר מִן־הָאֲדָמָה, *and the Lord God formed the man* [*out of the*] *dust of the earth,* Gen. II, 7. The preposition מִן, however, is commonly used to indicate the material (373, 3).

Strictly speaking, those objective complements are in apposition to the principal object.

357. 3. A secondary object is commonly used without preposition to indicate the part of the body especially affected by the action, *v. g.* הוּא יְשׁוּפְךָ רֹאשׁ וְאַתָּה תְּשׁוּפֶנּוּ עָקֵב, *he shall bruise thee on the head and thou shalt bruise him on the heel,* Gen. III, 15.

358. 4. Verbs indicating the activity of the senses, heart or mind frequently have an objective complement in the form of an undetermined adjective or participle, *v. g.* וַיִּשְׁמַע משֶׁה אֶת־הָעָם בֹּכֶה, *and Moses heard the people weeping,* Num. XI, 10. Often such objective complements are expressed by a co-ordinate or a subordinate clause with a suitable conjunction (see Lesson XXII; cp. 258, 231, 308).

C. Complement of a Passive Verb.

Examples:

1. וַיֻּגַּד לְרִבְקָה אֶת־דִּבְרֵי עֵשָׂו, *and the words of Esau were told to Rebecca,* lit. *and it was told Rebecca the words of Esau.* — 2. הֲלוֹא נָכְרִיּוֹת נֶחְשַׁבְנוּ לוֹ, *have we not been counted as strangers by him?*

359. 1. Verbs, which in the active have a direct object, are often construed impersonally (3 s. m.) with the object of the active construction still subordinated directly to the passive (with or without אֶת as above, 352), *v. g.* וַיֻּגַּד לְרִבְקָה אֶת־דִּבְרֵי עֵשָׂו, *and the words of Esau were told to Rebecca,* Gen. XXVII, 42. Of course, as in other languages, the object of the active may become the subject of the passive and the subject of the active (agent) is then expressed with the preposition לְ, more rarely by מִן or בְּ *Instrumenti* (see following Lesson), וַתִּקָּבֵר רָחֵל, *and Rachel was buried.*

360. 2. Verbs, which in the active take two objects without the help of prepositions (double accusative), retain with the passive the secondary object in the same form as with the active (355—357), *v. g.* הֲלוֹא נָכְרִיּוֹת נֶחְשַׁבְנוּ לוֹ, *have we not been counted as strangers by him?* Gen. XXXI, 15.

D. Adverbial Modifiers (Words or Phrases).

Examples:

1. וַיִּבְרַח מִצְרָיִם, *and he fled* [*to*] *Egypt;* הֲיֵשׁ בֵּית־אָבִיךְ מָקוֹם, *is there room* [*in*] *thy father's house?* הָלַךְ בַּמִּדְבָּר דֶּרֶךְ יוֹם, *he walked a day's journey in the wilderness.* — 2. כָּל־יְמֵי חַיֶּיךָ, *all the days of thy life.* — 3. מַר צֹרֵחַ שָׁם גִּבּוֹר, *the mighty man crieth there bitterly;* תִּשְׁפֹּט עַמִּים מִישֹׁר, *thou shalt judge the peoples* [*with*] *equity.* — 4. וָאֶצְעַק קוֹל־גָּדוֹל, *and I cried* [*with*] *a loud voice;* וַיִּרְגְּמוּ אֹתוֹ אֶבֶן, *and they stoned him* [*with*] *stones.* — 5. קוֹלִי אֶל־יְהוָה אֶקְרָא, *I will cry aloud to the Lord.*

Nouns denoting place, time, measure or manner, are often connected with the verbs without prepositions (accusative). These are called accusatives of nearer definition, specifying some immediate circumstance of the action.

361. 1. **Place.** a) Answering question 'whither', *v. g.* וַיִּבְרַח מִצְרָ֫יִם, *and he fled to Egypt,* 1 K. xi, 40 (cp. Latin: *eo domum*). The preposition אֶל־, however, is commonly used with the noun denoting place.

362. b) Answering question 'where'; the accusative in this case is generally followed by a genitive, *v. g.* הֲיֵשׁ בֵּית־אָבִיךָ מָקוֹם, *is there room in thy father's house?* Gen. xxiv 23. Commonly, however, the question 'where' is answered with the preposition בּ, *in.*

363. c) ־ָה *locale.* The accusative of place is often indicated by the old accusative ending ־ָה. This ־ָה is almost always toneless and, consequently, the vowels of the noun are seldom modified, except in the segolates in which the auxiliary vowel becomes unnecessary and the vowel of the first syllable in the *qaṭl* form occasionally reverts to its primitive quality and quantity. Most commonly this ־ָה is used in answer to the question 'whither', but sometimes also to the question 'where'. It can be used, though improperly, even with a noun preceded by the prepositions אֶל־ עַד־ or לְ. It is found sometimes in nouns denoting time. Examples: אַ֫רְצָה, *to the earth;* הַבַּ֫יְתָה, *to the house;* הָהָ֫רָה, *to the mountain;* מִדְבָּ֫רָה, *to the wilderness;* נֶ֫גְבָּה, *to the south;* הָאֹ֫הֱלָה, *to the tent;* לְמַ֫עְלָה, *upwards;* לְמַ֫טָּה, *downwards;* לַ֫יְלָה, *by night, night.*

364. d) The accusative is also used sometimes in answer to the question 'how far' 'how high', *v. g.* הָלַךְ בַּמִּדְבָּר דֶּ֫רֶךְ יוֹם, *he walked a day's journey in the wilderness,* 1 K. xix, 4.

365. 2. **Time.** In answer to the question 'when' or 'how long', *v. g.* הַיּוֹם, *to-day; at that time;* בֹּ֫קֶר, *in the morning;* כָּל־יְמֵי חַיֶּ֫יךָ, *all the days of thy life,* Gen. iii, 14 (see numerals, Lesson xxiv; cp. also 363).

366. 3. **Manner, Condition (Adverbial Accusative).** A noun is often directly subordinated to a verb, in order to indicate the manner or condition in which an action takes place. In English we generally use an adverb, or prepositional phrase with *in, with, in the form of, with regard, etc.* Both adjective and substantive can thus be used adverbially and can be either masc. or fem., sing. or plural, *v. g.* עָרוֹם הִלְּכוּ, *they go about naked* (*as one naked*), Job. xxiv, 10; מַר צֹרֵחַ שָׁם גִּבּוֹר, *the mighty man crieth there bitterly*, Zeph. i, 14; יִזְעֲקוּ מָרָה, *they shall cry bitterly*, Ez. xxvii, 30; תִּשְׁפֹּט עַמִּים מִישֹׁר, *thou shalt judge the peoples with equity*, Ps. lxvii, 5; בֶּ֫טַח, *with confidence;* לֵב אֶחָד, *uniformly;* מֵישָׁרִים, *uprightly.*

Often a noun denoting state, manner or condition is preceded by the prep. כְּ, *as, in the form of, according, like, etc., v. g.* כָּאֶבֶן מַ֫יִם יִתְחַבָּאוּ, [*the*] *waters are congealed like stone*, Job. xxxviii, 30.

367. 4. **Organ, Instrument.** Frequently, especially after verbs of speaking, crying, and after verbs denoting some external action, the noun expressing the organ, means or instrument by which the action is performed, is directly subordinated to the verb (cp. 370, 8). Such a noun is always undetermined and often accompanied by an adjective or genitive, *v. g.* וָאֶזְעַק קוֹל־גָּדוֹל, *and I cried with a loud voice*, Ez. xi, 13; דִּבְּרוּ אִתִּי לְשׁוֹן שָׁ֫קֶר, *they spoke with me with a deceitful tongue*, Ps. cix, 2; וַיִּרְגְּמוּ אֹתוֹ אָ֫בֶן, *and they stoned him with stones*, Lev. xxiv, 23.

368. 5. Apparently similar is the case in which the instrument or organ is determined by the suffix of the same person as the subject. In English, we often render such noun by an adverb, *v. g.* קוֹלִי אֶל־יְהוָה אֶקְרָא *I shall cry aloud to the Lord*, Ps. iii, 5; צַהֲלִי קוֹלֵךְ, *cry aloud*, Is. x, 30.

EXERCISES.

I. 1. שָׂבַ֫עְתִּי עֹלוֹת אֵילִים וְחֵ֫לֶב מְרִיאִים וְדַם פָּרִים וּכְבָשִׂים וְעַתּוּדִים לֹא חָפָ֫צְתִּי׃ — 2. כִּשְׁמֹעַ עֵשָׂו (Esau) אֶת־דִּבְרֵי אָבִיו וַיִּצְעַק צְעָקָה גְּדֹלָה וּמָרָה עַד־מְאֹד וַיֹּ֫אמֶר לְאָבִיו בָּרֲכֵ֫נִי גַם־אָ֫נִי (162) אָבִי׃ — 3. וַיִּסַּע מִשָּׁם אַבְרָהָם אַ֫רְצָה הַנֶּ֫גֶב וַיֵּ֫שֶׁב בֵּין־קָדֵשׁ (pr. n.) וּבֵין שׁוּר (pr. n.)׃ — 4. וַיִּשְׁלַח יַעֲקֹב וַיִּקְרָא (call) לְרָחֵל (pr. n.) וּלְלֵאָה (pr. n.) הַשָּׂדֶה אֶל־צֹאנוֹ׃ — 5. וַיִּשְׁלַח יְהוָה אֶת־שְׁמוּאֵל וַיַּצֵּל אֶתְכֶם מִיַּד אֹיְבֵיכֶם מִסָּבִיב (all around) וַתֵּשְׁבוּ בֶּטַח׃ — 6. יִשְׁאָל֫וּנִי מִשְׁפְּטֵי־צֶדֶק קִרְבַת אֱלֹהִים יֶחְפָּצוּן׃ — 7. אֲבָנִים שְׁלֵמוֹת תִּבְנֶה (thou shalt build) אֶת־מִזְבַּח יְהוָה׃ — 8. סָקוֹל יִסָּקֵל הַשּׁוֹר וְלֹא יֵאָכֵל אֶת־בְּשָׂרוֹ׃ — 9. וַיְבָרְכֵ֫הוּ וַיֹּאמַר בָּרוּךְ אַבְרָם לְאֵל עֶלְיוֹן׃ — 10. וַיַּעֲמֹד וַיְבָ֫רֶךְ אֵת כָּל־קְהַל יִשְׂרָאֵל קוֹל גָּדוֹל׃

II. 1. And now, come (fem.) let me, I pray, counsel thee a counsel and save thy life and the life of thy son, Solomon. —

2. And the Lord plagued Pharaoh with great plagues and also his house on account of (עַל־דְּבַר) Sarai, the wife of Abraham. — 3. For (כִּי) the children of Israel shall abide many days without (אֵין) king, and without captain, and without sacrifice. — 4. And Joseph was brought down to Egypt and Potiphar (וַיִּקְנֵהוּ פּוֹטִיפַר) an officer of Pharaoh, the captain of the guard, an Egyptian, bought him from the hands of the Ishmaelites, (הַיִּשְׁמְעֵאלִים) who had brought him down thither. — 5. Thou (thyself) shalt be (תִּהְיֶה) over my house; only in the throne shall I be greater than thou. — 6. Come, ye children, hearken unto me: I will teach you the fear of the Lord.

LESSON XVII.

PREPOSITIONS. ADVERBS.

Vocabulary. Verbs.

חָבַק, *Qal & Pi.* to embrace.
חָבַל, to bind, pledge; (*Niph.*); *Pi.* twist.
חָגַר, to gird, gird oneself.
אָשַׁר, (*Qal*) & *Pi.* to go straight, call blessed; (*Pu.*).
*אָנַף, *Qal & Hithp.*, to be angry.
אָרַךְ | *אָרֵךְ } to be long; *Hiph.* to prolong, last long.
שָׂכַר, to hire; (*Niph.*, *Hithp.*).
זָמַר, (to trim, prune; *Niph.*); *Pi.* make music (by singing or playing).
חָקַר, to search; (*Niph.*, *Pi.*).
נָתַץ, to pull down, break down; *Niph.*; *Pi.*; *Pu.*; *Hoph.*
טָרַף, to tear, rend, pluck; (*Niph.*, *Pu.*, *Hiph.*).
בָּרַח to flee; *Hiph.*
נָחַל, to get possession, inherit; (*Pi.* divide for a possession); *Hithp.* possess; *Hiph.* give possession; (*Hoph.*).
חָשַׂךְ, to withhold, refrain; (*Niph.*).
*חָשַׁךְ, to grow dark; (*Hiph.*).
פָּרַע, to let go, let alone; (*Niph.*, *Hiph.*).
חָמַס, to treat violently, wrong; (*Niph.*).
חָמַל, to spare (with עַל, have compassion).
רָדַף, (with prepos. אַחֲרֵי) to pursue in order to overtake; (with acc.) put to flight, hunt, persecute; (*Niph.*); *Pi.* pursue ardently; (*Pu.*, *Hiph.*).
מָרַד to rebel.

Nouns.

מַעְגָּל (iv) *m. entrenchment, track, course of life*
יֹשֶׁר (v) *m. uprightness*
[אֶשֶׁר (v) or אָשָׁר (iv)] *m. pl. const.* אַשְׁרֵי, *happiness (happy)*
אֹרַח (v) *m. way, path, mode of life*
צֶלֶם (v) *m. image*
דְּמוּת (i) *f. likeness*
תֹּמֶר (v) | תָּמָר (iv) } *m. palm-tree*
שָׂכָר (iv) *m. wages, hire*
שָׂכִיר (ii) *a. hired (servant)*
מְחִיר (i) *m. price, hire*
כֶּרֶם (v) *m.* (*f.*) *vineyard*
אוֹת (וֹת) (i) *m. sign, pledge*
קָרוֹב (ii) *adj. near*

Nouns.

דֶּ֫בֶר	(v) *m. pestilence*	חֹ֫שֶׁךְ	(v) *m. darkness*
רִיב (וּת)	(i) *m. strife, dispute*	כֶּ֫לֶב	(v) *m. dog*
רֹב	(iii) *m. multitude*	אֲרִי / אַרְיֵה	(v) *m. lion*
נַחֲלָה	(v) *f. property, inheritance*	חַיָּה	(iii) *f. beast, animal*
נַ֫חַל	(v) *m. torrent, valley*	חָלִ֫ילָה	*interj. far be it, absit!*
חֶרְפָּה	(v) *f. reproach*	שָׂטָן	(iv) *m. adversary, Satan*
מוֹלֶ֫דֶת	(v) *f. kindred, offspring*	עוֹף	(i) *m. coll. birds, flying creatures.*

I. Prepositions.

Very often nouns are subordinated to the verbs by means of prepositions. Most of these prepositions primarily indicate a relation of space, but have been gradually extended and adapted also to relations of time, cause, purpose, *etc.* We give here a list of the most common prepositions with their principal meanings. Their syntactical use will be illustrated by examples, but, for a full treatment, recourse must be had to Dictionaries.

A. List of Prepositions with their principal meanings.

1. Simple Prepositions.

369. אֶל־ (אֶל). אֶל indicates motion or direction (physical or moral) towards an object or place; hence, it corresponds to English *towards, to, unto, into, as far as, against.*

Examples.

1. וַיֵּ֫לֶךְ מִשָּׁם אֶל־הַר הַכַּרְמֶל, *and he went thence to Mount Carmel*, 2 K. II, 25; — 2. וַיֹּאמֶר אֱלִישָׁע אֶל־מֶ֫לֶךְ יִשְׂרָאֵל, *and Elisha said to the king of Israel*, 2 K. III, 13; — 3. עָזְרֵ֫נוּ כִּי נִקְבְּצוּ אֵלֵינוּ כָּל מַלְכֵי הָאֱמֹרִי יֹשְׁבֵי הָהָר, *help us, for all the kings of the Amorites that dwell in the mountain are gathered together against us*, Jos. X, 6; — 4. וַיֹּסֶף עוֹד לְדַבֵּר אֵלָיו, *and he spoke to him again*, Gen. XVIII, 29.

370. בְּ. בְּ primarily indicates the idea of being or moving within a certain place, or within a certain time. In English, according to verb and context, it may be rendered by *in, on, during, among, in the capacity of, as, with* (of instrument), *for* (of price); besides, it is often used after verbs of touching, striking, *etc.*, and also may, after verbs of motion, imply the idea of bringing.

Examples.

1. בַּמָּקוֹם, *in the place;* בַּבַּיִת, *in the house;* בַּיּוֹם, *during the day;* הַמֶּלֶךְ אֲשֶׁר מָלַךְ בְּחֶשְׁבּוֹן, *the king who reigned in Heshbon,* Jos. XIII, 10; — 2. יָשָׁר בָּאָדָם אָיִן, *there is none upright among men,* Micah VII, 2; — 3. *I appeared to Abraham* בְּאֵל שַׁדָּי, *as El-Shaddai,* Ex. VI, 3 (cp. French *il agit en honnête homme); —* 4. נֶפֶשׁ אֲשֶׁר תִּגַּע בּוֹ, *any one that touches him,* Lev. XXII, 6; — 5. וַאֲנִי בְּחַסְדְּךָ בָטַחְתִּי, *and I have trusted in thy kindness,* Ps. XIII, 6; — 6. כָּל־בֶּן־נֵכָר לֹא־יֹאכַל בּוֹ, *no foreigner shall eat thereof (share in it by eating),* Ex. XII, 43; — 7. פֶּן יִפְגָּעֵנוּ בַּדֶּבֶר אוֹ בֶחָרֶב, *lest he strike us with pestilence or with the sword,* Ex. V, 3; — 8. נֶפֶשׁ בְּנֶפֶשׁ עַיִן בְּעַיִן, *life for life, eye for eye,* Deut. XIX, 21; — 9. וַיִּפְקֹד שִׁמְשׁוֹן אֶת־אִשְׁתּוֹ בִּגְדִי, *and Samson visited his wife, bringing her a kid,* lit. *in* or *with a kid,* Jud. XV, 1.

On בּ with Infinit. constr., see 209.

371. כּ. כּ (poet. כְּמוֹ), indicates conformity and comparison, hence occurs in the sense of *as, like, according, about, something like,* and is frequently used instead of the adverbial accusative (366).

Examples.

1. כְּדֶרֶךְ יוֹם, *about a day's journey;* — 2. אִישׁ כִּלְבָבוֹ, *a man according to his heart;* — 3. כַּכָּתוּב, *as it is written,* lit. *according to the written;* — 4. וְהָיָה כַצַּדִּיק כָּרָשָׁע, *(far be it that) the righteous should be as the wicked,* Gen. XVIII, 25.

On כּ with Infinit. constr., see 209.

372. ל. ל is used to indicate a great variety of relations between an action or state and some person or object, its most common use being to introduce the indirect object. In English, according to verb and context, ל will be rendered by *to, into, with reference to, with regard to, in respect of, with, by, etc.*

Examples.

1. וַיִּתֵּן לוֹ *and he gave to him,* וַיֹּאמֶר לוֹ, *and he said to him;* — 2. וַיִּשְׁאֲלוּ אַנְשֵׁי הַמָּקוֹם לְאִשְׁתּוֹ *and the men of the place asked [him] con-*

cerning his wife, Gen. xxvi, 7; — 3. וַיְהִי הָאָדָם לְנֶפֶשׁ חַיָּה, *and man became (was made into) a living soul,* Gen. ii, 7 (356); — 4. וְנִבְחַר מָוֶת מֵחַיִּים (373, 10) לְכֹל הַשְּׁאֵרִית הַנִּשְׁאָרִים, *and death shall be chosen rather than life by all the residue that remain,* Jer. viii, 3 (cp. 359); — 5. לְכֶלֶב חַי הוּא טוֹב מִן־הָאַרְיֵה הַמֵּת, *a living dog is better than a dead lion,* lit. *as to a living dog, it is better* . . . (cp. 487), Eccles. ix, 4. — 6. בְּרַח לְךָ, *flee thou* (*Dativus ethicus,* cp. colloquial English *run away with yourself*); עִבְרוּ לָכֶם, *pass ye over;* וַתֵּשֶׁב לָהּ, *and she sat down, etc.*

373. מִן. In a general way, מִן indicates physical or moral motion from, separation from an object, and hence, removal, privation, origin, starting point, source, authorship, *etc.*; accordingly, it may correspond to the English prepositions or prepositional phrases *from, of, out of, away from, on account of, for, for the sake of, more than, rather than, etc.*

Examples.

1. וַיֵּרֶד מֹשֶׁה מִן־הָהָר אֶל־הָעָם, *and Moses went down from the mountain unto the people,* Ex. xix, 14; — 2. מִיָּמִין, מִימִין, *on the right* (*a dextris*); מִשְּׂמֹאול, *on the left* (*a sinistris*); מִחוּץ, *outside;* — 3. וַיִּצֶר יְהוָה אֱלֹהִים מִן־הָאֲדָמָה כָּל־חַיַּת הַשָּׂדֶה, *and out of the ground the Lord God formed every beast of the field,* Gen. ii, 19; — 4. וְאָבִיו וְאִמּוֹ לֹא יָדְעוּ כִּי מֵיְהוָה הִיא, *but his father and his mother knew not that it was from the Lord,* Jud. xiv, 4; — 5. כָּבוֹד לָאִישׁ שֶׁבֶת מֵרִיב, *it is an honor for a man to (live) remain away from strife* (*i. e. without strife*), Prov. xx, 3; — 6. הַצֻּרִים נִתְּצוּ מִמֶּנּוּ, *the rocks are broken asunder by him (by a power coming from),* Nah. i, 6; — 7. הֵם הִמְלִיכוּ וְלֹא מִמֶּנִּי, *they have set up kings, but not at my prompting* (lit. *from me*), Hos. viii, 4; — 8. כִּי־מַר־לִי מְאֹד מִכֶּם, *for it grieveth me much for your sake,* Ruth i, 13; — 9. וַיִּקַּח מֵאַבְנֵי הַמָּקוֹם, *and he took one of the stones of the place,* Gen. xxviii, 11; — 10. וְהַנָּחָשׁ הָיָה עָרוּם מִכֹּל חַיַּת הַשָּׂדֶה, *now the serpent was more subtle than any beast of the field* (lit. *subtle away from any beast,* cp. 493), Gen. iii, 1; — 11. מֵרוֹב, *on account of the multitude, etc.*

374. עַל־. עַל indicates primarily position or motion over an object physically or morally, and hence has the various senses of the English prepositions *on, upon, over, above;* often it may be rendered by *besides, in addition to, together with, with, in behalf of, against, by, near (standing over), etc.*

Examples.

1. עַל־פְּנֵי הַמָּיִם, *over the face of the waters,* Gen. I, 2; — 2. הַמֶּלֶךְ אֲשֶׁר מָלַךְ עֲלֵיכֶם, *the king that reigneth over you,* 1 Sam. XII, 14; — 3. עָלַי לָתֵת, *it is my duty to give,* lit. *upon me to give;* — 4. נִלְחַם אָבִי עֲלֵיכֶם, *my father fought for you,* lit. *had a fight over you,* Jud. IX, 17; — 5. וּפַרְעֹה עֹמֵד עַל־הַיְאֹר, *and Pharaoh was standing by the Nile,* Gen. XLI, 1; — 6. וַיִּקַּח עֵשָׂו אֶת־מַחֲלַת עַל־נָשָׁיו לוֹ לְאִשָּׁה, *and Esau took to himself Mahalath for a wife, in addition to his [other] wives,* lit. *over and above his other wives,* Gen. XXVIII, 9; — 7. יָעַצְתִּי הֵאָסֹף יֵאָסֵף עָלֶיךָ כָל־יִשְׂרָאֵל, *I counsel that all Israel be gathered unto thee,* 2 Sam. XVII, 11; — 8. *They shall be called* עַל שֵׁם אֲחֵיהֶם, *after the name of their brethren,* Gen. XLVIII, 6; — 9. לֹא תַעֲמֹד עַל־דַּם רֵעֶךָ, *thou shalt not stand against the blood of thy neighbor,* Lev. XIX, 16, *etc.*

375. Other simple prepositions are the following: אַחַר, אַחֲרֵי, *behind, after;* אֵצֶל, *beside;* אֵת, *with;* בֵּין, *between;* בִּלְתִּי, בְּלִי, *without;* בַּעַד, *behind, on behalf of;* בְּעַד, *through;* זוּלַת, *except;* יַעַן, *on account of;* מוּל and מוֹל, *in front of;* נֶגֶד, *in front of, opposite to;* נֹכַח, *in front of, before;* עַד, *unto;* עִם, *with;* תַּחַת, *under, in place of.* Many of these were originally nouns and a few are occasionally still used as such.

2. Compound Prepositions.

376. Compound prepositions consist of:

a) two prepositions, *v. g.* מֵאַחֲרֵי, *from (from after);* מֵאֵת, מֵעִם, *from (from with)*; מֵעַל, *from (from upon);* מִתַּחַת, *from (from under);* לְמִן, *from;* לְנֶגֶד, לְנֹכַח, *before;* אֶל־מוּל, *towards;* מִבְּלִי, *for lack,* or *want of;*

b) a noun and a preposition, *v. g.* לְבַד, מִלְּבַד, *besides* (בַּד, *separation*); לִפְנֵי, *before,* מִפְּנֵי, *from (from before)* (פָּנִים, *face*); בִּגְלַל, *for the sake of* (גָּלָל, *account*); בַּעֲבוּר, *on account of* (עֲבוּר, *account*); בְּיַד, *through* (יָד, *hand*); אֶל־עֵבֶר, *beyond* (עֵבֶר, *country across*); מֵעֵבֶר לְ, *from beyond;* לְעֻמַּת, *together with* (עֻמָּה, *juxtaposition*); לְמַעַן, *on account of* (מַעַן, *purpose*); עַל־עֵקֶב, *on account of* (עֵקֶב, *consequence*); עַל־פִּי, לְפִי, כְּפִי, *according to, according to the tenor of, as* (פִּי, *mouth*); לִקְרַאת, *towards* (קְרֹאת, Inf. constr.).

B. Inflection.

377. Review. בּ, כּ, ל are generally pronounced with *Sh·wa (passim)*; before a consonant with *Sh·wa*, they are sounded with *Ḥireq* (46, 108); when followed by *Ḥaṭeph*, they take the vowel of the *Ḥaṭeph* (48, 120); before אֱלֹהִים and אֱמֹר, they take *Ṣere* with quiescent *Aleph* (120, note), before אֲדֹנָי (יְהוָה), they are sounded with *Pathaḥ* and silent *Aleph* (120, note), before the article, they take the vowel of the article (109).

378. Before monosyllables and dissyllabic *Mil'el*, בּ, כּ, ל are often sounded with pretonic *Qameṣ*, not however when such words are closely connected with a following word, *v. g.* when they are in the construct state or marked with a conjunctive accent (40, 3) because, in that case, the prepositions are not before the main tone. This occurs: a) before the Inf. constr. of verbs פ"ו, פ"י, ע"ו, ע"ע, *v. g.* לָתֵת, *to give;* לָלֶכֶת, *to go;* b) before monosyllabic pronouns, *v. g.* בָּזֶה, בָּכֶם, לָכֶם, לָמָה, לָמָּה; c) in certain expressions, *v. g.* לָעַד, *to eternity,* לָרֹב, *in multitude,* לָבֶטַח, *in security,* לָנֶצַח, *forever;* but לְנֵצַח נְצָחִים, because נֵצַח is joined to what follows.

379. The prepositions כ and מִן (110, 111, 121) have special forms with suffixes, see Paradigm H. The other prepositions take the suffixes of the noun, mostly like a singular noun; some, however, have suffixes like plural nouns, such as תַּחַת, אַחַר (אַחֲרֵי), אֶל, עַל, עַד; finally others may be treated like singular nouns, or like nouns in the masculine plural or in the feminine plural, such as בֵּין, סָבִיב.

380. Compound prepositions are inflected invariably according to the requirements of their simple last element, *v. g.* מֵאַחֲרֶיךָ, *from behind thee, etc.*

C. Syntactical Remarks.

381. 1. The use of the prepositions is sufficiently clear from their lexicographical meaning. When several words are under the government of the same preposition, the preposition is often, although not necessarily, repeated before every one of them, *v. g.* וַיֹּאמֶר יְהוָה אֶל־אַבְרָם לֶךְ־לְךָ מֵאַרְצְךָ וּמִמּוֹלַדְתְּךָ וּמִבֵּית אָבִיךָ, *now Yahweh said unto Abram, Get thee out of thy country, and from thy kindred, and from thy father's house,* Gen. xii, 1.

382. 2. Certain prepositions appear to be under the immediate government of a verb which by its nature excludes such a combination; thus, prepositions indicating motion are used after verbs of rest. In such cases, the verb on which the prep. really depends has been left out and must be inferred from the context (cp. English *he cried himself to sleep, he laughed him to scorn*). This is called by grammarians *Constructio Pregnans, v. g.* וַיַּשְׁכֵּם אַבְרָהָם בַּבֹּקֶר אֶל־הַמָּקוֹם, *and Abraham rose early in the morning* (*to go*) *to the place,* Gen. xix, 27.

II. Adverbs.

383. Hebrew is comparatively poor in Adverbs. Only a few are primitive; the great majority of them are real nouns (subst. or adjectives in the accusative, 351 ff., or infinitives absolute, 197) most of which are still used as ordinary substantives, *etc.*

Hebrew adverbs, like prepositions, are either simple or compound; in this latter case, their meaning is derived from the combination of the elements that enter into their composition.

The most common adverbs are:

384. Place.

פֹּה	here.	אַחַר	behind.
שָׁם	there.	אֲחֹורַנִּית	backward.
הֲלֹם	here, there.	לְפָנִים	beforehand.
שָׁמָּה	thither.	מַעְלָה, מַעַל (וָמַעְלָה)	upward.
הֵנָּה	hither.	מִמַּעַל, לְמַעְלָה	above, *desuper*.
הֵנָּה וָהֵנָּה	hither and thither.	לְמַטָּה, מַטָּה	downward.
חוּץ, חוּצָה, מִחוּץ	outside.	מִלְמַטָּה	beneath.
מִבַּיִת	inside.	מִסָּבִיב, סָבִיב	around.
פְּנִימָה	towards, within.		
אָחוֹר	backward.		

385. Time.

אָז	then.	שִׁלְשׁוֹם	day before yesterday.	לַיְלָה	by night.
הַיּוֹם	to-day.			עַתָּה, עַתָּה	now.
מָחָר	to-morrow.	עוֹד	again, still, yet.	כְּבָר	already.
אֶתְמוֹל	yesterday.	יוֹמָם	by day.	טֶרֶם	not yet.
				מְהֵרָה	soon.

386. **Manner.**

- יַ֫חַד, יַחְדָּו together.
- לְבַד separately.
- בַּלָּט secretly.
- שָׁוְא uselessly.
- הֵיטֵב well.
- חִנָּם gratis, in vain.
- טוֹב well.
- כֹּה thus.
- רֵיקָם in vain.
- כָּ֫כָה thus.
- כֵּן thus, so, rightly.
- לְאַט, לָאַט gently.
- פִּתְאֹם suddenly.
- לָכֵן, עַל־כֵּן consequently, therefore.
- אֵפוֹא, אֵפוֹ now, then.
- הֵן, הִנֵּה, הֶן־ lo! behold!

387. **Quantity and Number.**

- מְאֹד much.
- הַרְבֵּה much.
- יוֹתֵר too much.
- מְעַט a little.
- כִּמְעַט somewhat.
- אַחַת once.
- שֵׁנִית again (cp. 525 ff.).

388. **Affirmation and Negation.**

- אָכֵן certainly.
- אָמְנָם, אֻמְנָם truly.
- כִּי verily, truly.
- יֵשׁ there (is, was).
- אֵין, אַ֫יִן not.
- לֹא not.
- בַּל not (poet. for לֹא).
- אַל not, *ne*.
- בְּלִי not.
- בִּלְתִּי not.
- אֶ֫פֶס no longer.
- טֶ֫רֶם not yet.

389. **Interrogation.**

- הֲ, הַ, הֶ (413) *num, utrum?*
- הֲלֹא, הֲלוֹא *nonne?*
- אַי, אַיֵּה where?
- אֵיפֹה where? of what kind?
- אַ֫יִן whence?
- אָן where? whither?
- אָ֫נָה where? whither? how long?
- אֵיךְ, אֵיכָה how? where?
- אִם *num?*
- מַדּוּעַ why?
- מָתַי when?
- עַד־מָתַי how long?
- מָה . . . (415f.) how! how?
- לָ֫מָּה, לָמָה why?
- בַּמֶּה, בַּמָּה wherein?
- כַּמָּה, כַּמֶּה how much? how often?
- אֵי־מִזֶּה whence?
- אֵי־לָזֹאת on what account?
- עַד־מָה how long?
- הֲכִי is it that? is it because... that?

A few adverbs are capable of receiving suffixes in the form of verbal suffixes even with *Nun Energicum* (see 334 and Paradigm H), thus, אַיֵּ, הֵן, הִנֵּה, עוֹד, אֵין.

לְבַד (Lesson XI) takes nominal suffixes.

Instead of using adverbs, Hebrew has often recourse to various constructions, when in English an adverb or adverbial phrase would be preferred, (see Inf. absol. 195—196; Inf. constr. 211d, 457).

EXERCISES.

I. To us; to you; to thee; to thee (P.); from me; from them; from him; greater than he; he said to him; like thee; like us; like you; around us; near them; except you; in my presence; with you; you (acc.): under them; in them; through us; from (under) you; before him; for the sake of all of us; towards them; for the lack of a god; according to the precept; on account of her.

Above; downwards; backward; where? whither? here; hither; there; thither; when; how long? why? certainly; in vain; well; together; now; already; not yet; again; again he went; he is very good; and he was still standing; somewhat; by night.

II. 1. מִי כָמֹוךָ בָּאֵלִם יְהוָה׃ — 2. חֻקָּה אַחַת לָכֶם וְלַגֵּר אֲשֶׁר
בָּאָרֶץ, כָּכֶם כַּגֵּר יִהְיֶה (it shall be) לִפְנֵי יְהוָה׃ — 3. לָכַד דָּוִד אֶת־
עִיר בְּנֵי עַמּוֹן וְאֶת־הָעָם אֲשֶׁר בָּהּ הָרַג בֶּחָרֶב כִּי אָנַף בָּם מְאֹד׃ —
4. וַיֹּאמֶר אֱלֹהִים זֹאת (this) אוֹת־הַבְּרִית אֲשֶׁר־אֲנִי נֹתֵן בֵּינִי וּבֵינֵיכֶם׃ —
5. וְאָכַל הָעוֹף אֶת־בְּשָׂרְךָ מֵעָלֶיךָ׃ — 6. לֹא נוּכַל דַּבֵּר אֵלֶיךָ רַע אוֹ (or)
טוֹב׃ — 7. וַיֹּאמְרוּ בְנֵי־יִשְׂרָאֵל אֶל־שְׁמוּאֵל אַל־תַּחֲרֵשׁ מִמֶּנּוּ מִזְּעֹק אֶל־
יְהוָה אֱלֹהֵינוּ וְיוֹשִׁעֵנוּ מִיַּד פְּלִשְׁתִּים׃ — 8. וַיִּגְדַּל הַמֶּלֶךְ שְׁלֹמֹה מִכֹּל
מַלְכֵי הָאָרֶץ לְעֹשֶׁר וּלְחָכְמָה׃ — 9. וַיֹּאמֶר הַשָּׂטָן אֶל־יְהוָה שְׁלַח־נָא יָדְךָ
וְגַע בְּכָל־אֲשֶׁר לְאִיּוֹב׃ — 10. עוֹד מְעַט וְאֵין רָשָׁע׃ — 11. וַיֹּאמְרוּ
אֶל־דָּוִד לֵאמֹר הִנְנוּ עַצְמְךָ וּבְשָׂרְךָ אֲנָחְנוּ וַיִּמְשְׁחוּהוּ לְמֶלֶךְ עֲלֵיהֶם׃ —
12. וַיֹּאכְלוּ שָׁם לֶחֶם יַחְדָּו׃ — 13. וַיְדַבֵּר אַחְאָב (Ahab) אֶל־נָבוֹת
(Naboth) לֵאמֹר תְּנָה־לִּי כַּרְמְךָ . י הוּא קָרוֹב אֵצֶל בֵּיתִי וְאֶתְּנָה לְךָ תַּחְתָּיו
כֶּרֶם טוֹב מִמֶּנּוּ אִם טוֹב בְּעֵינֶיךָ אֶתְּנָה־לְּךָ כֶסֶף מְחִיר זֶה׃ וַיֹּאמֶר נָבוֹת
אֶל־אַחְאָב חָלִילָה לִּי מֵיְהוָה מִתִּתִּי אֶת־נַחֲלַת אֲבֹתַי לָךְ׃

III. 1. And Deborah, a prophetess, was judging Israel at that time, and she was sitting under the palm-tree of Deborah, between

Ramah (הָרָמָה) and Bethel (בֵּית־אֵל) in Mount Ephraim. — 2. Hezechias (חִזְקִיָּה) trusted in Jehovah, the God of Israel, and after him there was not [one] like him among all the kings of Judah. — 3. Thou shalt not oppress a hired servant [that is] poor and needy [whether he be] of thy brethren, or of thy resident strangers that are in the land; in his day thou shalt give him his hire, neither shall the sun go down upon it. — 4. Man has forgotten thee but God has remembered thee. — 5. He that trusteth in his own heart is a fool; but whoso walketh in wisdom, he shall be delivered. — 6. Because thou hast rejected the word of the Lord, He hath also rejected thee from [being] a king. — 7. Let the Lord judge between me and thee.

LESSON XVIII.

VERBS *LAMEDH-HE* (ל"ה); DEMONSTRATIVE PRONOUNS.

Vocabulary. Verbs.

גָּלָה to uncover, remove, go into exile; *Niph.; Pi.* uncover, reveal; *Pu.*; (*Hithp.*); *Hiph.* take into exile; (*Hoph.*).

שָׁבָה to take captive; *Niph.*

עָשָׂה to do, make, prepare; *Niph.*; (*Pu.*).

שָׁתָה to drink.

[שָׁקָה] *Hiph.* to give to drink, water; (*Pu.*).

רָבָה to be much, many, great; *Pi.* & *Hiph.* multiply, increase.

שָׁחָה (to bow down; *Hiph.* depress); *Hithpa'lel* (irreg.) prostrate oneself, bow down.

עָנָה to answer, respond; (*Niph.*; *Hiph.*).

עָנָה (to be low, depressed); (*Niph.*); *Pi.* afflict, humble; *Pu.*; *Hithp.*; (*Hiph.*).

בָּנָה to build; *Niph.*

חָשָׁה *Qal* & *Hiph.* to be silent.

רָעָה to pasture, tend (trans.), graze.

רָעָה to associate with; *Hithp.* id.

בָּכָה to weep; (*Pi.* lament).

רָאָה to see; *Niph.* appear; (*Pu.* be detected); *Hithp.* look at one another; *Hiph.* show; *Hoph.*

[צָוָה] *Pi.* to command; (*Pu.*).

קָוָה *Qal* & *Pi.* to wait for; *Niph.* be collected.

קָשָׁה to be hard, severe; (*Niph.*); *Pi.* & *Hiph.* make hard, difficult.

כָּסָה (to cover); (*Niph.*); *Pi.* cover, conceal.

חָרָה to burn, be kindled (of anger); (*Niph.*; *Hiph.*); *Hithp.* to become angry.

תָּעָה to err; (*Niph.* wander about); *Hiph.* to cause to wander.

עָלָה to go up, ascend; *Niph.* be brought up; *Hiph.* cause to go up, bring up, offer; (*Hoph.*); (*Hithp.* lift oneself up).

*גָּבַר to be strong; *Pi.* & *Hiph.* make strong, confirm; *Hithp.* show oneself strong.

פָּרַץ to break through; (*Niph.*; *Hithp.*; *Pu.*).

Nouns.

רֹ֫תֶם (v) *m.* broom-plant	יָבֵשׁ (iv) *a.* dry	יַבָּשָׁה (iv) *f.* land
חֶ֫רֶט (v) *m.* graving tool, stylus	מַסֵּכָה (i) *f.* molten metal	עֵ֫גֶל (v) *m.* calf
		דַּ֫עַת (v) *m.* knowledge

I. Verbs *Lāmeḏh-Hē* (Paradigm S).

390. These verbs are properly ל״י or ל״ו. *Yoḏh* and *Waw*, when final, were not pronounced; the vowel of the second radical, being now in an open syllable, was lengthened: *ă* to *ā*; *ĭ* to *ē* or *æ̆*. As it is generally not allowed in Hebrew to have a word ending in a vowel unless it is fully written, *He* was added as *mater lectionis*. Thus, verbs which ought to be גָּלַי or עָנַו were pronounced and written גָּלָה, עָנָה.

From the fact that in the above forms no difference was found between verbs primitively ל״י and those primitively ל״ו, they remain alike in the various inflectional peculiarities and are all treated as if from a root ל״י.

391. A. **Forms without afformatives.** When there are no afformatives, *Yoḏh* is kept only in the participle passive *Qal*, גָּלוּי, fem. גְּלוּיָה; in all the other cases it is elided and we have the following forms:

1. All the Perfects have ָה, *v. g.* גָּלָה, נִגְלָה, גִּלָּה, הִגְלָה, *etc.*

2. All the Indicative Imperfects have ֶה, *v. g.* יִגְלֶה, תִּגְלֶה, יִגָּלֶה, יְגַלֶּה, *etc.*

3. All Participles have ֶה, construct ֵה, like nouns of class VI (296, 297), except Part. pass. *Qal.*, *v. g.* גֹּלֶה, constr. גֹּלֵה, fem. גֹּלָה; נִגְלֶה, מְגַלֶּה, *etc.*

4. All Imperat. have ֵה, *v. g.* גְּלֵה, הִגָּלֵה, הַגְלֵה, גַּלֵּה, *etc.*

5. All Infin. Constr. have fem. ending וֹת, *v. g.* גְּלוֹת, הִגָּלוֹת, *etc.*

6. Infin. Absol. has ֹה or וֹ in *Qal* and sometimes *Niph.* and *Pi.* (see regular verb, Paradigms I-L), *v. g.* גָּלֹה, (גָּלוֹ), נִגְלֹה. It has ֵה in all other cases: גַּלֵּה, הִגָּלֵה, הַגְלֵה, *etc.*

B. **With afformatives beginning with a consonant** (ת, נ), the primitive *Yoḏh* remains:

392. 1. Perfect. a) In passive stems, *Pu.*, *Hoph.* and generally *Niph.*, the primitive *Yoḏh* contracts with a preceding *a*-sound to

ֵי (61). This occurs sometimes also with active derivative stems especially before תִי probably to avoid too many *i*-sounds. Ex.: גִּלֵּית, גִּלֵּיתִי; הִגְלֵיתָ, הִגְלֵיתֶם; הִגְלֵינוּ, נִגְלֵיתָ, (נִגְלֵיתָ); occasionally גִּלֵּיתִי, for גִּלִּיתִי; הִגְלֵיתִי, for הִגְלִיתִי.

393. In the active stems, (always in *Qal*, generally in *Pi.*, *Hiph.*, *Hithp.*, and sometimes in *Niph.* especially before תָ), *Yodh* quiesces in *Hireq*, *v. g.* גָּלִיתָ, גְּלִיתֶם, גָּלִינוּ; גִּלִּיתָ, גִּלִּינוּ; הִגְלִיתָ, הִגְלִיתִי, (הִגְלֵיתִי); הִתְגַּלִּיתָ; *Niph.* נִגְלֵיתָ and נִגְלִיתָ.

394. 2. In Imperf. Indic. and Imperative, before נָה, *Yodh* quiesces in ֶי (æ̂), *v. g.* תִּגְלֶינָה, תְּגַלֶּינָה, תִּתְגַּלֶּינָה, *etc.*

395. C. **Before afformatives beginning with a vowel,** *Yodh* regularly falls out and the afformatives are added directly to the second radical, *v. g.* גָּלוּ, גְּלִי, יִגְלוּ, תִּגְלוּ, *etc.* (cp. nouns, class VI, of the same origin, 296).

396. **The 3f. s. Perf.** has sometimes the old fem. ending ַת, גָּלַת, and so always before verbal suffixes; generally, however, by analogy with the other verbs, the fem. ending ָה is used, being further added to ת, and thus a form arises with double femin. ending, *v. g.* גָּלְתָה, גִּלְּתָה, הִגְלְתָה, *etc.*

397. D. **With Suffixes.** Suffixes are regularly added as in the strong verb (Lesson XIV) but, when the form has no afformatives, they are added directly to the second radical as in C (395), *v. g.* גָּלַנִי, עָשְׂךָ, עָשָׂנוּ, יִגְלֵנִי, יַעֲשׂוֹנִי. On 3f. s. Perfect, see C (396), *v. g.* צִוַּתָּה, הֶעֱלָתַם.

398. E. **Apocopated forms.** On account of the tone moving backward (233, 247), final ֶה is dropped, often in the Jussive and always after *Waw Consecutivum* (occasionally, Imperat. *Pi'el*, *Hithpa'el* and *Hiph.* are treated likewise). This is called Apocopated Imperfect. The form then ends in a doubly closed syllable. This doubly closed syllable is either kept, or, as is more common, a helping vowel is used (50, 276); in either case, *Hireq* of the preformative of *Qal* can be kept short or may be lengthened to *Sere* (cp. סֵפֶר for סִפְר, 276), *v. g.* וַיִּשְׁבְּ, וַיֵּבְךְּ, וַיִּגֶל, וַיִּבֶן, יֶרֶב, וַתֶּרֶב. With a gutt. of course, we have *Pathah* as helping vowel, and, with a first guttural, also as vowel of the preformatives, וַיַּעַשׂ, for וַיַּעְשׂ.

In *Hiph.*, when the helping vowel *S'ghol* is used, *Pathah* of the first syllable is generally heightened to *S'ghol* (cp. מֶלֶךְ, for מַלְךְ), *v. g.* וַיֶּשֶׁק, וַיֶּגֶל, for וַיַּשְׁק, for וַיַּשְׁקְ. Imper. הֶרֶב from הַרְבֵּה.

With a first gutt., *Qal* and *Hiph.* have the same form; the context will generally show which one is meant, *v. g.* וַיַּעַל, *and he went up*, וַיַּעַל, *and he brought up.*

399. **Remarks.** 1. The verb רָאָה, *to see*, has Imperf. Indic. יִרְאֶה, Jussive, יֵרֶא, but with *Waw Consec.* וַיַּרְא; 3 f. s. is וַתֵּרֶא and 1 s. is generally וָאֶרְאֶה, sometimes וָאֵרֶא.

400. 2. The verb שָׁחָה, *to bow down*, is used especially in the *Hithpa'lel.* The final stem-letter appears twice, first as ו and then as ה. Hence, Perf. is הִשְׁתַּחֲוָה; Imperf. Ind. יִשְׁתַּחֲוֶה; Apocopated Imperf. יִשְׁתַּחוּ.

401. 3. We append the forms of the two verbs הָיָה, *to be*, and חָיָה, *to live*: *Qal* Perf. הָיָה, חָיָה, Imperf. Ind. יִהְיֶה, יִחְיֶה; Juss. יְהִי, יְחִי; *Waw Consec.* וַיְהִי, וַיְחִי; Imperat. הֱיֵה, חֲיֵה; Inf. abs. הָיֹה, חָיֹה; Inf. constr. הֱיוֹת, (לְ)חְיוֹת; *Niph.* נִהְיָה; *Pi.* חִיָּה, יְחַיֶּה, חַיֵּה, חַיּוֹת, מְחַיֶּה, *Hiph.* הֶחֱיָה, הַחֲיוֹת, הַחֲיֵה.

II. Demonstrative Pronouns and Adjectives.

402. A. **Form.** The demonstrative adjectives and pronouns are:

1. Sing. m. זֶה, f. זֹאת, *this*; pl. אֵלֶּה, (אֵל) *these.*

2. Rarer forms: a) comm. זוּ invariable, used in poetry, and then mostly as a relative.

b) f. זֹה, זוֹ, *this.*

c) m. הַלָּזֶה; f. הַלֵּזוּ; c. הַלָּז, *yonder.*

3. The separate personal pronouns of the 3 p. הוּא, הִיא, הֵם, הֵמָּה, הֵן, הֵנָּה, are used also as demonstrative adjectives in the sense of *that, those* (149), and then always take the article. As pronouns they can be used only in the nominative (144).

403. B. **Syntactical Remarks.** 1. Demonstratives, when used as adjectives, are placed after the substantive, and after other adjectives if there are any; they take the article when the substantive is determined, *v. g.* הָאִישׁ הַזֶּה, *this man*; הַיּוֹם הַהוּא, *that day.* When the substantive is determined by a suffix (159), the demonstrative is sometimes found without the article *v. g.* אֹתֹתַי אֵלֶּה, *these my signs*, Ex. x, 1. As predicates, they do not take the article (89), זֶה הָאִישׁ, *this is the man*, lit. *the man is this* [*one*].

404. 2. When used for the neuter pronouns *it, this, that,* זֹאת and הוּא are more common than זֶה or הִיא, *v. g.* זֹאת עֲשׂוּ *this do ye.*

405. 3. זֶה and sometimes הוּא are used as enclitics to emphasize interrogative particles, מִי־זֶה, *who now?* מַה־זֶּה or מַה־זֹּאת, *what now?* מִי הוּא־זֶה, *who? who is he that..?*

406. 4. זֶה is also added to emphasize adverbial and especially temporal expressions, *v. g.* עַתָּה זֶה יָדַעְתִּי, *now indeed I know,* 1 K. XVII, 24; וְהִנֵּה־זֶה מַלְאָךְ נֹגֵעַ בּוֹ, *and behold, an angel touched him,* 1 K. XIX, 5.

407. 5. When זֶה is repeated, it is equivalent to *this . . . that; the one . . . the other, v. g.* וְקָרָא זֶה אֶל־זֶה, *and the one called unto the other,* Is. VI 3.

408. 6. זֶה, זוֹ and especially זוּ can be used as relative pronouns (501), *v. g.* לִוְיָתָן זֶה־יָצַרְתָּ, *Leviathan, whom thou hast formed,* Ps. CIV, 26; זֶה־אָהַבְתִּי נֶהְפְּכוּ־בִי, *those whom I have loved are turned against me,* Job XIX, 19.

EXERCISES.

I. He answered; and he answered; revealing (part.); in revealing; thou hast built; you have built; they have taken into exile; he has multiplied; you (f.) have wept; we shall see; and I shall see; he has commanded us; the waters were collected; he shall bring them up; do (ye) this and live; it is he who shall make us strong; this thing is too hard for me; these men built the house; they shall become numerous; I have made; I have commanded.

II. 1. בְּחָכְמָה יִבָּנֶה בָּיִת׃ — 2. אֱכֹל בְּשִׂמְחָה לַחְמֶךָ וּשְׁתֵה בְלֶב־טוֹב יֵינֶךָ׃ — 3. עֵת לִפְרוֹץ וְעֵת לִבְנוֹת עֵת לִבְכּוֹת וְעֵת לִשְׂחוֹק עֵת לַחֲשׁוֹת וְעֵת לְדַבֵּר׃ — 4. וַיַּרְא אֱלֹהִים אֶת־כָּל־אֲשֶׁר עָשָׂה וְהִנֵּה טוֹב מְאֹד׃ — 5. וַיִּבֶן נֹחַ מִזְבֵּחַ לַיהוָה׃ — 6. וַיַּעַשׂ מֹשֶׁה וְאַהֲרֹן כַּאֲשֶׁר צִוָּה יְהוָה אֹתָם כֵּן עָשׂוּ׃ — 7. וַיֹּאמֶר אֱלֹהִים יִקָּווּ הַמַּיִם מִתַּחַת הַשָּׁמַיִם אֶל־מָקוֹם אֶחָד וְתֵרָאֶה הַיַּבָּשָׁה וַיְהִי כֵן׃ — 8. וַיִּגְבְּרוּ הַמַּיִם וַיִּרְבּוּ מְאֹד עַל־הָאָרֶץ וַיְכֻסּוּ כָּל־הֶהָרִים׃ — 9. אֶת־הָאָרֶץ הַטּוֹבָה הַזֹּאת נָתַן אֱלֹהִים לְעַם־יִשְׂרָאֵל׃ — 10. בַּיּוֹם הַהוּא יָדַע יִשְׂרָאֵל כִּי גָדוֹל יְהוָה׃ — 11. מִי (who) רָאָה גִּבּוֹרִים כָּהֵמָּה׃ — 12. וְאֵלֶּה הָלְכוּ מִן־

הָעִיר לִקְרַאת יִשְׂרָאֵל וַיִּהְיוּ לְיִשְׂרָאֵל בַּתָּוֶךְ אֵלֶּה מִזֶּה וְאֵלֶּה מִזֶּה וַיַּכּוּ
(נָכָה) אוֹתָם עַד־בִּלְתִּי הִשְׁאִיר־לָהֶם שָׂרִיד וּפָלִיט׃ — 13. וַיִּשְׁכַּב וַיִּישַׁן
תַּחַת עֵץ אֶחָד וְהִנֵּה־זֶה מַלְאָךְ נֹגֵעַ בּוֹ וַיֹּאמֶר לוֹ קוּם (arise) אֱכוֹל׃

III. 1. And Noah built an altar to the Lord. — 2. And the anger of the Lord was kindled against the people. — 3. And Abraham sent away Hagar (הָגָר), and she went and she wandered in the desert of Beersheba (בְּאֵר שָׁבַע). — 4. And when the queen of Sheba had seen all the wisdom of Solomon and the house which he had built, then she said to the king: Truth was the report that I had heard in my own land. — 5. And Abraham came up from Egypt, he and his wife and all that belonged to him. — 6. And Aaron took the gold from their hand and fashioned it with a graving tool and made it a molten calf, and they said: These are thy gods, O Israel, who brought thee up out of the land of Egypt.

LESSON XIX.

VERBS *LAMEDH-ALEPH* (ל״א).

INTERROGATIVE PARTICLES AND PRONOUNS.

Vocabulary. Verbs.

בָּרָא to create; *Niph.* (*Pi.* cut down).

[חָבָא] *Niph.* & *Hithp.* to withdraw, hide oneself, (thicken); (*Hiph.* hide, conceal); (*Hoph.*).

[חָבָה] *Niph.* to hide oneself.

חָטָא to go wrong, sin; *Pi.* make a sin-offering, purify; *Hithp.*; *Hiph.*

טָמֵא to be unclean; *Niph.* defile oneself; *Pi.* defile, declare unclean; *Pu.*; *Hithp.*

כָּלָא to shut up, restrain; (*Niph.*).

כָּלָה to be complete; *Pi.* complete, completely destroy; (*Pu.*).

מָלֵא to be full, fill; *Niph.* be filled; *Pi.* fill; (*Pu.*; *Hithp.*).

מָצָא to find, attain to; *Niph.*; *Hiph.*

[קָנָא] *Pi.* to be jealous; *Hiph.* provoke to jealousy.

קָנָה to acquire, buy; (*Niph.*; *Hiph.*).

קָרָא to call, proclaim, read; *Niph.*; (*Pu.*).

קָרָא to encounter; (*Niph.*; *Hiph.*).

קָרָה to encounter, meet; (*Niph.*; *Hiph.*).

רָפָא to heal; *Niph.*; *Pi.* repair; (*Hithp.*).

רָפָה to sink, relax; (*Pi.* let drop); (*Hithp.* show oneself slack); *Hiph.* abandon.

שָׂנֵא to hate; (*Niph.*); *Pi.* hate an enemy.

[נָכַר] *Hiph.* to observe; (*Niph.* be recognized; *Pi.* recognize).

פָּשַׁע to rebel, transgress; (*Niph.* be offended).

*דָּלַק to burn, hotly pursue; *Hiph.* inflame.

*חָרַד to be terrified, tremble; *Hiph.* terrify.

[חָרַם] *Hiph.* to devote to extermination, destroy; (*Hoph.*).

שָׁעָה (שָׁאָה) to gaze; (*Hiph.*; *Hithp.*).

עָרַךְ to arrange, set in order; *Niph.*

נָשַׁל to drop off, draw off; (*Pi.*).

צָפָה to watch, spy; *Pi.*

Nouns.

זָכָר (iv) *m. male*
נְקֵבָה (iv) *f. female*
כְּתֹנֶת, כֻּתֹּנֶת (v) *f. tunic*
פֶּשַׁע (v) *m. transgression*
נָעִים (ii) *a. pleasant*
חַטָּאת, constr. חַטַּאת (i) *f. sin, sin-offering*
אֹכֶל (v) *m. food*

אַדִּיר (i) *a. majestic, lofty*
תְּהוֹם (i) *f. & m. abyss, deep sea, depth*
מְעָרָה (i) *f. cave.*
עֶרֶב (v) *m. evening*
עֶלֶם (v) *m. young man.*
עָוֹן (ii) *m. iniquity*
אָכְלָה (v) *f. food, eating*

סָכָל (iv) *m. fool*
חֵרֶם (v) *m. devoted thing (involving destruction)*
כָּלָה (iv) *f. completion, annihilation*
עֵרֶךְ (v) *m. order, valuation, price.*
מַאֲכָל (iv) *m. food*

I. Verbs *Lamedh-Aleph* (Paradigm T).

Verbs *Lamedh-Aleph* are treated like the ordinary strong verb, whenever *Aleph* retains its consonantal value. The irregularities are due to the fact that *Aleph,* being a weak letter, occasionally quiesces in the preceding vowel (2, 3). Most of those verbs have an Imperfect in *a* (Infin. Constr. *ō*, 201).

409. A. *Aleph* retains its consonantal value whenever the last radical of the verb (Paradigms I-L) has a vowel or a vocal *Sh·wa, i. e.* when *Aleph* begins a syllable, *v. g.* מָצְאוּ, יִמְצְאוּ, יִמְצָאֵנִי, מֹצְאִים, *etc.*

410. B. When the last radical of the verb comes at the end of a syllable, *Aleph* quiesces in the preceding vowel which is consequently lengthened, if not already long *(Pathah* to *Qameṣ; Ḥireq* to *Ṣere)* thus:

1. In all cases where *Aleph* is final, *v. g.* מָצָא, for מָצַא; יִמְצָא; נִמְצָא; יִמָּצֵא; הִמְצִיא; יַמְצִיא, *etc.*

411. 2. Before afformatives beginning with a consonant, a) *Aleph* quiesces in *Qameṣ* in Perfect *Qal* of the active verbs, *v. g.* מָצָאתִי, מָצָאתָ, מְצָאתֶם, מָצָאנוּ; b) *Aleph* quiesces in *Ṣere* in Perfect *Qal* of the stative verbs and in the Perfect of all the Derivative Stems, *v. g.* מָלֵאתִי, מָלֵאתָ; נִמְצֵאתָ, הִמְצֵאתִי, *etc.*; c) *Aleph* quiesces in *S·ghol* before the ending נָה of the Imperf. (Indic., Jussive and Imperat.) in all stems (cp. *Lamedh-He*), *v. g.* תִּמְצֶאנָה, תִּמָּצֶאנָה. תַּמְצֶאנָה, תִּתְמַצֶּאנָה, *etc.*

(See Lesson XXII about some very common ל״א verbs which are doubly weak, as יָצָא, *to go out,* נָשָׂא, *to lift,* יָרֵא, *to fear*).

412. C. MIXED FORMS. Verbs ל"א sometimes show some forms borrowed from verbs ל"ה and *vice versa;* thus especially רָפָא and רָפָה; קָרָה and קָרָא, *etc.*

II. Interrogative Sentence.

A. Interrogative Particles and Pronouns.

413. 1. Interrogative particles. A list of the Interrogative particles is given in Lesson xvii, 389; a few remarks on the vocalization of the interrogative הֲ may be made here:

a) It is הֲ before non-gutturals and *Resh* with a full vowel, *v. g.* הֲמָצָאתָ, *hast thou found?* הֲרָדַפְתִּי, *have I pursued?*

b) It is הַ before all consonants with *Sh·wa* (48) and before gutturals with vowels other than *Qameṣ* or *Ḥateph Qameṣ, v. g.* הַמְקַנֵּא אַתָּה, *art thou jealous?* הַאַף, *also?* הַאֵלֵךְ, *shall I go?*

In about ten passages, perhaps owing to a confusion with the article, הַ is followed by *Daghesh Forte, v. g.* Gen. xvii, 17 .

c) It is הֶ before gutturals with *Qameṣ* or *Ḥateph Qameṣ* (not merely like the article הֶ (113) before חָ or unaccented הָ and עָ), *v. g.* הֶהָיְתָה, *was it? did it happen?* הֶחָכָם הוּא, *was he a wise man?*

414. 2. Interrogative Pronouns and Adjectives.

a) מִי, *who?* generally used of persons (invariable), מִי אַתָּה, *who art thou?*

b) אֵי־זֶה, *which, what?* adj., אֵי־זֶה הַדֶּרֶךְ, *which is the way?*

c) מַה־, מַה, מָה, מֶה, *what?* used of things. It is vocalized in various ways according to the nature of the following consonant (cp. article, 87, 113; interrogative הֲ, 413) and according to the place it occupies in the sentence.

415. *α*) In close connection with what follows (connected by *Maqqeph* or marked with a conjunctive accent), it is:

מַה־ with *Daghesh Forte* in the following consonant, except gutturals and *Resh, v. g.* מַה־מָּצָאתָ, *what didst thou find?* The ה may be dropped and מַ prefixed to the following word, *v. g.* מַלָּכֶם, *what have you?* (*what is to you?*); מַזֶּה, *what is this?*

מַה־, מַה, with Implicit *Daghesh Forte* before ה and often before ח with any vowel but *Qameṣ, v. g.* מַה־הוּא, *what is he?* מַה־חֶפְצוֹ, *what is his pleasure?* מַה חַטָּאתִי, *what is my sin?*

מָה־, מָה, without *Daghesh Forte* always before the article הַ, and הֵמָּה, הֵנָּה, *they*; generally before א, ר, and often before ע with vowels other than *Qameṣ, v. g.* מָה־הַדָּבָר הַזֶּה, *what is this thing?* מָה־אֲדַבֵּר, *what shall I say?* מָה אֹמַר, *what shall I say?*

מֶה־, מֶה, without *Daghesh Forte* before הָ, חָ, עָ, and often before ח and ע even with vowels other than *Qameṣ, v. g.* מֶה־עָשָׂה, *what did he do?* מֶה־עָשִׂיתָ, *what hast thou done?*

416. β) Not in close connection with what follows:

מָה, always in a Pause and regularly with the principal disjunctive accents, *v. g.* וְנַחְנוּ מָה, *and what are we?* lit. *and we, what?* Ex. xvi, 8; עַל־מָה הִכִּיתָ אֶת־אֲתֹנְךָ, *wherefore hast thou smitten thy she-ass?* Num. xxii, 32.

מֶה, with smaller disjunctive accents when far removed from the main accent, *v. g.* מֶה מִשְׁפַּט הָאִישׁ אֲשֶׁר עָלָה לִקְרַאתְכֶם, *what manner of a man (was he) that came up to meet you?* (accent *Y.thibh*) 2 K. i, 7.

In combination with בְּ, כְּ, לְ, the forms are בַּמֶּה, & בַּמָּה; כַּמָּה & כַּמֶּה; לָמָּה and, mostly before gutturals, לָמָה.

B. Syntax.

Examples:

1. הֲתוֹדֵךְ מַחֲזִיק בָּם, *wilt thou hold them still?* הֲתֵלְכִי עִם־הָאִישׁ הַזֶּה, *wilt thou go with this man?* הֲלֹא כָל־הָאָרֶץ לְפָנֶיךָ, *is not all the land before thee?* בֶּן־מִי־זֶה הָעָלֶם, *whose son is this young man?* הֲשֹׁמֵר אָחִי אָנֹכִי, *am I my brother's keeper?* הַאַחֵיכֶם יָבֹאוּ לַמִּלְחָמָה וְאַתֶּם תֵּשְׁבוּ פֹה, *shall you stay here while your brethren go to the fight?* — 2. הֲלָנוּ אַתָּה אִם־לְצָרֵינוּ, *art thou for us or for our enemies?* — 3. לָדַעַת הֲיִשְׁמְעוּ, *to know whether they would hearken;* לֹא יָדַעְתִּי מִי עָשָׂה, *I know not who did it.* — 4. מִי־אֵפוֹא הוּא, *who then is he?* — 5. הֲשָׁלוֹם לוֹ, שָׁלוֹם, *is he well? he is.*

1. Direct questions.

417. a) The interrogation may be made without any interrogative particle, by the mere inflection of the voice; this is particularly the case in animated speech, *v. g.* וְאַתָּה תִּירָשֶׁנּוּ, *and shouldst thou possess him?* Jud. XI, 23; עוֹדְךָ מַחֲזִיק בָּם, *wilt thou hold them still?* Ex. XI, 2.

418. b) However, a simple affirmative question is generally introduced by הֲ, sometimes elliptically by אִם, properly *if*, the first clause of an indirect question being understood (*art thou?* = [*tell us*] *if thou art*), *v. g.* הֲתֵלְכִי עִם־הָאִישׁ הַזֶּה, *wilt thou go with this man?* Gen. XXIV, 58; אִם־תִּהְיֶה רָעָה בְּעִיר, *shall evil befall a city?* Amos III, 6.

419. c) A simple negative question is expressed by הֲלֹא, and by הַאֵין when the existence itself of the subject is questioned, *v. g.* הֲלֹא כָל־הָאָרֶץ לְפָנֶיךָ, *is not all the land before thee?* Gen. XIII, 9; וַיֹּאמֶר יְהוֹשָׁפָט הַאֵין פֹּה נָבִיא לַיהוָה עוֹד, *and Josaphat said, Is there not still here a prophet of the Lord?* 1 K. XXII, 7.

420. d) When another interrogative particle or an interrogative pronoun is used, הֲ is of course left out. The pronouns מִי and מָה can be used in oblique cases, *v. g.* בַּת־מִי אַתְּ, *whose daughter art thou?* Gen. XXIV, 23; בֶּן־מִי־זֶה הָעָלֶם, *whose son is this young man?* 1 Sam. XVII, 56. Note that when direct object, מִי always takes the directive particle אֵת, but מָה never does, *v. g.* אֶת־מִי אַעֲלֶה־לָּךְ, *whom shall I bring up unto thee?* 1 Sam. XXVIII, 11; מֶה עָשִׂיתָ, *what hast thou done?* Gen. IV, 10.

מָה is also used adverbially in an exclamatory sentence, *v. g.* הִנֵּה מַה־טּוֹב וּמַה־נָּעִים שֶׁבֶת אַחִים גַּם־יָחַד, *ecce quam bonum et quam iucundum habitare fratres in unum!* Ps. CXXXIII, 1.

421. e) Very often an interrogation is only rhetorical for a positive and emphatic statement; הֲ (and sometimes אִם) is used when a negative answer is expected or suggested, and הֲלֹא when an assertion is intended, הֲשֹׁמֵר אָחִי אָנֹכִי, *am I my brother's keeper?* Gen. IV, 9; הֲלֹא־הֵם כְּתוּבִים, *are they not written?* cp. הִנָּם כְּתוּבִים, *behold, they are written,* 1 K. XI, 41; XIV, 19.

422. f) Two clauses are often co-ordinated in Hebrew after one interrogative particle, when in our modern languages they would be subordinated, *v. g.* הַאַחֵיכֶם יָבֹאוּ לַמִּלְחָמָה וְאַתֶּם תֵּשְׁבוּ פֹה, *shall your brethren go to the war and shall ye sit here? i. e. shall ye sit here while your brethren go to the war?* Num. XXXII, 6; cp. 258.

2. Disjunctive Questions.

423. A disjunctive question is introduced by הֲ in the first clause, and אִם or וְאִם in the second (seldom by אוֹ or וְאוֹ); when negative,

אִם־לֹא (or אִם אַיִן, if יֵשׁ is in the first clause) is used in the second clause, *v. g.* הֲלָנוּ אַתָּה אִם־לְצָרֵינוּ, *art thou for us or for our adversaries?* Jos. v, 13.

3. Indirect Questions.

424. Indirect questions, whether simple or disjunctive resemble the direct questions in all points; in the simple clause, however, אִם is more common here than in direct interrogation, see 418. לָדַעַת הֲיִשְׁמְעוּ אֶת־מִצְוֹת יְהוָֹה, *to know whether they would hearken unto the commandments of Jehovah,* Jud. III, 4; לְכוּ דִרְשׁוּ . . . אִם אֶחְיֶה מֵחֳלִי זֶה, *go, inquire . . . whether I shall recover of this sickness,* 2 K. I, 2; וְהָאִישׁ מִשְׁתָּאֵה לָהּ לָדַעַת הַהִצְלִיחַ יְהוָֹה דַּרְכּוֹ אִם־לֹא, *and the man looked at her to know whether God had made his journey prosperous or not,* Gen. XXIV, 21; לֹא יָדַעְתִּי מִי עָשָׂה, *I know not who did it,* Gen. XXI, 26.

425. 4. Greater vividness is given to a question by adding זֶה, זאת, הוּא or אֵפוֹא to the interrogative particle or pronoun, *v. g.* מִי־אֵפוֹא הוּא, *who then is he?* Gen. XXVII, 33.

426. 5. The answer to a question is made by repeating the emphatic word with the corresponding change of person if necessary *v. g.* הֲתֵלְכִי עִם־הָאִישׁ הַזֶּה וַתֹּאמֶר אֵלֵךְ, *wilt thou go with this man? and she said, I will (go);* הֲשָׁלוֹם לוֹ, שָׁלוֹם, *is he well? yes,* lit. *[he is] well.*

EXERCISES.

I. Did he go? Didst thou not find? Will he be clean? Didst thou complete? Is this a thing devoted to destruction? it is. Is this the tunic? What hast thou done? Where have they hidden themselves? Whither shall I flee? Whom shall I call? Why should she be jealous? On what account did you rebel? Did you go or not? Whose son laughed yesterday? Didst thou send him or me? Have you sinned against God? we have. Is there peace in the land? there is.

II. 1. וַיִּבְרָא אֱלֹהִים אֶת־הָאָדָם בְּצַלְמוֹ בְּצֶלֶם אֱלֹהִים בָּרָא אֹתוֹ זָכָר וּנְקֵבָה בָּרָא אֹתָם׃ — 2. הֲלוֹא אָב אֶחָד לְכֻלָּנוּ הֲלוֹא אֵל אֶחָד בְּרָאָנוּ׃ — 3. עֵת לַהֲרוֹג וְעֵת לִרְפּוֹא עֵת לֶאֱהֹב וְעֵת לִשְׂנֹא׃ — 4. בַּיָּמִים הָהֵם וּבָעֵת הַהִיא נְאֻם־יְהוָֹה יְבֻקַּשׁ אֶת־עֲוֹן יִשְׂרָאֵל וְאֵינֶנּוּ וְאֶת־חַטֹּאת

יְהוּדָה וְלֹא תִמְּצֶאנָה׃ — 5. וַיְשַׁלְּחוּ בְנֵי־יַעֲקֹב אֶת־כְּתֹנֶת הַפַּסִּים אֶל־
אֲבִיהֶם וַיֹּאמְרוּ זֹאת מָצָאנוּ הַכֶּר־נָא הַכְּתֹנֶת בִּנְךָ הִיא אִם־לֹא׃ —
6. וַיַּעַן יַעֲקֹב וַיֹּאמֶר לְלָבָן (Laban) מַה־פִּשְׁעִי וּמַה חַטָּאתִי כִּי דָלַקְתָּ
אַחֲרָי׃ — 7. יְהוָה אֲדֹנֵינוּ מָה־אַדִּיר שִׁמְךָ בְּכָל־הָאָרֶץ׃ — 8. וְהַחָכְמָה
מֵאַיִן תִּמָּצֵא וְאֵי־זֶה מְקוֹם בִּינָה׃ לֹא־יָדַע אֱנוֹשׁ עֶרְכָּהּ וְלֹא תִמָּצֵא בְּאֶרֶץ
הַחַיִּים׃ תְּהוֹם אָמַר לֹא בִי־הִיא וְיָם אָמַר אֵין עִמָּדִי׃

III. 1. And they said: The man asked us persistently (Inf. abs.) concerning ourselves and concerning our kindred, saying, Is your father yet alive? have you [another] brother? and we answered him according to the tenor of these words; could we know in any wise (Inf. abs.) that he would say, Bring your brother down. — 2. Heal me, o Lord, and I shall be healed; save me, and I shall be saved. — 3. Let the whole earth be filled with his glory. — 4. Whosoever does touch them when they are dead, shall be unclean until the evening. — 5. And Saul said to Samuel, I have sinned because I have transgressed the commandment of Jehovah and thy words. — 6. Is not all the land before thee? — 7. And they said unto him, Where is Sarah, thy wife? and he said, Behold, in the tent. — 8. Who does not know among all these, that the hand of Jehovah has wrought this? — 9. Who is like Thee among the gods, O Jehovah?

LESSON XX.

VERBS *'AYIN-'AYIN* (ע"ע). INDEFINITE PRONOUNS. PRONOMINAL SUBSTITUTES.

Vocabulary. Verbs.

אָרַר to curse; (*Niph.* & *Hoph.*) be cursed; *Pi.* lay under a curse.

קָלַל* to be slight, simple; *Niph.* appear slight; *Pi.* curse; (*Pu.*); *Hiph.* lighten; (*Pilpel*, shake; *Hithpalpel*).

חָנַן† to show favor, be gracious; (*Po'el*); *Hithpo'el*, implore favor; (*Hoph.*).

גָּלַל to roll; (*Niph.*; *Po'al*; *Hithpo'el*; *Pilpel*, *Hithpalpel*; *Hiph.*).

סָבַב to turn about, surround; *Niph.* turn oneself; (*Pi.*); *Po'el*, encompass; *Hiph'il.*

מָרַר* to be bitter; *Pi.* & *Hiph.* make bitter, show bitterness; (*Hithpalpel*).

רָבַב to become many, great (see רבה, Lesson xviii).

הָלַל (to be boastful); *Pi.* praise; *Pu.*; *Hithpa.*; *Po'el*, make fool of; *Po'al*; *Hithpo'el.*

חָלַל to bore, pierce; (*Pi.*; *Pu.*; *Po'el*).

[חָלַל] *Pi.* to defile, profane; *Niph.* defile oneself, be defiled; (*Pu*); *Hiph.* begin.

כָּתַת to beat, crush; *Pi.* and (*Hiph.*) id.; (*Pu.* and *Hoph.* be crushed).

[עָלַל] *Po'el*, to act severely; (*Po'al*); *Hithpa'el*, busy oneself, deal wantonly; (*Hithpo'el*).

סָרַר to be stubborn, rebellious.

צָרַר† to bind, be narrow, distressed; *Pu.*; *Hiph.*

צָרַר to show hostility towards.

רָעַע to break, be broken; *Hithpo'el.*

רָעַע* to be evil, bad; (*Niph.*); *Hiph.* do evil, do an injury.

שָׁחַח to bow, be bowed down; (*Hiph.* lay low; *Hithpo'el*) (see שָׁחָה, Lesson xviii).

תָּמַם to be complete; *Hiph.*

[פָּרַר] *Hiph.* to break, frustrate; *Hoph.*

פָּרַד (to divide); *Niph.*; (*Pi.*; *Pu.*); *Hithp.* *Hiph.*

אָשַׁם / אָשֵׁם to offend; become guilty; (*Niph.*; *Hiph.*).

חָפַר to dig, search for.

חָפֵר† to be ashamed; *Hiph.* display shame.

Vocabulary. Verbs.

חָגַג to keep as a feast.

שָׁמֵם to be desolate, appalled; (*Niph.*); *Po'el*, appal; (*Hithpo'el*); *Hiph.* appal, devastate; (*Hoph.*).

בָּתַר to cut in two; *Pi.* id.

רָחַם (to love); *Pi.* have compassion; *Pu.*

מָנָה to count; *Niph.*; *Pi.* appoint.

Nouns.

אִי (iii) *m.* {*region, coast, island*}

עָצֵל (iv) *a. sluggish*

בֶּתֶר (v) *m. part, piece*

לָשׁוֹן (וֹת) (ii) *m.* & *f. tongue*

כִּכָּר (iv) *f. talent, district, loaf*

כַּר (iii) *m. he-lamb, battering-ram*

רָשׁ (i) *pt. poor*

צִיר (i) *m. messenger; pang; hinge*

קַל (iii) *a light, swift, simple* (*Qal*)

שַׁדַּי, אֵל שַׁדַּי, *pr. n. the Almighty*

דֶּלֶת (v) *f.* (*m.*) *door, gate* (*Daleth*)

מָאוֹר (וֹת) (ii) *m. luminary*

אָשָׁם (iv) *m. offence, guilt.*

I. Verbs *'Ayin-'Ayin* (Paradigm U).

The weakness and irregularity of these verbs arises from the fact that the second and third radical letters are identical, and that consequently they are often contracted. The main principles of contraction seem to be the following:

1. The second radical is contracted with the third whenever it is or has become vowelless, and often when it should be sounded with vocal *Sh'wa*, *v. g.* סַבָּה, for סָבְבָה; סַבּוּ, for סָבְבוּ; see below, 431.

2. Whenever the first radical is without a full vowel, the second radical yields its vowel to it and is itself contracted with the third, *v. g.* סֹב, for סְבֹב; יָסֹב, for יִסְבֹב, *etc.*

3. When neither of these principles applies the forms remain uncontracted, except in *Qal* Perfect where the contraction is found often in the third person singular and regularly with afformatives beginning with a consonant, *v. g.* צָרַר and צַר; סַבּוֹתָ, *etc.*

A. Uncontracted Forms.

According to the principles just given, the contraction does not take place:

427. 1. in the intensive stems *Pi'el*, *Pu'al*, *Hithpa'el*, *v. g.* חִלֵּל, *he profaned;* חֻלַּל, *he was profaned, etc.* These forms are entirely regular: חִלְּלָה, חִלַּלְתָּ, *etc.*

Pi'el occurs in about 25 of these verbs, *Pu'al* in about 15, and *Hithpa'el* in 5 or 6.

428. 2. in the forms *Pô'el, Pô'al, Hithpô'el,* which, in this class of verbs, are often used as substitutes for *Pi'el, Pu'al* and *Hithpa'el.* These forms are also regularly inflected, *v. g.* סוֹבֵב, *he encompassed;* סוֹבְבָה, סוֹבַבְתָּ, סוֹבַבְתִּי, *etc.*

The forms *Pô'el, Pô'al, Hithpô'el* are found as regular formations for the ordinary strong verb in some Semitic languages, and indicate the effort towards an end; hence they are called 'Conative' (171). *Pô'el* occurs in about 20 verbs, *Pô'al* in about 5, and *Hithpô'el* in about 25.

429. 3. in the forms *Pilpel* and *Hithpalpel* obtained by the repetition of the primitively biliteral stem and generally indicating repetition. They are used as substitutes for *Pi'el, etc.,* and are regularly inflected, *v. g.* גִּלְגֵּל, *he rolled,* from גָּלַל; גִּלְגְּלוּ; גִּלְגַּלְתִּי, *etc.*

Pilpel and *Hithpalpel* occur in over 10 verbs of this class.

430. 4. in the Infinitive absolute, and participles of *Qal, v. g.* סָבוֹב; סָבוּב; סוֹבֵב.

431. In the 3 p. s. (m. & f.) and 3 p. pl. *Qal* (sometimes also Inf. Constr.) of about 25 verbs, the contraction is not found, *v. g.* צָרַר, צָרֲרָה, צָרֲרוּ. Sometimes the contracted form occurs side by side with the uncontracted form; the contracted form has generally an intransitive, the uncontracted form a transitive meaning, *v. g.* צָרַר, *he bound;* צָרֲרוּ; but צָרָה, (it) *was narrow.*

432. In the uncontracted forms, the second radical often receives a *Hateph Pathah* instead of a simple Vocal *Sh'wa* to safeguard the pronunciation, *v. g.* צָרֲרוּ, הַלְלוּ, *praise ye;* the same is true of the nouns in which the contraction does not take place, *v. g.* קִלְלַת, *the curse of . . .*

B. Contracted Forms.

433. All the other forms are contracted and the last radical marked with *Daghesh Forte* unless it is final (22, cp. 261 ff.); the vowel that precedes *Daghesh Forte* may be long if the sharpened syllable is accented, but it must be shortened if that syllable becomes unaccented (53).

434. 1. Vowel of the Stem. a) As a rule, the contracted monosyllabic stem has the same vowel as the last syllable of the strong verb (characteristic vowel, 185, 201), *v. g.* Perf. *Qal* סַב; Inf. Constr. סֹב; Imperf. Indic. יָסֹב;. *Hoph.* יוּסַב, *etc.*

Stative verbs have *a* in Imperf. *Qal, v. g.* יֵקַל.

435. b) In *Niph*. Imperf. (Imperat., Indic.) the vowel is *a* instead of *e, v. g.* Perf. נָסַב; Imperf. Indic. יִסַּב, for יִנָּסֵב; Imperat. הִסַּב. In some verbs, the Perf. *Niph.* has *ē, v. g.* נָמֵס, from מָסַס, *to melt.*

c) *Hiph'il* has *ē* instead of *î* in an accented syllable, which is shortened to *ĭ* in an unaccented syllable; *ē* and *ĭ* are sometimes replaced by *a* under the influence of a gutt., *v. g.* הֵסֵב, הֲסִבֹּנִי, הֲסִבּוֹתָ, הֵפֵר.

436. d) The Jussive has the same form as the Indic. After *Waw Consecutivum*, the tone is drawn backward except in a pause (247), and the vowels *ō* and *ē*, being in an unaccented closed syllable, are shortened to *ŏ* and *ǣ* respectively (248), *v. g.* יָסֹב; Juss. יָסֹב, but וַיָּסָב P. וַיָּסֹב; *Hiph.* יָסֵב, וַיָּסֶב; *Hoph.* וַיּוּסַב, 247; see further under 439.

437. 2. Preformatives and Stem-formative Prefixes. When Preformatives, *etc.*, are pretonic in an open syllable, they must be lengthened (134, 136), *ă* to *ā* (Imperf. *Qal* and *Hiph'il*, generally Perfect *Niph'al*), *ĭ* to *ē* (Imperf. *Qal* of stative verbs, Perf. and Part. *Hiph.*), *ŭ* to *û* (*Hoph.*). These, except *û*, are only tone-long and consequently are volatilized as often as they are not pretonic (135), Ex.: Imperf. *Qal* יָסֹב, נָסֹב; Imperf. *Hiph.* יָסֵב, תָּסֵב; Part. *Niph.* נָסַב; Imperf. *Qal* of stative verbs, יֵקַל, תֵּקַל; Perf. *Hiph.* הֵסֵב, הֲסִבּוֹתָ; Part. *Hiph.* מֵסֵב, *Hoph'al,* הוּסַב, יוּסַב, הוּסַבּוֹתָ

438. 3. Afformatives. a) In the contracted forms, the vowel-afformatives ָה, וּ, ִי remain generally unaccented, the exceptions occurring mostly after *Waw Consecutivum* of the Perfect, *v. g.* תַּמּוּ, יָסֹבּוּ, הֵסַבָּה, תְּסֻבּוּ; but וְקַלּוּ.

b) In the contracted forms, consonantal afformatives are preceded by an accented connective long vowel וֹ, in the Perfects and ֶי in the Imperfects, so that instead of תָ, תִי, נוּ, נָה, *etc.*, we have וֹתָ, וֹתִי, וֹנוּ, ֶינָה. The afformatives תֶם and תֶן, however, retain the tone וֹתֶם, וֹתֶן (Paradigm U).

439. C. Aramaïzing Forms.

In the Imperf. Indic. (Juss.) of *Qal*, *Hiph.* and *Hoph.*, some verbs occasionally take a *Daghesh Forte* in the first radical as if derived from a root *Pe-Nun;* in that case, the preformative remains short, the last radical is often not doubled, and the connective vowel is not used (Paradigm U). Besides, the tone cannot be drawn backward after *Wāw consecutivum* (38) and *ō* and *ē* remain long. Among these verbs may be mentioned סָבַב, כָּתַת, תָּמַם, דָּמַם (be dumb), מָרַר, שָׁמֵם, חָלַל, *etc., v. g.* יִסֹּב, יִסַּב, וַיִּסֹּב, וַיִּסֶּב, וַיִּכְּתוּ, יִכַּתּוּ.

II. Indefinite Pronouns.

440. A. **Morphology.** 1. The Interrogative pronouns מִי and מָה are used also as indefinite pronouns or adjectives in the sense of *whoever, whatever, anything, v. g.* וַיֹּאמֶר משֶׁה מִי לַיהוָה אֵלָי, *and Moses said, Whoever is for Jehovah, [let him come] to me,* Ex. xxxii, 26; מִי יִמְצָא, *whoever finds.* In connection with negatives, מָה may be translated by *not . . . anything, nothing whatever, v. g.* לֹא יָדַעְתִּי מָה, *I know nothing at all [about it],* 2 Sam. xviii, 29.

441. 2. כֹּל, כָּל־ (*totality*).

a) In the construct state, α) כֹּל, followed by a determinate noun, means *all the, the whole, v. g.* כָּל־הָאָרֶץ, *the whole earth;* β) with an indeterminate noun it is equivalent to English *any, of all kinds, every, each,* and with a negative *none, not . . . any, v. g.* אַל־תֹּאכְלִי כָּל־טָמֵא, *eat not of any unclean thing,* Jud. xiii, 4; γ) followed by אֲשֶׁר it means *all that which, all those who, any one who, whosoever, whatsoever*; cp. כֹּל in the same sense with a participle (307); with suffixes, see 483.

b) In the absolute state, כֹּל corresponds to English *all, everything, anything,* and with a negative, *nothing, not, . . anything, v. g.* נָתַתִּי לָכֶם אֶת־כֹּל, *I have given you everything,* Gen. ix, 3; וְלָרָשׁ אֵין־כֹּל, *and the poor man had nothing,* 2 Sam. xii, 3; לֹא־תֶחְסַר כֹּל בָּהּ, *thou shalt not lack anything in it (the land),* Deut. viii, 9.

442. B. The **indefinite personal subject** *one, they, men* (*French on*) is expressed:

1. by the 3 p. m. s., *v. g.* קָרָא שְׁמָהּ בָּבֶל, *they called its name Babel,* Gen. xi, 9;

2. by the 3 p. m. pl., *v. g.* מֵעוֹלָם לֹא שָׁמְעוּ, *one has never heard,* Is. lxiv, 3;

3. more rarely by the 2 m. s., *v. g.* לֹא־תָבוֹא שָׁמָּה, *one cannot come* (בוא) *thither,* Is. vii, 25;

4. by the plural participle, *v. g.* וְאֶת־כָּל־נָשֶׁיךָ וְאֶת־בָּנֶיךָ מוֹצִאִים אֶל־הַכַּשְׂדִּים *and they shall bring out* (יָצָא, go out) *all thy wives and thy children to the Chaldeans,* Jer. xxxviii, 23;

5. by the impersonal passive (359), *v. g.* אָז הוּחַל לִקְרֹא בְּשֵׁם יְהוָה, *then men began to call upon the name of Jehovah,* Gen. iv, 26;

6. sometimes by אִישׁ, אָדָם, *etc.*; cp. 444.

443. C. The **impersonal pronoun 'it'** as subject of a verb is generally left out, thus especially when *it* is the anticipative subject of a verb the real subject of which is a word or expression that follows, *v. g.* וַיִּחַר לְיַעֲקֹב, *and it became hot to Jacob, i. e. and Jacob became angry,* Gen. xxxi, 36; לֹא־טוֹב הֱיוֹת הָאָדָם לְבַדּוֹ, *it is not good that man should be alone,* lit. *the being of man alone is not good,* Gen. ii, 18; cp. 404.

III. Substitutes for Pronouns.

444. 1. אִישׁ (*man*) *some one, any one, each, every* (with negatives אִישׁ . . . לֹא, אַל . . . אִישׁ *nobody*), *v. g.* אִם יוּכַל אִישׁ לִמְנוֹת, *if any one can count,* Gen. xiii, 16.

2. אָדָם (*man*), is used in the same sense, *v. g.* אָדָם כִּי יַקְרִיב, *if any one brings,* Lev. i, 2.

3. נֶפֶשׁ (*soul*), same sense, *v. g.* נֶפֶשׁ כִּי תֶחֱטָא, *if any one sins,* Lev. iv, 2. נֶפֶשׁ is also used as a reflexive pronoun, *v. g.* קֹנֶה־לֵּב אֹהֵב נַפְשׁוֹ, *he that possesses wisdom* (*heart*) *loves himself* (*his own soul*), Prov. xix, 8.

4. דָּבָר (*word, thing*), *something, anything* (with negative, *nothing*), *v. g.* הֲיִפָּלֵא מֵיְהוָה דָּבָר, *could anything be too hard for the Lord?* Gen. xviii, 14.

כֹּל often precedes אִישׁ, אָדָם, נֶפֶשׁ, in the sense of *everybody, anybody* (with negative, *nobody*), and דָּבָר, in the sense of *everything, anything.*

5. מְאוּמָה (*something*) is used mostly with negatives, *v. g.* אַל־תִּשְׁלַח יָדְךָ אֶל־הַנַּעַר וְאַל־תַּעַשׂ לוֹ מְאוּמָה, *lay not thy hand upon the lad, neither do thou anything unto him,* Gen. xxii, 12.

6. The indeterminate plural of some nouns denoting time often means *some, a few, v. g.* יָמִים, *some days;* שָׁנִים, *a few years.* Sometimes אֲחָדִים, *some,* is added, *v. g.* יָמִים אֲחָדִים, *a certain number of days,* Gen. xxvii, 44.

7. The reciprocal (sometimes distributive) is expressed by אִישׁ . . . אָחִיו; אִישׁ . . . אִישׁ; הָאֶחָד . . . הָאֶחָד; זֶה . . . זֶה; *a man . . . his brother;* אִישׁ . . . רֵעֵהוּ, *a man . . . his companion, his friend;* אִישׁ . . . קְרוֹבוֹ, *a man . . . his neighbor;* אִשָּׁה . . . אֲחוֹתָהּ, *a woman . . . her sister;* אִשָּׁה . . . רְעוּתָהּ, *a woman . . . her friend, v. g.* וְלֹא קָרַב זֶה אֶל־זֶה כָּל־הַלָּיְלָה, *and the one came not near the other all the night,* Ex. xiv, 20; וַיַּךְ הָאֶחָד אֶת הָאֶחָד, *and the one smote the other,*

cp. 2 Sam. xiv, 6; הִרְגוּ אִישׁ־אֶת־אָחִיו וְאִישׁ אֶת־רֵעֵהוּ וְאִישׁ אֶת־קְרֹבוֹ, *slay every man his brother, and every man his friend, and every man his neighbor*, Ex. xxxii, 27.

8. The reflexive is generally expressed by one of the reflexive Stems (170 ff.; 330); sometimes by נֶפֶשׁ, *soul*, or לֵב, *heart*, with proper suffix, *v. g.* וַיֹּאמֶר אֱלֹהִים אֶל־לִבּוֹ, *and God said to himself*, Gen. viii, 21.

9. עֶצֶם, (*bone substance*) is used in the sense of *self, selfsame, very same*, in reference to things, *v. g.* בְּעֶצֶם הַיּוֹם הַזֶּה, *in that selfsame day*, Gen. vii, 13.

EXERCISES.

I. He shall surround; I shall curse; thou hast profaned; they have acted severely; she was bitter; he shall be bitter; they shall be ashamed; roll ye; they became numerous; who is cursed? Any one who bows; whoever is rebellious (part.); whoever has shown hostility to us shall be crushed; he shall encompass me; thou hast done an injury; did you find anything? We found nothing; thou shalt not curse anybody; if any one has compassion on the poor, he shall be blessed; and God has shown favor to His people; he devastated the land; and he began to count; can any one count?

II. 1. וַיֹּאמֶר אֱלֹהִים אֶל־בִּלְעָם לֹא תֵלֵךְ עִמָּהֶם וְלֹא תָאֹר אֶת־הָעָם
כִּי בָרוּךְ הוּא׃ — 2. אַל־תִּקְרֶאנָה לִי נָעֳמִי (Naomi) קְרֶאןָ לִי מָרָה כִּי־
הֵמַר שַׁדַּי לִי מְאֹד׃ — 3. הַדֶּלֶת תִּסּוֹב עַל־צִירָהּ וְעָצֵל עַל־מִטָּתוֹ׃ —
4. רָחֲקָה מִמֶּנּוּ הַיְשׁוּעָה כִּי רַבּוּ פְשָׁעֵינוּ׃ — 5. נֶפֶשׁ אֲשֶׁר תִּגַּע בְּכָל־
דָּבָר טָמֵא אוֹ בְנִבְלַת חַיָּה טְמֵאָה אוֹ בְּנִבְלַת בְּהֵמָה טְמֵאָה וְהוּא טָמֵא
וְאָשֵׁם׃ — 6. הֵחֵל הָאָדָם לָרֹב עַל־פְּנֵי הָאֲדָמָה׃ — 7. בְּתוֹכִי יִשְׁתּוֹמֵם
לִבִּי׃ — 8. וְחַנֹּתִי אֶת־אֲשֶׁר אָחֹן וְרִחַמְתִּי אֶת־אֲשֶׁר אֲרַחֵם׃ — 9. וַיָּגֶל
יַעֲקֹב אֶת־הָאֶבֶן מֵעַל פִּי הַבְּאֵר׃ — 10. וַיִּבְחַר־לוֹ לוֹט (Lot) אֵת כָּל־כִּכַּר
הַיַּרְדֵּן וַיִּסַּע לוֹט מִקֶּדֶם וַיִּפָּרְדוּ אִישׁ מֵעַל אָחִיו׃ — 11. עוֹלֵל לְאֹיְבַי
כַּאֲשֶׁר עוֹלַלְתָּ לִי עַל כָּל פְּשָׁעָי׃ — 12. וַיִּקַּח־לוֹ אֶת־כָּל־אֵלֶּה וַיְבַתֵּר אֹתָם
בַּתָּוֶךְ וַיִּתֵּן אִישׁ־בִּתְרוֹ לִקְרַאת רֵעֵהוּ׃ — 13. הֲיֵשׁ דָּבָר מֵאֵת־יְהוָֹה
וַיֹּאמֶר יֵשׁ׃

III. 1. Turn thy way to the Lord and trust in Him. — 2. I shall bless those that bless thee and I shall curse him that curses thee and in thee shall all the families of the earth be blessed. — 3. And this day shall be unto you for a memorial and you shall keep it a feast to the Lord; throughout your generations, you shall keep it a feast [by] an ordinance forever. — 4. The soul of the wicked desireth evil, his neighbor is not favored in his eyes. — 5. And they rolled the stone from the mouth of the well and watered the sheep. — 6. By these (מֵאֵלֶּה) were the islands of the nations divided in their lands, every one after his tongue, after their families. — 7. Speak unto the children of Israel and say unto them, If any man of you brings an oblation to the Lord, of the cattle of the herd and of the flock you shall bring your oblation. — 8. And Laban said, What shall I give thee? and Jacob said, Thou shalt not give me anything. — 9. You shall not afflict any widow or fatherless child. — 10. Nothing failed (נָפַל) of any good thing which the Lord had spoken to the house of Israel.

LESSON XXI.

VERBS *'AYIN-WAW.* *'AYIN-YODH.*
VERBAL IDEAS as COMPLEMENTARY OBJECT of a Verb.

Vocabulary. *Verbs.*

שׁוּב to turn back, return; *Polel* & *Hiph.* bring back, restore (*Polal*) *Hoph.*

בּוֹא to come, come in, go in; *Hiph.* bring; *Hoph.*

קוּם to arise, stand up; *Pi'el*, confirm; (*Polel*) & *Hiph.* raise up, erect, build; (*Hithpolel*, *Hoph'al*).

נוּס to flee, escape; (*Polel*, drive); (*Hithpolel*); *Hiph.* put to flight.

[כּוּן] *Hiph.* & *Polel*, to setup, prepare; *Niph.* (*Polal*, *Hithpolel*, & *Hoph-'al*, be established, be ready).

שׂוּר סוּר to turn aside, depart; *Hiph.* remove; *Hoph.*

גּוּר to sojourn; (*Hithpolel*).

נוּעַ to quiver, tremble, totter; (*Niph.*); *Hiph.* cause to totter.

טוֹב to be pleasing, good; (*Hiph.*) (this verb occurs only in *Qal* Perfect, Imperat., Inf. Constr. and sometimes *Hiph.*; see יָטַב, Lesson **xv**).

שִׂים שׂוּם to put, place, transform; *Hiph.*; (*Hoph.*).

מוּת to die; *Hiph.* kill; *Hoph.*

נוּחַ to rest; *Hiph.* cause to rest, place, put, leave; *Hoph.*

דִּין to judge; *Niph.*

בִּין to discern, understand; *Niph.* be intelligent; (*Polel* & *Hithpolel*, consider diligently; *Hiph.* understand, give understanding.)

לִיץ to scorn; *Hiph.* deride; (*Pol.*; *Hithpol.*)

רוּם to be high, exalted; *Polel*, rear, extol; (*Polel*, *Hithpol.*); *Hiph.* raise, erect, offer; (*Hoph.*).

בּוֹשׁ to be ashamed; *Polel*, delay; *Hiph.* put to shame.

בָּעָה to inquire, trouble, cause to boil up; (*Niph.*).

אָדַר (*Niph.* to be glorious; *Hiph.* make glorious).

רָעַשׁ to quake; (*Niph.*); *Hiph.*

[פָּלַל] *Pi'el*, to mediate; *Hithpa'el*, pray, intercede.

Vocabulary. Verbs.

- שִׂית to set, put; (*Hoph.*).
- לִין לוּן to lodge, pass the night, remain; (*Hiph.*; *Hithpalpel*;) *Niph.* & *Hiph.* murmur.
- הָמָה to murmur, roar, be boisterous
- [חָתַן] *Hithp.* to form marriage alliance.
- [יָאַל] *Hiph.* to show willingness.
- שִׁיר to sing; *Polel*, sing by profession; *Hoph.*
- עָוָה *Qal* & *Hiph.* to commit iniquity, do wrong.
- שׁוּג סוּג to move away; *Niph.* turn oneself away; *Hiph.* remove, displace; (*Hoph.*).

Nouns.

- נָחָשׁ (iv) *m. serpent*
- מָלוֹן (ii) *m. lodging*
- (עֲבֹדָה) עֲבוֹדָה (i) *f. labor, service*
- עֵדָה (iv) *f. congregation*
- רַעַשׁ (v) *m. earthquake*
- אֶרֶז (v) *m. cedar*
- בַּר. (iii) *a. pure, clean, m. grain*
- תְּרוּמָה (i) *f. contribution, offering*
- כֶּבֶשׂ (v) *m. lamb*
- כִּבְשָׂה (v) *f. ewe-lamb*
- דַּי (constr.) דֵּי (iii) *m. sufficiency*
- נֵס (iii) *m. standing, ensign, banner*
- יַעַר (v) *forest, wood; honey comb.*

I. Verbs ʿAyin-Wāw (*Mediæ Waw*; Paradigm V).

445. 1. Although it is not certain whether these verbs are essentially biliteral, or whether they have been reduced from a triliteral root the middle radical of which was *Waw*, it is advantageous to treat them as monosyllabic and biliteral verbs.

The verbs belonging to this class are quoted, not in the 3 p. s. m. Perfect *Qal*, but in the Infinitive Construct and are so given in the Dictionaries, *v. g.* קוּם, not קָם.

2. The verbs *Mediæ Waw*, which are at the same time *Lamedh-He*, do not belong to this class and have no other irregularity besides the one connected with *Lamedh-He*, *v. g.* צִוָּה, *he commanded.*

Besides these, a certain number of verbs, which have a guttural for the first or last radical, are strong and are inflected like a strong verb with a guttural; they are: גָּוַע, *to expire;* עָוַל, *Pi. to act wrongly;* צָוַח, *to cry aloud;* שִׁוַּע, *Pi. to cry for help;* רָוַח, *to be wide;* עִוֵּר, *Pi. to make blind;* עִוֵּת, *Pi. to be bent, crooked* (*Pu. Hithp.*); אָיַב, *to be hostile.*

A. Non-Intensive Stems.

446. 1. Vowel of the Stem. a) The stem is always monosyllabic and receives the vowel corresponding to the second syll. of the strong verb (characteristic vowel). This vowel, however, is always lengthened, except in *Hophʿal* throughout and in Perfect *Qal,* before consonantal afformatives, *v. g.* קָם, הֵקִים, קָ֫מוּ; הוּקַם, קַמְתָּ, קַמְתִּי, *etc.*

One stative verb מוּת, *to die*, has *e* before vowel-afformatives, but *a* before consonantal afformatives, *v. g.* מֵת, מֵ֫תָה, מֵ֫תוּ; מַ֫תִּי, מַ֫תְנוּ.

447. b) In the Imperfect *Qal,* the original *u* (Inf. Constr., Imper., Indic.) is anomalously lengthened to *Shureq* (וּ) instead of *Ḥolem* which is found in the strong verb and verbs ע״ע, *v. g.* קוּם, קוּ֫מִי, יָקוּם, תָּקוּ֫מִי, נָקוּם, *etc.* However, there are five or six verbs with Imperf. *ô, v. g.* בּוֹא, יָבוֹא, *etc.*

448. c) According to 233, *û* and *î* (*Hiph.*) are reduced to *ō* and *ē* in the Jussive, *v. g.* יָקֹם, יָקֵם. After *Waw Consecutivum* the tone moves backward and *ō* and *ē* are further shortened to *ŏ* and *ĕ* respectively, except in a pause (247, 248), *v. g.* וַיָּ֫קָם, P. וַיָּקֹם; וַיָּ֫קֶם, but וָאָקוּם (247). With third gutt. or *Resh, a* is almost always found instead of *ŏ* and *ĕ*, *v. g.* וַיָּ֫סַר, for וַיָּ֫סָר and וַיָּ֫סֶר.

449. d) In *Niphʿal, Pathaḥ* was probably first lengthened to *Qameṣ*, which in turn has been further obscured to *Ḥolem* (וֹ); in a pretonic syllable, this *Ḥolem* becomes *Shureq, v. g.* נָקוֹם, נְקוּמוֹתֶם, יִקּוֹם, נְקוּמוֹ֫תָ, *etc.*

450. e) Participles are always found with a long vowel which corresponds to the Perfect, *v. g.* קָם (Part. pass. קוּם), נָקוֹם, מוּקָם.

451. 2. Preformatives. a) As in verbs ע״ע (437), the preformatives, whenever pretonic in an open syllable, have long vowels, *a* to *ā; i* to *ē; u* to *û;* this vowel, except *û*, is only tone long and is volatilized when not pretonic, *v. g.* יָקוּם, הוּקַם, הֵקִים, יָבוֹא, הֲקִימ֫וֹתָ. Note Part. *Hiph.* מֵקִים, not מָקִים; cp. מֵסֵב in verbs ע״ע.

452. b) As observed in verbs ע״ע (439), some of the ע״ו verbs, *v. g.* שׂוּג, נוּחַ, occasionally take a *Daghesh Forte* after the preformatives which consequently retain a short vowel, *v. g.* יַשִּׂ֫יגוּ, יַנִּ֫יחַ *etc.*

453. 3. Afformatives. a) Vowel afformatives remain unaccented except in *Hophʿal* and plural וּן (cp. ע״ע, 439), *v. g.* קָ֫מָה, קָ֫מוּ, הֵקִ֫ימוּ, תָּקוּ֫מִי.

454. b) As in ע״ע verbs (439) before consonantal afformatives, there is generally a connective vowel, וֹ in Perf. *Niph.* and *Hiph.*, and ◌ֵי in the Imperf. Ind. (not Imperatives). Perf. *Qal,* the whole *Hophʿal* and the intensive Stems have no connective vowels. The consonantal afformatives are unaccented except תֶּם and תֶּן, *v. g.* תְּקֻמֶּנָה and תְּקִימֶינָה (תָּשֹׁבְנָה) תְּקוּמֶינָה; הֲקִימוֹתָ; נְקוּמוֹתֶם, נְקוּמוֹתָ *etc.*

B. Intensive Stems.

455. Besides the verbs mentioned under 445, a few others have a regular *Pi'el, Pu'al* and *Hithpa'el, v. g.* קִיֵּם. Most of the ע"ו verbs, however, repeat the last radical and lengthen the vowel of the first radical, thus giving rise to the forms *Pôlel, Pôlal* and *Hithpôlel* (171). In these names the repetition of the *Lamedh* indicates the repetition of the last radical. It will be seen that these forms are identical with those of the ע"ע verbs, סוֹבֵב, קוֹמֵם, (428). They are inflected regularly. Some verbs have the forms *Pilpel* and *Hithpalpel*, 429.

II. Verbs *'Ayin-Yodh*, ע"י, (Paradigm W).

456. Verbs *'Ayin-Yodh* are treated exactly like verbs *'Ayin-Waw;* the only difference is that they have the vowel ִי instead of וּ in all the Modes of the Imperfect *Qal, v. g.* Perf. בָּן, בָּנָה, בַּנְתָּ; Infin. Constr. בִּין; Imperative בִּין; Indicative יָגִיל, יָגִילוּ, תָּגִילִי, יָשִׂים; Juss. יָשֵׂם, וַיָּשֶׂם; Participle Active לָן and שָׂם; Participle Passive שִׂים and שׂוּם.

III. Verbal Ideas as complementary object of a Verb.

Examples:

1. וַיֹּוסֶף לַחֲטֹא, *and he continued to sin;* מַרְבִּים הָעָם לְהָבִיא מִדַּי, *the people are bringing too much.* — 2. לִמְדוּ הֵיטֵב, *learn to do well;* לֹא יִצְלַח מִזַּרְעוֹ אִישׁ יוֹשֵׁב עַל־כִּסֵּא דָוִד, *no more shall any man of his seed succeed in sitting on the throne of David;* זֶה הַדָּבָר אֲשֶׁר־צִוָּה יְהוָה תַּעֲשׂוּ, *this is the thing that the Lord commanded (that) you should do.* — 3. הוֹאֶל־נָא וְלִין, *be content, I pray, to stay.* — 4. לְכָה נֵלְכָה, *come, let us go;* עוֹד תָּשׁוּב תִּרְאֶה, *thou shalt see yet.* — 5. וַיַּרְא יְהוָה כִּי רַבָּה רָעַת הָאָדָם, *and Jehovah saw that the wickedness of man was great;* וַיַּרְא אֱלֹהִים אֶת־הָאוֹר כִּי טוֹב, *and the God saw that the light was good;* הִגִּיד לָהֶם אֲשֶׁר־הוּא יְהוּדִי, *he told them that he was a Jew.*

When a verb receives its complement in the form of a verb or verbal clause the latter can be subordinated in various ways.

457. 1. It is very commonly in the Infin. Constr. with, and sometimes, without לְ. This is especially common after הֵחֵל, *to begin;* הוֹאִיל, *to be willing;* הוֹסִיף, *to continue;* חָדַל, *to cease;* כָּלָה, *to finish, complete;* אָבָה, *to be willing;* חָפֵץ, *to desire;* יָכֹל, *to be able;* שׁוּב, *to do again* (see above 211 γ); and also after the *Hiph'il* stem of some verbs indicating a motion in a certain direction, as הִגְדִּיל, *to do greatly;* הִרְחִיק, *to make it distant;* הִרְבָּה, *to make it much.* All these verbs are often best rendered in English by an adverb or adverbial phrase (389) *v. g.* וַיֹּסֶף לַחֲטֹא, *and he continued to sin,* Ex. IX 34; מַרְבִּים הָעָם לְהָבִיא מִדֵּי הָעֲבֹדָה, *the people are bringing too much for the service,* lit. *are multiplying to bring more than necessary,* Ex. XXXVI, 5.

458. 2. It is sometimes found in the Infin. Absol., Participle, or (as often in English) Imperf. Ind. without conjunction, *v. g.* לִמְדוּ הֵיטֵב, *learn to do well,* Is. I, 17; לְדַעְתּוֹ מָאוֹס בָּרָע וּבָחוֹר בַּטּוֹב, *that he may know to refuse the evil and to choose the good,* Is. VII, 15; לֹא יִצְלַח מִזַּרְעוֹ אִישׁ יֹשֵׁב עַל־כִּסֵּא דָוִד וּמֹשֵׁל עוֹד בִּיהוּדָה, *no more shall any man of his seed succeed in sitting on the throne of David, and in ruling Judah,* Jer. XXII, 30; זֶה הַדָּבָר אֲשֶׁר צִוָּה יְהוָה תַּעֲשׂוּ, *this is the thing which the Lord commanded* [*that*] *you should do,* Lev. IX, 6.

459. 3. The two verbs may be simply co-ordinated by *Waw* (see the use of וְ instead of the subordinating conjunctions, Lesson XXII; cp. English *I shall go and see you; be sure and come*); Ex.: הוֹאֶל־נָא וְלִין, *be willing, I pray, to tarry all night,* Jud. XIX, 6; לְמַעַן יִלְמְדוּ וְיָרְאוּ אֶת־יְהוָה, *that they may learn to fear the Lord,* Deut. XXXI, 12. Sometimes the verbal complement is added in the form of an historical statement, *v. g.* וַיְצַו יוֹסֵף וַיְמַלְאוּ אֶת־כְּלֵיהֶם בָּר, *and Joseph commanded to fill their vessels with grain,* lit.: *commanded and they filled* . . . Gen. XLII, 25. See also 240—242.

460. 4. The two verbs may be simply juxtaposed in the same mode, without *Waw Copulativum* (*asyndeton*). This is especially common with קוּם, *arise,* לֵךְ, לְכָה, *go, come,* which are used almost as real interjections, *v. g.* עוֹד תָּשׁוּב תִּרְאֶה, *thou shalt see yet,* lit.: *thou shalt return, thou shalt see,* Ezech. VIII, 6; לְכָה ׀ נֵלְכָה *come, let us go,* 1 Sam. IX, 10.

In all the above cases, very often the second verb, which is grammatically secondary, contains the principal idea, and must be rendered accordingly.

461. 5. The most common way of subordinating a verbal complement to the principal verb, is to use the conjunction כִּי and sometimes אֲשֶׁר or אֵת אֲשֶׁר, *v. g.* וַיַּרְא יְהוָה כִּי רַבָּה רָעַת הָאָדָם, *and the Lord saw that* *the wickedness of man was great,* Gen. vi, 5; הִגִּיד לָהֶם אֲשֶׁר־הוּא יְהוּדִי, *he told them that he was a Jew,* Esther iii, 4; כִּי שָׁמַעְנוּ אֵת אֲשֶׁר־הוֹבִישׁ יְהוָה אֶת־מֵי יַם־סוּף מִפְּנֵיכֶם, *for we have heard that the Lord dried up the waters of the Red Sea before you,* lit.: *the circumstance that . . .,* Jos. ii, 10.

462. Very often, כִּי is placed not before what for us would be the subject of the complementary clause, but before its predicate, while the subject of the secondary clause becomes the direct object of the principal verb, *v. g.* וַיַּרְא אֱלֹהִים אֶת־הָאוֹר כִּי־טוֹב, *and God saw that the light was good,* lit.: *God saw the light that it was good,* Gen. i, 4.

כִּי is often used to introduce a direct quotation, *v. g.* וַיֹּאמֶר כִּי אֶת־שֶׁבַע כְּבָשֹׂת תִּקַּח מִיָּדִי, *and he said, these seven ewe-lambs shalt thou take of my hand,* Gen. xxi, 30.

EXERCISES.

I. He returned; she returned; he shall bring back; they shall put to flight; to flee; he came to pray; he placed him captain over the army; depart from me and let me die; I removed; pray to the Lord and he shall deliver thee; do not put me to shame; the Lord shall judge the nations; bring back thy people from Babylon; they cut down cedar trees and erected a house; let him raise his standard and the earth shall quake; the earth shall totter like a drunken man; command him to turn back; they came to put the inhabitants to flight; I have sojourned; thou hast set up; come ye in to rest; thou hast scorned; and he came again; an intelligent mind (heart); we have been established; they shall consider diligently.

II. 1. וַיֹּאמֶר אָבִינוּ שֻׁבוּ שִׁבְרוּ־לָנוּ מְעַט־אֹכֶל׃ — 2. וְעַתָּה יְהוָה
אֱלֹהָי אַתָּה הִמְלַכְתָּ אֶת־עַבְדְּךָ תַּחַת דָּוִד אָבִי וְאָנֹכִי נַעַר קָטֹן לֹא אֵדַע
צֵאת (the going out) וָבֹא׃ — 3. אַיֵּה הָאֲנָשִׁים אֲשֶׁר בָּאוּ אֵלֶיךָ׃ —
4. לֹא יָקֻמוּ רְשָׁעִים בַּמִּשְׁפָּט וְחַטָּאִים בַּעֲדַת צַדִּיקִים׃ — 5. וַיָּנָס אֲרָם
(Aram = the Syrians) מִפְּנֵי יִשְׂרָאֵל׃ — 6. כָּל־לְבָבוֹ הֵכִין חִזְקִיָּהוּ
לִדְרֹשׁ יְהוָה אֱלֹהֵי אֲבוֹתָיו׃ — 7. וַיָּבֹא הָעָם אֶל־מֹשֶׁה וַיֹּאמְרוּ הִתְפַּלֵּל
אֶל־יְהוָה וְיָסֵר מֵעָלֵינוּ אֶת־הַנָּחָשׁ׃ — 8. יָדַעְתָּ אֶת־דָּוִד אָבִי כִּי לֹא
יָכֹל לִבְנוֹת בַּיִת לְשֵׁם יְהוָה אֱלֹהָיו׃ — 9. וַיַּרְא שָׁאוּל אֲשֶׁר־דָּוִד מַשְׂכִּיל
מְאֹד׃ — 10. וְעַתָּה צַוֵּה וְיִכְרְתוּ־לִי אֲרָזִים מִן־הַלְּבָנוֹן׃ — 11. וַיִּתְחַתֵּן
שְׁלֹמֹה אֶת־פַּרְעֹה מֶלֶךְ מִצְרָיִם וַיִּקַּח אֶת־בַּת־פַּרְעֹה וַיְבִיאֶהָ אֶל־עִיר דָּוִד
עַד כַּלֹּתוֹ לִבְנוֹת אֶת־בֵּיתוֹ וְאֶת־בֵּית יְהוָה׃ — 12. וַיֹּאמְרוּ אֶל־מֹשֶׁה

לֵאמֹר מַרְבִּים הָעָם לְהָבִיא מִדֵּי הָעֲבֹדָה לַמְּלָאכָה אֲשֶׁר־צִוָּה יְהוָה לַעֲשֹׂת
אֹתָהּ׃ וַיְצַו מֹשֶׁה וַיַּעֲבִירוּ קוֹל בַּמַּחֲנֶה לֵאמֹר אִישׁ וְאִשָּׁה אַל־יַעֲשׂוּ־
עוֹד מְלָאכָה לִתְרוּמַת הַקֹּדֶשׁ וַיִּכָּלֵא הָעָם מֵהָבִיא׃

III. 1. The Spirit of the Lord departed from Saul and a spirit of evil from the Lord troubled him. — 2. And you shall flee as you fled from the earthquake in the days of Osias (עֻזִּיָּה), king of Judah. — 3. His heart trembled and the heart of his people, as the trees of the forest tremble before the wind. — 4. And there was set (food) before him to eat: but he said, I will not eat. — 5. And Abrahm again took a wife. — 6. Reprove not a scoffer lest (פֶּן) he hate thee; reprove a wise man and he will love thee. — 7. And the Levite consented to dwell with the man; and the young man was unto him as one of his sons. — 8. And all the children of Israel murmured against Moses and against Aaron; and the whole congregation said unto them, Would that (לוּ) we had died in the land of Egypt! or would that we had died in the wilderness! And why hath Jehovah brought us unto this land, to fall by the sword? And they said one to another, Let us make a captain (a head) and let us return to Egypt.

LESSON XXII.

WEAK VERBS (Conclusion); CONJUNCTIONS.

Vocabulary. Verbs.

נָטָה to stretch out, extend, bend; *Hiph.* *id.*; (*Niph.*)

[נָכָה] *Hiph.* to smite, strike; (*Niph.*; *Pu.*).

יָדָה (to throw, cast; *Pi.*); *Hiph.* praise, give thanks, confess.

יָרָה to throw, shoot; (*Niph.*); *Hiph.* throw, point out, teach, instruct.

יָרֵא to fear; *Niph.* cause astonishment, be fearful; (*Pi.*).

יָצָא to go out, come out; *Hiph.* bring out.

נָשָׂא to lift, carry, take; *Niph.* be lifted; *Pi.* exact; *Hithp.* lift oneself; (*Hiph.*).

נָשָׁא lend on interest *Hiph.*

[נָשָׁא] *Hiph.* deceive (*Niph.*).

[אָנָה] *Pi.* to meet; *Pu.*; *Hithp.* seek a quarrel.

מָרָה to be rebellious; *Hiph.* show disobedience.

[קִיץ] *Hiph.* to awake (see יָקַץ XV).

קוּץ to feel a loathing; (*Hiph.*).

[יָחַל] (*Niph.* to wait); *Pi.* await; *Hiph.* wait.

נָהַג to drive, conduct; *Pi.* drive away, guide.

עָטָה to wrap oneself; *Hiph.* wrap.

צוּד to hunt; *Polel*, hunt eagerly.

צָרַע *Qal* & *Pu.* to be struck with leprosy.

פּוּץ to be dispersed; *Niph.* be scattered; *Hiph.* scatter.

נָפַץ to be scattered, dispersed.

נָפַץ to shatter; *Pi.* dash to pieces; (*Pu.*).

פּוּחַ to breathe; *Hiph.* snort, excite.

נָפַח to breathe, blow; (*Pu.*); *Hiph.*

[קָלָה] *Niph.* to be lightly esteemed; *Hiph.* treat with contempt (see קָלַל, XX).

נָקַף (to go around); *Hiph.* go around, complete the circuit, come around.

[נָקַף] *Pi.* to strike; *Niph.* be struck.

שׁוּט to rove about; *Polel* & (*Hithpolel*) run to and fro.

חָרַשׁ to engrave, plough; (*Niph.*; *Hiph.*).

*חָרֵשׁ to be silent; *Hiph.* be silent, exhibit silence.

Nouns.

מַטֶּה (vi) *m. staff, rod; branch; tribe*
אַרְבֶּה (vi) *m. locust*
חֵמָה (iv) *f. heat, anger, rage*
צַיִד (v) *m. hunting, venison*
חֵן (iii) *m. favor, grace*
צָרַעַת (v) *f. leprosy*
מַעֲלָל (iv) *m. deed, pratice*
קֶדֶם (v) *m. front, east, aforetime*
קָדִים (ii) *m. east, east wind.*
תֹּם (iii) *m. completeness, integrity*
תָּם (iii) *a. perfect, complete*
פִּנָּה (iii) *f. corner*
קֶרֶב (v) *m. inward part, midst*
לְחִי (v) *m. jaw, cheek, jawbone.*

I. Conclusion of Weak Verbs.

A. Doubly Weak Verbs.

463. A certain number of verbs have two weak radicals; in that case the verb undergoes the modifications proper to each one of the weak radicals (see, however, 445, 2). We give here the chief forms of the more common of these verbs.

1. פ״ן and ל״ה. נָטָה *to stretch out: Qal,* Perf. נָטִיתָ; Imperf. Ind. יִטֶּה for יִנְטֶה; Apocopated Imperf. וַיֵּט, וַתֵּט. *Hiph.* Perf. הִטָּה, Imperf. וַיַּט; Imperat. הַט, etc.

   נָכָה *to smite: Hiph.* Perf. הִכִּיתָ; Imperf. Ind. יַכֶּה; Juss. יַךְ, etc.

2. פ״ן and ל״א. נָשָׂא *to lift: Qal,* Imperf. Ind. יִשָּׂא; Imperat. שָׂא; Inf. constr. (נְשֹׂא) and שְׂאֵת (לָשֵׂאת). *Niph.* Perf. נִשָּׂא; Inf. constr. הִנָּשֵׂא, etc.

3. פ״א and ל״ה. אָבָה *to be willing: Qal,* Imperf. יֹאבֶה, etc.

   אָפָה *to bake: Qal,* Imperf. 3 p pl., יֹאפוּ, etc.

4. פ״י and ל״א. יָצָא *to go out: Qal,* Imperf. Ind. יֵצֵא; Imperat. צֵא, Inf. constr. צֵאת. *Hiph.* Perf. הוֹצִיא, etc.

   יָרֵא *to fear: Qal,* Imperf. Ind. יִירָא; Imperat. יְרָא; Inf. constr. יְרֹא. *Niph.* Imperf. תִּוָּרֵא, Part. נוֹרָא, etc.

5. פ"י and ל"ה. יָדָה *to throw: Hiph.* Imperf. יוֹדֶה; Imperat. (2 pl.) הוֹדוּ; Inf. constr. הוֹדוֹת, etc.

יָרָה *to throw: Qal,* Perf. (1 p. s.); יָרִיתִי Imperf. Imperat. יְרֵה; Inf. constr. יְרוֹת. *Hiph.* Perf. (1 s.) הוֹרֵיתִי; Imperf. Ind. יוֹרֶה; Inf. constr. הוֹרוֹת; Part. מוֹרֶה, etc.

B. **Relation of Weak Verbs to one another.**

464. A certain number of weak verbs were primitively biliteral; this is still witnessed by the fact that, while the two original radicals have been retained, they have been increased with the help of various weak letters, sometimes without any perceptible difference of meaning, at other times, with some shade of difference, *v. g.* יָצַב (*Hithp.*) and נָצַב (*Niph.*), *to take one's stand;* טוֹב and יָטַב, *to be good;* פּוּחַ and נָפַח, *to breathe;* נָפַץ and פּוּץ, *to be dispersed;* דָּכָה and דָּכָא, *to crush;* שָׁחָה and שָׁחַח, *to bend down, worship;* רָבַב and רָבָה, *be much, many;* קָלָה (*Niph.*) and קָלַל, *to be trifling, lightly esteemed;* כָּלָה, *to be complete,* and כָּלַל, *to complete;* מוּל, מָהַל and מָלַל, *to circumcise, etc.*

C. **Defective Verbs.**

465. Some verbs which occur in two or more kindred roots, are inflected occasionally partly according to the one and partly according to the other, each one being defective and completing the other, *v. g.* טוֹב and יָטַב; טוֹב occurs only in the *Qal* Perf., Imperat. and Infinitive Construct while *Hiph.* is generally הֵיטִיב from יָטַב; קוּץ & יָקַץ, *Qal* Imperf. Ind. יִיקַץ from יָקַץ, *Hiph.* הֵקִיץ from קוּץ, *etc.*

D. **Less common Formations.**

466. 1. Apart from the forms *Po'el, Po'al, Hithpo'el* which occur in the ע"ע stems (428); *Polel, Polal, Hithpolel* common in the ע"ו stems (455); the forms *Pilpel, Hithpalpel* which occur in both (429, 455), there are still other less common formations which are found occasionally in Hebrew, *v. g. Pa'lel* or *Pi'lel, Pu'lal* (repetition of the last radical), *v. g.* שַׁאֲנַן, *to be greenish;* אֻמְלַל, *be withered.*

P·'al'al repetitition of the last two radicals, (קְטַלְטַל) indicates quick succession of movements, *v. g.* סָחַר, *go about,* סְחַרְחַר, *palpitate* (of the heart).

Besides these, the forms *Tiph'el* and *Shaph'el* are found as rare, and in most cases doubtful, substitutes for *Hiph'il.*

The forms *Pi'la'*, *Pa'pal*, & *Nithpa''el* (קִטְלַט, קְטַלְטַל & נִתְקַטֵּל), are very rare in the Bible although the latter is common in post-Biblical Hebrew.

E. How to find out the root of a verb.

467. 1. To find the radical letters, we must eliminate all preformatives, informatives and afformatives. When three letters remain, they constitute the root and the word should be looked for under that form in the Dictionary. It may be of some help to know that eleven letters contained in the three proper names: אֵיתָן מֹשֶׁה וְכָלֵב, *'Êthan, Moses and Caleb,* can be both radicals and formative (often called servile) letters, while the others are always radicals, *v. g.* in יַשְׁמִיעֻנִי, י is the personal preformative of Imperf. Ind.; ִי, infix of the *Hiph.*; ו ending of 3 p. pl.; נִי, suffix of 1 p. sing. Hence, the root is שמע.

2. If after eliminating all formative letters, only two consonants remain, the stem belongs to one of the weak verbs פ"ן, פ"י, ע"ע, ע"ו, ע"י, ל"ה. If the first of these two letters has *Daghesh Forte,* it will be generally פ"ן, less frequently פ"י (343), ע"ע (439) ע"ו or ע"י (452).

3. If only one letter remains it is a doubly weak verb and generally פ"ן and ל"ה.

II. Principal Conjunctions in Hebrew.

A. Co-ordinating Conjunctions

468. (often subordinating in meaning).

1. Copulative: וְ, *and;* גַּם, *also;* אַף, *even, also.*
2. Alternative: וְ, *or;* אוֹ, *or;* אִם, *or,* often in disjunctive questions (423).
3. Adversative: וְ, *but;* כִּי, כִּי אִם, *but, except;* רַק, *only;* אַךְ, *yet, but;* אֶפֶס כִּי, *except that;* אוּלָם, *but indeed.*
4. Correlative: וְ . . . וְ, גַּם, . . . גַּם, *both . . . and; as well . . . as.*
5. Disjunctive: אוֹ . . . אוֹ, אִם . . . אִם, *either . . . or;* לֹא . . . וְלֹא. גַּם . . . וְגַם לֹא, *neither . . . nor.*

B. Subordinating Conjunctions and conjunctive phrases.

469. In Hebrew, mere juxtaposition or co-ordination often takes the place of subordination; hence the conjunction וְ may replace any one of the others which we are going to give; cp. 238 ff.; 249 ff.; 259, 459.

470.   1. Conjunctions denoting time.

כִּי, כְּמוֹ, אֲשֶׁר, אִם, כַּאֲשֶׁר, *when, as often as;*

עַד אֲשֶׁר, עַד־כִּי, ⎱ *until, until*
עַד־אֲשֶׁר אִם, עַד־אִם, ⎰ *the time when;*

אַחַר אֲשֶׁר, אַחֲרֵי־אֲשֶׁר, אַחֲרֵי, *after;*

עַד־אֲשֶׁר לֹא, בְּטֶרֶם, מֶרֶם, לִפְנֵי (228), קָדְמַת *before (not yet);*

מִדֵּי, *as often as;*

מֵאָז, *since.*

471.   2. Conjunctions denoting purpose, aim
(final, telic conjunctions), generally with Imperfect.

אֲשֶׁר, לְמַעַן אֲשֶׁר, לְמַעַן (228), *so that, in order that, to the end that;*

עַל־דִּבְרַת שֶׁלֹּא, אֲשֶׁר לֹא, *so that . . not, for the purpose that . . not;*

בַּעֲבוּר אֲשֶׁר, בַּעֲבוּר, *for the purpose of;*

פֶּן, *lest* (218);

לְבִלְתִּי, *so that . . not.*

472.   3. Conjunctions denoting result.

כִּי, אֲשֶׁר, *so that;*

אֲשֶׁר לֹא, *so that . . not.*

473.   4. Conjunctions denoting concession (concessive).

אִם, גַּם כִּי, גַּם, *although;*

כִּי גַם, *even though.*

474.   5. Conjunctions denoting cause, reason for statements, *etc.*

כִּי, יַעַן כִּי, יַעַן אֲשֶׁר, יַעַן;
עַל, עַל־אֲשֶׁר, עַל כִּי;
תַּחַת אֲשֶׁר, עַל־דְּבַר אֲשֶׁר;
תַּחַת כִּי;
⎱ *because, since, on the ground that, for the reason that, etc.;*

עַל־כָּל־אֹדוֹת אֲשֶׁר, *for the very reason that;*

עֵקֶב, עֵקֶב כִּי, עֵקֶב אֲשֶׁר; מֵאֲשֶׁר, *from the fact that, because;*

מִבְּלִי; עַל־בְּלִי, *because . . . not.*

475. 6. Conjunctions denoting condition.

אִם (הֵן), *if,* for conditions fulfilled or capable of fulfilment;

לוּ; (אִם לוּ) אִלּוּ, *if,* for conditions unfulfilled or incapable of fulfilment;

אִם לֹא, *if . . . not;*

לוּלֵא, (לוּלֵי), *unless;*

כִּי, *supposing that, in case that, if.*

476. 7. Conjunctions denoting comparison, preference, substitution.

כַּאֲשֶׁר; אֲשֶׁר, *as;*	תַּחַת אֲשֶׁר, *whereas, while (potius-quam);*
כַּאֲשֶׁר . . . כֵּן, *as . . . so;*	יוֹתֵר שֶׁ, *besides that.*
כָּל־עֻמַּת שֶׁ, *in all points as;*	

כּ is not properly a conjunction but a substantive used as preposition. Note also כּ . . . כּ; כּ . . . וְכ; כֵּן . . . כּ, *as . . . so; so . . . as.*

477. 8. Conjunctions denoting oath and asseveration.

אִם, (*if*) *certainly not;* אִם־לֹא, (*if not*) *certainly.*

These are properly conjunctions indicating condition. In some cases, they are preceded by the clause, כֹּה יַעֲשֶׂה־לִּ(י) אֱלֹהִים וְכֹה יוֹסִיף אִם (*a*), . . אִם לֹא (*b*) *the Lord do so to (me) and more also! if* (*a*) *I do (this);* . . . (*b*) *if I do not (do this) i. e.* (*a*) *I will certainly not do it;* (*b*) *I will certainly do it.* Very often, the imprecative clause is understood especially after the clauses חַי־יְהוָה, or חַי־יְהוָה וְחֵי נַפְשְׁךָ, [*as*] *the Lord liveth and* [*as*] *thy soul liveth.*

478. 9. Conjunctions denoting desire.

אִם, לוּ = *if only, utinam: would that . . .* (cp. 475).

EXERCISES.

I. He smote; he smote them; confess the Lord that you may live; and he lifted up his voice; and he waited some days; and God shall scatter you among the peoples; Satan roved about the earth; when God stretches his hand the earth quakes; fear the Lord and depart from evil; do not fear (f. s.), for, God has heard thy voice; help me, so that it may be well with me; for the reason that you have heard my voice; go out into the field and hunt for me some venison; whoever lifts himself up; they were dispersed; praise the Lord.

II. 1. יוֹדוּךָ עַמִּים ׀ אֱלֹהִים יוֹדוּךָ עַמִּים כֻּלָּם׃ — 2. וְהַנַּעַר שְׁמוּאֵל
הֹלֵךְ וְגָדֵל וָטוֹב גַּם עִם־יְהוָֹה וְגַם עִם־אֲנָשִׁים׃ — 3. וַיִּקְרָא דָוִד לְאַחַד
מֵהַנְּעָרִים וַיֹּאמֶר גַּשׁ פְּגַע־בּוֹ וַיַּכֵּהוּ וַיָּמֹת׃ — 4. וַיְהִי בְּשׁוּב דָּוִד מֵהַכּוֹת
אֶת־הַפְּלִשְׁתִּי וַתֵּצֶאנָה הַנָּשִׁים מִכָּל־עָרֵי יִשְׂרָאֵל׃ — 5. הַט אָזְנְךָ וּשְׁמַע
דִּבְרֵי חֲכָמִים וְלִבְּךָ תָּשִׁית לְדַעְתִּי׃ — 6. וַיֹּאמֶר לֹא יַעֲקֹב יֵאָמֵר עוֹד
שִׁמְךָ כִּי אִם־יִשְׂרָאֵל׃ — 7. בְּרַח לְךָ אֶל־לָבָן אָחִי וְיָשַׁבְתָּ עִמּוֹ יָמִים
אֲחָדִים עַד אֲשֶׁר־תָּשׁוּב חֲמַת אָחִיךָ׃ — 8. וַיֹּאמֶר יִצְחָק הַגִּשָׁה לִּי
וְאֹכְלָה מִצֵּיד בְּנִי לְמַעַן תְּבָרֶכְךָ נַפְשִׁי וַיַּגֶּשׁ לוֹ וַיֹּאכַל וַיָּבֵא לוֹ יַיִן
וַיֵּשְׁתְּ׃ — 9. כֹּה אָמַר יְהוָֹה יַעַן כִּי מָרִיתָ פִּי יְהוָֹה וְלֹא שָׁמַרְתָּ אֶת־
הַמִּצְוָה אֲשֶׁר צִוְּךָ יְהוָֹה אֱלֹהֶיךָ לֹא־תָבוֹא נִבְלָתְךָ אֶל־קֶבֶר אֲבֹתֶיךָ׃ —
10. וַיָּבֵא מֶלֶךְ־אֲרָם סֵפֶר אֶל־מֶלֶךְ יִשְׂרָאֵל לֵאמֹר וְעַתָּה כְּבוֹא הַסֵּפֶר הַזֶּה
אֵלֶיךָ הִנֵּה שָׁלַחְתִּי אֵלֶיךָ אֶת־נַעֲמָן (pr. n.) עַבְדִּי וַאֲסַפְתּוֹ מִצָּרַעְתּוֹ׃
וַיְהִי כִּקְרֹא מֶלֶךְ־יִשְׂרָאֵל אֶת־הַסֵּפֶר וַיִּקְרַע בְּגָדָיו וַיֹּאמֶר הַאֱלֹהִים אָנִי
לְהָמִית וּלְהַחֲיוֹת כִּי־זֶה שֹׁלֵחַ אֵלַי לֶאֱסֹף אִישׁ מִצָּרַעְתּוֹ כִּי אַךְ־דְּעוּ־נָא
וּרְאוּ כִּי־מִתְאַנֶּה הוּא לִי׃ — 11. וְכַאֲשֶׁר יְעַנּוּ אֹתוֹ כֵּן יִרְבֶּה וְכֵן יִפְרֹץ
וַיָּקֻצוּ מִפְּנֵי בְּנֵי יִשְׂרָאֵל׃ — 12. גַּם כִּי־תַרְבּוּ תְפִלָּה אֵינֶנִּי שֹׁמֵעַ׃ —
13. וַיֵּט מֹשֶׁה אֶת־מַטֵּהוּ עַל־אֶרֶץ מִצְרַיִם וַיהוָֹה נִהַג רוּחַ־קָדִים בָּאָרֶץ
כָּל־הַיּוֹם הַהוּא וְכָל־הַלָּיְלָה הַבֹּקֶר הָיָה וְרוּחַ הַקָּדִים נָשָׂא אֶת־
הָאַרְבֶּה׃

III. 1. Only do not rebel against the Lord. — 2. If now I have found grace in your eyes, speak, I pray you, in the ear of Pharaoh. — 3. And the people refused to hear the voice of Samuel, and they said, Nay, but let a king be over us. — 4. And it came to pass, when man began to be numerous on the face of the earth, that the sons of God saw the daughters of men that they were fair [good]. — 5. Say (f.) that thou art my sister, so that it may be well with me for thy sake. — 6. For, I have known him, to the end that he may command his children and his household after him, that they may keep the way of Jehovah by doing righteousness and justice. —

7. Not to us, o Lord, not to us but to thy name give glory. — 8. Say ye to the righteous, because (he is) good, that he shall eat the fruit of his doings. — 9. Hear, my son, and receive my sayings: and the years of thy life shall be many. I have taught thee in the way of wisdom, I have led thee in paths of uprightness. — 10. And Samson said, with the jawbone of an ass, have I smitten a thousand men. — 11. And ye shall be left few in number (בִּמְתֵי מְעָט) whereas you were as the stars of heaven for multitude.

LESSON XXIII.

APPOSITION. REPETITION OF NOUNS. COMPARISON OF ADJECTIVES. RELATIVE SENTENCE.

Vocabulary. Verbs.

שִׂישׂ, שׂוּשׂ to exult, rejoice.
גָּבַהּ to be high, exalted, haughty; *Hiph.*
מָכַר to sell; *Niph.* & (*Hithp.*) sell oneself.
חָמַם to be or become warm; (*Niph.*; *Pi.*; *Hithp.*).
עָתַק* to move, proceed; *Hiph.* move forward, transcribe.
לָהַט (to blaze up, flame); *Pi.* set ablaze.
טָעַם to taste.
חָסָה to seek refuge.
[אוה] *Pi.* to desire; *Hithp.*
[כָּנַע] *Niph.* to humble oneself, be humbled; *Hiph.* humble.
[קָבַל] *Pi.* to receive.
עוּר to rouse oneself, awake (int.); *Niph.* be roused: *Polel*, rouse, incite; (*Pilpel*); *Hithpolel*; *Hiph.* rouse, stir up.
[פָּלָא] *Niph.* to be wonderful, difficult; *Hiph.* do wondrously; (*Hithp.*).
קָצַץ (to cut off); *Pi.* cut to pieces; *Pu.*
יָתַר (to remain over); *Niph.* be left over; *Hiph.* leave over, show excess.

Nouns.

כְּרוּב (i) *m. cherub*
עֲבֹת (i) *m. & f. cord, cordage*
סְאָה (i) *f. seah (measure)*
סֹלֶת (v) *f. fine flour*
קֵץ (iii) *m. end*
קָצֶה (vi) *m. end, extremity*
קָצָה (vi) *f.* (pl. m.) *end*
בָּשָׂר (iv) *m. flesh*
חַרְטֹם (iii) *m. magician*
נָדִיב (ii) *a.* {*noble, generous*}
צֶ֫דֶק (v) *m. righteousness*
גָּבֹהַּ (ii) *a. high, haughty*
חֵמָר (iv) *m.* {*bitumen, asphalt*}
מְכֹנָה (i) *f. basis*
מְכַשֵּׁף (iv) *pt. sorcerer*
שְׁכֶם for שֶׁ֫כֶם (v) *m. shoulder*
מַבּוּל (i) *m. flood, deluge*
עֵ֫דֶר (v) *m. flock, herd*
רֶ֫וַח (v) *m. space, inrveal*

Nouns.

נָהָר (iv) *m. river, stream*	מְדִינָה (i) *f. province*	שֶׁמֶשׁ (v) *f. & m. sun*
מְתִים (מַת) / מְתֵי } (i) *m. male, man*	שִׁיר (i) *m. song*	שָׂשׂוֹן (ii) *m. exultation*
טַף (iii) *m. little ones*	בָּרִיא (ii) *a. fat*	מָשׂוֹשׂ (ii) *m. rejoicing*
אֲחֻזָּה (i) *f. possession*	יָפֶה (vi) *a. beautiful*	לָאט, לָט (i) *m. secrecy, mystery, enchantment*
בַּהֶרֶת (v) *f. brightness (sore)*	מָן (i) *manna*	רָעָב (iv) *m. famine, hunger*
לָבָן (iv) *a. white*	הָרָה (vi) *a. f. pregnant*	תֻּמָּה (iii) *f. perfection*
שָׂפָה (iv) *f. lip, tongue*	מִסְגֶּרֶת (v) *f. border, fastness*	מִשְׁמָר (iv) *m. prison; watch*
עֵמֶק (v) *m. vale, valley*	שֹׂבַע (v) *m.* / שָׂבָע (iv) *m.* } *plenty, abundance, satiety*	
גֶּבֶר (v) *m. man*		

I. Apposition.

Examples:

1. אִשָּׁה אַלְמָנָה, *a woman, a widow.* — 2. הַמֶּלֶךְ דָּוִד, *king David.* — 3. הַכְּרוּבִים זָהָב, *the Cherubim of gold.* — 4. סְאָה סֹלֶת, *a seah of flour.* — 5. וְיֵדְעוּ הָעָם כֻּלּוֹ, *and let all the people know.* — 6. וַיַּעֲשׂוּ גַם־הֵם חַרְטֻמֵּי מִצְרַיִם כֵּן, *and they also, (viz.) the magicians of Egypt, did in like manner.* שִׁיתֵמוֹ נְדִיבֵמוֹ כְּעֹרֵב, *make them (or rather) their nobles like Oreb.* — 7. וַתֹּסֶף לָלֶדֶת אֶת־אָחִיו אֶת־הָבֶל, *and further she brought forth his brother Abel.* — 8. וַיְהִי כָל־הָאָרֶץ שָׂפָה אֶחָת, *and the whole earth was of one language.* — 9. הָאֵל תָּמִים דַּרְכּוֹ, *the way of God is perfect.*

By apposition is meant the juxtaposition of two substantives, in the same case, one, generally the second, modifying the other. Substantives are often found in apposition in Hebrew, when in our languages, an adjective or a genitive would be preferred. This is especially the case in the determination of number, measure, weight and time.

Apposition is used in Hebrew:

479. 1. between a person or thing and its class, species or genus, *v. g.* אִשָּׁה אַלְמָנָה, *a woman, a widow.* Akin to this is the apposition between a thing and its quality, *v. g.* אֲמָרִים אֱמֶת, *words of truth* (*words which are true*);

480. 2. between a person or thing and its name, *v. g.* הַמֶּלֶךְ דָּוִד, *king David;* הַנָּהָר פְּרָת, *the river Euphrates;*

481. 3. between a thing and its material, *v. g.* הַכְּרוּבִים זָהָב, *the Cherubim of gold;* הָעֲבֹתֹת הַזָּהָב, *the cords of gold;*

482. 4. between the thing measured, weighed or counted and the measure, weight or number, *v. g.* סְאָה סֹלֶת וְסָאתַיִם שְׂעֹרִים בְּשֶׁקֶל, *a seah of flour and two seahs of barley for a shekel,* 2 K. VII, 1; חֹדֶשׁ יָמִים, *a month of days, i. e. a full month,* Gen. XXIX, 14; יָמִים מִסְפָּר, *days, a number, i. e. a few days,* Num. IX, 20.

In almost all the above cases, the constr. state with a following genitive could be used, *v. g.* נְהַר פְּרָת, *the river Euphrates;* כְּסִיל אָדָם, *a foolish man,* lit. *a fool of a man,* Prov. XV, 20.

483. 5. כֹּל (*entirely*) *all* (441), instead of being in the constr. state with a following genitive as is generally the case, is often placed in apposition to the noun with a suffix corresponding to it, וְיָדְעוּ הָעָם כֻּלּוֹ, *and the whole people shall know,* lit. *and the people, all of it, shall know,* Is. IX, 8.

484. 6. Very frequently, a subst. is placed in apposition to another, not to complete it, but to limit and to define it more accurately; very often it corresponds to "*i. e.*", "viz.", or to "*or rather,*" *v. g.* וַיַּעֲשׂוּ גַם־הֵם חַרְטֻמֵּי מִצְרַיִם כֵּן, *and they also, the magicians of Egypt, did in like manner,* Ex. VII, 11; וַתִּרְאֵהוּ אֶת־הַיֶּלֶד, *and she saw him, namely the child,* Ex. II, 6; עֲבֹר אֶת־הַיַּרְדֵּן הַזֶּה אַתָּה וְכָל־הָעָם הַזֶּה אֶל־הָאָרֶץ אֲשֶׁר אָנֹכִי נֹתֵן לָהֶם לִבְנֵי יִשְׂרָאֵל, *go over this Jordan, thou and all this people, unto the land which I do give to them, even to the children of Israel,* Jos. I, 2; שִׁיתֵמוֹ נְדִיבֵמוֹ כְּעֹרֵב, *make them* [*or rather*] *their nobles like Oreb,* Ps. LXXXIII, 12.

485. 7. When אֶת or a preposition precedes the first noun or pronoun, it may be repeated before the second noun in apposition, *v. g.* וַתֹּסֶף לָלֶדֶת אֶת־אָחִיו אֶת־הָבֶל, *and further she brought forth his brother Abel,* Gen. IV, 2.

486. 8. The fact that nouns of so divergent meanings can be placed in apposition, explains how Hebrew can use the one as predicate of the other in a nominal sentence, whereas in our languages we would adopt a different construction, *v. g.* וַיְהִי כָל־הָאָרֶץ שָׂפָה אֶחָת, *and the whole earth was of one language,* Gen. XI, 1; עֵמֶק הַשִּׂדִּים בֶּאֱרֹת בֶּאֱרֹת, *the vale of Siddim was full of pits,* lit. *was pits, pits*; cp. Gen. XIV, 10.

487. 9. A kind of inverted apposition occurs when a noun (or phrase), logically forming part of a sentence, is placed at the beginning without being grammatically connected with what follows, and is resumed by a suitable pronoun in the sentence proper. Such a noun or phrase is called **casus pendens** and corresponds to the English construction with *as for, as to, concerning, etc.* The *casus pendens* is generally emphatic. Ex.: הָאֵל תָּמִים דַּרְכּוֹ, *the way of God is perfect,* lit. *God his way* ... 2 Sam. xxii, 31; אִישׁ זְרוֹעַ לוֹ הָאָרֶץ, *to the man of power, belongs to earth,* lit.: *the man of power to him belongs the earth,* Job, xxii, 8; וּמֵעֵץ הַדַּעַת טוֹב וָרָע לֹא תֹאכַל מִמֶּנּוּ, *but of the tree of the knowledge of good and evil, thou shalt not eat (of it),* Gen. ii, 17, cp. 146, 307, 372.

II. Repetition of Nouns.

Examples:

1. צֶדֶק צֶדֶק תִּרְדֹּף, *thou shalt follow strict justice.* — 2. וְעֵמֶק הַשִּׂדִּים בֶּאֱרֹת בֶּאֱרֹת חֵמָר, *the vale of Siddim was full of bitumen pits.* — 3. שָׁנָה שָׁנָה, *every year.* — 4. קַח מֵאִתָּם מַטֶּה מַטֶּה, *take of them a rod from each.* — 5. אֶבֶן וָאָבֶן, *two kinds of stone,* lit.: *stone and stone.*

The repetition of words may indicate:

488. 1. the strengthening of an idea, *v. g.* צֶדֶק צֶדֶק תִּרְדֹּף, *thou shalt follow strict justice,* Deut. xvi, 20, lit. *justice (and only) justice;* עָמֹק עָמֹק, *very deep,* Eccl. vii, 24;

489. 2. a great number, *v. g.* וְעֵמֶק הַשִּׂדִּים בֶּאֱרֹת בֶּאֱרֹת חֵמָר, *the vale of Siddim (was) full of bitumen pits,* Gen. xiv, 10;

490. 3. totality, continuity, repetition, especially with expressions of time, *all, every, v. g.* שָׁנָה שָׁנָה, *every year;* בַּבֹּקֶר בַּבֹּקֶר, *every morning;* בְּיוֹם הַשַּׁבָּת בְּיוֹם הַשַּׁבָּת, *every Sabbath day,* Lev. xxiv, 8;

491. 4. distribution, *each, v. g.* קַח מֵאִתָּם מַטֶּה מַטֶּה לְבֵית אָב, *take from them rods, one for each father's house,* Num. xvii, 17 (2);

492. 5. diversity and variety, inasmuch as the same object is of a different quality; in this case the second word is generally preceded by וְ, *v. g.* אֶבֶן וָאָבֶן, *two kinds of stone;* בְּלֵב וָלֵב יְדַבֵּרוּ, *they speak with a double heart,* Ps. xii, 3.

III. Comparison of adjectives.

Examples:

A. 1. גָּבֹהַּ מִכָּל־הָעָם, *taller than any of the people.* — 2. וַיֶּאֱהַב אֶת־רָחֵל מִלֵּאָה, *and he loved Rachel more than Leah.* — B. 1. בְּנוֹ הַקָּטָן,

his youngest son; גְּדֹלֵי הָעִיר, *the greatest men of the city;* שִׁיר הַשִּׁירִים *the most excellent song (song of songs).* — 2. בָּרִיא מְאֹד, *very fat;* הַנַּעֲרָה יָפָה עַד־מְאֹד, *the damsel was extremely comely;* טוֹבָה הָאָרֶץ מְאֹד מְאֹד, *the land is exceedingly good.*

A. Comparative.

493. Hebrew possesses no special form for the comparative or superlative of the adjective. To show that a person or thing excels, or is inferior to, another, the second term of comparison is preceded by מִן, ־מִ, מֵ, *away from, prae, v. g.* גָּבֹהַּ מִכָּל־הָעָם, *taller than any of the people,* 1 Sam. IX, 2; cp. 373.

494. The use of מִן is very common after verbs, in the sense of *more than, v. g.* וַיֶּאֱהַב אֶת־רָחֵל מִלֵּאָה, *and he loved Rachel more than Leah,* Gen. XXIX, 30.

Some times מִן after adjectives and verbs may be rendered by *too . . . for, or rather . . . than, v. g.* הַמְעַט מִכֶּם, *is it too small for you?* Is. VII, 3; יָרוּם מִמֶּנִּי, *it is too high for me,* Ps. LXI, 3.

B. Superlative.

495. 1. Relative Superlative. The relative superlative is expressed:

a) by the simple adjective with the article, *v. g.* בְּנוֹ הַקָּטָן, *his youngest son,* Gen. IX, 24; גְּדֹלֵי הָעִיר, *the greatest men of the city,* 2 K. X, 6;

b) by using the construct state of a noun before the genitive plural of the same noun, *v. g.* שִׁיר הַשִּׁירִים, *the song of songs, i. e. the most excellent song;* קֹדֶשׁ הַקֳּדָשִׁים, *the holy of holies, i. e. the most holy place.*

496. 2. Absolute Superlative. The absolute superlative is expressed:

a) by the adverb מְאֹד, *very, much,* which may be still intensified by עַד, בְּ, or another מְאֹד, *v. g.* בָּרִיא מְאֹד, *very fat,* Jud. III, 17; הַנַּעֲרָה יָפָה עַד־מְאֹד, *the damsel was extremely comely,* 1 K. I, 4; טוֹבָה הָאָרֶץ מְאֹד מְאֹד, *the land is exceedingly good,* Num. XIV, 7;

b) by repeating the adjective as above, 488, *v. g.* קָדוֹשׁ | קָדוֹשׁ | קָדוֹשׁ יְהוָה צְבָאוֹת, *holy, holy, holy, is Jehovah of hosts, i. e. exceedingly holy,* Is. VI, 3.

IV. Relative Sentence (cp. 122, 123, 408).

Examples:

1. הָאֲנָשִׁים אֲשֶׁר בָּאוּ אֵלֶיךָ, *the men who came to thee;* הֶעָרִים אֲשֶׁר יָשַׁב בָּהֵן לוֹט, *the cities in which Lot dwelt;* הָאָרֶץ אֲשֶׁר־יָצָאתָ מִשָּׁם, *the land whence thou hast come;* הַמְּלָכִים אֲשֶׁר אִתּוֹ, *the kings who were with him;* הָאָדָם אֲשֶׁר יָצַר, *the man whom He had created.* — 2. הַדֶּרֶךְ־זוּ אֵלֵךְ, *the way wherein I should walk.* — 3. יְהוָה הַמּוֹצִאֲךָ מֵאֶרֶץ מִצְרַיִם, *the Lord who brought thee out of the land of Egypt;* כֹּל הַהִקְדִּישׁ שְׁמוּאֵל, *all that Samuel has dedicated.* — 4. אִיּוֹב שְׁמוֹ, *a man whose name was Job;* אֱלֹהִים לֹא יְדָעוּם, *gods whom they knew not.* — 5. מְקַצֶּה רַגְלַיִם שֹׁלֵחַ דְּבָרִים בְּיַד־כְּסִיל, *he who ends a message through a fool cuts out his own feet.*

In some Semitic languages, notably Arabic, a distinction is made between relative clauses attached to a determinate substantive and those attached to an indeterminate substantive; the former is generally introduced by a relative particle, the latter is merely juxtaposed. In Hebrew, although the rule often applies (503), yet, it is not absolute.

497. 1. The relative clause, most frequently introduced by אֲשֶׁר, 122 (sometimes by שֶׁ 123), is constructed as an independent sentence, *v. g.* (independent: בָּאוּ אֵלֶיךָ, *they came to thee*) הָאֲנָשִׁים אֲשֶׁר בָּאוּ אֵלֶיךָ, *the men who came to thee,* Gen. xix, 5; (יָצָאתָ מִשָּׁם, *thou hast come thence*), הָאָרֶץ אֲשֶׁר־יָצָאתָ מִשָּׁם, *the land from whence thou hast come,* Gen. xxiv, 5; (יִמָּצֵא אִתּוֹ, *it shall be found with him*), אֲשֶׁר יִמָּצֵא אִתּוֹ וָמֵת, (*he*) *with whom it* (*the cup*) *shall be found shall die,* Gen. xliv, 9; (יָשַׁב בָּהֵן לוֹט, *Lot dwelt in them*), הֶעָרִים אֲשֶׁר־יָשַׁב בָּהֵן לוֹט, *the cities in which Lot dwelt,* Gen. xix, 29.

498. The pronoun or adverb referring back to the antecedent is called retrospective. The retrospective pronoun is omitted:

a) almost always, when it would be a pronoun in the nominative, *v. g.* אִתּוֹ הֵם, *they are with him,* but הַמְּלָכִים אֲשֶׁר אִתּוֹ, *the kings who are with him,* not אִתּוֹ הֵם.

However, the retrospective pronoun in the nominative is sometimes found when the sentence is negative, *v. g.* הַבְּהֵמָה אֲשֶׁר לֹא טְהוֹרָה הִיא, *the animals which are not clean.*

499. b) commonly, when it would be in the accusative, *v. g.* יָצַר אֹתוֹ, *he made him,* but הָאָדָם אֲשֶׁר יָצָר, *the man whom he had made,* Gen. ii, 8. The retrospective pronoun, however, is often found, *v. g.* אֲנִי יוֹסֵף אֲשֶׁר־מְכַרְתֶּם אוֹתִי, *I am Joseph whom you sold,* Gen. xlv, 4.

500. c) occasionally, when the pronoun would be preceded by a preposition, *v. g.* בַּמָּקוֹם אֲשֶׁר דִּבֶּר אִתּוֹ, *in the place where he had spoken with him,* Gen. xxxv, 13, instead of אֲשֶׁר דִּבֶּר אִתּוֹ בּוֹ (שָׁם); generally, however, the retrospective pronoun or adverb is found in such cases, cp. examples under 497.

501. 2. Instead of אֲשֶׁר, the demonstratives זוּ and less frequently זֶה (408) are also used, with or without the retrospective pronouns, as just explained, *v. g.* דֶּֽרֶךְ־זוּ אֵלֵךְ, *the way wherein I should walk,* Ps. cxliii, 8.

502. 3. The article is found in the same sense, generally with participle but also with a finite verb, *v. g.* וְשָׁכַחְתָּ אֶת־יְהוָה אֱלֹהֶיךָ הַמּוֹצִיאֲךָ מֵאֶרֶץ מִצְרַיִם, *and (lest) thou forget Jehovah, thy God, who brought thee out of the land of Egypt,* Deut. viii, 14; כֹּל הַֽהִקְדִּישׁ שְׁמוּאֵל, *all that Samuel had consecrated,* 1 Chron. xxvi, 28.

503. 4. Frequently, especially after an undetermined noun, the relative particle is omitted and the relation indicated by mere juxtaposition, either in a nominal or verbal sentence (231) and with or without the retrospective pronoun, *v. g.* אִישׁ הָיָה בְאֶֽרֶץ־עוּץ אִיּוֹב שְׁמוֹ, *there was a man in the land of Hus whose name was Job,* Job i, 1; עָם לֹא־יָבִין, *a people who does not understand,* Hos. iv, 14; אֱלֹהִים לֹא יְדָעוּם, *gods whom they knew not,* Deut. xxxii, 17; שְׁלַח־נָא בְּיַד־תִּשְׁלָח, *send, I pray thee, by the hand of the one whom thou shalt send,* Ex. iv, 13.

504. 5. Very often, an independent relative clause is expressed by a participle (307), *v. g.* רְאֵה מָה־אָשִׁיב שֹׁלְחִי דָּבָר, *consider what answer I shall return to the one who sent me,* 2 Sam. xxiv, 13; מְקַצֶּה רַגְלַיִם שֹׁלֵחַ דְּבָרִים בְּיַד־כְּסִיל, *he who sends a message through a fool cuts out his own feet,* Prov. xxvi, 6.

EXERCISES.

I. 1. וַיֻּגַּד לְרִבְקָה אֶת־דִּבְרֵי עֵשָׂו בְּנָהּ הַגָּדֹל׃ — 2. וַיֹּאמֶר מַלְאַךְ יְהוָה לְהָגָר (pr. n.) הִנָּךְ הָרָה וְיֹלַדְתְּ בֵּן וְקָרָאת שְׁמוֹ יִשְׁמָעֵאל׃ — 3. הַמִּצְוָה הַזֹּאת אֲשֶׁר אָנֹכִי מְצַוְּךָ הַיּוֹם לֹא־נִפְלֵאת הִוא מִמְּךָ וְלֹא־רְחֹקָה הִוא׃ — 4. וַיֹּאמֶר מִיכָיְהוּ (Micaias) אִם־שׁוֹב תָּשׁוּב בְּשָׁלוֹם לֹא־דִבֶּר יְהוָה בִּי וַיֹּאמֶר שִׁמְעוּ עַמִּים כֻּלָּם׃ — 5. וַיִּקְרָא גַּם־פַּרְעֹה לַחֲכָמִים וְלַמְכַשְּׁפִים וַיַּעֲשׂוּ גַם־הֵם חַרְטֻמֵּי מִצְרַיִם בְּלַהֲטֵיהֶם כֵּן׃ — 6. וּלְקִישׁ

(pr. n.) הָיָה בֵן וּשְׁמוֹ שָׁאוּל בָּחוּר וָטוֹב וְאֵין אִישׁ מִבְּנֵי יִשְׂרָאֵל טוֹב
מִמֶּנּוּ מִשִּׁכְמוֹ וָמַעְלָה גָּבֹהַּ מִכָּל הָעָם׃ — 7. וְלֹא־יִוָּדַע הַשָּׂבָע בָּאָרֶץ מִפְּנֵי
הָרָעָב הַהוּא אַחֲרֵי־כֵן כִּי־כָבֵד הוּא מְאֹד׃ — 8. כָּל־מָקוֹם אֲשֶׁר תִּדְרֹךְ
כַּף־רַגְלְכֶם בּוֹ לָכֶם נְתַתִּיו כַּאֲשֶׁר דִּבַּרְתִּי אֶל־מֹשֶׁה׃ — 9. וַיִּלְקְטוּ אֶת־
הַמָּן בַּבֹּקֶר אִישׁ כְּפִי אָכְלוֹ וְחַם הַשֶּׁמֶשׁ וְנָמָס׃ — 10. טַעֲמוּ וּרְאוּ
כִּי־טוֹב יְהוָה אַשְׁרֵי הַגֶּבֶר יֶחֱסֶה־בּוֹ׃

II. 1. And behold I myself bring a flood of waters upon the earth, to destroy all flesh wherein is the breath of life. — 2. And he bought the hill of Samaria for two talents of silver. — 3. And it came to pass, when they were in the field, that Cain rose up against Abel his brother and slew him. — 4. And one cried unto another, and said, Holy, holy, holy is the Lord of hosts: the whole earth is full of His glory. — 5. Thou (thyself) shalt be over my house, only with reference to the throne will I be greater than thou. — 6. And the Lord shall return his blood upon his own head, because he fell upon men more righteous and better than he. — 7. I am Joseph, your brother, whom you sold unto Egypt. — 8. We accept good from God and we will not accept evil! and in all this Job did not sin with his lips. — 9. But of the tree of the knowledge of good and evil thou shalt not eat (of it). — 10. Because Ahab has humbled himself before me, I will not bring the evil in his days; but in his son's day will I bring the evil upon his house.

LESSON XXIV.

NUMERALS.

Vocabulary. Verbs.

† פָּשַׁט to strip off, make a raid; (*Pi.*); *Hiph.* strip one of.

יָעַד (to appoint); *Niph.* meet by appointment; (*Po'el*; *Hiph.*; *Hoph.*).

[סוּת] *Hiph.* incite, instigate.

חָנַט to spice, make spicy, embalm.

גָּזָה (to cut, sever).

גָּזַז to shear; (*Niph.*).

חָצָה to divide; *Niph.*

תָּקַע to thrust, drive, blow, clap hands; *Niph.* be blown.

נָדַד to retreat, flee; (*Po'el; Hithpo'el; Hiph.; Hoph.*).

רוּץ to run; *Pôlel; Hiph.* bring quickly.

נוּד to move to and fro; show grief; sympathize; *Hiph.*; (*Hoph.; Hithpolel*).

[נָחַם] *Niph.* (נִחַם, § 340) to be sorry, console oneself; *Pi.* comfort; (*Pu.*); *Hithp.* have compassion.

[רוּעַ] *Hiph.* to raise a shout, shout; (*Polāl*); *Hithpolel.*

גָּוַע to expire.

מָנָה to count; *Niph.*; *Pi.* appoint; (*Pu.*).

שָׁנָה to change (intrans.); *Pi.*; change (trans.); (*Pu.; Hithp.*).

שָׁנָה to repeat, do again; (*Niph.*).

זָרַק to toss, scatter.

Nouns.

מַצֵּבָה (v) / מַצֶּבֶת (iv) } *f. pillar*

רֶכֶב (v) *m. chariot*

שָׁבוּעַ (ii) *m. week*

שֵׁבֶט (v) *m. rod, sceptre, tribe*

פַּעַם (ים◌ָ-) (v) *f. beat, occurrence, time*

חֲצִי, חֵצִי (v) *m. half*

רָחָב (iv) *a. wide*

כֹּר (i) *m. kor (measure)*

קֶמַח (v) *m. flour*

מְרַגֵּל (iv) *pt. spy*

שָׁכֵן (iv) *a. neighbor, inhabitant*

חֵיק, חֵק (i) *m. bosom*

צֶמֶד (v) *m. couple, pair, yoke*

רָחוֹק (ii) *a. far, distant*

חֶרֶשׂ (v) *m. earthenware*

אֵפֶר (v) *m. ashes*

אַמָּה (iii) *f. cubit, ell*

מָנָה (iv) *f. part, portion*

מָנֶה (vi) *m. maneh, mina (weight)*

עֶצֶם (וֹת & ים◌ָ-) (v) *f bone, body, self*

מַעֲשֶׂה (vi) *m. work, deed*
פֶּסַח (v) *m. Passover*
עֶרֶב (v) *m. evening, sunset*
אֹרֶךְ (v) *m. length*
רֹחַב (v) *m. width*
מְעִיל (i) *m. robe*

נָבָל (iv) *a. senseless*
רֹפֵא (iv) *pt. physician*
שַׁחַר (v) *m. dawn*
שׁוֹפָר / שֹׁפָר (iv) *m. horn, trumpet*
קוֹמָה (i) *f. height*
חָמָס (iv) *m. violence, wrong*

כְּאֵב (i) *m. pain*
עוֹר (ות) (i) *m. skin, hide*
בֶּטֶן (v) *f. womb, body*
עֵירֹם (iii) *a. naked; m. nakedness*
עָרֹם (iii) *a. naked*
שֵׁנָה (vi) *f. sleep.*

I. Morphology.

505. **1. Table.**

		Cardinals. with masc. nouns. abs.	with masc. nouns. constr.	with fem. nouns. abs.	with fem. nouns. constr.	Ordinals.
א'	1	אֶחָד	אַחַד	אַחַת	אַחַת	רִאשׁוֹן
ב'	2	שְׁנַיִם	שְׁנֵי	שְׁתַּיִם	שְׁתֵּי	שֵׁנִי
ג'	3	שְׁלֹשָׁה	שְׁלֹשֶׁת	שָׁלֹשׁ	שְׁלֹשׁ	שְׁלִישִׁי
ד'	4	אַרְבָּעָה	אַרְבַּעַת	אַרְבַּע	אַרְבַּע	רְבִיעִי
ה'	5	חֲמִשָּׁה	חֲמֵשֶׁת	חָמֵשׁ	חֲמֵשׁ	חֲמִישִׁי
ו'	6	שִׁשָּׁה	שֵׁשֶׁת	שֵׁשׁ	שֵׁשׁ	שִׁשִּׁי
ז'	7	שִׁבְעָה	שִׁבְעַת	שֶׁבַע	שְׁבַע	שְׁבִיעִי
ח'	8	שְׁמֹנָה	שְׁמֹנַת	שְׁמֹנֶה	שְׁמֹנֶה	שְׁמִינִי
ט'	9	תִּשְׁעָה	תִּשְׁעַת	תֵּשַׁע	תְּשַׁע	תְּשִׁיעִי
י'	10	עֲשָׂרָה	עֲשֶׂרֶת	עֶשֶׂר	עֶשֶׂר	עֲשִׂירִי

		with masc. nouns.	with fem. nouns.
יא'	11	אַחַד עָשָׂר / עַשְׁתֵּי עָשָׂר	אַחַת עֶשְׂרֵה / עַשְׁתֵּי עֶשְׂרֵה
יב'	12	שְׁנֵים עָשָׂר / שְׁנֵי עָשָׂר	שְׁתֵּים עֶשְׂרֵה / שְׁתֵּי עֶשְׂרֵה
יג'	13	שְׁלֹשָׁה עָשָׂר	שְׁלֹשׁ עֶשְׂרֵה
יד'	14	אַרְבָּעָה עָשָׂר	אַרְבַּע עֶשְׂרֵה
טו'	15	etc.	etc.

Above ten, cardinals are used instead of ordinals.

כ'	20	עֶשְׂרִים	נ'	50	חֲמִשִּׁים	פ'	80	שְׁמֹנִים
ל'	30	שְׁלֹשִׁים	ס'	60	שִׁשִּׁים	צ'	90	תִּשְׁעִים
מ'	40	אַרְבָּעִים	ע'	70	שִׁבְעִים			

ק'	100	מְאַת, מֵאָה	ר'	200	מָאתַיִם	ש'	300	שְׁלֹשׁ מֵאוֹת
א̈	1000	אֶלֶף	ב̈	2000	אַלְפַּיִם	ג̈	3000	שְׁלֹשֶׁת אֲלָפִים

10000	עֲשֶׂרֶת אֲלָפִים (רִבּוֹא, רִבּוֹ) רְבָבָה	20000	עֶשְׂרִים אֶלֶף רִבּוֹתַיִם

2. Remarks.

506. A peculiarity of the Semitic languages is that for the numbers 3—10 a fem. form is used with masc. nouns, while a masc. form is used with fem. nouns.

Note שְׁתַּיִם and שְׁתֵּי not שְׁתַיִם or שְׁתֵי.

507. The numerals from 11 to 19 are formed by placing the units, without the copula, before the number ten (masc. עָשָׂר and fem. עֶשְׂרֵה). It is to be noted that in the fem. the unit is regularly in the constr. st. *i. e. three of the decad, etc.*

508. The decads. 20 is the plural of עֶשֶׂר, *ten*, עֶשְׂרִים; the other decads are the plural of the corresponding units, *v. g.* שָׁלֹשׁ, *three*, שְׁלֹשִׁים, *thirty, etc.* Note עֶשְׂרִים, שִׁבְעִים, תִּשְׁעִים, instead of עֲשָׂרִים, שְׁבָעִים, תְּשָׁעִים. These numerals are all of common gender. The compound numerals from 20 upwards are formed from decads and units by means of the conjunction וְ, *v. g.* עֶשְׂרִים וּשְׁלֹשָׁה, *23*. The units may precede or follow the decads.

509. Suffixes may be added to the numerals as to the other nouns, *v. g.* חֲמִשָּׁיו, *his fifty.*

510. Ordinals. *First* is expressed by רִאשׁוֹן. The ordinals from 2—10 are formed by adding ־ִי to the corresponding cardinal and by inserting another ־ִי before the last radical, *v. g.* שְׁלִישִׁי, *third, etc.* The fem. is formed by adding ת, *v. g.* שְׁלִישִׁית. The ending ־ָה is rare and found only in 3 and 10, שְׁלִשִׁיָּה.

II. Syntax.

A. Cardinals.

511. 1. אֶחָד is generally an adjective and treated as such, *v. g.* בְּיוֹם אֶחָד, *in one day;* as substantive, it can be in the constr. state, *v. g.* אַחַד הֶהָרִים, *one of the mountains.*

512. 2. **Numbers from 2 to 10.** These numerals, being real substantives, can be either in the constr. state or remain in the absolute; in the latter case, they are in apposition to the thing numbered and either precede or follow it.

a) With a determinate noun, with יוֹם or with another numeral, the numeral generally precedes in the constr. state, *v. g.* חֲמֵשֶׁת הַמְּלָכִים *the five kings;* שְׁלֹשֶׁת יָמִים, *three days;* שְׁלֹשֶׁת אֲלָפִים, *three thousand.*

513. b) With an undetermined noun, except יוֹם or another numeral, the numeral generally remains in the abs. st. and precedes the thing numbered, *v. g.* שֶׁבַע שָׁנִים, *seven years;* עֲשָׂרָה גְמַלִּים, *ten camels.* In some sections of the Bible, more particularly in the later books, the numeral follows the thing numbered, *v. g.* פָּרִים שְׁלֹשָׁה, *three bullocks.*

514. c) The thing numbered is generally in the plural, with very few exceptions, *v. g.* חָמֵשׁ שָׁנִים, *five years;* עֲשָׂרָה גְמַלִּים, *ten camels, etc.*

515. 3. **Numerals from 11 to 19.** a) They are always in the abs. st. in apposition to the thing numbered and generally stand before, but sometimes after, especially in later books, *v. g.* שְׁתֵּי־עֶשְׂרֵה, אֲבָנִים, *12 stones,* Jos. IV, 8.

516. b) The thing numbered is regularly in the plural, but certain common substantives of time, measure, weight, and a few collectives remain in the singular. The more common of these are: יוֹם, *day;* שָׁנָה, *year;* אִישׁ, *man;* נֶפֶשׁ, *soul, person;* שֵׁבֶט, *tribe;* מַצֵּבָה, *pillar;* אַמָּה, *cubit,* חֹדֶשׁ, *month,* עִיר, *city,* שֶׁקֶל, *shekel,* רֶכֶב, *chariot,* רַגְלִי, *infantry* (cp. English: ten foot long), *v.g.* אַחַד עָשָׂר יוֹם, *11 days;* וַיִּמְלֹךְ שְׁתֵּים־עֶשְׂרֵה שָׁנָה *and he reigned 12 years,* 2 K. III, 1.

517. 4. **Numerals above 20. Decads, hundreds and thousands.** They take the object numbered either after them in the plural or singular; or (especially in later books) before them in the plural; or finally, the thing numbered is repeated in the plural with the units and generally in the singular with the decads and hundreds, *v. g.* שְׁלֹשִׁים וּשְׁמֹנֶה שָׁנָה, *38 years,* Deut. II, 14; מֵאָה שָׁנָה וְעֶשְׂרִים שָׁנָה וְשֶׁבַע שָׁנִים, *127 years,* Gen. XXIII, 1; וְאַחֲרֵי הַשָּׁבֻעִים שִׁשִּׁים וּשְׁנַיִם, *and after the 62 weeks,* Dan. IX, 26;

518. 5. . . . . *years old* is rendered by בֶּן־ *son of* followed by the number of years, *v. g.* בֶּן־שְׁלֹשִׁים שָׁנָה דָּוִד בְּמָלְכוֹ, *David was 30 years old when he began to reign,* 2 Sam. V, 4.

519. 6. When a numerical phrase is to be made definite, the article usually is prefixed to the thing numbered, not to the numeral; if however the numeral is not accompanied by the object numbered, the article is prefixed to the numeral, *v. g.* שְׁלֹשׁ מֵאוֹת הָאִישׁ, *the 300 men,* Jud. VII, 7; but אַרְבָּעָה מְלָכִים אֶת־הַחֲמִשָּׁה, *four kings against the five,* Gen. XIV, 9.

Words that can easily be supplied in expressions of time, weight or measure, are commonly understood after numerals, *v. g. ephah, day, shekel, etc.*

B. **Ordinals.**

520. 1. The ordinals from 1 to 10 are treated exactly as adjectives, *v. g.* בַּשָּׁנָה הָרְבִיעִית, *in the fourth year.*

521. 2. Above 10, cardinals are used instead of ordinals and may stand either before or after the thing numbered, *v. g.* בְּאַרְבָּעִים שָׁנָה, *in the fortieth year.*

522. 3. In stating dates, some peculiarities are to be noted:

a) The genitive *of the month* is commonly rendered by לְ, with the cardinal number even from 1 to 10, and יוֹם is often omitted, *v. g.* בַּחֲמִשָּׁה עָשָׂר יוֹם לַחֹדֶשׁ, *on the 15th day of the month,* Ex. XVI, 1; בְּשִׁבְעָה לַחֹדֶשׁ, *on the seventh day of the month,* 2 K. XXV, 8.

523. b) The word שָׁנָה, *year* is often put in the constr. st. at the beginning of the phrase, and is repeated regularly but not necessarily after the numerals; here also cardinals are frequently used for the ordinals, *v. g.* בִּשְׁנַת שְׁתֵּים־עֶשְׂרֵה שָׁנָה לְיוֹרָם, *in the 12th year of Joram,* 2 K. VIII, 25; בִּשְׁנַת שְׁתַּיִם לְאָסָא מֶלֶךְ יְהוּדָה, *in the second year of Asa, king of Judah,* 1 K. XV, 25.

C. **Distributives.**

524. Distributives are expressed:

1. by repeating the cardinal number, *v. g.* שֵׁשׁ וָשֵׁשׁ, *six each;*

2. by repeating the thing numbered along with the numeral, *v. g.* אִישׁ־אֶחָד אִישׁ־אֶחָד לַשָּׁבֶט, *one man for every tribe,* Jos. III, 12;

3. by the cardinal with ל, *v. g.* אִישׁ אֶחָד לַשָּׁבֶט, *one man to the tribe,* i. e. *one man for every tribe,* Deut. I, 23;

4. in certain cases by ל alone, *v. g.* וְכָל־הָעָם יָצְאוּ לְמֵאוֹת וְלַאֲלָפִים, *and all the people went out by hundreds and by thousands*, 2 Sam. xviii, 4.

D. Multiplicatives.

1. English *'times'* may be rendered in Hebrew:

525. a) by the cardinals and

α) פַּעַם, (f.) lit. *beat* (cp. French *coup*), *v. g.* הַפַּעַם, *this time;* פַּעַם or פַּעַם אַחַת, *once;* פַּעֲמַיִם, *twice;* שָׁלֹשׁ פְּעָמִים, *three times, etc.*

β) פַּעַם understood, *v. g.* אַחַת or בְּאַחַת, *once;* שֶׁבַע, *seven times, etc.*

γ) Instead of פַּעַם, other words are occasionally used, such as רֶגֶל, (*foot*), עֵת (*time, duration*), *v. g.* שָׁלֹשׁ רְגָלִים, *three times*, Num. xxii, 28; רַבּוֹת עִתִּים, *many times*, Neh. ix, 28.

526. b) by the ordinals and פַּעַם understood, or sometimes expressed, *v. g.* שֵׁנִית, *a second time;* בַּשְּׁבִיעִית, *on the seventh time;* פַּעַם חֲמִישִׁית, *a fifth time;* בַּפַּעַם הַשְּׁבִיעִית, *on the seventh time.*

2. English *' . . . . fold'* is rendered in Hebrew:

527. a) by the dual fem. of cardinals, *v. g.* אַרְבַּעְתַּיִם, *fourfold,* שִׁבְעָתַיִם, *sevenfold, etc.*

528. b) *Double* is expressed either by the dual masc. *v. g.* שְׁנַיִם, *v. g.* שְׁנַיִם יְשַׁלֵּם, *he shall pay double*, Ex. xxii, 3; or by מִשְׁנֶה, *repetition,* placed in apposition to the noun; also by מִשְׁנֶה עַל, *repetition over, v. g.* וְכֶסֶף מִשְׁנֶה קְחוּ בְיֶדְכֶם, *and take double the money in your hand*, Gen. xliii, 12; וְהָיָה בַּיּוֹם הַשִּׁשִּׁי וְהֵכִינוּ אֵת אֲשֶׁר־יָבִיאוּ וְהָיָה מִשְׁנֶה עַל אֲשֶׁר־יִלְקְטוּ יוֹם ׀ יוֹם, *and it shall come to pass on the sixth day, that they shall prepare that which they shall have brought in, and it shall be twice as much as they gather daily*, Ex. xvi, 5.

E. Fractions.

529. 1. *'Half'* is generally expressed by חֲצִי, חֵצִי, (חֶצְיוֹ), *v. g.* וַיִּקַּח מֹשֶׁה חֲצִי הַדָּם, *and Moses took half of the blood*, Ex. xxiv, 6; אַמָּתַיִם וָחֵצִי אָרְכּוֹ, *two cubits and a half shall be the length thereof*, Ex, xxv,10.

2. The other fractions are expressed by the ordinal (or cardinal above ten, 521); the article generally precedes the thing measured, *v. g.* בְּרְבִעִית הַהִין שֶׁמֶן, *with the fourth part of a hin of oil*, Num. xv, 4.

Some special words occasionally occur, *v. g.* רֹבַע, *a fourth;* חֹמֶשׁ, *a fifth;* עִשָּׂרוֹן ,עֶשָּׂרוֹן, *a tenth;* מַעֲשֵׂר, *tithe.*

EXERCISES.

I. 1. תּוֹרָה אַחַת וּמִשְׁפָּט אֶחָד יִהְיֶה לָכֶם וְלַגֵּר הַגָּר אִתְּכֶם׃ —
2. בַּחֹדֶשׁ הָרִאשׁוֹן בְּאַרְבָּעָה עָשָׂר לַחֹדֶשׁ בֵּין הָעַרְבַּיִם פֶּסַח לַיהוָֹה׃ —
3. וַיִּהְיוּ כָּל־יְמֵי אָדָם אֲשֶׁר־חַי תְּשַׁע מֵאוֹת שָׁנָה וּשְׁלֹשִׁים שָׁנָה וַיָּמֹת׃ —
4. וַיְהִי לֶחֶם־שְׁלֹמֹה לְיוֹם אֶחָד שְׁלֹשִׁים כֹּר סֹלֶת וְשִׁשִּׁים כֹּר קָמַח׃ —
5. וַיְחִי־שֵׁת אַחֲרֵי הוֹלִידוֹ אֶת־אֱנוֹשׁ שֶׁבַע שָׁנִים וּשְׁמֹנֶה מֵאוֹת שָׁנָה
וַיּוֹלֶד בָּנִים וּבָנוֹת׃ — 6. וַיָּשֻׁבוּ הַמְרַגְּלִים אֶל־יְהוֹשֻׁעַ וַיֹּאמְרוּ אֵלָיו
אַל־יַעַל כָּל־הָעָם כְּאַלְפַּיִם אִישׁ אוֹ כִּשְׁלֹשֶׁת אֲלָפִים אִישׁ יַעֲלוּ וְיַכּוּ אֶת־
הָעָי (Ai, pr. n.)׃ — 7. הָשֵׁב לִשְׁכֵנֵינוּ שִׁבְעָתַיִם אֶל־חֵיקָם חֶרְפָּתָם
אֲשֶׁר חֵרְפוּךָ אֲדֹנָי׃ — 8. וַיְהִי בִשְׁמוֹנִים שָׁנָה וְאַרְבַּע מֵאוֹת שָׁנָה לְצֵאת
בְנֵי־יִשְׂרָאֵל מֵאֶרֶץ־מִצְרַיִם בַּשָּׁנָה הָרְבִיעִית בְּחֹדֶשׁ זִו (Ziv) הוּא הַחֹדֶשׁ
הַשֵּׁנִי לִמְלֹךְ שְׁלֹמֹה עַל־יִשְׂרָאֵל וַיִּבֶן הַבַּיִת לַיהוָֹה׃

II. 1. And there were born unto Job seven sons and three daughters. His cattle was seven thousand sheep and three thousand camels, and five hundred yoke of oxen, and five hundred she-asses. — 2. Joseph died, being a hundred and ten years old. — 3. And Joseph commanded his servants, the physicians, to embalm his father, and they fulfilled forty days for him; and the Egyptians wept for him seventy days. — 4. And Seth lived one hundred and five years, and he begat Enosh; and Seth, after he begat Enosh, lived 807 years; and all the days of Seth were 912 years, and he died. — 5. And David's anger was greatly kindled against the man, and he said to Nathan, As Jehovah liveth, the man that hath done this is worthy of death (a son of death) and he shall restore the lamb (f.) fourfold. — 6. And a river went out of Eden to water the garden: and from there it was parted and became four heads. The name of the first is Pishon; the name of the second river is Gihon; the name of the third river is Hiddekel (Tigris); and the fourth river is the Euphrates. — 7. And it came to pass on the seventh day, that they rose early at the dawning of the day and compassed the city after the same manner seven times: and it came to pass at the seventh time the priests blew the trumpets, and Joshua said unto the people: Shout.

JOB I.

1 איש היה בארץ עוץ איוב שמו והיה האיש ההוא תם וישר וירא
אלהים וסר מרע: 2 ויולדו לו שבעה בנים ושלוש בנות: 3 ויהי מקנהו שבעת
אלפי צאן ושלשת אלפי גמלים וחמש מאות צמד בקר וחמש מאות אתונות
ועבדה רבה מאד ויהי האיש ההוא גדול מכל בני קדם: 4 והלכו בניו ועשו
משתה בית איש יומו ושלחו וקראו לשלשת אחיתיהם לאכל ולשתות עמהם:
5 ויהי כי הקיפו ימי המשתה וישלח איוב ויקדשם והשכים בבקר והעלה
עלות מספר כלם כי אמר איוב אולי חטאו בני וקללו[1] אלהים בלבבם ככה
יעשה איוב כל הימים: 6 ויהי היום ויבאו בני האלהים להתיצב על יהוה
ויבוא גם השטן בתוכם: 7 ויאמר יהוה אל השטן מאין תבא ויען השטן
את יהוה ויאמר משוט בארץ ומהתהלך בה: 8 ויאמר יהוה אל השטן
השמת לבך אל עבדי איוב כי אין כמהו בארץ איש תם וישר ירא אלהים
וכר מרע: 9 ויען השטן את יהוה ויאמר החנם ירא איוב אלהים: 10 הלא
את שכת[2] בעדו ובעד ביתו ובעד כל אשר לו מסביב מעשה ידיו ברכת
ומקנהו פרץ בארץ: 11 ואולם שלח נא ידך וגע בכל אשר לו אם לא על
פניך יקללך: 12 ויאמר יהוה אל השטן הנה כל אשר לו בידך רק אליו אל
תשלח ידך ויצא השטן מעם פני יהוה: 13 ויהי היום ובניו ובנתיו אכלים
ושתים יין בבית אחיהם הבכור: 14 ומלאך בא אל איוב ויאמר הבקר היו
חרשות והאתנות רעות על ידיהם: 15 ותפל שבא[3] ותקחם ואת הנערים
הכו לפי חרב ואמלטה רק אני לבדי להגיד לך: 16 עוד זה מדבר וזה בא
ויאמר אש אלהים נפלה מן השמים ותבער בצאן ובנערים ותאכלם ואמלטה
רק אני לבדי להגיד לך: 17 עוד זה מדבר וזה בא ויאמר כשדים שמו
שלשה ראשים ויפשטו על הגמלים ויקחום ואת הנערים הכו לפי חרב
ואמלטה רק אני לבדי להגיד לך: 18 עד זה מדבר וזה בא ויאמר בניך

---

[1] The Massoretic text here and elsewhere reads ברכו, which is a euphemism. [2] שׂוּךְ to fence about, protect. [3] Sheba i. e. marauders from Sheba.

ובנותיך אכלים ושתים יין בבית אחיהם הבכור: 19 והנה רוח גדולה באה
מעבר המדבר ויגע בארבע פנות הבית ויפל על הנערים וימותו ואמלטה
רק אני לבדי להגיד לך: 20 ויקם איוב ויקרע את מעלו ויגז את ראשו ויפל
ארצה וישתחו: 21 ויאמר ערם יצתי מבטן אמי וערם אשוב שמה יהוה
נתן ויהוה לקח יהי שם יהוה מברך: 22 בכל זאת לא חטא איוב ולא נתן
תפלה לאלהים:

JOB II.

1 ויהי היום ויבאו בני האלהים להתיצב על יהוה ויבא גם השטן בתכם
להתיצב על יהוה: 2 ויאמר יהוה אל השטן אי מזה תבא ויען השטן את
יהוה ויאמר משט בארץ ומהתהלך בה: 3 ויאמר יהוה אל השטן השמת
לבך אל עבדי איוב כי אין כמהו בארץ איש תם וישר ירא אלהים וסר מרע
ועדנו מחזיק בתמתו ותסיתני בו לבלעו חנם: 4 ויען השטן את יהוה ויאמר
עור בעד עור וכל אשר לאיש יתן בעד נפשו: 5 אולם שלח נא ידך וגע אל
עצמו ואל בשרו אם לא אל פניך יקללך: 6 ויאמר יהוה אל השטן הנו בידך
אך את נפשו שמר: 7 ויצא השטן מאת פני יהוה ויך את איוב בשחין[1]
רע מכף רגלו ועד קדקדו: 8 ויקח לו חרש להתגרד[2] בו והוא ישב בתוך
האפר: 9 ותאמר לו אשתו עדך מחזיק בתמתך קלל אלהים ומת: 10 ויאמר
אליה כדבר אחת הנבלות תדברי גם את הטוב נקבל מאת האלהים
ואת הרע לא נקבל בכל זאת לא חטא איוב בשפתיו: 11 וישמעו שלשת
רעי איוב את כל הרעה הזאת הבאה עליו ויבאו איש ממקמו אליפז התימני[3]
ובלדד השוחי[4] וצופר הנעמתי[5] ויועדו יחדו לבוא לנוד לו ולנחמו: 12 וישאו
את עיניהם מרחוק ולא הכירהו וישאו קולם ויבכו ויקרעו איש מעלו ויזרקו
עפר על ראשיהם השמימה: 13 וישבו אתו לארץ שבעת ימים ושבעת
לילות ואין דבר אליו דבר כי ראו כי גדל הכאב מאד:

PROVERBS IV.

1 שמעו בנים מוסר אב והקשיבו לדעת בינה: 2 כי לקח טוב נתתי
לכם תורתי אל תעזבו: 3 כי בן הייתי לאבי רך[6] ויחיד לפני אמי: 4 וירני
ויאמר לי יתמך דברי לבך שמר מצותי וחיה: 5 קנה חכמה קנה בינה אל
תשכח ואל תט מאמרי פי: 6 אל תעזבה ותשמרך אהבה ותצרך: 7 ראשית

---

[1] Boil, eruption. [2] To scrape. [3] Eliphaz the Temanite. [4] Bildad the Shuhite. [5] Ṣophar the Naamathite. [6] Tender, delicate.

חכמה קנה חכמה ובכל קנינך קנה בינה: 8 סלסלה[1] ותרוממך תכבדך כי
תחבקנה: 9 תתן לראשך לוית[2] חן עטרת תפארת תמגנך: 10 שמע בני
וקח אמרי וירבו לך שנות חיים: 11 בדרך חכמה הריתיך הדרכתיך במעגלי
ישר: 12 בלכתך לא יצר צעדך ואם תרוץ לא תכשל: 13 החזק במוסר
אל תרף נצרה כי היא חייך: 14 בארח רשעים אל תבא ואל תאשר בדרך
רעים: 15 פרעהו אל תעבר בו שטה[3] מעליו ועבר: 16 כי לא ישנו אם
לא ירעו ונגזלה שנתם אם לא יכשילו: 17 כי לחמו[4] לחם רשע ויין חמסים
ישתו: 18 וארח צדיקים כאור נגה[5] הולך ואור[6] עד נכון היום: 19 דרך
רשעים כאפלה[7] לא ידעו במה יכשלו: 20 בני לדברי הקשיבה לאמרי הט
אזנך: 21 אל יליזו[8] מעיניך שמרם בתוך לבבך: 22 כי חיים הם למצאיהם
ולכל בשרו מרפא[9]: 23 מכל משמר נצר לבך כי ממנו תוצאות חיים:
24 הסר ממך עקשות[10] פה ולזות[11] שפתים הרחק ממך: 25 עיניך לנכח
יביטו ועפעפיך[12] יישרו נגדך: 26 פלס[13] מעגל רגלך וכל דרכיך יכנו:
27 אל תט ימין ושמאול הסר רגלך מרע:

---

[1] To exalt. [2] Wreath. [3] To turn aside. [4] To eat. [5] Brightness. [6] To shine. [7] Darkness. [8] To depart. [9] Healing, cure. [10] Crookedness. [11] Deviation. [12] Eyelid. [13] To make level, weigh.

PARADIGMS.

The Personal

	A. Separate Pronoun. Nominative of the Pronoun (Lesson v).		B. Verbal Suffix.[2] Accusative of the Pronoun (Lessons xiv and xvii). a.		b.	c. α.
Sing. 1.	common אָנֹכִי, in pause אָנֹכִי; אֲנִי, in pause אָנִי	I	־נִי	me	ַ־נִי, (ַ־נִּי)	ֵ־נִי
2. m.	אַתָּה, (אַתְּ), in pause אָתָּה	thou	ךָ, (כָה)	thee	ְ־ךָ, (ְ־כָה), pause ֶ־ךָ, ָ־ךְ	
2. f.	אַתְּ (אַתִּי)		ךְ	thee	(ָ־ךְ), ֵ־ךְ, ֶ־ךְ	
3. m.	הוּא	he	הוּ, ו	him	ָ־הוּ, (ה), ו	ֵ־הוּ
3. f.	הִיא	she	הָ	her	ָ־הּ	ֶ־הָ
Plur. 1.	common אֲנַחְנוּ, (נַחְנוּ), (אֲנוּ), pause אֲנָחְנוּ, (נָחְנוּ)	we	נוּ	us	ָ־נוּ	ֵ־נוּ
2. m.	אַתֶּם	you	כֶם	you	ְ־כֶם	
2. f.	אַתֵּנָה, אַתֶּן		[כֶן]	you	[ְ־כֶן]	
3. m.	הֵמָּה, הֵם	they	ם, (הֶם)	them	ָ־ם, ַ־ם, ָ־מוֹ *	ֵ־ם, (ֶ־ם), ֵ־מוֹ *
3. f.	הֵנָּה		ן, [הֶן]	them	ָ־ן, (ַ־ן)	[ֵ־ן]

[1] Forms in curved brackets are rare; those in square brackets do not in column Ba are used after forms ending in a vowel; those in column b are and cβ are used after forms of the Imperfect ending in a consonant, cα being nominal suffixes see lesson vi, 150, 151.

A.

Pronouns.[1]

β.	C. Nominal Suffix.[3] Genitive of the Pronoun (Lessons vi and xvii). a.		b.	c.
—ֶנִּי	—ִי	*my* (*mei*)	—ִי	—ַי, P. —ָי
—ֶךָּ (—ֶנְךָּ)	—ְךָ, (—ְכָה)	*thy* (*tui*)	—ְךָ, (כָה), P. —ֶךָ, (—ָךְ)	—ֶיךָ
	ךְ		—ֵךְ, (—ָךְ)	—ַיִךְ
(—ֶנְהוּ), —ֶנּוּ	—הוּ, ו	*his* (*ejus, suus*)	ו (ה), —ֵהוּ	—ָיו, —ָו, (—ֵיהוּ*)
—ֶנָּה	—ָהּ	*her*	—ָהּ, —ֶהָ	—ֶיהָ
—ֶנּוּ	—נוּ	*our*	—ֵנוּ, (—ָנוּ)	—ֵינוּ
	כֶם	*your*	—ְכֶם	—ֵיכֶם
	כֶן		—ְכֶן	—ֵיכֶן
	הֶם	*their*	—ָם, —ָמוֹ*	—ֵיהֶם
	—מוֹ*			—ֵימוֹ*
	הֶן		—ָן, (הֶן)	—ֵיהֶן

occur; those marked with an asterisk are poetical. [2] Verbal suffixes used after forms of the Perfect ending in a consonant; those in columns cα the ordinary suffixes, and cβ the suffixes with *Nun energicum*. [3] On.

B. Nouns, Class I: Nouns with unchangeable

	Singular			
	absol.	constr.	light suff.	heavy suff.
1	סוּס	סוּס	סוּסִי	סֽוּסְכֶם
2	סוּסָה	סוּסַת	סֽוּסָתִי	סֽוּסַתְכֶם
3	כּוֹס	כּוֹס	כּוֹסִי	כּֽוֹסְכֶם
4	רוּחַ	רוּחַ	רוּחִי	רֽוּחֲכֶם

C. Nouns, Class II: Nouns with changeable

1	גָּדוֹל	גְּדוֹל	גְּדוֹלִי	גְּדֽוֹלְכֶם
2	גְּדוֹלָה	גְּדוֹלַת	גְּדֽוֹלָתִי	גְּדֽוֹלַתְכֶם

D. Nouns, Class III: Monosyllables in *a*, *e*, *o*;

	Singular			
	absol.	constr.	light suff.	heavy suff.
1	עַם, (P. עָם), *m. people,*	עַם	עַמִּי	—
2	כַּף, (P. כָּף), *f. palm of the hand,*	כַּף	כַּפִּי	—
3	יָם, *m. sea,*	יַם־, יָם	יַמִּי	יַמְּכֶם
4	גָּמָל, *m. camel,*	—	—	—
5	שֵׁן, *f.* (*m.*) *tooth, ivory,*	שֶׁן־, שֵׁן	שִׁנּוֹ	—
6	אֵם, *f. mother,*	אֵם	אִמִּי	אִמְּכֶם
7	לֵוִי, *m. Levite,*	—	—	—
8	חֹק, *m. precept,*	חָק־, חֹק	חֻקִּי	חָקְכֶם חֻקְּכֶם
9	לְאֹם, *m. people,*	—	לְאֻמִּי	—
10	פַּר, (P. פָּר), *m. bull* (see 118),	פַּר	—	—
11	חֻקָּה, *f. precept,*	חֻקַּת	—	—
12	פְּקֻדָּה, *f. office, visitation,*	פְּקֻדַּת	פְּקֻדָּתְךָ	—
13	פָּרָה, *f. heifer,*	—	פָּרָתוֹ	—

Vowels. (Lesson V).

Plural				Dual	
absol.	constr.	light suff.	heavy suff.	absol.	constr.
סוּסִים	סוּסֵי	סוּסַי	סֽוּסֵיכֶם		
סוּסוֹת	סוּסוֹת	סֽוּסוֹתַי	סוּסֽוֹתֵיכֶם		
כּוֹסוֹת	כּוֹסוֹת	כּֽוֹסוֹתַי	כּוֹסֽוֹתֵיכֶם		
רוּחוֹת	רוּחוֹת	רֽוּחוֹתַי	רוּחֽוֹתֵיכֶם		

Vowel in the Penult. (Lesson V).

גְּדוֹלִים	גְּדוֹלֵי	גְּדוֹלַי	גְּֽדוֹלֵיכֶם	שְׁבוּעַ֫יִם	שְׁבוּעֵי
גְּדוֹלוֹת	גְּדוֹלוֹת	גְּֽדוֹלוֹתַי	גְּדוֹלֽוֹתֵיכֶם	(*two weeks*)	

Dissylables following their analogy. (Lesson XI).

Plural.				Dual	
absol.	constr.	light suff.	heavy suff.	absol.	constr.
עַמִּים	עַמֵּי	עַמָּיו	—		
כַּפּוֹת	כַּפּוֹת	כַּפּוֹתָיו	—		
		כַּפַּי	כַּפֵּיהֶם	כַּפַּ֫יִם	כַּפֵּי
יַמִּים	יַמֵּי	יַמַּי	יַמֵּיכֶם		
גְּמַלִּים	גְּמַלֵּי	גְּמַלָּיו	גְּמַלֵּיהֶם		
--	—	שִׁנָּיו	שִׁנֵּיהֶם	שִׁנַּ֫יִם	שִׁנֵּי
אַמּוֹת	אַמּוֹת	אַמּוֹתָיו	אַמְּֽוֹתֵיהֶם		
לְוִיִּם	—	לְוִיֵּ֫נוּ	—		
חֻקִּים	חֻקֵּי	חֻקַּי	חֻקֵּיכֶם		
לְאֻמִּים	—	—	—		
פָּרִים	—	פָּרֶ֫יהָ	—		
חֻקּוֹת	חֻקּוֹת	חֻקּוֹתַי	{ חֻקּוֹתֵיהֶם חֻקֹּתָם		
פְּקֻדּוֹת	—	—	—		
פָּרוֹת	—	—	—		

[A brace spans the light suff. through dual constr. columns over the row beginning כַּפַּי.]

E. Nouns, Class IV:

*Milra*ʿ Nouns with changeable

	Singular				
	abs.		constr.	l. suff.	heavy suff.
1	עוֹלָם	*m. eternity,*	עוֹלַם	עוֹלָמִי	עוֹלַמְכֶם
2	כָּנָף	*f. (m.) wing,*	כְּנַף	כְּנָפִי	
3	דָּבָר	*m. word,*	דְּבַר	דְּבָרִי	דְּבַרְכֶם
4	חָכָם	*a. wise,*	חֲכַם	חֲכָמִי	חֲכַמְכֶם
5	זָקֵן	*a. old,*	זְקַן	זְקֵנִי	—
6	לֵבָב	*m. (f.) heart,*	לְבַב	לְבָבִי	לְבַבְכֶם
7	נְבֵלָה	*f. corpse,*	נִבְלַת	נִבְלָתִי	—
8	צְדָקָה	*f. justice,*	צִדְקַת	צִדְקָתִי	—
9	שְׁאֵלָה	*f. petition,*	שְׁאֵלַת	שְׁאֵלָתִי	—
10	שֹׁפֵט	*pt. judging, judge,*	שֹׁפֵט	שֹׁפְטִי	—
11	אֹיֵב	*pt. enemy,*	אֹיֵב	אֹיְבִי	{ אֹיִבְכֶם יֹצֶרְךָ
12	כֹּהֵן	*m. priest,*	כֹּהֵן	—	—

F. Nouns, Class V:

		Singular				
		abs.		constr.	l. suff.	heavy suff.
A and B	1	מֶ֫לֶךְ	*m. king,*	מֶ֫לֶךְ	מַלְכִּי	מַלְכְּכֶם
	2	רֶ֫גֶל	*f. foot,*	רֶ֫גֶל	רַגְלִי	רַגְלְכֶם
	3	נַ֫עַר	*m.* { *child, youth,* *servant,*	נַ֫עַר	נַעֲרִי	נַעַרְכֶם
	4	סֵ֫פֶר	*m. book, letter,*	סֵ֫פֶר	סִפְרִי	סִפְרְכֶם
	5	קֹ֫דֶשׁ	*m.* { *sacredness,* *sanctuary,*	קֹ֫דֶשׁ	קָדְשִׁי	קָדְשְׁכֶם
	6	פֹּ֫עַל	*m. work,*	פֹּ֫עַל	פָּעֳלִי	פָּעָלְכֶם
	7	מַלְכָּה	*f. queen,*	מַלְכַּת	[מַלְכָּתִי]	[מַלְכַּתְכֶם]
	8	עֶזְרָה	*f. help,*	עֶזְרַת	עֶזְרָתִי	—
	9	חָרְבָּה	*f.* { *waste, ruin,* *desolation,*	[חָרְבַּת]	[חָרְבָּתִי]	[חָרְבַּתְכֶם]

Qameṣ and *Ṣere*. (Lesson XI).

Plural abs.	Plural constr.	Plural light suff.	Plural heavy suff.	Dual abs.	Dual constr.
עוֹלָמִים	עוֹלְמֵי	עוֹלָמַי	עוֹלְמֵיכֶם		
כְּנָפִים	כַּנְפֵי	כְּנָפָיו	כַּנְפֵיהֶם	כְּנָפַ֫יִם	כַּנְפֵי
דְּבָרִים	דִּבְרֵי	דְּבָרַי	דִּבְרֵיכֶם		
חֲכָמִים	חַכְמֵי	חֲכָמַי	חַכְמֵיכֶם		
זְקֵנִים	זִקְנֵי	זְקֵנַי	זִקְנֵיכֶם		
לְבָבוֹת	—	—	—	יְרֵכַ֫יִם *thighs*	
	(generations)				
(תּוֹלֵדֶת)	תּוֹלְדֹת	תּוֹלְדֹתָיו	תּוֹלְדֹתָם	יַרְכָתַ֫יִם *thighs*	יַרְכְּתֵי
צְדָקוֹת	צִדְקֹת	צִדְקֹתָיו	—		
—	—	—	—		
שֹׁפְטִים	שֹׁפְטֵי	שֹׁפְטָיו	שֹׁפְטֵיהֶם		
אֹיְבִים	אֹיְבֵי	אֹיְבַי	אֹיְבֵיכֶם	מֹאזְנַ֫יִם *balance*	מֹאזְנֵי
כֹּהֲנִים	כֹּהֲנֵי	כֹּהֲנַי	כֹּהֲנֵיהֶם		

Segolates. (Lesson XII).

Plural abs.	Plural constr.	Plural light suff.	Plural heavy suff.	Dual abs.	Dual constr.
מְלָכִים	מַלְכֵי	מְלָכַי	מַלְכֵיכֶם		
רְגָלִים	רַגְלֵי	רְגָלַי	רַגְלֵיכֶם	רַגְלַ֫יִם	רַגְלֵי
נְעָרִים	נַעֲרֵי	נְעָרַי	נַעֲרֵיכֶם	נַעֲלַ֫יִם *sandal*	נַעֲלֵי
סְפָרִים	סִפְרֵי	סְפָרַי	סִפְרֵיכֶם		
קֳדָשִׁים / קֳדָשִׁים	קָדְשֵׁי	קֳדָשַׁי / קֳדָשַׁי	קָדְשֵׁיכֶם		
פְּעָלִים	פָּעֳלֵי	פְּעָלַי	פָּעֳלֵיכֶם		
מְלָכוֹת	[מַלְכוֹת]	[מַלְכוֹתַי]	[מַלְכְוֹתֵיכֶם]		
—	—	—	—		
חֲרָבוֹת	חָרְבוֹת	חָרְבוֹתָיו	חָרְבוֹתֵיהֶם		

		Singular			
		abs.	constr.	l. suff.	heavy suff.
C	10	יוֹנֶ֫קֶת, *f. sprout,*	יוֹנֶ֫קֶת	יוֹנַקְתּוֹ	[יוֹנַקְתְּכֶם]
	11	גֻּלְגֹּ֫לֶת, *f. skull,*	[גֻּלְגֹּ֫לֶת]	גֻּלְגָּלְתִּי	[גֻּלְגָּלְתְּכֶם]
D	12	מִלְחָמָה, *f. war, battle,*	מִלְחֶ֫מֶת	מִלְחַמְתִּי	מִלְחַמְתָּם
E	13	מָ֫וֶת, *m. death,*	מוֹת	מוֹתִי	[מוֹתְכֶם]
	14	זַ֫יִת, *m. olive, olive tree,*	זֵית	זֵיתְךָ	[זֵיתְכֶם]
	15	עַ֫יִן, *f. eye, fountain,*	עֵין	עֵינִי	עֵינְכֶם
F	16	פְּרִי, / P. פֶּ֫רִי, *m. fruit,*	פְּרִי	פִּרְיִי	פֶּרְיְכֶם
	17	גְּדִי, *m. kid,*	גְּדִי	—	—
	18	חֳלִי, *m. sickness,*	חֳלִי	חָלְיוֹ	—

G. Nouns, Class VI: *Milraʿ* Nouns in ה ֶ.

	Singular			
	abs.	constr.	l. suff.	heavy suff.
1	רֹעֶה, *pt. shepherd,*	רֹעֵה	רֹעֵ֫הוּ / רֹעִי	—
2	שָׂדֶה, *m. field,*	שְׂדֵה	שָׂדֵ֫הוּ / שָׂדִי	—
3	יָד, *f. (m.) hand,*	יַד	יָדוֹ / יָדֵ֫הוּ	יֶדְכֶם
4	שָׂפָה, *f. lip,*	שְׂפַת	שְׂפָתוֹ	[שְׂפַתְכֶם]
5	שָׁנָה, *f. year,*	שְׁנַת	שְׁנָתִי	שְׁנַתְכֶם

Plural				Dual	
abs.	constr.	light suff.	heavy suff.	abs.	constr.
[יְוֹנְקוֹת]	[יוֹנְקוֹת]	יוֹנְקוֹתָיו	[יוֹנְקוֹתֵיכֶם]		
[גֻּלְגָּלוֹת]	[גֻּלְגְּלוֹת]	גֻּלְגְּלוֹתָם	[גֻּלְגְּלוֹתֵיכֶם]		
מִלְחָמוֹת	מִלְחֲמוֹת	מִלְחֲמוֹתָיו	[מִלְחֲמוֹתֵיכֶם]		
[מוֹתִים]	מוֹתֵי	מוֹתָיו			
זֵיתִים	[זֵיתֵי]	[זֵיתַי]	זֵיתֵיכֶם		
—	עֵינֵי	עֵינַי	עֵינֵיהֶם	עֵינַ֫יִם	עֵינֵי
—	—	—	—		
גְּדָיִים	גְּדָיֵי	—	—		
חֲלָיִים	חֲלָיֵי	חֲלָיֵ֫נוּ	—		

(Lesson XII).

Plural				Dual	
abs.	constr.	light suff.	heavy suff.	abs.	constr.
רֵעִים	רֵעֵי	רֵעַי	רֵעֵיהֶם		
שָׂדִים שָׂדוֹת	שְׂדֵי שְׂדוֹת	שָׂדַי שְׂדוֹתַי	שְׂדוֹתֵיכֶם		
יָדוֹת	יְדוֹת	יָדַי	יְדֵיכֶם	יָדַ֫יִם	יְדֵי
[שְׂפָתוֹת]	שִׂפְתוֹת	שִׂפְתוֹתָיו	שִׂפְתוֹתֵיכֶם		
		שְׂפָתַי	שִׂפְתֵיהֶם	שְׂפָתַ֫יִם	שִׂפְתֵי
שָׁנוֹת שָׁנִים	שְׁנוֹת שְׁנֵי	שְׁנוֹתַי שָׁנָיו	— —		

H. Particles

		1. c.	2. m.	2. f.	3. m.	3. f.
לְ,	*to*	לִי	(לְכָה) לְךָ לָךְ P.	לָךְ	לוֹ	לָהּ
כְּ,	*as, like*	כָּמוֹנִי	כָּמוֹךָ	—	כָּמוֹהוּ	כָּמוֹהָ
מִן,	*from*	(מִנִּי) מִמֶּנִּי (מֶנִּי P.)	מִמְּךָ מִמֶּךָּ P.	מִמֵּךְ	מִמֶּנּוּ (מֶנְהוּ)	מִמֶּנָּה
אֶל־,	*to*	אֵלַי	אֵלֶיךָ	אֵלַיִךְ	אֵלָיו	אֵלֶיהָ
אֵת אֶת־	(*Accus.*)	אוֹתִי אֹתִי	אֹתְךָ (אֹתָךְ P.)	אֹתָךְ	אֹתוֹ	אֹתָהּ
אֵת אֶת־	*with*	(אתי) אִתִּי	(אִתְּךָ) אִתְּךָ אִתָּךְ P.	אִתָּךְ	אִתּוֹ (אתו)	אִתָּהּ (אתה)
בֵּין,	*between*	בֵּינִי	בֵּינְךָ בֵּינֶךָ P.	—	בֵּינוֹ	—
יֵשׁ יֶשׁ־	*there is*	—	יֶשְׁךָ	—	יֶשְׁנוֹ	—
אַיִן אֵין	*there is not*	אֵינֶנִּי	אֵינְךָ	אֵינֵךְ	אֵינֶנּוּ	אֵינֶנָּה
הִנֵּה, הֵן, הֶן־	*behold*	הִנְנִי, הִנֵּנִי הִנֶּנִּי P.	הִנְּךָ הִנֶּךָּ P.	הִנָּךְ	הִנּוֹ	—
עוֹד,	*still*	עוֹדֶנִּי עוֹדִי	עוֹדְךָ	עוֹדָךְ	עוֹדֶנּוּ	עוֹדָהּ עוֹדֶנָּה
אֵי, אַיֵּה,	*where*	—	אַיֶּכָּה	—	אַיּוֹ	—

The prepositions בְּ, עִם (עִמָּדִי and עִמִּי) are inflected like לְ. The prepositions אַחַר, אַחֲרֵי, *after*, תַּחַת, *under*, סָבִיב, *around* (before suffixes: סְבִיבֵי and סְבִיבוֹת), עַד, *unto*, עַל, *upon* and many others are inflected like אֶל.

with suffixes.

1. c.	2. m.	2. f.	3. m.	3. f.
לָ֫נוּ	לָכֶם	[לָכֶן] לָכֵ֫נָה	לָ֫מוֹ, לָהֶם לָהֵ֫מָּה	לָהֵ֫נָּה, לָהֵן
כָּמ֫וֹנוּ	כָּכֶם, כָּכֵם (כְּמוֹכֶם)	—	כְּמוֹהֶם, כָּהֵם (כָּהֵ֫מָּה, כָּהֶם)	(כָּהֵן) כָּהֵ֫נָּה
מִמֶּ֫נּוּ	מִכֶּם	מִכֶּן	(מֵהֵ֫מָּה) מֵהֶם	(מֵהֵ֫נָּה) מֵהֶן
אֵלֵ֫ינוּ	אֲלֵיכֶם	אֲלֵיכֶן	אֲלֵהֶם, אֲלֵיהֶם אֵלֵ֫ימוֹ	אֲלֵהֶן, אֲלֵיהֶן
אֹתָ֫נוּ	אֶתְכֶם	אֶתְכֶן	(אֶתְהֶם) אֹתָם	(אֹתָן) אֶתְהֶן
אִתָּ֫נוּ	אִתְּכֶם	אִתְּכֶן	(אִתָּם) אִתָּם	—
בֵּינֵ֫ינוּ בֵּינוֹתֵ֫ינוּ	בֵּינֵיכֶם	—	בֵּינֵיהֶם בֵּינוֹתָם	—
—	יֶשְׁכֶם	—	—	—
—	אֵינְכֶם	—	(אֵינֵ֫ימוֹ) אֵינָם	—
הִנֶּ֫נּוּ, הִנְנוּ הִנֶּ֫נּוּ P.	הִנְּכֶם	—	הִנָּם	—
—	—	—	עוֹדָם	עוֹדֶ֫נָּה
—	—	—	אַיָּם	—

I. Strong Verb. 1. Regular

קָטַל, *to kill* (Pay special attention

			Qal active	Qal stative middle e	Qal stative middle o	*Niph'al* passive, reflexive
PERFECT	Indic. *Sing.*	3. m.	*קָטַל	*כָּבֵד	*קָטֹן	*נִקְטַל
		3. f.	*קָֽטְלָה	*כָּֽבְדָה	*קָֽטְנָה	נִקְטְלָה
		2. m.	*קָטַ֫לְתָּ	*כָּבַ֫דְתָּ	*קָטֹ֫נְתָּ	*נִקְטַ֫לְתָּ
		2. f.	קָטַלְתְּ	כָּבַדְתְּ	קָטֹנְתְּ	נִקְטַלְתְּ
		1. c.	קָטַ֫לְתִּי	כָּבַ֫דְתִּי	קָטֹ֫נְתִּי	נִקְטַ֫לְתִּי
	Plur.	3. c.	קָֽטְלוּ	כָּֽבְדוּ	קָֽטְנוּ	נִקְטְלוּ
		2. m.	*קְטַלְתֶּם	*כְּבַדְתֶּם	*קְטָנְתֶּם	נִקְטַלְתֶּם
		2. f.	קְטַלְתֶּן	כְּבַדְתֶּן	קְטָנְתֶּן	נִקְטַלְתֶּן
		1. c.	קָטַ֫לְנוּ	כָּבַ֫דְנוּ	קָטֹ֫נּוּ	נִקְטַ֫לְנוּ
	Inf. absol.		*קָטוֹל			*הִקָּטֹל, *נִקְטֹל
IMPERFECT	Inf. construct		*קְטֹל	*כְּבַד		*הִקָּטֵל
	Imper. *Sing.*	2. m.	קְטֹל	כְּבַד		הִקָּטֵל
		2. f.	*קִטְלִי	כִּבְדִי		*הִקָּֽטְלִי
	Plur.	2. m.	קִטְלוּ	כִּבְדוּ		הִקָּֽטְלוּ
		2. f.	קְטֹ֫לְנָה	כְּבַ֫דְנָה		הִקָּטַ֫לְנָה
	Indic. *Sing.*	3. m.	*יִקְטֹל	*יִכְבַּד	*יִקְטַן	*יִקָּטֵל
		3. f.	תִּקְטֹל	תִּכְבַּד		תִּקָּטֵל
		2. m.	תִּקְטֹל	תִּכְבַּד		תִּקָּטֵל
		2. f.	*תִּקְטְלִי	תִּכְבְּדִי		תִּקָּֽטְלִי
		1. c.	אֶקְטֹל	אֶכְבַּד		אֶקָּטֵל (אִקָּטֵל)
	Plur.	3. m.	יִקְטְלוּ	יִכְבְּדוּ		יִקָּֽטְלוּ
		3. f.	*תִּקְטֹ֫לְנָה	תִּכְבַּ֫דְנָה		*תִּקָּטַ֫לְנָה
		2. m.	תִּקְטְלוּ	תִּכְבְּדוּ		תִּקָּֽטְלוּ
		2. f.	תִּקְטֹ֫לְנָה	תִּכְבַּ֫דְנָה		תִּקָּטַ֫לְנָה
		1. c.	נִקְטֹל	נִכְבַּד		נִקָּטֵל
	Jussive		Same as Indicative			
	Cohortative		אֶקְטְלָה			
	Participle act.		*קֹטֵל	כָּבֵד	קָטֹן	*נִקְטָל
	pass.		*קָטוּל			

(Lessons VII-XI).
to forms with an asterisk).

Pi‘el active	Pu‘al passive	Hithpa‘el reflexive	Hiph‘il active	Hoph‘al passive
*קִטֵּל, קִטַּל	*קֻטַּל	*הִתְקַטֵּל	*הִקְטִיל	*הָקְטַל
קִטְּלָה	קֻטְּלָה	הִתְקַטְּלָה	הִקְטִילָה	הָקְטְלָה
*קִטַּ֫לְתָּ	*קֻטַּ֫לְתָּ	*הִתְקַטַּ֫לְתָּ	*הִקְטַ֫לְתָּ	*הָקְטַ֫לְתָּ
קִטַּלְתְּ	קֻטַּלְתְּ	הִתְקַטַּלְתְּ	הִקְטַלְתְּ	הָקְטַלְתְּ
קִטַּ֫לְתִּי	קֻטַּ֫לְתִּי	הִתְקַטַּ֫לְתִּי	הִקְטַ֫לְתִּי	הָקְטַ֫לְתִּי
קִטְּלוּ	קֻטְּלוּ	הִתְקַטְּלוּ	הִקְטִ֫ילוּ	הָקְטְלוּ
קִטַּלְתֶּם	קֻטַּלְתֶּם	הִתְקַטַּלְתֶּם	הִקְטַלְתֶּם	הָקְטַלְתֶּם
קִטַּלְתֶּן	קֻטַּלְתֶּן	הִתְקַטַּלְתֶּן	הִקְטַלְתֶּן	הָקְטַלְתֶּן
קִטַּ֫לְנוּ	קֻטַּ֫לְנוּ	הִתְקַטַּ֫לְנוּ	הִקְטַ֫לְנוּ	הָקְטַ֫לְנוּ
*קַטֵּל, *קַטֶּל	קֻטַּל	*הִתְקַטֵּל	*הַקְטֵל	*הָקְטַל
*קַטֵּל	wanting	הִתְקַטֵּל	*הַקְטִיל	wanting
קַטֵּל		הִתְקַטֵּל	*הַקְטֵל	
*קַטְּלִי	wanting	*הִתְקַטְּלִי	*הַקְטִ֫ילִי	wanting
קַטְּלוּ		הִתְקַטְּלוּ	הַקְטִ֫ילוּ	
קַטֵּ֫לְנָה		הִתְקַטֵּ֫לְנָה	הַקְטֵ֫לְנָה	
*יְקַטֵּל	*יְקֻטַּל	*יִתְקַטֵּל	*יַקְטִיל	*יָקְטַל
תְּקַטֵּל	תְּקֻטַּל	תִּתְקַטֵּל	תַּקְטִיל	תָּקְטַל
תְּקַטֵּל	תְּקֻטַּל	תִּתְקַטֵּל	תַּקְטִיל	תָּקְטַל
תְּקַטְּלִי	תְּקֻטְּלִי	תִּתְקַטְּלִי	*תַּקְטִ֫ילִי	תָּקְטְלִי
אֲקַטֵּל	אֲקֻטַּל	אֶתְקַטֵּל	אַקְטִיל	אָקְטַל
יְקַטְּלוּ	יְקֻטְּלוּ	יִתְקַטְּלוּ	יַקְטִ֫ילוּ	יָקְטְלוּ
*תְּקַטֵּ֫לְנָה	*תְּקֻטַּ֫לְנָה	*תִּתְקַטֵּ֫לְנָה	*תַּקְטֵ֫לְנָה	*תָּקְטַ֫לְנָה
תְּקַטְּלוּ	תְּקֻטְּלוּ	תִּתְקַטְּלוּ	תַּקְטִ֫ילוּ	תָּקְטְלוּ
תְּקַטֵּ֫לְנָה	תְּקֻטַּ֫לְנָה	תִּתְקַטֵּ֫לְנָה	תַּקְטֵ֫לְנָה	תָּקְטַ֫לְנָה
נְקַטֵּל	נְקֻטַּל	נִתְקַטֵּל	נַקְטִיל	נָקְטַל
			*יַקְטֵל	
		אֶתְקַטְּלָה	אַקְטִ֫ילָה	
*מְקַטֵּל		*מִתְקַטֵּל	*מַקְטִיל	*מְקֻטָּל, *מָקְטָל
	*מְקֻטָּל			

J. Strong Verb. 2. Verb First-guttural (Lessons VII—XI).
עָמַד, *to stand.*
(*Pi‘el, Pu‘al* and *Hithpa‘el* are regular).

			Qal		Niph‘al	Hiph‘il	Hoph‘al
PERFECT	Indic. *Sing.*	3. m.	עָמַד		נֶעֱמַד*	הֶעֱמִיד*	הָעֳמַד*
		3. f.	עָמְדָה		נֶעֶמְדָה	הֶעֱמִ֫ידָה	הָעָמְדָה*
		2. m.	עָמַ֫דְתָּ		נֶעֱמַ֫דְתָּ	הֶעֱמַ֫דְתָּ	הָעֳמַ֫דְתָּ
		2. f.	עָמַדְתְּ		נֶעֱמַדְתְּ	הֶעֱמַדְתְּ	הָעֳמַדְתְּ
		1. c.	עָמַ֫דְתִּי		נֶעֱמַ֫דְתִּי	הֶעֱמַ֫דְתִּי	הָעֳמַ֫דְתִּי
	Plur.	3. c.	עָמְדוּ		נֶעֶמְדוּ	הֶעֱמִ֫ידוּ	הָעָמְדוּ
		2. m.	עֲמַדְתֶּם*		נֶעֱמַדְתֶּם	הֶעֱמַדְתֶּם	הָעֳמַדְתֶּם
		2. f.	עֲמַדְתֶּן*		נֶעֱמַדְתֶּן	הֶעֱמַדְתֶּן	הָעֳמַדְתֶּן
		1. c.	עָמַ֫דְנוּ		נֶעֱמַ֫דְנוּ	הֶעֱמַ֫דְנוּ	הָעֳמַ֫דְנוּ
	Inf. absol.		עָמוֹד		נַעֲמוֹד, הֵאָסֹף	הַעֲמֵד	הָעֳמֵד*
	Inf. constr.		עֲמֹד*		הֵעָמֵד*	הַעֲמִיד*	
	Imper. *Sing.*	2. m.	עֲמֹד	חֲזַק	הֵעָמֵד	הַעֲמֵד	
		2. f.	עִמְדִי	חִזְקִי	הֵעָמְדִי	הַעֲמִ֫ידִי	wanting
	Plur.	2. m.	עִמְדוּ	חִזְקוּ	הֵעָמְדוּ	הַעֲמִ֫ידוּ	
		2. f.	עֲמֹ֫דְנָה	חֲזַ֫קְנָה	הֵעָמַ֫דְנָה	הַעֲמֵ֫דְנָה	
IMPERFECT	Indic. *Sing.*	3. m.	יַעֲמֹד*	יֶחֱזַק*	יֵעָמֵד*	יַעֲמִיד*	יָעֳמַד*
		3. f.	תַּעֲמֹד	תֶּחֱזַק	תֵּעָמֵד	תַּעֲמִיד	תָּעֳמַד
		2. m.	תַּעֲמֹד	תֶּחֱזַק	תֵּעָמֵד	תַּעֲמִיד	תָּעֳמַד
		2. f.	תַּעַמְדִי	תֶּחֶזְקִי	תֵּעָמְדִי	תַּעֲמִ֫ידִי	תָּעָמְדִי
		1. c.	אֶעֱמֹד	אֶחֱזַק	אֵעָמֵד	אַעֲמִיד	אָעֳמַד
	Plur.	3. m.	יַעַמְדוּ	יֶחֶזְקוּ	יֵעָמְדוּ	יַעֲמִ֫ידוּ	יָעָמְדוּ
		3. f.	תַּעֲמֹ֫דְנָה	תֶּחֱזַ֫קְנָה	תֵּעָמַ֫דְנָה	תַּעֲמֵ֫דְנָה	תָּעֳמַ֫דְנָה
		2. m.	תַּעַמְדוּ	תֶּחֶזְקוּ	תֵּעָמְדוּ	תַּעֲמִ֫ידוּ	תָּעָמְדוּ
		2. f.	תַּעֲמֹ֫דְנָה	תֶּחֱזַ֫קְנָה	תֵּעָמַ֫דְנָה	תַּעֲמֵ֫דְנָה	תָּעֳמַ֫דְנָה
		1. c.	נַעֲמֹד	נֶחֱזַק	נֵעָמֵד	נַעֲמִיד	נָעֳמַד
Juss.						יַעֲמֵד	
Cohort.			אֶעֶמְ֫דָה			אַעֲמִ֫ידָה	
Part. act.			עֹמֵד		נֶעֱמָד*	מַעֲמִיד*	
pass.			עָמוּד				מָעֳמָד

K. Strong Verb. 3. Verb Middle-guttural (Lessons VII—XI).

שָׁחַט, *to slaughter;* בָּרַךְ, *to bless.*

(*Hiph'il* and *Hoph'al* are regular).

			Qal	*Niph'al*	*Pi'el*	*Pu'al*	*Hithpa'el*
PERFECT	INDIC. *Sing.*	3. m.	שָׁחַט	נִשְׁחַט	*בֵּרַךְ	*בֹּרַךְ	*הִתְבָּרֵךְ
		3. f.	*שָׁחֲטָה	*נִשְׁחֲטָה	בֵּרְכָה	[בֹּרְכָה]	הִתְבָּרְכָה
		2. m.	שָׁחַ֫טְתָּ	נִשְׁחַ֫טְתָּ	בֵּרַ֫כְתָּ	בֹּרַ֫כְתָּ	הִתְבָּרַ֫כְתָּ
		2. f.	שָׁחַטְתְּ	נִשְׁחַטְתְּ	בֵּרַכְתְּ	בֹּרַכְתְּ	הִתְבָּרַכְתְּ
		1. c.	שָׁחַ֫טְתִּי	נִשְׁחַ֫טְתִּי	בֵּרַ֫כְתִּי	בֹּרַ֫כְתִּי	הִתְבָּרַ֫כְתִּי
	Plur.	3. c.	*שָׁחֲטוּ	*נִשְׁחֲטוּ	בֵּרְכוּ	בֹּרְכוּ	הִתְבָּרְכוּ
		2. m.	שְׁחַטְתֶּם	נִשְׁחַטְתֶּם	בֵּרַכְתֶּם	בֹּרַכְתֶּם	הִתְבָּרַכְתֶּם
		2. f.	שְׁחַטְתֶּן	נִשְׁחַטְתֶּן	בֵּרַכְתֶּן	בֹּרַכְתֶּן	הִתְבָּרַכְתֶּן
		1. c.	שָׁחַ֫טְנוּ	נִשְׁחַ֫טְנוּ	בֵּרַ֫כְנוּ	בֹּרַ֫כְנוּ	הִתְבָּרַ֫כְנוּ
	INF. absol.		שָׁחוֹט	נִשְׁחוֹט	*בָּרֵךְ	wanting	
IMPERFECT	INF. constr.		שְׁחֹט	הִשָּׁחֵט	*בָּרֵךְ		*הִתְבָּרֵךְ
	IMPER. *Sing.*	2. m.	*שְׁחַט	הִשָּׁחֵט	*בָּרֵךְ		*הִתְבָּרֵךְ
		2. f.	*שַׁחֲטִי	*הִשָּׁחֲטִי	*בָּרְכִי	wanting	*[הִתְבָּרְכִי
	Plur.	2. m.	שַׁחֲטוּ	הִשָּׁחֲטוּ	בָּרְכוּ		הִתְבָּרְכוּ]
		2. f.	שְׁחַ֫טְנָה	הִשָּׁחַ֫טְנָה	*בָּרֵ֫כְנָה		הִתְבָּרֵ֫כְנָה
	INDIC. *Sing.*	3. m.	*יִשְׁחַט	יִשָּׁחֵט	*יְבָרֵךְ	*יְבֹרַךְ	*יִתְבָּרֵךְ
		3. f.	תִּשְׁחַט	תִּשָּׁחֵט	תְּבָרֵךְ	תְּבֹרַךְ	תִּתְבָּרֵךְ
		2. m.	תִּשְׁחַט	תִּשָּׁחֵט	תְּבָרֵךְ	תְּבֹרַךְ	תִּתְבָּרֵךְ
		2. f.	*תִּשְׁחֲטִי	*תִּשָּׁחֲטִי	תְּבָרְכִי	תְּבֹרְכִי	תִּתְבָּרְכִי
		1. c.	אֶשְׁחַט	אֶשָּׁחֵט	אֲבָרֵךְ	אֲבֹרַךְ	אֶתְבָּרֵךְ
	Plur.	3. m.	יִשְׁחֲטוּ	יִשָּׁחֲטוּ	יְבָרְכוּ	יְבֹרְכוּ	יִתְבָּרְכוּ
		3. f.	תִּשְׁחַ֫טְנָה	תִּשָּׁחַ֫טְנָה	תְּבָרֵ֫כְנָה	תְּבֹרַ֫כְנָה	תִּתְבָּרֵ֫כְנָה
		2. m.	תִּשְׁחֲטוּ	תִּשָּׁחֲטוּ	תְּבָרְכוּ	תְּבֹרְכוּ	תִּתְבָּרְכוּ
		2. f.	תִּשְׁחַ֫טְנָה	תִּשָּׁחַ֫טְנָה	תְּבָרֵ֫כְנָה	תְּבֹרַ֫כְנָה	תִּתְבָּרֵ֫כְנָה
		1. c.	נִשְׁחַט	נִשָּׁחֵט	נְבָרֵךְ	נְבֹרַךְ	נִתְבָּרֵךְ
	with suff.		יִשְׁחָטֵ֫הוּ				
	JUSS.		Same as regular verb				
	COHORT.		אֶשְׁחֲטָה		אֲבָרְכָה		
	PART. act.		שֹׁחֵט	נִשְׁחָט	*מְבָרֵךְ		*מִתְבָּרֵךְ
	pass.		שָׁחוּט			*מְבֹרָךְ	

L. Strong Verb. 4. Verb Third guttural

שָׁלַח, *to send.*

				Qal	*Niph'al*	*Pi'el*
PERFECT	INDIC.	*Sing.*	3. m.	שָׁלַח	נִשְׁלַח	שִׁלַּח
			3. f.	שָֽׁלְחָה	נִשְׁלְחָה	שִׁלְּחָה
			2. m.	שָׁלַ֫חְתָּ	נִשְׁלַ֫חְתָּ	שִׁלַּ֫חְתָּ
			2. f.	*שָׁלַ֫חַתְּ	*נִשְׁלַ֫חַתְּ	*שִׁלַּ֫חַתְּ
			1. c.	שָׁלַ֫חְתִּי	נִשְׁלַ֫חְתִּי	שִׁלַּ֫חְתִּי
		Plur.	3. c.	שָֽׁלְחוּ	נִשְׁלְחוּ	שִׁלְּחוּ
			2. m.	שְׁלַחְתֶּם	נִשְׁלַחְתֶּם	שִׁלַּחְתֶּם
			2. f.	שְׁלַחְתֶּן	נִשְׁלַחְתֶּן	שִׁלַּחְתֶּן
			1. c.	שָׁלַ֫חְנוּ	נִשְׁלַ֫חְנוּ	שִׁלַּ֫חְנוּ
	INF. absol.			*שָׁלוֹחַ	*נִשְׁלֹחַ	*שַׁלֵּחַ
IMPERFECT	INF. constr.			*שְׁלֹחַ	*הִשָּׁלַח	*שַׁלַּח
	IMPER.	*Sing.*	2. m.	*שְׁלַח	*הִשָּׁלַח	*שַׁלַּח
			2. f.	שִׁלְחִי	הִשָּֽׁלְחִי	*שַׁלְּחִי
		Plur.	2. m.	שִׁלְחוּ	הִשָּֽׁלְחוּ	שַׁלְּחוּ
			2. f.	שְׁלַ֫חְנָה	הִשָּׁלַ֫חְנָה	*שַׁלַּ֫חְנָה
	INDIC.	*Sing.*	3. m.	*יִשְׁלַח	*יִשָּׁלַח	*יְשַׁלַּח
			3. f.	תִּשְׁלַח	תִּשָּׁלַח	תְּשַׁלַּח
			2. m.	תִּשְׁלַח	תִּשָּׁלַח	תְּשַׁלַּח
			2. f.	תִּשְׁלְחִי	תִּשָּֽׁלְחִי	תְּשַׁלְּחִי
			1. c.	אֶשְׁלַח	אִשָּׁלַח	אֲשַׁלַּח
			3. m.	יִשְׁלְחוּ	יִשָּֽׁלְחוּ	יְשַׁלְּחוּ
			3. f.	*תִּשְׁלַ֫חְנָה	תִּשָּׁלַ֫חְנָה	תְּשַׁלַּ֫חְנָה
			2. m.	תִּשְׁלְחוּ	תִּשָּֽׁלְחוּ	תְּשַׁלְּחוּ
			2. f.	תִּשְׁלַ֫חְנָה	תִּשָּׁלַ֫חְנָה	תְּשַׁלַּ֫חְנָה
			1. c.	נִשְׁלַח	נִשָּׁלַח	נְשַׁלַּח
	with suff.			*יִשְׁלָחֵ֫נִי		*יְשַׁלְּחֵ֫הוּ, אֲשַׁלֵּֽחֲךָ
	JUSS.					
	COHORT.			אֶשְׁלְחָה		
	PART. act.			*שֹׁלֵחַ	*נִשְׁלָח	*מְשַׁלֵּחַ
	pass.			*שָׁלוּחַ		

Pu'al	*Hithpa'el*	*Hiph'il*	*Hoph'al*
שֻׁלַּח	הִשְׁתַּלַּח	הִשְׁלִיחַ	הָשְׁלַח
שֻׁלְּחָה	הִשְׁתַּלְּחָה	הִשְׁלִיחָה	הָשְׁלְחָה
שֻׁלַּחְתָּ	הִשְׁתַּלַּחְתָּ	הִשְׁלַחְתָּ	הָשְׁלַחְתָּ
* שֻׁלַּחַתְּ	* הִשְׁתַּלַּחַתְּ	*הִשְׁלַחַתְּ	*הָשְׁלַחַתְּ
שֻׁלַּחְתִּי	הִשְׁתַּלַּחְתִּי	הִשְׁלַחְתִּי	הָשְׁלַחְתִּי
שֻׁלְּחוּ	הִשְׁתַּלְּחוּ	הִשְׁלִיחוּ	הָשְׁלְחוּ
שֻׁלַּחְתֶּם	הִשְׁתַּלַּחְתֶּם	הִשְׁלַחְתֶּם	הָשְׁלַחְתֶּם
שֻׁלַּחְתֶּן	הִשְׁתַּלַּחְתֶּן	הִשְׁלַחְתֶּן	הָשְׁלַחְתֶּן
שֻׁלַּחְנוּ	הִשְׁתַּלַּחְנוּ	הִשְׁלַחְנוּ	הָשְׁלַחְנוּ
		* הַשְׁלֵחַ	
* שֻׁלַּח	* הִשְׁתַּלַּח	* הַשְׁלִיחַ	* הָשְׁלֵחַ
	* הִשְׁתַּלַּח	* הַשְׁלַח	
wanting	הִשְׁתַּלְּחִי	הַשְׁלִיחִי	wanting
	הִשְׁתַּלְּחוּ	הַשְׁלִיחוּ	
	הִשְׁתַּלַּחְנָה	הַשְׁלַחְנָה	
*יְשֻׁלַּח	*יִשְׁתַּלַּח	*יַשְׁלִיחַ	* ישְׁלַח
תְּשֻׁלַּח	תִּשְׁתַּלַּח	תַּשְׁלִיחַ	תָּשְׁלַח
תְּשֻׁלַּח	תִּשְׁתַּלַּח	תַּשְׁלִיחַ	תָּשְׁלַח
תְּשֻׁלְּחִי	תִּשְׁתַּלְּחִי	תַּשְׁלִיחִי	תָּשְׁלְחִי
אֲשֻׁלַּח	אֶשְׁתַּלַּח	אַשְׁלִיחַ	אָשְׁלַח
יְשֻׁלְּחוּ	יִשְׁתַּלְּחוּ	יַשְׁלִיחוּ	יָשְׁלְחוּ
תְּשֻׁלַּחְנָה	*תִּשְׁתַּלַּחְנָה	תַּשְׁלַחְנָה	*תָּשְׁלַחְנָה
תְּשֻׁלְּחוּ	תִּשְׁתַּלְּחוּ	תַּשְׁלִיחוּ	תָּשְׁלְחוּ
תְּשֻׁלַּחְנָה	תִּשְׁתַּלַּחְנָה	תַּשְׁלַחְנָה	תָּשְׁלַחְנָה
נְשֻׁלַּח	נִשְׁתַּלַּח	נַשְׁלִיחַ	נָשְׁלַח
		יַשְׁלַח	
	*מִשְׁתַּלֵּחַ	*מַשְׁלִיחַ	
מְשֻׁלָּח			מָשְׁלָח

PERFECT

Qal		3. p. m.	3. f.	2. m.	2. f.	1. c.	3. c.	2. c.	1. c.
Verbal forms		קְטָלַ֫ (קָטַל)	קְטָלַ֫ת (קְטָלָ֫ת)	קְטַלְתָּ֫ (קְטַלְתָּ֫)	קְטַלְתִּ֫	קְטַלְתִּ֫	קְטָלוּ֫	קְטַלְתּ֫וּ	קְטַלְנ֫וּ
Suffixes, *Sing.*	1. c.	קְטָלַ֫נִי, שְׁכֵחַ֫נִי	קְטָלַ֫תְנִי	קְטַלְתַּ֫נִי	קְטַלְתִּ֫ינִי	—	קְטָלוּ֫נִי	קְטַלְתּ֫וּנִי	—
	2. m.	קְטָלְךָ	קְטָלַ֫תְךָ	—	—	קְטַלְתִּ֫יךָ	קְטָלוּ֫ךָ	—	קְטַלְנ֫וּךָ
	2. f.	קְטָלֵךְ	קְטָלָ֫תֶךְ	—	—	קְטַלְתִּיךְ	קְטָלוּךְ	—	קְטַלְנוּךְ
	3. m.	קְטָלָ֫הוּ / קְטָלוֹ	קְטָלַ֫תְהוּ / קְטָלַ֫תּוּ	קְטַלְתָּ֫הוּ / קְטַלְתּוֹ	קְטַלְתִּ֫יהוּ / —	קְטַלְתִּ֫יהוּ / קְטַלְתִּיו	קְטָלוּ֫הוּ / —	קְטַלְתּ֫וּהוּ / —	קְטַלְנ֫וּהוּ / —
	3. f.	קְטָלָ֫הּ	קְטָלַ֫תָּה	קְטַלְתָּ֫הּ	קְטַלְתִּ֫יהָ	קְטַלְתִּ֫יהָ	קְטָלוּ֫הָ	—	קְטַלְנ֫וּהָ
Plur.	1. c.	קְטָלָ֫נוּ	קְטָלַ֫תְנוּ	קְטַלְתָּ֫נוּ	קְטַלְתִּ֫ינוּ	—	קְטָלוּ֫נוּ	קְטַלְתּ֫וּנוּ	—
	2. m.	—	—	—	—	קְטַלְתִּיכֶם	—	—	קְטַלְנוּכֶם
	2. f.	—	—	—	—	—	—	—	—
	3. m.	קְטָלָם, לְבֵשָׁם	קְטָלָ֫תַם	קְטַלְתָּם	קְטַלְתִּים	קְטַלְתִּים	קְטָלוּם	—	קְטַלְנוּם
	3 f.	קְטָלָן	—	—	—	קְטַלְתִּין	קְטָלוּן	—	—

	suff.	1 c.	2. m.	2. f.	3. m.	3. f.	1. pl.	3. m.	3. f.
Pi'el	3. m. s.	קִטְּלַ֫נִי	קִטֶּלְךָ	קִטְּלֵךְ	קִטְּלוֹ	קִטְּלָהּ	קִטְּלָ֫נוּ	קִטְּלָם	קִטְּלָן
Hiph'il	3. m. s.	הִקְטִילַ֫נִי	הִקְטִילְךָ	הִקְטִילֵךְ	הִקְטִילוֹ	הִקְטִילָהּ	הִקְטִילָ֫נוּ	הִקְטִילָם	הִקְטִילָן

IMPERFECT

Qal INDIC.

Forms ending in a consonant: יִקְטְלֵ֫נִי, יִלְבָּשֵׁ֫נִי; יִקְטָלְךָ, יִלְבָּשְׁךָ; יִקְטְלֵ֫נוּ, יִלְבָּשֵׁ֫נוּ; יִקְטָלְכֶם; יִקְטְלֶ֫הָ; יִלְבָּשֶׁ֫הָ.

Forms ending in a vowel: יִקְטְלוּ֫נִי, יִשְׁמָעוּ֫נִי.

With *Nun energicum*: יִקְטְלֶ֫נִּי, יִקְטְלֶ֫ךָּ, יִקְטְלֶ֫נָּה, יִקְטְלֶ֫נּוּ; יְשַׁלְּחֶ֫נּוּ.

INF. CONSTR. קָטְלִי, קָטְלֵ֫נִי, קְטָלֵ֫נִי; קָטְלְךָ (קְטָלְךָ); קָטְלוֹ; (פִּגְעוֹ, שָׁלְחוֹ). IMPER. קָטְלֵ֫נִי, שָׁמְעֵ֫נִי; קִטְלוּ֫נִי, שִׁמְעוּ֫נִי. PART. שֹׁמְרֵ֫נִי, שֹׁמְרִי.

N. Weak Verb. 1. Verb *Pê-Nûn* (Lesson XV).

נָגַשׁ, *to approach.*

(*Pi'el*, *Pu'al* and *Hithpa'el* are regular).

			Qal		*Niph'al*	*Hiph'il*	*Hoph'al*
PERFECT	INDIC. *Sing.*	3. m.	נָגַשׁ	נָפַל	*נִגַּשׁ	*הִגִּישׁ	*הֻגַּשׁ
		3. f.			נִגְּשָׁה	הִגִּ֫ישָׁה	הֻגְּשָׁה
		2. m.			נִגַּ֫שְׁתָּ	הִגַּ֫שְׁתָּ	הֻגַּ֫שְׁתָּ
		2. f.			נִגַּשְׁתְּ	הִגַּשְׁתְּ	הֻגַּשְׁתְּ
		1. c.			נִגַּ֫שְׁתִּי	הִגַּ֫שְׁתִּי	הֻגַּ֫שְׁתִּי
	Plur.	3. c.	regular.		נִגְּשׁוּ	הִגִּ֫ישׁוּ	הֻגְּשׁוּ
		2. m.			נִגַּשְׁתֶּם	הִגַּשְׁתֶּם	הֻגַּשְׁתֶּם
		2. f.			נִגַּשְׁתֶּן	הִגַּשְׁתֶּן	הֻגַּשְׁתֶּן
		1. c.			נִגַּ֫שְׁנוּ	הִגַּ֫שְׁנוּ	הֻגַּ֫שְׁנוּ
	INF. absol.		נָגוֹשׁ		נִגּוֹף, הִנָּגֵשׁ	*הַגֵּשׁ	*הֻגֵּשׁ
	INF. constr.		*גֶּ֫שֶׁת	*נְפֹל	הִנָּגֵשׁ	*הַגִּישׁ	*הֻגַּשׁ
	IMPER. *Sing.*	2. m.	*גַּשׁ	*נְפֹל	הִנָּגֵשׁ	*הַגֵּשׁ	wanting
		2. f.	גְּשִׁי	נִפְלִי	הִנָּגְשִׁי	הַגִּ֫ישִׁי	
	Plur.	2. m.	גְּשׁוּ	נִפְלוּ	הִנָּגְשׁוּ	הַגִּ֫ישׁוּ	
		2. f.	גַּ֫שְׁנָה	נְפֹ֫לְנָה	הִנָּגַ֫שְׁנָה	הַגֵּ֫שְׁנָה	
IMPERFECT	INDIC. *Sing.*	3. m.	*יִגַּשׁ	*יִפֹּל	*[יִנָּגֵשׁ]	*יַגִּישׁ	*יֻגַּשׁ
		3. f.	תִּגַּשׁ	תִּפֹּל		תַּגִּישׁ	תֻּגַּשׁ
		2. m.	תִּגַּשׁ	תִּפֹּל		תַּגִּישׁ	תֻּגַּשׁ
		2. f.	תִּגְּשִׁי	תִּפְּלִי		תַּגִּ֫ישִׁי	תֻּגְּשִׁי
		1. c.	אֶגַּשׁ	אֶפֹּל		אַגִּישׁ	אֻגַּשׁ
	Plur.	3. m.	יִגְּשׁוּ	יִפְּלוּ	regular.	יַגִּ֫ישׁוּ	יֻגְּשׁוּ
		3. f.	תִּגַּ֫שְׁנָה	תִּפֹּ֫לְנָה		תַּגֵּ֫שְׁנָה	תֻּגַּ֫שְׁנָה
		2. m.	תִּגְּשׁוּ	תִּפְּלוּ		תַּגִּ֫ישׁוּ	תֻּגְּשׁוּ
		2. f.	[תִּגַּ֫שְׁנָה]	[תִּפֹּ֫לְנָה]		[תַּגֵּ֫שְׁנָה]	[תֻּגַּ֫שְׁנָה]
		1. c.	נִגַּשׁ	נִפֹּל		נַגִּישׁ	נֻגַּשׁ
	with suff.		יִתְּנֶ֫נּוּ, יִתְּנֵ֫נוּ				
	with l. cons.					*וַיַּגֵּשׁ, וַיַּגֶּשׁ־	
	JUSS.					*יַגֵּשׁ	
	COHORT.		אֶגְּשָׁה				
	PART. act.		נֹגֵשׁ		*נִגָּשׁ	*מַגִּישׁ	
	pass.		נָגוּשׁ				מֻגָּשׁ

O. Weak Verb. 2. *Pê-Yôdh* (פ״י) 1 Class: Verbs originally *Pê-Wāw*. (Lesson XV). יָשַׁב, *to settle down, dwell*; יָרַשׁ, *to possess, inherit*.

(*Piʿel*, *Puʿal* and *Hithpaʿel* are regular).

		Qal	Qal	*Niphʿal*	*Hiphʿil*	*Hophʿal*
PERFECT	INDIC. *Sing.* 3. m.	יָשַׁב		נוֹשַׁב*	הוֹשִׁיב*	הוּשַׁב*
	3. f.			נוֹשְׁבָה	הוֹשִׁיבָה	הוּשְׁבָה
	2. m.			נוֹשַׁבְתָּ	הוֹשַׁבְתָּ	הוּשַׁבְתָּ
	2. f.	regular.		נוֹשַׁבְתְּ	הוֹשַׁבְתְּ	הוּשַׁבְתְּ
	1. c.			נוֹשַׁבְתִּי	הוֹשַׁבְתִּי	הוּשַׁבְתִּי
	Plur. 3. c.			נוֹשְׁבוּ	הוֹשִׁיבוּ	הוּשְׁבוּ
	2. m.			נוֹשַׁבְתֶּם	הוֹשַׁבְתֶּם	הוּשַׁבְתֶּם
	2. f.			נוֹשַׁבְתֶּן	הוֹשַׁבְתֶּן	הוּשַׁבְתֶּן
	1. c.			נוֹשַׁבְנוּ	הוֹשַׁבְנוּ	הוּשַׁבְנוּ
	INF. absol.	יָשׁוֹב			הוֹשֵׁב, הוֹשִׁיב*	
IMPERFECT	INF. constr.	שֶׁבֶת*, יְסֹד		הִוָּשֵׁב*	הוֹשִׁיב*	הוּשַׁב*
	IMPER. *Sing.* 2. m.	שֵׁב*	יְרַשׁ*	הִוָּשֵׁב*	הוֹשֵׁב*	wanting
	2. f.	שְׁבִי	יְרְשִׁי	הִוָּשְׁבִי	הוֹשִׁיבִי	
	Plur. m.	שְׁבוּ	יְרְשׁוּ	הִוָּשְׁבוּ	הוֹשִׁיבוּ	
	f.	שֵׁבְנָה	יְרַשְׁנָה	הִוָּשַׁבְנָה	הוֹשֵׁבְנָה	
	INDIC. *Sing.* 3. m.	יֵשֵׁב*	יִירַשׁ*	יִוָּשֵׁב*	יוֹשִׁיב*	יוּשַׁב*
	3. f.	תֵּשֵׁב	תִּירַשׁ	תִּוָּשֵׁב	תּוֹשִׁיב	תּוּשַׁב
	2. m.	תֵּשֵׁב	תִּירַשׁ	תִּוָּשֵׁב	תּוֹשִׁיב	תּוּשַׁב
	2. f.	תֵּשְׁבִי	תִּירְשִׁי	תִּוָּשְׁבִי	תּוֹשִׁיבִי	תּוּשְׁבִי
	1. c.	אֵשֵׁב	אִירַשׁ	אִוָּשֵׁב*	אוֹשִׁיב	אוּשַׁב
	Plur. 3. m.	יֵשְׁבוּ	יִירְשׁוּ	יִוָּשְׁבוּ	יוֹשִׁיבוּ	יוּשְׁבוּ
	3. f.	תֵּשַׁבְנָה	תִּירַשְׁנָה	תִּוָּשַׁבְנָה	תּוֹשֵׁבְנָה	תּוּשַׁבְנָה
	2. m.	תֵּשְׁבוּ	תִּירְשׁוּ	תִּוָּשְׁבוּ	תּוֹשִׁיבוּ	תּוּשְׁבוּ
	2. f.	תֵּשַׁבְנָה	תִּירַשְׁנָה	תִּוָּשַׁבְנָה	תּוֹשֵׁבְנָה	תּוּשַׁבְנָה
	1. c.	נֵשֵׁב	נִירַשׁ	נִוָּשֵׁב	נוֹשִׁיב	נוּשַׁב
	with ו cons.	וַיֵּשֶׁב*	וַיִּירַשׁ		וַיּוֹשֶׁב*	
	JUSS.				יוֹשֵׁב*	
	COHORT.	אֵשְׁבָה	אִירְשָׁה		אוֹשִׁיבָה	
	PART. act.	יֹשֵׁב		נוֹשָׁב*	מוֹשִׁיב*	
	pass.	יָשׁוּב				מוּשָׁב*

	P. Weak Verb. 2 b. *Pê-Yôdh* 2 Class: Verbs originally *Pê-Yôdh* (Lesson XV). יָטַב, *to be good.* Qal	Hiph'il	Q. Weak Verb. 2 c. *Pê-Yôdh* and *'Ayin-Sādhê* (Lesson XV). יָצַר, *to fashion.* Qal	Niph'al	Hiph'il	Hoph'al	R. Weak Verb. 3. *Pê-'Aleph* (Lesson XV). אָכַל, *to eat.* Qal
[P]ERF. INDIC. *Sing.* 3. m.	יָטַב	הֵיטִיב*	Qal regular	נִצַּר* etc. like *Pe-Nun*	הִצִּיר*	הֻצַּר* etc.	אָכַל
3. f.		הֵיטִ֫יבָה					like verbs first guttural
2. m.		הֵיטַ֫בְתָּ					
2. f.		הֵיטַבְתְּ					
1. c.	regular	הֵיטַ֫בְתִּי					
Plur. 3. c.		הֵיטִ֫יבוּ					
2. m.		הֵיטַבְתֶּם					
2. f.		הֵיטַבְתֶּן					
1. c.		הֵיטַ֫בְנוּ					
INF. absol.	יָטוֹב	הֵיטֵב*					אָכוֹל
INF. constr.	יְטֹב	הֵיטִיב*					אֱכֹל*, אֲכֹל
IMPER. *Sing.* 2. m.		הֵיטֵב*					אֱכֹל
2. f.		הֵיטִ֫יבִי					אִכְלִי
Plur. 2. m.		הֵיטִ֫יבוּ					אִכְלוּ
2. f.		[הֵיטֵ֫בְנָה]			הַצֵּר		[אֱכֹ֫לְנָה]
IMPF. INDIC. *Sing.* 3. m.	יִיטַב*	יֵיטִיב*					יֹאכַל* (in P. יֹאכֵל)
3. f.	תִּיטַב	תֵּיטִיב					תֹּאכַל
2. m.	תִּיטַב	תֵּיטִיב			הַצֵּר		תֹּאכַל
2. f.	תִּיטְבִי	תֵּיטִ֫יבִי					תֹּאכְלִי
1. c.	אִיטַב	אֵיטִיב					אֹכַל*
Plur. 3. m.	יִיטְבוּ	יֵיטִ֫יבוּ					יֹאכְלוּ
3. f.	תִּיטַ֫בְנָה	[תֵּיטֵ֫בְנָה]	יִצֹּר etc. like *Pe-Nun*	יִוָּצֵר etc.	יַצִּיר etc. like *Pe-Nun*	יֻצַּר etc. like *Pe-Nun*	תֹּאכַ֫לְנָה
2. m.	תִּיטְבוּ	תֵּיטִ֫יבוּ					תֹּאכְלוּ
2. f.	[תִּיטַ֫בְנָה]	[תֵּיטֵ֫בְנָה]					[תֹּאכַ֫לְנָה]
1. c.	נִיטַב	[נֵיטִיב]					נֹאכַל
with ו cons.	וַיִּיטַב	וַיֵּיטֶב					וַיֹּ֫אמֶר,* וַיֹּ֫אכַל*
with suff.							יֹאכְלֶ֫נּוּ, יֹאכְלֵם
JUSS.		יֵיטֵב					
COHORT.							
PART. act.	יֹטֵב	מֵיטִיב					אֹכֵל
pass.	יָטוּב						אָכוּל

S. Weak Verb. 4. Verb *Lāmedh-Hē*
גָּלָה, *to mani-*

			Qal	*Niph'al*	*Pi'el*
PERFECT	Indic. *Sing.*	3. m.	* גָּלָה	* נִגְלָה	* גִּלָּה
		3. f.	* גָּלְתָה	נִגְלְתָה	גִּלְּתָה
		2. m.	* גָּלִ֫יתָ	* נִגְלֵ֫יתָ, ־ִ֫יתָ	* גִּלִּ֫יתָ
		2. f.	גָּלִית	נִגְלֵית	גִּלִּית
		1. c.	גָּלִ֫יתִי	נִגְלֵ֫יתִי	גִּלִּ֫יתִי, גִּלֵּ֫יתִי
	Plur.	3. c.	* גָּלוּ	נִגְלוּ	גִּלּוּ
		2. m.	גְּלִיתֶם	[נִגְלֵיתֶם]	גִּלִּיתֶם
		2. f.	גְּלִיתֶן	[נִגְלֵיתֶן]	[גִּלִּיתֶן]
		1. c.	גָּלִ֫ינוּ	נִגְלֵ֫ינוּ	גִּלִּ֫ינוּ
	with suff.		גָּלְךָ, גְּלִיתִיו, גְּלִיתַ֫נִי, גָּלָ֫נִי		
	Inf. absol.		* גָּלֹה	נִגְלֹה, הִגָּלֵה	גַּלֹּה, גַּלֵּה
IMPERFECT	Inf. constr.		גְּלוֹת	* הִגָּלוֹת	גַּלּוֹת
	Imper. *Sing.*	2. m.	* גְּלֵה	הִגָּלֵה	גַּלֵּה, גַּל
		2. f.	* גְּלִי	הִגָּלִי	גַּלִּי
	Plur.	2. m.	גְּלוּ	הִגָּלוּ	גַּלּוּ
		2. f.	* גְּלֶ֫ינָה	[הִגָּלֶ֫ינָה]	[גַּלֶּ֫ינָה]
	Indic. *Sing.*	3. m.	* יִגְלֶה	* יִגָּלֶה	* יְגַלֶּה
		3. f.	תִּגְלֶה	תִּגָּלֶה	תְּגַלֶּה
		2. m.	תִּגְלֶה	תִּגָּלֶה	תְּגַלֶּה
		2. f.	* תִּגְלִי	[תִּגָּלִי]	תְּגַלִּי
		1. c.	אֶגְלֶה	אֶגָּלֶה, אִגָּלֶה	אֲגַלֶּה
	Plur.	3. m.	יִגְלוּ	יִגָּלוּ	יְגַלּוּ
		3. f.	* תִּגְלֶ֫ינָה	* תִּגָּלֶ֫ינָה	* תְּגַלֶּ֫ינָה
		2. m.	תִּגְלוּ	תִּגָּלוּ	תְּגַלּוּ
		2. f.	תִּגְלֶ֫ינָה	תִּגָּלֶ֫ינָה	תְּגַלֶּ֫ינָה
		1. c.	נִגְלֶה	[נִגָּלֶה]	נְגַלֶּה
	with ו cons.		וַיִּ֫גֶל, (וַיֵּ֫בְךְּ, וַיֵּ֫שְׁבְּ), (וַתֵּ֫רֶב)	וַיִּגָּל	וַיְגַל
	with suff.		יִגְלְךָ, יִגְלֵ֫נִי		יְגַלְּךָ, יְגַלֵּ֫נִי
	Juss.		* יִ֫גֶל	* יִגָּל	יְגַל
	Cohort.		Generally same as Indicative, rarely אֶשְׁעָה		
	Part. act.		* גֹּלֶה	נִגְלֶה	מְגַלֶּה
	pass.		* גָּלוּי		

(ל״ה). (Lesson XVIII).

fest, reveal.

Pu'al	*Hithpa'el*	*Hiph'il*	*Hoph'al*
* גֻּלָּה	* הִתְגַּלָּה	* הִגְלָה	* הָגְלָה
גֻּלְּתָה	[הִתְגַּלְּתָה]	הִגְלְתָה	הָגְלְתָה
* גֻּלֵּיתָ	* הִתְגַּלֵּיתָ	* הִגְלֵיתָ, ־ֵ־יתָ	* הָגְלֵיתָ
[גֻּלֵּית]	[הִתְגַּלֵּית]	הִגְלֵית, ־ִ־ית	[הָגְלֵית]
גֻּלֵּיתִי	הִתְגַּלֵּיתִי	הִגְלֵיתִי, ־ִ־יתִי	הָגְלֵיתִי
גֻּלּוּ	הִתְגַּלּוּ	הִגְלוּ	הָגְלוּ
[גֻּלֵּיתֶם	הִתְגַּלֵּיתֶם	הִגְלֵיתֶם, ־ִ־יתֶם	הָגְלֵיתֶם]
גֻּלֵּיתֶן	[הִתְגַּלֵּיתֶן]	[הִגְלֵיתֶן]	הָגְלֵיתֶן
[גֻּלֵּינוּ	[הִתְגַּלֵּינוּ	הִגְלֵינוּ	[הָגְלֵינוּ
		הַגְלֵה	הָגְלֵה
גֻּלּוֹת	הִתְגַּלּוֹת	הַגְלוֹת	
wanting	[הִתְגַּלֵּה] הִתְגַּל הִתְגַּלִּי הִתְגַּלּוּ [הִתְגַּלֶּינָה]	הַגְלֵה, (הֶגֶל) הַגְלִי הַגְלוּ [הַגְלֶינָה]	wanting
* יְגֻלֶּה	* יִתְגַּלֶּה	* יַגְלֶה	* [יָגְלֶה]
תְּגֻלֶּה	[תִּתְגַּלֶּה]	תַּגְלֶה	תָּגְלֶה
תְּגֻלֶּה	תִּתְגַּלֶּה	תַּגְלֶה	תָּגְלֶה
[תְּגֻלִּי]	תִּתְגַּלִּי	תַּגְלִי	תָּגְלִי
[אֲגֻלֶּה	אֶתְגַּלֶּה	אַגְלֶה	אָגְלֶה
יְגֻלּוּ	יִתְגַּלּוּ	יַגְלוּ	יָגְלוּ
* [תְּגֻלֶּינָה]	* [תִּתְגַּלֶּינָה]	* תַּגְלֶינָה	* תָּגְלֶינָה
תְּגֻלּוּ	תִּתְגַּלּוּ	תַּגְלוּ	תָּגְלוּ
תְּגֻלֶּינָה	[תִּתְגַּלֶּינָה]	תַּגְלֶינָה	תָּגְלֶינָה
[נְגֻלֶּה	נִתְגַּלֶּה	נַגְלֶה	נָגְלֶה]
	וַיִּתְגַּל	וַיֶּגֶל, וַיַּעַל	
		יַגְלְךָ, יַגְלֵנִי	
	יִתְגַּל	יֶגֶל, (יַפְתְּ)	
	מִתְגַּלֶּה	מַגְלֶה	
מְגֻלֶּה			מָגְלֶה

T. Weak Verb. 5. Verb *Lāmedh-Aleph* מָצָא,

		Qal		Niph'al	Pi'el
PERFECT	INDIC. *Sing.* 3. m.	מָצָא*	מָלֵא*	נִמְצָא*	מִצֵּא
	3. f.	מָֽצְאָה	מָֽלְאָה	נִמְצְאָה	מִצְּאָה
	2. m.	מָצָ֫אתָ*	מָלֵ֫אתָ*	נִמְצֵ֫אתָ*	מִצֵּ֫אתָ*
	2. f.	מָצָאת	תָלֵאת	נִמְצֵאת	מִצֵּאת
	1. c.	מָצָ֫אתִי	מָלֵ֫אתִי	נִמְצֵ֫אתִי	מִצֵּ֫אתִי
	Plur. 3. c.	מָֽצְאוּ	מָֽלְאוּ	נִמְצְאוּ	מִצְּאוּ
	2. m.	מְצָאתֶם	מְלֵאתֶם	נִמְצֵאתֶם	מִצֵּאתֶם
	2. f.	מְצָאתֶן	מְלֵאתֶן	[נִמְצֵאתֶן]	[מִצֵּאתֶן]
	1. c.	מָצָ֫אנוּ	מָלֵ֫אנוּ	[נִמְצֵ֫אנוּ	מִצֵּ֫אנוּ
	with suff.	מְצָאתִ֫יהָ, מְצָאַ֫תְנוּ, מְצָאוֹ			
	INF. absol.	מָצוֹא		נִמְצֹא	מַצֹּא
IMPERFECT	INF. constr.	מְצֹא		הִמָּצֵא	מַצֵּא
	IMPER. *Sing.* 2. m.	מְצָא*		הִמָּצֵא	מַצֵּא
	2. f.	מִצְאִי		[הִמָּֽצְאִי]	[מַצְּאִי]
	Plur. 2. m.	מִצְאוּ		הִמָּֽצְאוּ	מַצְּאוּ
	2. f.	מְצֶ֫אנָה*		*[הִמָּצֶ֫אנָה]	*[מַצֶּ֫אנָה]
	INDIC. *Sing.* 3. m.	יִמְצָא*		יִמָּצֵא*	יְמַצֵּא
	3. f.	תִּמְצָא		תִּמָּצֵא	תְּמַצֵּא
	2. m.	תִּמְצָא		תִּמָּצֵא	תְּמַצֵּא
	2. f.	תִּמְצְאִי		תִּמָּֽצְאִי	תְּמַצְּאִי
	1. c.	אֶמְצָא		אֶמָּצֵא	אֲמַצֵּא
	Plur. 3. m.	יִמְצְאוּ		יִמָּֽצְאוּ	יְמַצְּאוּ
	3. f.	תִּמְצֶ֫אנָה*		תִּמָּצֶ֫אנָה*	תְּמַצֶּ֫אנָה*
	2. m.	תִּמְצְאוּ		תִּמָּֽצְאוּ	תְּמַצְּאוּ
	2. f.	תִּמְצֶ֫אנָה		תִּמָּצֶ֫אנָה	תְּמַצֶּ֫אנָה
	1. c.	נִמְצָא		נִמָּצֵא	נְמַצֵּא
	with 1. consec.	וַיִּמְצָא etc.			
	with suff.	יִמְצָאֲךָ, יִמְצָאֵ֫נִי			יְמַצְּאֵ֫נִי
	JUSS.				
	COHORT.	אֶמְצְאָה			
	PART. act.	מֹצֵא		נִמְצָא	מְמַצֵּא
	pass.	מָצוּא			

(ל״א). (Lesson XIX).

to find.

Pu'al		*Hithpa'el*	*Hiph'il*		*Hoph'al*
*מֻצָּא]	קֹרָא	הִתְמַצֵּא]	הִמְצִיא	(הָמְצָא)	*הֻמְצָא,
מֻצְּאָה		הִתְמַצְּאָה	הִמְצִיאָה	etc.	הֻמְצְאָה
*מֻצֵּאתָ		*הִתְמַצֵּאתָ	*הִמְצֵאתָ		*[הֻמְצֵאתָ
מֻצֵּאת		הִתְמַצֵּאת]	הִמְצֵאת		הֻמְצֵאת
מֻצֵּאתִי		הִתְמַצֵּאתִי	הִמְצֵאתִי		הֻמְצֵאתִי
מֻצְּאוּ		הִתְמַצְּאוּ	הִמְצִיאוּ		הֻמְצְאוּ
מֻצֵּאתֶם		הִתְמַצֵּאתֶם]	הִמְצֵאתֶם		הֻמְצֵאתֶם
מֻצֵּאתֶן		הִתְמַצֵּאתֶן	הִמְצֵאתֶן]		הֻמְצֵאתֶן
מֻצֵּאנוּ]		הִתְמַצֵּאנוּ]	הִמְצֵאנוּ]		הֻמְצֵאנוּ]
			הַמְצֵא		
		הִתְמַצֵּא	הַמְצִיא		הָמְצָא
wanting		הִתְמַצֵּא] הִתְמַצְּאִי הִתְמַצְּאוּ *[הִתְמַצֶּאנָה	הַמְצֵא הַמְצִיאִי הַמְצִיאוּ *הַמְצֶאנָה		wanting
יְמֻצָּא		יִתְמַצֵּא	יַמְצִיא		[יֻמְצָא
תְּמֻצָּא]		תִּתְמַצֵּא	תַּמְצִיא		תֻּמְצָא
תְּמֻצָּא		תִּתְמַצֵּא	תַּמְצִיא		תֻּמְצָא
תְּמֻצְּאִי		תִּתְמַצְּאִי]	תַּמְצִיאִי		תֻּמְצְאִי
אֲמֻצָּא		אֶתְמַצֵּא]	אַמְצִיא		אֻמְצָא
יְמֻצְּאוּ		יִתְמַצְּאוּ	יַמְצִיאוּ		יֻמְצְאוּ
*תְּמֻצֶּאנָה		*[תִּתְמַצֶּאנָה]	*תַּמְצֶאנָה		*תֻּמְצֶאנָה
תְּמֻצְּאוּ		תִּתְמַצְּאוּ	תַּמְצִיאוּ		תֻּמְצְאוּ
תְּמֻצֶּאנָה		תִּתְמַצֶּאנָה]	תַּמְצֶאנָה		תֻּמְצֶאנָה
נְמֻצָּא]		נִתְמַצֵּא]	נַמְצִיא		נֻמְצָא]
			וַיַּמְצֵא		
			*יַמְצִיאֵנִי		
			יַמְצֵא		
			אַמְצִיאָה		
		מִתְמַצֵּא	מַמְצִיא		
מְמֻצָּא					מֻמְצָא

U. Weak Verb. 6. Verb *ʿAyin*-
(Lesson XX, XXII). סָבַב, *to turn;* סָכַךְ, *to screen;* קַל, *to*

			Qal		*Niphʿal*	*Hiphʿil*
PERFECT	INDIC. *Sing.*	3. m.	*סָבַב, תַּם		*נָסַב, נָמֵס	*הֵסֵב, הֵסַב
		3. f.	סָבֲבָה, תַּ֫מָּה		*נָסַ֫בָּה	*הֵסֵ֫בָּה
		2. m.	*סַבּ֫וֹתָ		*נְסַבּ֫וֹתָ	*הֲסִבּ֫וֹתָ
		2. f.	סַבּוֹת		נְסַבּוֹת	הֲסִבּוֹת
		1. c.	סַבּ֫וֹתִי		נְסַבּ֫וֹתִי	הֲסִבּ֫וֹתִי
	Plur.	3. c.	סָבֲבוּ, תַּ֫מּוּ		נָסַ֫בּוּ	הֵסַ֫בּוּ, הֵחֵ֫לּוּ
		2. m.	סַבּוֹתֶם		נְסַבּוֹתֶם	הֲסִבּוֹתֶם
		2. f.	סַבּוֹתֶן		נְסַבּוֹתֶן	הֲסִבּוֹתֶן
		1. c.	סַבּ֫וֹנוּ		נְסַבּ֫וֹנוּ	הֲסִבּ֫וֹנוּ
	with suff.		סַבּ֫וּנִי, סְבָבֻ֫נִי			
	INF. absol.		סָבוֹב		הִמֵּס, הִסּוֹב	*הָסֵב
IMPERFECT	INF. constr.		*סֹב		*הִסֵּב	הָסֵב
	IMPER. *Sing.*	2. m.	*סֹב		הִסַּב	*הָסֵב
		2. f.	*סֹ֫בִּי		*הִסַּ֫בִּי	הָסֵ֫בִּי
	Plur.	2. m.	סֹ֫בּוּ		הִסַּ֫בּוּ	הָסֵ֫בּוּ
		2. f.	[סֻבֶּ֫ינָה]		[הִסַּבֶּ֫ינָה]	[הֲסִבֶּ֫ינָה]
	INDIC. *Sing.*	3. m.	*יָסֹב (יֵקַל)	*יִסֹּב	*יִסַּב	*יָסֵב, יַסֵּב
		3. f.	תָּסֹב	תִּסֹּב	תִּסַּב	תָּסֵב
		2. m.	תָּסֹב	תִּסֹּב	תִּסַּב	תָּסֵב
		2. f.	*תָּסֹ֫בִּי	תִּסְּבִי	*תִּסַּ֫בִּי	[תָּסֵ֫בִּי]
		1. c.	אָסֹב	אֶסֹּב	אֶסַּב	אָסֵב
	Plur.	3. m.	יָסֹ֫בּוּ (יֵקַ֫לּוּ)	יִסְּבוּ	יִסַּ֫בּוּ	יָסֵ֫בּוּ, יַסֵּ֫בּוּ
		3. f.	*תְּסֻבֶּ֫ינָה	[תִּסֹּ֫בְנָה]	[תִּסַּבֶּ֫ינָה]	*תְּסִבֶּ֫ינָה
		2. m.	תָּסֹ֫בּוּ	תִּסְּבוּ	תִּסַּ֫בּוּ	תָּסֵ֫בּוּ
		2. f.	[תְּסֻבֶּ֫ינָה]	[תִּסֹּ֫בְנָה]	[תִּסַּבֶּ֫ינָה]	תְּסִבֶּ֫ינָה
		1. c.	נָסֹב	נִסֹּב	נִסַּב	נָסֵב
	with ו consec.		*וַיָּ֫סָב (*P.* וַיָּסֹב)			וַיָּ֫סֶב
	with suff.		*יְסֻבֵּ֫נִי			*יְסִבֵּ֫נִי (יְסִבְּכֶם)
	JUSS.		יָסֹב			יָסֵב
	COHORT.		אָסֹ֫בָּה			אָסֵ֫בָּה
	PART. act.		סֹבֵב		נָסָב	*מֵסֵב
	pass.		*סָבוּב		(*fem.* נְסַבָּה)	

'*Ayin* (ע״ע) or *Mediae geminatae*
תַּם, *to be complete;* חִלֵּל, *to defile;*
be slight; מָסַס, *to melt.*

Reinforced stems

Hoph'al	*Pi'el* חִלֵּל / *Pu'al* חֻלַּל / *Hithpa'el* הִתְחַלֵּל — regular	*Po'el*	*Po'al*	*Hithpo'el*	*Pilpel*	*Hithpalpel* הִתְקַלְקֵל etc.
*הוּסַב		*סוֹבֵב	*סוֹבַב	הִסְתּוֹבֵב	סִכְסֵךְ	
הוּסַבָּה		סוֹבְבָה	סוֹבְבָה	הִסְתּוֹבְבָה	סִכְסְכָה	
הוּסַבּוֹתָ]		סוֹבַבְתָּ	סוֹבַבְתָּ	הִסְתּוֹבַבְתָּ	סִכְסַכְתָּ	
הוּסַבּוֹת		סוֹבַבְתְּ	סוֹבַבְתְּ	הִסְתּוֹבַבְתְּ	סִכְסַכְתְּ	
הוּסַבּוֹתִי]		סוֹבַבְתִּי	סוֹבַבְתִּי	הִסְתּוֹבַבְתִּי	סִכְסַכְתִּי	
הוּסַבּוּ		סוֹבְבוּ	סוֹבְבוּ	הִסְתּוֹבְבוּ	סִכְסְכוּ	
הוּסַבּוֹתֶם]		סוֹבַבְתֶּם	סוֹבַבְתֶּם	הִסְתּוֹבַבְתֶּם	סִכְסַכְתֶּם	
הוּסַבּוֹתֶן		סוֹבַבְתֶּן	סוֹבַבְתֶּן	הִסְתּוֹבַבְתֶּן	סִכְסַכְתֶּן	
הוּסַבּוֹנוּ]		סוֹבַבְנוּ	סוֹבַבְנוּ	הִסְתּוֹבַבְנוּ	סִכְסַכְנוּ	
		סוֹבֵב	סוֹבַב	הִסְתּוֹבֵב	סַכְסֵךְ	
		סוֹבֵב			סַכְסֵךְ	
wanting		סוֹבֵב	wanting	הִסְתּוֹבֵב	סַכְסֵךְ	
		סוֹבְבִי		הִסְתּוֹבְבִי	סַכְסְכִי	
		סוֹבְבוּ		הִסְתּוֹבְבוּ	סַכְסְכוּ	
		סוֹבֵבְנָה		הִסְתּוֹבֵבְנָה	סַכְסֵכְנָה	
*יוּסַב, יֻסַּב		יְסוֹבֵב	יְסוֹבַב	יִסְתּוֹבֵב	יְסַכְסֵךְ	
תּוּסַב]		תְּסוֹבֵב	תְּסוֹבַב	תִּסְתּוֹבֵב	תְּסַכְסֵךְ	
תּוּסַב		תְּסוֹבֵב	תְּסוֹבַב	תִּסְתּוֹבֵב	תְּסַכְסֵךְ	
*תּוּסַבִּי		תְּסוֹבְבִי	תְּסוֹבְבִי	תִּסְתּוֹבְבִי	תְּסַכְסְכִי	
אוּסַב]		אֲסוֹבֵב	אֲסוֹבַב	אֶסְתּוֹבֵב	אֲסַכְסֵךְ	
יוּסַבּוּ		יְסוֹבְבוּ	יְסוֹבְבוּ	יִסְתּוֹבְבוּ	יְסַכְסְכוּ	
*תּוּסַבֶּינָה]		תְּסוֹבֵבְנָה	תְּסוֹבַבְנָה	תִּסְתּוֹבֵבְנָה	תְּסַכְסֵכְנָה	
תּוּסַבּוּ		תְּסוֹבְבוּ	תְּסוֹבְבוּ	תִּסְתּוֹבְבוּ	תְּסַכְסְכוּ	
תּוּסַבֶּינָה		תְּסוֹבֵבְנָה	תְּסוֹבַבְנָה	תִּסְתּוֹבֵבְנָה	תְּסַכְסֵכְנָה	
נוּסַב]		נְסוֹבֵב	נְסוֹבַב	נִסְתּוֹבֵב	נְסַכְסֵךְ	
			יְסוֹבְבֵנִי			
		מְסוֹבֵב		מִסְתּוֹבֵב	מְסַכְסֵךְ	
מוּסָב			מְסוֹבָב			

V. Weak Verb. 7. Verb *'Ayin-Wā*

קוּם, *to arise*; מוּת, *to di*

			Qal		*Niph'al*	*Hiph'il*	*Hoph'al*
PERFECT	Indic. *Sing.*	3. m.	* קָם	* מֵת	* נָקוֹם	* הֵקִים	הוּקַם
		3. f.	* קָמָה	* מֵתָה	* נָקוֹמָה	* הֵקִימָה	[הוּקְמָה]
		2. m.	* קַמְתָּ	* מַתָּה	[נְקוּמוֹתָ]	הֲקִימוֹתָ	הוּקַמְתָּ
		2. f.	קַמְתְּ	[מַתְּ]	[נְקוּמוֹת]	הֲקִימוֹת	הוּקַמְתְּ
		1. c.	קַמְתִּי	מַתִּי	נְקוּמוֹתִי	הֲקִימוֹתִי	[הוּקַמְתִּי]
	Plur.	3. c.	קָמוּ	מֵתוּ	נָקוֹמוּ	הֵקִימוּ	הוּקְמוּ
		2. m.	קַמְתֶּם	[מַתֶּם]	נְקוּמוֹתֶם	הֲקִימוֹתֶם	[הוּקַמְתֶּם]
		2. f.	[קַמְתֶּן]	[מַתֶּן]	[נְקוּמוֹתֶן]	[הֲקִימוֹתֶן]	הוּקַמְתֶּן
		1. c.	קַמְנוּ	מַתְנוּ	[נְקוּמוֹנוּ]	הֲקִימוֹנוּ	[הוּקַמְנוּ]
	with suff.		שָׂמָהוּ, שָׂמוֹ			הֱמִיתָהוּ	
	Inf. absol.		* קוֹם		* הִקּוֹם, נָסוֹג	* הָקֵם	
IMPERFECT	Inf. constr.		* קוּם		* הִקּוֹם	* הָקִים	הוּקַם
	Imp. *Sing.*	2. m.	* קוּם		* הִקּוֹם	* הָקֵם	wanting
		2. f.	* קוּמִי		[הִקּוֹמִי]	* הָקִימִי	
	Plur.	2. m.	קוּמוּ		הִקּוֹמוּ	הָקִימוּ	
		2. f.	קֹמְנָה		[הִקּוֹמֶינָה]	[הָקֵמְנָה]	
	Indic. *Sing.*	3. m.	* יָקוּם, יָבוֹא		* יִקּוֹם	* יָקִים	* יוּקַם
		3. f.	תָּקוּם		תִּקּוֹם	תָּקִים	תּוּקַם
		2. m.	תָּקוּם		תִּקּוֹם	תָּקִים	[תּוּקַם]
		2. f.	* תָּקוּמִי		[תִּקּוֹמִי]	תָּקִימִי	תּוּקְמִי
		1. c.	אָקוּם		אֶקּוֹם	אָקִים	[אוּקַם]
	Plur.	3. m.	יָקוּמוּ		יִקּוֹמוּ	יָקִימוּ	יוּקְמוּ
		3. f.	* תְּקוּמֶינָה, תָּשֹׁבְנָה		[תִּקּוֹמֶינָה]	תָּקֵמְנָה, תְּקִימֶינָה	[תּוּקַמְנָה]
		2. m.	תָּקוּמוּ		תִּקּוֹמוּ	תָּקִימוּ	תּוּקְמוּ
		2. f.	תְּקוּמֶינָה		[תִּקּוֹמֶינָה]	[תָּקֵמְנָה]	[תּוּקַמְנָה]
		1. c.	נָקוּם		נִקּוֹם	נָקִים	נוּקַם
	with ו cons.		וַיָּקָם, P. וַיָּקֹם			וַיָּקֶם	
	with suff.		יְשׁוּפֵנִי			יְקִימֵנִי	
	Juss.		* יָקֹם			* יָקֵם	
	Cohort.		אָקוּמָה				
	Part. act.		קָם		* נָקוֹם	* מֵקִים	
	pass.		קוּם				* מוּקָם

(ע"ו). (Lesson XXI, XXII.)

עָוַת, *to be bent.*

Reinforced stems

Piʿel עִוֵּת, *Puʿal* עֻוַּת, *Hithpaʿel* הִתְעַוֵּת — regular

Hithpalpel הִתְחַלְחֵל, *to writhe*; *Polpal (Pulpal)*, *Pilpel* כִּלְכֵּל, *to sustain, contain*; *Hithpôlel* הִתְבּוֹשֵׁשׁ, *to be ashamed* — see Paradigm U

W. Weak Verb.

8. Verb ʿ*Ayin-Yôdh* (ע"י). (Lesson XXI, XXII.)

בִּין, *to understand*; גִּיל, *to rejoice.*

Polel	*Polal*	*Qal*	*Niphʿal*
* קוֹמֵם	* קוֹמַם	* בָּן	נָבוֹן
קוֹמְמָה	[קוֹמְמָה]	* בָּנָה	[נָבוֹנָה]
קוֹמַמְתָּ	קוֹמַמְתָּ	* בַּנְתָּ	נְבוּנוֹתָ
[קוֹמַמְתְּ]	[קוֹמַמְתְּ]	בַּנְתְּ	[נְבוּנוֹת]
קוֹמַמְתִּי	קוֹמַמְתִּי	[בַּנְתִּי]	נְבוּנוֹתִי
קוֹמְמוּ	קוֹמְמוּ	בָּנוּ	etc.
[קוֹמַמְתֶּם]	[קוֹמַמְתֶּם]	[בַּנְתֶּם]	like ע"ו
קוֹמַמְתֶּן	קוֹמַמְתֶּן	[בַּנְתֶּן]	
[קוֹמַמְנוּ]	קוֹמַמְנוּ	בַּנּוּ	
עוֹרַרְתִּיךָ			
		* בֹּן	
קוֹמֵם		* בִּין	
קוֹמֵם	wanting	* בִּין	
[קוֹמְמִי]		בִּינִי	
קוֹמְמוּ		בִּינוּ	
[קוֹמֵמְנָה]		בֵּנָּה	
יְקוֹמֵם	יְקוֹמַם	* יָגִיל	
תְּקוֹמֵם	[תְּקוֹמַם]	תָּגִיל	
תְּקוֹמֵם	תְּקוֹמַם	תָּגִיל	
[תְּקוֹמְמִי]	תְּקוֹמְמִי	תָּגִילִי	
אֲקוֹמֵם	[אֲקוֹמַם]	אָגִיל	
יְקוֹמְמוּ	יְקוֹמְמוּ	יָגִילוּ	
תְּקוֹמֵמְנָה	תְּקוֹמַמְנָה	תְּגֵלְנָה	
תְּקוֹמְמוּ	[תְּקוֹמְמוּ]	תָּגִילוּ	
תְּקוֹמֵמְנָה	תְּקוֹמַמְנָה	תְּגֵלְנָה	
[נְקוֹמֵם]	נְקוֹמַם]	נָגִיל	
		וַיָּגֶל	
		יְרִיבֵנִי	
		יָגֵל	
מְקוֹמֵם		לֵץ (לֵצִים), שָׂב	נָבוֹן
	מְקוֹמָם	שִׂים, שׂוּם	

			strong verb				
			Regular	1 guttural	2 guttural	3 guttural	verb פ״ן.
Qal	PERF.	Indic.	קָטַל	עָמַד	שָׁחַט	שָׁלַח	גַשׁ
	IMPERF.	Inf. c.	קְטֹל	עֲמֹד	שְׁחֹט	שְׁלֹחַ	שֶׁת
		Indic.	יִקְטֹל	יַעֲמֹד	יִשְׁחַט	יִשְׁלַח	גַּשׁ
Niphʿal	PERF.	Indic.	נִקְטַל	נֶעֱמַד	נִשְׁחַט	נִשְׁלַח	גַּשׁ
	IMPERF.	Inf. c.	הִקָּטֵל	הֵעָמֵד	הִשָּׁחֵט	הִשָּׁלַח	נָּגֵשׁ
		Indic.	יִקָּטֵל	יֵעָמֵד	יִשָּׁחֵט	יִשָּׁלַח	גֵשׁ
Piʿel	PERF.	Indic.	קִטֵּל	עִמֵּד	בֵּרַךְ	שִׁלַּח	גֵּשׁ
	IMPERF.	Inf. c.	קַטֵּל	עַמֵּד	בָּרֵךְ	שַׁלַּח	גֵּשׁ
		Indic.	יְקַטֵּל	יעַמֵּד	יְבָרֵךְ	יְשַׁלַּח	גֵּשׁ
Puʿal	PERF.	Indic.	קֻטַּל	עֻמַּד	בֹּרַךְ	שֻׁלַּח	גַּשׁ
	IMPERF.	Inf. c.	קֻטַּל	עֻמַּד	בֹּרַךְ	שֻׁלַּח	גַּשׁ
		Indic.	יְקֻטַּל	יְעֻמַּד	יְבֹרַךְ	יְשֻׁלַּח	גַּשׁ
Hithpaʿel	PERF.	Indic.	הִתְקַטֵּל	הִתְעַמֵּד	הִתְבָּרֵךְ	הִשְׁתַּלַּח	תְנַגֵּשׁ
	IMPERF.	Inf. c.	הִתְקַטֵּל	הִתְעַמֵּד	הִתְבָּרֵךְ	הִשְׁתַּלַּח	תְנַגֵּשׁ
		Indic.	יִתְקַטֵּל	יִתְעַמֵּד	יִתְבָּרֵךְ	ישְׁתַּלַּח	תְנַגֵּשׁ
Hiphʿil	PERF.	Indic.	הִקְטִיל	הֶעֱמִיד	הִשְׁחִיט	הִשְׁלִיחַ	גִּישׁ
	IMPERF.	Inf. c.	הַקְטִיל	הַעֲמִיד	הַשְׁחִיט	הַשְׁלִיחַ	גִּישׁ
		Indic.	יַקְטִיל	יַעֲמִיד	יַשְׁחִיט	יַשְׁלִיחַ	גִּישׁ
Hophʿal	PERF.	Indic.	הָקְטַל	הָעֳמַד	הָשְׁחַט	הָשְׁלַח	גַּשׁ
	IMPERF.	Inf. c.	הָקְטַל	הָעֳמַד	הָשְׁחַט	הָשְׁלַח	גַּשׁ
		Indic.	יָקְטַל	יָעֳמַד	יָשְׁחַט	יָשְׁלַח	גַּשׁ

weak verb

	verb		verb	verb		verb	verb	verb	
	פ״י.		ל״ה.	ל״א.		ע״ע.	ע״ו.	ע״י.	
	יָשַׁב		גָּלָה	מָצָא		סַב	קָם	בָּן	
יְטַב	שֶׁבֶת		גְּלוֹת	מְצֹא		סֹב	קוּם	בִּין	
יִיטַב	יֵשֵׁב	יִצַּר	יִגְלֶה	יִמְצָא		יָסֹב	יָקוּם	יָבִין	
	נוֹשַׁב	נִצַּר	נִגְלָה	נִמְצָא		נָסַב	נָקוֹם	נָבוֹן	
	הִוָּשֵׁב	הִוָּצֵר	הִגָּלוֹת	הִמָּצֵא		הִסַּב	הִקּוֹם	הִבּוֹן	
	יִוָּשֵׁב	יִוָּצֵר	יִגָּלֶה	יִמָּצֵא		יִסַּב	יִקּוֹם	יִבּוֹן	
	יִשֵּׁב		גִּלָּה	מִצֵּא		סוֹבֵב	קוֹמֵם	בּוֹנֵן	סִכְסֵךְ
	יַשֵּׁב		גַּלּוֹת	מַצֵּא		סוֹבֵב	קוֹמֵם	בּוֹנֵן	סַכְסֵךְ
	יְיַשֵּׁב		יְגַלֶּה	יְמַצֵּא		יְסוֹבֵב	יְקוֹמֵם	יְבוֹנֵן	יְסַכְסֵךְ
	יֻשַּׁב		גֻּלָּה	מֻצָּא		סוֹבַב	קוֹמַם	בּוֹנַן	כֻּלְכַּל
	יֻשַּׁב		גֻּלּוֹת	מֻצָּא	regular or:	סוֹבַב	קוֹמַם	בּוֹנַן	כָּלְכַּל
	יְיֻשַּׁב		יְגֻלֶּה	יְמֻצָּא		יְסוֹבַב	יְקוֹמַם	יְבוֹנַן	יְכָלְכַּל
	הִתְיַשֵּׁב		הִתְגַּלָּה	הִתְמַצֵּא		הִסְתּוֹבֵב	הִתְקוֹמֵם	הִתְבּוֹנֵן	הִתְקַלְקֵל
	הִתְיַשֵּׁב		הִתְגַּלּוֹת	הִתְמַצֵּא		הִסְתּוֹבֵב	הִתְקוֹמֵם	הִתְבּוֹנֵן	הִתְקַלְקֵל
	יִתְיַשֵּׁב		יִתְגַּלֶּה	יִתְמַצֵּא		יִסְתּוֹבֵב	יִתְקוֹמֵם	יִתְבּוֹנֵן	יִתְקַלְקֵל
הֵיטִיב	הוֹשִׁיב	הִצִּיר	הִגְלָה	הִמְצִיא		הֵסֵב	הֵקִים	הֵבִין	
הֵיטִיב	הוֹשִׁיב	הַצִּיר	הַגְלוֹת	הַמְצִיא		הָסֵב	הָקִים	הָבִין	
יֵיטִיב	יוֹשִׁיב	יַצִּיר	יַגְלֶה	יַמְצִיא		יָסֵב	יָקִים	יָבִין	
	הוּשַׁב	הֻצַּר	הָגְלָה	הֻמְצָא		הוּסַב	הוּקַם	הוּבַן	
	הוּשַׁב	הֻצַּר	הָגְלוֹת	הֻמְצָא		הוּסַב	הוּקַם	הוּבַן	
	יוּשַׁב	יֻצַּר	יָגְלֶה	יֻמְצָא		יוּסַב	יוּקַם	יוּבַן	

ENGLISH-HEBREW VOCABULARY.

This Vocabulary includes only the English words found in the Exercises with their Hebrew equivalents as they occur in the Biblical passage that are quoted. The Arabic figure refers to the lesson, while the Roman figure designates the class to which the various nouns belong.

A

Aaron, אַהֲרֹן, pr. n.
Abel, הֶבֶל pr. n.
Abimelech, אֲבִימֶלֶךְ pr. n.
Abraham, אַבְרָהָם, pr. n.
able, be be, יָכֹל, (15).
abomination, תּוֹעֵבָה, (iv) f.
act treacherously, בָּגַד, (8).
act severely with, [עלל], (20), *Po'el.*
add, to, יָסַף, (15).
adjure, to, [שׁבע] (10), *Hiph.*
Ahab, אַחְאָב, pr. n.
altar, מִזְבֵּחַ, (iv), m.
alive, חַי, (iii), a.
alone, . . . לְבַד, (iii) prep.
angel, מַלְאָךְ, (iv), m.
anger, אַף, (iii), m.
animal, בְּהֵמָה, (§ 260), f.
anoint, to, מָשַׁח, (8).
answer, to, עָנָה, (18).
appoint, to, יָעַד, (24); נָתַן, (15).
approach, to, קָרַב, קָרֵב (10); נָגַשׁ (15).
ark, אֲרוֹן, (i, § 118).
arm, זְרוֹעַ, (i), f. (m.)
army, צָבָא, וֹת . . (iv), m.; חַיִל (v), m.
ashamed, to be, בּוֹשׁ, (21); חָפֵר (20).
ask, שָׁאַל, (8).
ass, חֲמוֹר, (i), m.
ass, she-ass, אָתוֹן, (ii) f.
attend, be attentive, קָשַׁב, (9), *Hiph.*

B

Babylon, בָּבֶל, pr. n.
Balaam, בִּלְעָם, pr. n.
be, to, הָיָה, (§ 401).
bed, מִטָּה, (i), f.
Beersheba, בְּאֵר־שֶׁבַע, pr. n.
beget, to, יָלַד, (16), *Hiph.*
begin, to, חָלַל, (20), *Hiph.*
beginning, רֵאשִׁית, (i), f.; תְּחִלָּה, (i), f.
believe, אָמַן, (9), *Hiph.*
Bethel, בֵּית־אֵל, pr. n.
bitter, to be, מָרַר, (20).
bless, to, בָּרַךְ, (7), *Pi.*
blessed, בָּרוּךְ, (ii), pt., (*Baruch*).
blessing, בְּרָכָה, (iv, § 271), f.
blood, דָּם, (vi), m.
blow, to, תָּקַע, (24).
book, סֵפֶר (v), m.
booth, סֻכָּה, (iii), f.
border, גְּבוּל, (i), m.
born, to be, יָלַד, (16), *Niph.*
bosom, חֵק, חֵיק, (i), m.
bow, to, שָׁחַח, (20); שָׁחָה, (18).
boy, נַעַר, (v), m.
bread, לֶחֶם, (v), m.
break, to, שָׁבַר (9), כָּרַת, (8).
breath, רוּחַ, (i), f. (m.)
bring, to, קָרַב, (10), *Hiph.*; בּוֹא, (21), *Hiph.*
bring back, to, שׁוּב, (21), *Hiph.*

bring down, to, יָרַד, (15), *Hiph.*
bring forth, to, יָלַד (16).
bring up, to, עָלָה, (18), *Hiph.*
brother, אָח, (§ 260).
build, to, בָּנָה, (18).
bull, פַּר, (iii), m.
burnt-offering, עֹלָה, (i), f.
bury, to, קָבַר, (9).
buy, to, קָנָה, (19).

C

Cain, קַיִן, pr. n.
calf, עֵגֶל, (v), m.
calf, molten, עֵגֶל מַסֵּכָה.
call, to, קָרָא, (19).
camel, גָּמָל, (iii), m.
captain, שַׂר, (iii), m., ראשׁ, (§ 260).
capture, to, לָכַד, (10).
cattle, מִקְנֶה (vi), m.; בְּהֵמָה, (§ 260) f.
cattle, small, צֹאן, (i), f., (m.).
cedar-tree, אֶרֶז, (v), m.
chastise, to, יָסַר, (15).
child, יֶלֶד, (v), m. נַעַר, (v), m., בֵּן (§ 260), m.
choose, to, בָּחַר, (7).
chosen, בָּחוּר, (ii), pt.
city, עִיר, (§ 260), f.
clean, to be, טָהַר, (10).
cling, to, דָּבַק, (9).
close, to, סָגַר, (8).
clothed, to be, לָבֵשׁ, (7).
cloud, עָב, ות (i), m. & (f.).
collect, to, אָסַף, (8); קָבַץ, (10).
collected, to be, אָסַף, קָבַץ, קָוָה, (18), *Niph.*
come, to, בּוֹא, (21).
come up, to, עָלָה, (18).
command, to, [צוה], (18), *Pi.*
command, מִצְוָה, (i), f.; חֹק (iii), m.; חֻקָּה, (iii), f.; פִּקּוּדִים, (i), m. pl. פֶּה (פִּי), (i), m.
compass, סָבַב, (20).
compassion, to have, רָחַם, (20), *Pi.*
complete, to, כָּלָה, (19), *Pi.*
congregation, עֵדָה, (iv), f.
consecrate, to, קָדַשׁ, (7), *Hiph.*
consider, to, בִּין. (21), *Hithpolel.*
consult, to, דָּרַשׁ, (9).
controversy, enter into a, שָׁפַט, (7), *Niph.*
converse, to, דָּבַר, (7), *Hithp.*
corpse, נְבֵלָה, (iv), f.
counsel, to, יָעַץ, (15).
counsel, עֵצָה, (iv), f.
count, to, מָנָה, (20).
courage, to take, חָזַק, (9), *Hithp.*
covenant, בְּרִית, (i), f.
covenant, make a, כָּרַת בְּרִית.
crazy, אֱוִיל (i), a.; כְּסִיל, (i), a.
create, to, בָּרָא, (19).
crush, to, כָּתַת, (20).
cry, to, קָרָא (19); צָעַק, זָעַק, (16).
cup, כּוֹס, (i), f.
curse, to, אָרַר, (20); קָלַל, (20), *Pi.*

D

Dagon, דָּגוֹן, pr. n.
daughter, בַּת, (§ 260), f.
David, דָּוִד, pr. n.
dawn, שַׁחַר, (v), m.
day, יוֹם, (§ 260), m.
dead, מֵת, (i), pt.
death, מָוֶת, (v), m.
Deborah, דְּבוֹרָה, pr. n.
deep, עָמֹק, (iii), a.
delight in, to, חָפֵץ, (13).
deliver, to, [מלט], (10), *Pi.*; יָשַׁע, (15), *Hiph.*

delivered, to be, [מלט], (10), *Niph.*

deliver up, to, סָגַר, (8), *Hiph.*

depart, to, סוּר, (21).

desert, מִדְבָּר, (iv), m.

desire, to, חָמַד, (13); [אוה], (23), *Pi.*

desirable, נֶחְמָד, (iv), pt.

desolation, חָרְבָּה, (v), f.

despoil, to, גָּזַל, (9).

destroy, to, שָׁחַת, (8), *Pi. & Hiph.*; שָׁבַת, (7), *Hiph.*; כָּרַת, (8), *Hiph.*

devastate, to, שָׁמֵם, (20), *Hiph.*

die, to, מוּת, (21).

dispersed, to be, נָפַץ, (22).

divide, to, חָלַק, (14); פָּרַד, (20).

do, to, עָשָׂה, (18).

doctrine, לֶקַח, (v), m.

doing, מַעֲלָל, (iv), m.

door, דֶּלֶת, (v), m.; פֶּתַח, (v), m.

dry up, to, (be dried), יָבֵשׁ, (15).

dry land, חָרָבָה, (i), f.; יַבָּשָׁה, (i), f.

drunk, שִׁכּוֹר, (i), a.

drunk, to be or become, שָׁכַר, (10).

dwell, to, יָשַׁב, (15); שָׁכַן, (8).

E

ear, אֹזֶן, (v), f.

earth, אֶרֶץ, (v), f. (m.); אֲדָמָה, (iv), f.

earthquake, רַעַשׁ, (v), m.

eat, אָכַל, (15).

Eden, עֵדֶן, pr. n.

Egypt, Egyptians, } מִצְרַיִם, pr. n. (f., m.)

Egyptian, מִצְרִי, (i, iii), a.

Eli, עֵלִי, pr. n.

embalm, חָנַט, (24).

encompass, סָבַב, (20), *Po'el.*

enemy, אֹיֵב, (iv), pt.

Ephraim, אֶפְרַיִם, pr. n.

Ephron, עֶפְרוֹן, pr. n.

erect, to, קוּם, (21), *Hiph.*; רוּם (21), *Hiph.*; בָּנָה, (18).

err, to, תָּעָה, (18).

Esau, עֵשָׂו, pr. n.

established, to be, כּוּן, (21), *Niph.*

evening, עֶרֶב, (v), m.

evil, רַע, (iii), m.; רָעָה, (iii), f.

exile, to take into, גָּלָה, (18), *Hiph.*

eye, עַיִן (v), f.

F

Face, פָּנִים, (vi), pl. m. & f.

fail, נָפַל, (15).

faithful, נֶאֱמָן, (iv), pt.

faithfulness, אֱמֶת, (§ 260), f.

fall, to, נָפַל, (15).

fall upon, to, פָּגַע, (16).

family, מִשְׁפָּחָה, (v), f.

far be it, חָלִילָה, interj.

fashion, to, יָצַר, (15).

father, אָב, (§ 260).

fatherless, יָתוֹם, (ii), m.

favor, to, חָנַן, (20).

favor, חֵן, (iii), m.

fear, to, יָרֵא, (22).

fear, יִרְאָה, (i), f.

feast, to keep a, חָגַג, (20)

feast, חַג, (iii, § 118), m.

field, שָׂדֶה, { ־ִים (vi), m.; ־וֹת }

fierce, עָרִיץ, (i), a.

fight, to, לָחַם. (8), *Niph.*

find, to, מָצָא, (19).

fire, אֵשׁ, (iii), f. (m.).

first-born, בְּכוֹר, (i), m.

flee, to, בָּרַח (17); נוּם, (21).

flesh, בָּשָׂר, (iv), m.

flight, put to, נוּם, (21), *Hiph.*

flock, צֹאן, (i) m. & f.

flood, מַבּוּל, (i), m.
fool, foolish, אֱוִיל, (i), a.;
כְּסִיל, (i) a; נָבָל (iv) a.
foot, רֶגֶל, (v) f.
forget, to, שָׁכַח, (8),
former, first, רִאשׁוֹן, (i), a.
forsake, to, עָזַב, (8).
fruit, פְּרִי, (v), m.
full, to be, מָלֵא, (19).
fulfill, to, מָלֵא, (19).

G

Garden, גַּן, (iii), m.
garment, בֶּגֶד, (v), m.; לְבוּשׁ, (i), m.
gather, to, קָבַץ, (10); אָסַף, (8).
generation, דּוֹר, וֹת... ים— (i), m.
give, to, נָתַן, (15).
gladden, to, שִׂמֵּחַ, שָׂמַח, (10), *Pi.*
glory, כָּבוֹד, (ii) m. & f.
go, to, הָלַךְ, יָלַךְ, (15); יָצָא, (22).
go around, to, נָקַף, (22).
go down, to, יָרַד, (15); בּוֹא (21).
go out, to, יָצָא, (22).
go up, to, עָלָה, (18).
god, God, אֵל, (i); אֱלֹהַּ, (i); אֱלֹהִים (i).
Godolias, גְּדַלְיָהוּ, pr. n.
gold, זָהָב, (iv), m.
good, to be, טוֹב, (21); יָטַב, (15).
good, טוֹב, (i), a.
grace, חֵן, (iii), m.
grasp, to, אָחַז, (15).
graving tool, חֶרֶט, (v), m.
great, גָּדוֹל, (ii), a.
grief, תּוּגָה, (i), f.
ground, אֲדָמָה, (iv), f.
grow up, to, גָּדַל, (7).
growing large, גָּדֵל, (iv), a.
guard, טַבָּח, (i), m.
guard, to be on one's, שָׁמַר, (7), *Niph.*

H

Hagar, הָגָר, pr. n.
hand, יָד, (vi), f. (m.)
handmaid, אָמָה, (§ 260), f.
hard, to be, קָשָׁה, (18).
hasten, [מהר], (8), *Pi.*
hate, to, שָׂנֵא, (19); אָיַב, (§ 445).
head, רֹאשׁ, (§ 260), m.
heal, to, רָפָא, (19).
hear, to, שָׁמַע, (7).
hearken, to, שָׁמַע, (7); קָשַׁב, (9), *Hiph.*
heart, לֵב, וֹת (iii), m.; לֵבָב, וֹת (iv), m.
heaven, שָׁמַיִם, (§ 260), m.
heifer, פָּרָה, (iii), f.
help, to, עָזַר, (9).
help, עֵזֶר, (v), m.
herd, בָּקָר, (iv), m.
Hezechias, חִזְקִיָּה(וּ), pr. n.
hide oneself, to, [חבא], (19), *Niph.* & *Hithp.*
high, Most High, עֶלְיוֹן, (i), a. & pr. n.
high, רָם, (i), pt.
Hiram, חִירָם, pr. n.
hire, to, שָׂכַר, (17).
hired servant, שָׂכִיר, (ii), a.
hold, lay ... of, תָּפַשׂ, (14).
holiness, קֹדֶשׁ, (v), m.
holy, קָדוֹשׁ, (ii), a.
honest, כֵּן, (i), a.
honour, to, כִּבֵּד, (7), *Pi.*
horse, סוּס, (i), m.
hostility, to show .. to, צָרַר, (20).
house, household, בַּיִת, (§ 260), m.
humble oneself, to, [כנע], (23), *Niph.*
hunt, to, צוּד, (22).

I

Incense, to offer, קָטַר, (8), *Hiph.*
inform, to, שָׁמַע, (7), *Hiph.*
inhabitant, יוֹשֵׁב, (iv), pt.

inherit, יָרַשׁ, (15).
injury, to do an, רָעַע, (20), *Hiph.*
innocent, נָקִי, (iii), a.
insolent, זֵד, (i), a.
instruction, מוּסָר, (iv), m.
Isaac, יִצְחָק, יִשְׂחָק, pr. n.
island, אִי, (iii), m., (f.).
Ismaelites, יִשְׁמְעֵאלִים, pr. n.
Israel, יִשְׂרָאֵל, pr. n.

J

Jacob, יַעֲקֹב, pr. n.
jawbone, לְחִי, (v), m.
jealous, to be, [קנא], (19), *Pi.*
Jehovah, (Yahweh), the Lord, יְהוָֹה, pr. n.
Jehu, יֵהוּא, pr. n.
Jerusalem, יְרוּשָׁלַםִ, יְרוּשָׁלַיִם, pr. n.
Jezabel, אִיזֶבֶל, pr. n.
Joachim, יְהוֹיָקִים, pr. n.
Job, אִיּוֹב, pr. n.
Jordan, הַיַּרְדֵּן, pr. n.
Joseph, יוֹסֵף, pr. n.
Joshua, Josue, יְהוֹשֻׁעַ, pr. n.
Judah, יְהוּדָה, pr. n.
judge, to, שָׁפַט, (7); דִּין, (21).
judge, שֹׁפֵט, (iv), pt.
judgment, מִשְׁפָּט, (iv), m.; דִּין, (i), m.
just, צַדִּיק, (i), a.
just, to be, צָדֵק, (7).
justice, צְדָקָה, (iv), f.
justify, to, צָדֵק, (7), *Pi.* & *Hiph.*

K

Keep, to, שָׁמַר, (7).
keep as a feast, to, חָגַג, (20).
kindled, to be, (of anger), חָרָה, (18).
kindred, תּוֹלְדוֹת, (iv), f. pl.
king, מֶלֶךְ, (v), m.
king, to make, . . מָלַךְ, (7), *Hiph.*
kingdom, מַלְכוּת, (i), f.; מַמְלָכָה (v), f.
know, יָדַע, (15).

L

Lamb, כֶּבֶשׂ, (v), m.; כִּבְשָׂה, (v), f.
lampstand, מְנוֹרָה, (i), f.
land, אֶרֶץ, (v), f.
land, dry land, יַבָּשָׁה, (iv), f.
large, גָּדוֹל, (ii), a.
laugh, to, צָחַק, (14); שָׂחַק, (14).
law, תּוֹרָה, (i), f.
lay hold of, to, תָּפַשׂ, (14).
lead, to, דָּרַךְ (9), *Hiph.*
leave, to, [שׁאר], (11), *Hiph.*
letter, סֵפֶר, (v).
Levite, לֵוִי, (iii), m.
lie down, to, שָׁכַב, (7).
life, חַיִּים, (iii), m. pl.; נֶפֶשׁ, (v), f.
lift, to, נָשָׂא, (22).
lift oneself, to, נָשָׂא, (22), *Hithp.*
light, אוֹר, (i), m.
lip, שָׂפָה, (vi), f.
listen, קָשַׁב, (9), *Hiph.*
live, חָיָה, (§ 401).
living, חַי, (iii), a.
Lord, אֲדֹנָי, pr. n.
lord, אָדוֹן, (ii), m.
love, to, אָהַב, (15).

M

Magnify oneself, גָּדַל, (7), *Hithp.*
majesty, splendor, הוֹד, (i), m.
make, to, עָשָׂה, (18).
male, זָכָר, (iv), m.
man, אִישׁ, (§ 260); אָדָם, (iv); גֶּבֶר, (v); אֱנוֹשׁ, (i); מְתִים, (i), m. pl.; נֶפֶשׁ, (v), f.
manner, מִשְׁפָּט, (iv), m.
many, רַב, (iii), a.
mare, סוּסָה, (i), f.

master, אָדוֹן, (ii), m.
Melchisedech, מַלְכִּי־צֶדֶק, pr. n.
memorial, זִכָּרוֹן, (ii), m.
messenger, מַלְאָךְ, (iv), m.; צִיר, (i), m.
middle, midst, תָּוֶךְ, (v), m.
minister, to, [שׁרת], (10), *Pi.*
month, new moon, חֹדֶשׁ, (v), m.
Moses, מֹשֶׁה, pr. n.
mountain, הַר, (§ 260), m.
mouth, פֶּה, constr. פִּי, (§ 150), m.
mother, אֵם, (iii), f.
multiply, to, רָבָה, (18), *Hiph.*
murmur, to, הָמָה, (21); לוּן, (21), *Niph.*
must, new wine, תִּירוֹשׁ, (i), m.

N

Name, שֵׁם, (§ 260), m.
narrate, to, סָפַר, (8), *Pi.*
Nathan, נָתָן, pr. n.
near, to draw . . ., קָרֵב, קָרַב, (10); נָגַשׁ, (15).
needy, אֶבְיוֹן, (i), a.
neighbor, שָׁכֵן, (iv), m.; רֵעַ, (vi), m.
Noah, נֹחַ, pr. n.
numerous, to be or become . . ., רָבָה, (18); רָבַב, (20).

O

Oblation, קָרְבָּן, (iv), m.; מִנְחָה, (i), f.
observe (keep), to, שָׁמַר, (7).
observe (keep watch), to, צָפָה, (19).
occupation, מְלָאכָה, (v), f.
officer, סָרִיס, (ii), m.
old, זָקֵן, (iv), a.
olive, olive tree, זַיִת, (v), m.
open, to, פָּתַח, (9).
oppress, to, עָשַׁק, (9).
order, (see command), חֹק, (iii), m.
ordinance, (see command), חֻקָּה, (iii), f.
Osias, עֻזִּיָּהוּ, pr. n.
overthrow, to, הָפַךְ, (14).
ox, cattle, בָּקָר, (iv), m.

P

Pacify, to, [כפר], (14), *Pi.*
palm of the hand, sole, כַּף, (iii), f.
palm-tree, תֹּמֶר, (v), m.; תָּמָר, (iv), m.
part, to, פָּרַד, (20).
passed in review, to be . ., פָּקַד, (7), *Pu.*
pass over, to, עָבַר, (10).
path, נְתִיבָה, (i), f.; מַעְגָּל, (iv), m.
people, גּוֹי, (i), m.; עַם, (iii), m.; לְאֹם, (iii), m.
perfect, תָּם, (iii), a.
perish, אָבַד, (15).
Pharaoh, פַּרְעֹה, pr. n.
Philistines, פְּלִשְׁתִּים, pr. n.
physician, רֹפֵא, (iv), pt.
pious, חָסִיד, (ii), a.
place, מָקוֹם, (ii) m.
place, to, שׂוּם, שִׂים, (21).
plague, to, נָגַע, (15), *Pi.*
plague, נֶגַע, (v), m.
pool, בְּרֵכָה, (iv), f.
poor, אֶבְיוֹן, (i), a.; עָנִי, (iii), a.; רָשׁ, (i), pt.; דַּל, (iii), a.
possess, to, יָרַשׁ, (15).
possession, אֲחֻזָּה, (i) f.; רְכוּשׁ, (i) m.
posterity, זֶרַע, (v), m.
Potiphar, פּוֹטִיפַר, pr. n.
pour, to, שָׁפַךְ, (13).
praise, to, הִלֵּל, (20), *Pi.*; יָדָה, (22), *Hiph.*
pray, to, [פלל], (21), *Hithp.*
prayer, תְּפִלָּה, (i), f.

precept, חֹק, (iii), see command.
preserve, to, שָׁמַר, (7).
priest, כֹּהֵן, (iv), m.
prisoner, אָסִיר, (ii), m.
profane, to, חָלַל, (20), *Pi.*
prophet, נָבִיא, (ii) m.
prophetess, נְבִיאָה, (ii), f.
prophesy, to, [נבא], *Hithp.*
proverb, מָשָׁל, (iv), m.
provoke, to, כָּעַס, (11), *Hiph.*
psalm, מִזְמוֹר, (i), m.
put to flight, נוּס, (21), *Hiph.*
put forth, to, שָׁלַח, (7).
put off, (shoes), נָשַׁל, (19).
put on, to, לָבֵשׁ, (7).

Q

Qish, קִישׁ, pr. n.
Qorah, קֹרַח, pr. n.
quake, to, רָעַשׁ, (21).
queen,, מַלְכָּה, (iii), f.

R

Ramah, הָרָמָה, pr. n.
raise, to, רוּם, (21), *Hiph.*
rebel, to, פָּשַׁע, (19); מָרַד, (17).
rebellious, to be, סָרַר, (20).
rebuke, [יכח], (15), *Hiph.*
receive, to, לָקַח, (15); [קבל], (23), *Pi.*
recount, to סָפַר, (8), *Pi.*
redeem, to, גָּאַל, (14).
redeemer, גֹּאֵל, (iv), pt.
refuse, to, [מאן], (9), *Pi.*
reign, to, מָלַךְ, (7).
reign, מַלְכוּת, (i), f.
reject, to, מָאַס, (8).
rejoice, to, שָׂמַח, שָׂמֵחַ, (10).
remain, to, [שאר], (11), *Niph.*
remember, to, זָכַר, (7).
remind, to, זָכַר, (7), *Hiph.*
remnant, נִשְׁאָר, (iv), pt.
remove, to, סוּר, (21), *Hiph*; רָחַק, (10), *Hiph.*
report, דָּבָר, (iv), m.
reprove, to, [יכח], (15), *Hiph.*
request, שְׁאֵלָה, (i), f.
require, to, [בקשׁ], (10), *Pi.*
rest, to, נוּחַ, (21); שָׁבַת, (7).
rest, יֶתֶר, (v), m.
restore, to, שָׁלֵם, (9), *Pi.*
return, to, שׁוּב, (21).
Reuben, רְאוּבֵן, pr. n.
reveal, to, גָּלָה, (18), *Pi.*
review, to be passed in, פָּקַד, (7), *Pu.*
ride, to, רָכַב, (9).
righteous, to be, צָדֵק, (7).
righteous, צַדִּיק, (i), a.
righteousnes, צְדָקָה, (iv), f.
rise, to, קוּם, (21).
rise early, to, [שׁכם], (14), *Hiph.*
river, נָהָר, (iv), m.; יְאֹר, (i), m.
roll, to, גָּלַל, (20).
rove about, to, שׁוּט, (22).
rule, to, מָשַׁל, (13).

S

Sabbath, שַׁבָּת, f. (m.).
sacrifice, to, זָבַח, (8).
sacrifice, זֶבַח, (v), m.; עֹלָה, (i), f.
saith (utterance), נְאֻם, (i), m.
salvation, יְשׁוּעָה, (ii), f.
Samaria, שֹׁמְרוֹן, pr. n.
Samson, שִׁמְשׁוֹן, pr. n.
Samuel, שְׁמוּאֵל, pr. n.
sanctify, to, קָדַשׁ, (7), *Hiph.*
sanctify oneself, to, קָדַשׁ, (7), *Hithp.*

sanctuary, מִקְדָּשׁ, (iv), m.; קֹדֶשׁ, (v), m.
Sarah, שָׂרָה, pr. n.
Satan, שָׂטָן, (iv), m.
Saul, שָׁאוּל, pr. n.
save, to, [ישע], (15), *Hiph.*
say, to, אָמַר, (15).
saying, אֹמֶר & אֵמֶר, (v, 15) m.
scatter (tr.), to, פּוּץ, (22), *Hiph.*
scorn, to, לִיץ, (21).
scorner, לֵץ, (i), pt.
sea, יָם, (iii), m.
see, to, רָאָה, (18).
seek, to, [בקשׁ], (10), *Pi.*
seek out, to, דָּרַשׁ, (9).
seize, to, אָחַז, (15).
sell, to, מָכַר; (23).
send, to, שָׁלַח, (7).
servant, עֶבֶד, (v), m.
serve, to, עָבַד, (9).
set, to, שִׁית, (21); שִׂים, שׂוּם, (21),
set out on a journey, to, נָסַע, (16).
set up, to, כּוּן, (21), *Hiph*; קוּם, (21), *Hiph.*
settle down, to שָׁכַן, (8).
severely, to act, [עלל], (20), *Po'el*,
shame, put to, בּוֹשׁ. (21), *Hiph.*
she-ass, אָתוֹן, (ii), f.
Sheba, שְׁבָא, pr. n.
sheep, צֹאן, (i), f. (m.).
shepherd, רֹעֶה, (vi), pt.; רֹעֵה צֹאן.
shoe, נַעַל, (v), m.
shout, to, [רוע], (24), *Hiph.*
silent, to be, חָרֵשׁ, (9), *Hiph.*
Siloah, שִׁלֹחַ, pr. n.
silver, כֶּסֶף, (v), m.
sin, to, חָטָא, (19),.
sin, חַטָּאת, (i), f.
sister אָחוֹת, (§ 260), f.
sit, to, יָשַׁב, (15).
slaughter, שָׁחַט, (8).
slay, to, הָרַג, (9).
sleep, to, יָשֵׁן, (15).
slip, off, נָשַׁל, (19).
small, to be, קָטֹן, (7).
small, קָטוֹן, (ii), a.; קָטָן, (iii), a.
smite, to, [נכה], (22), *Hiph.*
sojourn, to, גּוּר, (21).
sojourner, גֵּר, (i), m.
Solomon, שְׁלֹמֹה, pr. n.
son, בֵּן, (§ 260), m.
soul, נֶפֶשׁ, (v), f.
sound, קוֹל, וֹת . . (i), m.
sow, to, זָרַע, (13).
speak, to, דִּבֶּר, (7), *Pi.*
spirit, רוּחַ, (i), f. (m.).
splendor, הוֹד, (i), m.
stand, to, עָמַד, (7).
stand, to take one's stand, [נצב], (15), *Niph.*
standard, נֵס, (iii), m.
start early, [שׁכם], (14), *Hiph.*
start, to . . . on a journey, נָסַע, (16).
statute, מִצְוָה, see command.
steal, גָּנַב, (8).
stone, אֶבֶן, ־ִים, (v), f., (m.).
straight, to be, יָשַׁר, (15).
straight, יָשָׁר, (iv), a.
stranger, resident, גֵּר, (i), m.
stranger, strange, זָר. (i), pt.
strength, גְּבוּרָה, (ii), f.
stretch, to, נָטָה, (22).
strong, to be, גָּבַר, (18); חָזַק, (9).
strong, becoming . . ., חָזֵק, (iv) a.
strong, גִּבּוֹר, (i), a.
stumble, to, כָּשַׁל, (10).
stumbling-block, מִכְשׁוֹל, (i), m.
sun, שֶׁמֶשׁ, (v), f. & m.
support, צוּר, (i), m.
surround, סָבַב, (20).

survivor, שָׂרִיד, (ii), m.
swallow, to, בָּלַע, (14).
swallow down, to, בָּלַע, (14), *Pi.*
swear, to, שָׁבַע, (10), *Niph.*
swine, חֲזִיר, (i), m.
sword, חֶרֶב, (v), f.

T

Tablet, לוּחַ, וֹת . . . (i), m.
take, to, לָקַח, (15).
talent, כִּכָּר, (iv), m.
tarry, to, עָמַד, (7).
teach, to, לָמַד, (8), *Pi.*; יָרָה, (22), *Hiph.*
tear, to, קָרַע, (13).
tell, נָגַד, (16), *Hiph.*
tent, אֹהֶל, (v), m.
terrible, עָרִיץ, (i), a.; נוֹרָא, (i), pt.
testimonies, עֵדוֹת, (i), f. pl.
testimony, עֵדוּת, (i), f.
thing, דָּבָר, (iv), m.
thing devoted (to destruction), חֵרֶם, (v), m.
think, to, חָשַׁב, (10).
throne, כִּסֵּא, (iv), m.
time, עֵת, (iii), m.
tin, בְּדִיל, (i), m.
tongue, לָשׁוֹן, וֹת . . . (ii), m. & f.
tooth, שֵׁן, (iii), f. (m).
totter, to, נוּעַ, (21).
touch, to, נָגַע, (15).
transgress, to, עָבַר, (10).
treacherously, act or deal . . ., בָּגַד, (8).
tree, עֵץ, (iv), m.
tremble, נוּעַ, (21).
trumpet, שׁוֹפָר, (iv), m.
trust, to, בָּטַח, (8).
truth, אֱמֶת, (§ 260), f.
turn, גָּלַל, (20).
Tyre, צוֹר, pr. n.

U

Unclean, to be, טָמֵא, (19).
unclean, טָמֵא, (iv), a.
understand, בִּין, (21).
understanding, בִּינָה, (i), f.
uphold, to, סָמַךְ, (10).
upright, כֵּן, (i), a.; יָשָׁר, (iv), a.
uprightness, יֹשֶׁר, (v), m.
utterance (divine message), נְאֻם, m.
Urias, אוּרִיָּהוּ, pr. n.

V

Vale, valley, עֵמֶק, (v), m.
vanity, הֶבֶל, (v), m.
venison, צַיִד, (v), m.
virgin, בְּתוּלָה, (ii), f.
visit, to, פָּקַד, (7).
voice, קוֹל, וֹת . . (i), m.

W

Wages, שָׂכָר, (iv), m.
wait, to, [יחל], (22), *Niph.*
wander, תָּעָה, (18.
war, מִלְחָמָה, (v), f.
warm, to be, חָמַם, (23).
warn, to, [זהר] (14), *Hiph.*
warrior, גִּבּוֹר, (i), a.
watch, to, נָצַר, (15).
water, מַיִם, (§ 260), m.
water, to, [שקה], (18), *Hiph.*
way, אֹרַח, (v), m.; דֶּרֶךְ, (v), m. (f.).
weak, דַּל, (iii), a.
weary, to be, יָעֵף, (15).
weep, to, בָּכָה, (18).
well, בְּאֵר, וֹת . . . (i), f.

well, to be, טוֹב, (21); יָטַב, (15).
wicked, to be, רָשַׁע, (14).
wicked, רָשָׁע, (iv), a.
wickedness, רִשְׁעָה, (v), f.
widow, אַלְמָנָה, (iv), f.
wilderness, מִדְבָּר, (iv), m.
willing, to be, [יאל], (15), *Hiph.*
wisdom, חָכְמָה, (v), f.
wise חָכָם, (iv), a.
woman, wife, אִשָּׁה, (§ 260), f.
wonderful, נוֹרָא, (i), pt.
wonderful things, נִוֹרָאוֹת, (i), f.
word, דָּבָר, (iv), m.
work, to, עָבַד, (9), עָשָׂה, (18).
work, פֹּעַל, (v), m.; מַעֲשֶׂה, (vi), m.
write, to, כָּתַב, (8).

Y

Young man, נַעַר, (v), m.; בָּחוּר, (ii, 5), m.; עֶלֶם, (v), m.
yoke, צֶמֶד, (v), m.
youth, נְעוּרִים, (ii), m. pl.
year, שָׁנָה, { ־ִים / וֹת } (vi), f.

Z

Zadok, צָדוֹק, pr. n.

INDEX OF HEBREW WORDS.

Proper names, adverbs and prepositions (Lesson xvii), ccnjunctions (Lesson xxii), and numerals (Lesson xxiv) are not included in this Index. The Arabic figures refer to the Lessons; letters refer to the Paradigms).

א

אָב § 260
אָבַד 15
אֶבְיוֹן 3
אֶבֶן 16
אָדוֹן 5
אַדִּיר 19
אָדָם 11
אֲדָמָה 13
אָהַב 15
אֹהֶל 16
[אוה] 23
אֱוִיל 4
אוֹצָר 11
אוֹר 3
מָאוֹר
אוֹת 17
אָח § 260
אֶחָד § 260
אָחַז 15
אֲחֻזָּה 23
אָחוֹת § 260
אִי § 264, 20
אָיַב § 445
אֹיֵב E
אַיִל 15
אִישׁ § 260
אָכַל 15
מַאֲכָל
אֹכֶל 19
אָכְלָה 19
אַלּוּף 13
אַלְמָנָה 11
אֵם D
אָמָה § 260
אָמַן 9
נֶאֱמָן
אֱמֶת § 260
אָמַר 15
אֹמֶר } 15
אֵמֶר } 15
אִמְרָה 15
[אנה] 22
אֱנוֹשׁ 14
אָנַף 17
אָסִיר 5
אָסַף 8
[אפק] 15
אֵפֶר 24
אַרְבֶּה 22
אֲרוֹן 4
אֶרֶז 21
אֹרַח 17
אֲרִי } 17
אַרְיֵה } 17
אֹרֶךְ 24
אָרֵךְ, אָרַךְ 17
אֶרֶץ 12, § 118
אָרַר 20
אֵשׁ 13
אִשָּׁה § 260
אָשַׁם } 20
אָשֵׁם } 20
אָשָׁם 20
אָשַׁר 17
אַשְׁרֵי 17
אָתוֹן 5

ב

בְּאֵר 6
בָּגַד 8
בֶּגֶד 12
בַּד 11
בְּדִיל 2
בְּהֵמָה § 260
בּוֹא 21
בּוֹשׁ 21
בָּחוּר 5
בָּחַר 7
בָּטַח 8
בֶּטֶן 24
בִּין 21
בִּינָה 1
בַּיִת § 260
בָּכָה 18
בְּכוֹר 2
בָּלַע 14
בָּמָה 6
בֵּן § 260
בָּנָה 18
בָּעָה 21
בָּעַר 10
בָּקָר 14
בֹּקֶר 12
[בקשׁ] 10
בַּר 21
בָּרָא 19
בָּרַח 17
בָּרִיא 23
בְּרִית 2
בָּרַךְ 7
בְּרָכָה 11
בְּרֵכָה 11
בָּשָׂר 23
בַּת § 260
בְּתוּלָה 5

ג

גָּאַל 14
גֹּאֵל 11
גָּבַהּ 23
גָּבֹהַּ 23
גְּבוּל 2
גִּבּוֹר 1
גְּבוּרָה 6
גָּבַר 18
גֶּבֶר 23
גָּדוֹל 5
גְּדִי F
גָּדַל 7

גָּדֵל 13
גּוֹי 3
גּוּר 21
גּוֹרָל 14
גָּזַז 24
גָּזַל 9
גֻּלְגֹּלֶת F
גָּלָה 18
גָּלַל 20
גְּמוּל 10
גְּמוּלָה 10
גָּמַל 14
גָּמָל D
גָּנַב 8
גֵּר 1

ד

דָּבַק 9
דָּבַר 7
מִדְבָּר
דָּבָר E
דֶּבֶר 17
דּוֹר 13
דַּי 21
דִּין 21
דִּין 12
דַּל 13
דָּלַק 19
דֶּלֶת 20
דָּם § 296, 13
דְּמוּת 17
דִּמְעָה 13
דַּעַת 18
דָּרַךְ 9
דֶּרֶךְ 13
דָּרַשׁ 9

ה

הֶבֶל 12
הוֹד 3
הָלַךְ 15
הָלַל 20
הָמָה 21
הָמוֹן 16
הָפַךְ 14
הַר § 260
הָרַג 9
הָרַס 13

ז

זָבַח 8
מִזְבֵּחַ
זֶבַח 14
זֵד 2
זָהָב 14
[זהר] 15
זַיִת F
זָכַר 7
זָכָר 19
זָמַר 17
מִזְמוֹר
זָעַק 16
זְעָקָה 16
זָקֵן E
זָר 1
זְרוֹעַ 9
זָרַע 13
זֶרַע 12
זָרַק 24

ח

[חבא] 19
[חבה] 19
חָבַל 17
חָבַק 17
חָבֵר 14
חָבַשׁ 8
חַג § 118
חָגַג 20
חָגַר 17
חָדַל 10
חֹדֶשׁ 12
חֲזִיר 3
חָזַק 9
חָזֵק 13
חָטָא 19
חַטָּאת 19
חַי 16
חַיָּה 17
חַיִּים 16
חַיִל 12
חֵיק 12
חָכָם E
חָכְמָה 12
חֵלֶב 16
חֲלוֹם 16
חֳלִי F
חָלִילָה 17
חָלַל 20
חָלַם 16
חָלַץ 14
חָלַק 14
חֵלֶק 14
חָם § 260
חָמַד 13
חֵמָה 22
חֲמוֹר 5
חָמַל 17
חָמַס 23
חָמֵס 17
חָמָס 24
חֵמֶר 23
חָנַט 24
חֵן 22
חָנַן 20
חָסָה 23
חָסִיד 5
חָסֵר 16
חָפֵץ 13
חֵפֶץ 13
חָפַר 20
חָצָה 24
חק D
חֻקָּה 3, D
חָקַר 17
חֹרֶב 12
חֶרֶב 12
חָרְבָּה F
חָרָבָה 3
חָרַד 19
חָרָה 18
חֹרֶט 18
חַרְטֹם 23
[חרם] 19
חֵרֶם 19
חֶרְפָּה 17
חָרַשׁ 9
חָרָשׁ 22
חֹרֶשׁ 24
חָשַׁךְ 17
חָשַׁב 10
חָשָׁה 18
חֹשֶׁךְ 17
חָשַׁךְ 17

ט

טָבַח 16
טָהַר 10
טוֹב 21
טוּב 1
טוֹבָה 9
טָמֵא 19
טָמֵא 11
טָעַם 23
טַף 23
טָרַף 17

י

[יאל] 15
יְאֹר 1
יָבֵשׁ 15
יָבֵשׁ 18
יַבָּשָׁה 18

יָגַע 15
יָד § 296, G
יָדָה 22
יָדַע 15
יוֹם § 260
יוֹנֶקֶת F
יָחִיד 13
[יחל] 22
יָטַב 15
יַיִן 12
יָכֹל 15
[יכח] 15
יָלַד 16
יֶלֶד 16
(יָלַךְ) 15
יָם § 261, D
יָמִין 15
יָסַף 15
יָסַר 15
מוּסָר
יָעַד 24
מוֹעֵד
יָעֵף 15
יָעַץ 15
יַעַר 21
יָפֶה 23
יָצָא 22
[יצב] 15
יָצַר 15
יֵצֶר 11
יָקַץ 15
יָרֵא 22
יִרְאָה 2
יָרַד 15
יָרָה 22
תּוֹרָה
יָרַשׁ 15
יָשַׁב 15
יְשׁוּעָה 6
יָשֵׁן 15
[ישע] 15
יָשַׁר 15
יָשָׁר 11
יֹשֶׁר 17
יָתוֹם 9
יָתַר 23
יֶתֶר 12

כ

כְּאֵב 24
כָּבֵד 7
כָּבֵד 11
כָּבוֹד 5
כָּבַשׁ 8
כֶּבֶשׂ 16
כֹּהֵן E
כּוּן 21
כֵּן 1
כּוֹס 1
כָּזָב 10
כִּכָּר 20
כָּלָא 19
כֶּלֶב 17
כָּלָה 19
כַּלָּה 19
כְּלִי § 260
כֵּן 1
[כנע] 23
כָּנָף E
כִּסֵּא 11
כָּסָה 18
כְּסִיל 2
כֶּסֶף 14
כָּעַס 11
כַּעַס 16
כַּף D
[כפר] 14
כַּר 20
כְּרוּב 23
כֶּרֶם 17
כָּרַת 8
כָּשַׁל 10
מִכְשׁוֹל
כָּתַב 8
כְּתֹנֶת, כֻּתֹּנֶת 19
כָּתַת 20

ל

לְאֹם D
לֵב 11
לֵבָב E
לָבָן 23
לְבוּשׁ 2
לָבֵשׁ 7
לוּחַ 4
לֵוִי D
לוּן, לִין 21
מָלוֹן
לָהַט 23
לְחִי 22
לָחַם 8
מִלְחָמָה
לֶחֶם 12
לִיץ 21
לָכַד 10
לָמַד 8
לֵץ 15
לָקַח 15
לֶקַח 13
לָשׁוֹן 20

מ

מָאוֹר 20
מַאֲכָל 19
[מאן] 9
מָאַס 8
מַבּוּל 23
[מגן] 16
מִדְבָּר 16
מַדּוּעַ 15
[מהר] 8
מוֹלֶדֶת 17
מוּסָר 11
מוֹעֵד 14
מוּת 21
מָוֶת F
מִזְבֵּחַ 11
מִזְמוֹר 1
מְחִיר 17
מַחֲנֶה 14
מַטֶּה 22
מִטָּה 1
מַיִם 260
מִישׁוֹר 16
מֵישָׁרִים 16
מָכַר 23
מִכְשׁוֹל 2
מְכַשֵּׁף 23
מָלֵא 19
מַלְאָךְ 11
מְלָאכָה 12
מָלוֹן 21
מִלְחָמָה F
[מלט] 10
מָלַךְ 7
מֶלֶךְ F
מַלְכָּה F
מְלוּכָה 6
מַלְכוּת 6
מַמְלָכָה 12
מִן § 261, 23
מָנָה 20, 24
מְנוֹרָה 1
מִסְפָּר 11
מַסֵּכָה 18
מַעְגָּל 17
מְעַט 11
מְעִיל 24
מַעֲלָל 22

מְעָרָה 19
מַעֲשֶׂה 24
מָצָא 19
מַצֵּבָה 24
מְצוּדָה 10
מִצְוָה 1
מִקְדָּשׁ 14
מָקוֹם 5
מִקְנֶה 12
מְרַגֵּל 24
מָרַד 17
מָרָה 22
מָרוֹם 15
מַר 15
מְרִיא 16
מָרַר 20
מָשׂוֹשׂ 23
מָשַׁח 8
מָשַׁךְ 13
מָשַׁל 13
מָשָׁל 11
מִשְׁמָר 23
מִשְׁפָּחָה 12
מַשְׁקֶה 14
מִשְׁתֶּה 14
[מַת] 23
מֵת 1

נ

נְאֻם 8
נֶאֱמָן 13
נָבִיא 5
[נבט] 15
נָבַל 15
נָבָל 24
נֵבֶל 15
נְבֵלָה E
נֶגֶב 16
[נגד] 16
נָגִיד 16
נָגַע 15
נֶגַע 16
נָגַשׂ 15
נָגַשׁ 15
נָדִיב 23
נָדַד 24
נָהַג 22
נָהָר 23
נוּד 24
נוּחַ 21
נוּם 21
נוּעַ 21
נוֹרָא 4
נָחַל 17
נַחֲלָה 17
נַחַל 17
[נחם] 24
נָחָשׁ 21
נָטָה 22
נָטַע 15
[נכה] 22
[נכר] 19
נֵכָר 16
נָכְרִי 16
נֵס 21
נָסַע 16
נַעַל F, 12
נָעִים 19
נַעַר F
נְעוּרִים 13
נָפַח 22
נָפַל 15
נָפַץ 22
נֶפֶשׁ 14
[נצב] 15
נֶצַח, נֵצַח 12
[נצל] 16
נָצַר 15
נְקֵבָה 19
נָקֹד 11
נָקִי 11
נָקַף 22
נֵר 6
נָשָׂא 22
נָשִׂיא 10
נָשָׁא 22
נִשְׁאַר 11
נָשַׁל 19
נְתִיבָה 2
נָתַן 15
נָתַץ 17

ס

סָבַב 20
סָגַר 8
סוּג, שׂוּג 21
סוּס 1
סוּסָה 1
סוּר 21
[סות] 24
סֻכָּה 2
סָבַל 19
סָלַח 10
סָמַךְ 10
סָפַר 8
מִסְפָּר
סֵפֶר F
סָקַל 16
סָרִיס 16
סָרַר 20
[סתר] 15

ע

עָב 3
עָבַד 9
עֶבֶד 13
עֲבוֹדָה 21
עָבַר 10
עֵגֶל 18
עַד § 260
עֵד 3
עֵדָה 21
עֵדוּת 3
עֵדוּת 4
עֵדֶר 23
עָוָה 21
עוֹלָם E
עָוֹן 14
עוֹף 17
עוּר 23
עוֹר 24
עָזַב 8
עָזַר 9
עֵזֶר 12
עֶזְרָה F
עָטָה 22
עֲטָרָה 16
עַי § 264
עַיִן F
עִיר § 260
עֵירֹם 24
עָלָה 18
עֹלָה 3
עֶלְיוֹן 3
[עלל] 20
עִם § 118, D
עָמַד 7
עַמּוּד 13
עָמֹק 11
עֵמֶק 23
עָנָה 18
עָנִי 11
עָפָר 16
עֵץ 11
עֵצָה 16
עֶצֶם 24
עָצֵל 20
עָקֵב 16

עֶרֶב 19
עָרִיץ 3
עָרַךְ 19
עֵרֶךְ 19
עָרֹם 24
עָשָׂה 18
עָשִׁיר 9
עָשַׁק 9
עֹשֶׁר 15
עֵת 11
עַתּוּד 15
עָתֵק 23

פ

[פאר] 16
תִּפְאָרָה
פָּגַע 16
פֶּה 6
פּוּחַ 22
פּוּץ 22
[פלא] 23
פָּלַט 10
[פלל] 21
תְּפִלָּה
פִּנָּה 22
פָּנִים 13
פֹּעַל F
פָּקַד 7
פְּקֻדָּה D
פִּקּוּדִים 2
פַּר D, § 118
פֶּרֶד 20
פָּרָה D
פְּרִי F
פָּרַע 17
פָּרַץ 18
פָּרַר 20
פַּר
פָּרָה
פָּשַׁט 24
פָּשַׁע 19
פֶּשַׁע 19
פַּת § 264
פָּתַח 9
פֶּתַח 16

צ

צֹאן 4
צָבָא 11
צַדִּיק 1
צָדֵק 7
צֶדֶק 23
צְדָקָה E
צוּד 22
צַיִד 22
[צוה] 18
מִצְוָה
צוּר 6
צָחַק 14
צִי § 264
צִיר 20
צָלַח, צָלֵחַ 13
צֶלֶם 17
צֶמֶד 24
צָעַד 14
צַעַד 14
צָעַק 16
צְעָקָה 16
צָפָה 19
צַר 16
צָרָה 16
צָרַח 16
צָרַע 22
צָרַעַת 22
צָרַר 20
צָרָה, צַר

ק

[קבל] 23
קָבַץ 10
קָבַר 9
קֶבֶר 12
קָדִים 22
קֶדֶם 22
קָדְקֹד § 265
קָדוֹשׁ 5
קָדַשׁ 7
קֹדֶשׁ F
קָהָל 16
קָוָה 18
קוֹל 6
קוּם 21
מָקוֹם
קוֹמָה 15
קוּץ 22
קָטוֹן 11
קָטֹן 7
קָטָן 11
[קטר] 8
קְטֹרֶת 12
[קיץ] 22
קַל 20
קָלָה 22
קָלַל 20
[קנא] 19
קָנָה 19
קִנֵּן 16
קֵץ 23
קָצֶה 23
קָצָה 23
קָצִיר 16
קָצַץ 23
קָצַר 13
קָרָא 19
קָרַב, קָרֵב 10
קֶרֶב 22
קָרְבָּן 20
קָרוֹב 17
קָרָה 19
קָרַע 13
קָשַׁב 9
קָשָׁה 18
קָשַׁר 16
קֶשֶׁר 16

ר

רָאָה 18
רֹאֶה 12
רֹאשׁ § 260
רִאשׁוֹן 6
רֵאשִׁית 3
רַב 11
רֹב 17
רָבַב 20
רָבָה 18
רֶגֶל F
רָגַם 16
רָדַף 17
רוּחַ 3
רָוַח 23
רוּם 21
מָרוֹם
תְּרוּמָה
[רוע] 24
רוּץ 24
רָחַב 24
רֹחַב 24
רָחוֹק 24
רָחַם 20
רֶחֶם 12
רַחֲמִים 12
רָחַץ 10
רָחַק 10
רִיב 17
רָבַב 9
רֶכֶב 24
רְכוּשׁ 14
רָם 3

13 רִנָּה
§ 296 רֵעַ
14 רַע
23 רָעָב
G רֹעֶה
18 רָעָה
14 רָעָה
20 רָעַע
21 רָעַשׁ
21 רַ֫עַשׁ
19 רָפָא
24 רֹפֵא
19 רָפָה
20 רָשׁ
14 רָשַׁע
14 רָשָׁע
14 רֶ֫שַׁע
14 רִשְׁעָה

שׂ

16 שָׂבֵעַ / שָׂבַע
23 שָׂבָע
23 שֹׂבַע
G שָׂדֶה
§ 260 שֶׂה
21 שׂוּם / שִׂים
23 שׂוּשׂ / שִׂישׂ
שָׂשׂוֹן
מָשׂוֹשׂ
14 שָׂחַק
17 שָׂטָן
13 שָׂכַל
17 שָׂכִיר
17 שָׂכַר
17 שָׂכָר
15 שְׂמֹאול
10 שָׂמַח
13 שָׂמֵחַ
13 שִׂמְחָה
19 שָׂנֵא
G, 23 שָׂפָה
11 שָׂרִיד
10 שָׂרַף
23 שָׂשׂוֹן

שׁ

8 שָׁאַל
E שְׁאֵלָה
11 [שׁאר]
18 שְׁבָה
24 שֵׁבֶט
24 שָׁבוּעַ
10 [שׁבע]
9 שָׁבַר
7 שָׁבַת
21 שׁוּב
22 שׁוּט
24 שׁוֹפָר
12 שׁוֹר
18 שָׁחָה
20 שָׁחַח
8 שָׁחַט
24 שַׁ֫חַר
8 [שׁחת]
21 שִׁיר
23 שִׁיר
21 שִׁית
7 שָׁכַב
8 שָׁכַח
16 שָׁכֹל / שָׁכַל
14 [שׁכם]
23 שְׁכֶם
8 שָׁכַן
24 שָׁכֵן
10 שָׁכַר
9 שָׁלוֹם
7 שָׁלַח
9 [שׁלך]
9 שָׁלֵם
16 שָׁלֵם
9 שָׁלַם
§ 260 שֵׁם
§ 260 שָׁמַ֫יִם
20 שָׁמֵם
7 שָׁמַע
7 שָׁמַר
23 שֶׁ֫מֶשׁ
D שֵׁן
24 שָׁנָה
24 שֵׁנָה
G שָׁנָה
19 שָׁעָה
16 שַׁ֫עַר
7 שָׁפַט
E שֹׁפֵט
13 שָׁפַךְ
18 [שׁקה]
מַשְׁקֶה
16 שֶׁ֫קֶר
10 [שׁרת]
18 שָׁתָה

ת

15 תְּאֵנָה
11 תּוּגָה
12 תָּוֶךְ
11 תּוֹלְדוֹת
11 תּוֹעֵבָה
1 תּוֹרָה
19 תְּחוּם
2 תְּחִלָּה
2 תִּירוֹשׁ
22 תָּם
23 תֹּם
23 תֻּמָּה
15 תָּמִים
10 תָּמַךְ
20 תָּמַם
17 תֹּ֫מֶר / תָּמָר
18 תָּעָה
16 תִּפְאָרָה
1 תְּפִלָּה
14 תָּפַשׂ
24 תָּקַע
21 תְּרוּמָה

LOGICAL INDEX.

(References are given to Paragraphs).

Part. I. **Orthography and Orthoëpy.**

(For this part, the order given in the Table of Contents is sufficiently logical; and the Student can follow it as it is).

Part. II. **Morphology.**

I. *Article.*

A. Ordinary form 87
B. With Gutturals . . . . 112—113

II. *Pronouns.*

A. Personal Pronouns (Paradigm A).
1. Separate Pronouns 143
2. Nominal Suffixes . . . . 150—156
3. Verbal Suffixes . . . . 315—334
B. Demonstrative Pronouns 149, 402
C. Relative Pronouns 122, 123, 408
D. Interrogative Pronouns . . . . 413—416
E. Indefinite Pronouns . . . . 440—441

III. *Nouns* (Substantives and Adjectives).

A. Gender . . . . 81—82
B. Number . . . . 83—85
C. Remnant of Accusative Case . . . . 363—364
D. Construct State . . . . 96—99
E. Flection
1. Previous Remarks
a) Changeable and Unchangeable Vowels . . . . 127—133
b) Rules for Nominal Flection . . . . 134—135
c) Various Classes of Nouns 140
2. Various Classes in particular
a) Class I 141
b) Class II 142
c) Class III . . . . 261—266
d) Class IV . . . . 267—275

e) Class V . . . . 276—295
f) Class VI . . . . 296—297
g) Unclassified Nouns 260
F. Numerals . . . . 505—510

IV. *Verbs.*

Preliminary Remarks: Radicals. Classification. Modifications of Fundamental Idea. Formations and Stems. Remarks on the Various Stems. Tenses Modes . . . . 163—174
Rules for Verbal Flection . . . . 136—139

I. Strong Verb.

A. Regular (Paradigm I)
1. Perfect
a) Indicative . . . . 175—188
b) Infinitive Absolute . . . . 193—194
2. Imperfect
a) Infinitive Construct . . . . 201—207
b) Imperative . . . . 215—218
c) Indicative . . . . 219—225
d) Jussive . . . . 233—234
e) Cohortative 232
f) Participles . . . . 298—303
3. *Waw Consecutivum* with Perf. and Imperfect Indicative . . . . 243—248
B. Strong Verb with Gutturals
1. First Guttural (Parad. J) 181, 182, 194, 204, 217, 224
2. Second Gutt. (Parad. K) 183, 188
3. Third Gutt. (Parad. L) 193, 203
C. Verbs with Pronominal Suffixes (Parad. M) 318—326, 331—333

II. Weak Verb.

A. Verbs *Pe-Aleph* (Parad. R) . . . . 336—337
B. Verbs *Pe-Nun* (Parad. N) . . . . 338—342
C. Verbs *Pe-Yodh* (Paradigms O, P, Q) . . . 343—351
D. Verbs *Lamedh-He* (Parad. S) . . . . 390—401
E. Verbs *Lamedh-Aleph* (Parad. T) . . . . . 409—412
F. Verbs *'Ayin-'Ayin* (Parad. U) . . . . 427—439
G. Verbs *'Ayin-Waw* & *'Ayin-Yodh* (Parad. V, W) . . . . 445—456
H. Verbs doubly Weak 463
I. Relations of Weak Verbs to one another 464
J. Defective Verbs 465
K. Less common Formations 466

V. *Particles.*

A. Prepositions . . . . 108—111; 369—380
B. Adverbs . . . . 124—126; 383—389
C. Conjunctions . . . . 88, 468—478

Part. III. **Syntax.**

I. Syntax of the *Article* 89, 90, 502

II. Syntax of the *Pronouns.*

A. Personal Pronouns.
1. Separate Pronouns . . . . 144—149
2. Nominal Suffixes . . . . 157—162
3. Verbal Suffixes . . . . 327—333
B. Demonstrative Pronouns . . . . 403—408
C. Relative Pronouns 122, 123, 408
D. Interrogative Pronouns 420
E. Indefinite Pronouns . . . . 440—443
F. Substitutes for Pronouns 444

III. Syntax of the *Noun.*

A. Various Meanings of the Plural 84
B. Repetition of Nouns and Phrases . . . . 488—492
C. Determination of the Noun 104, 117
D. Use of the Construct State . . . . 100—105
E. Expression of the Genitive by Circumlocution . . 106—107
F. Apposition . . . . 479—487
G. IV. Syntax of the *Adjective* . . . . . . 91, 92, 493—496
H. V. Syntax of the *Numeral* . . . . . . 511—529

VI. Syntax of the *Verb.*

A. Use of Tenses (?) and Modes.
1. Use of Perfect:
a) Indicative . . . . 189—192
b) Infinitive absolute . . . . 195—199
2. Use of Imperfect:
a) Indicative . . . . 226—231
b) Imperative, Jussive, Cohortative . . . . 235—237
c) Infinitive Construct . . . . 208—214
d) Participles . . . . 304—314
B. Use of *Waw Copulativum* . . . . 238—242
C. Use of *Waw Consecutivum* . . . . 249—260
D. Government of the Verb.
1. Direct Object . . . . 117, 352—354
2. Double Accusative . . . . 355—358

3. Object of a Passive Verb . . . . 359—360
4. Adverbial Modifiers . . . . 361—368
5. Use of Prepositions after verb . . 369—376, 381, 382

VII. The *Sentence.*

A. The Sentence in General.
1. Nominal Sentence . . . . 93—95
2. Verbal Sentence . . . . 114—117
3. Agreement between the various Members of a Sentence, especially between Subject and Predicate, in regard to Gender and Number 91, 116
4. The *Casus Pendens* 146, 307, 372, 487

B. Special Kinds of Sentences.
1. Interrogative Sentence . . . . . 389, 417—426
2. Negative Sentence 124, 126, 212, 234, 242, 388
3. Relative Clause . . . . 107, 122, 123, 231, 307, 497—504
4. Circumstantial Clause 115, 258, 310
5. Object Clause . . . . 457—462
6. Causal Clause . . . . 210, 211 β, 240—242, 253, 257, 469, 474
7. Conditional Clause . . . . 227, d, 240—242, 253, 257, 310, 469, 475
8. Final Clause . . . . 211 α; 228, 240—242, 469, 471
9. Concessive Clause . . . . 240—242, 253, 257, 310, 469, 473
10. Comparative Clause 469, 476
11. Disjunctive Clause . . . . 468, 2 & 5
12. Adversative Clause 468, 3
13. Temporal Clause . . . . 209, 228, 240—242, 253, 257, 310, 470
14. Exclamatory Sentence with מָה, אֵיךְ or אֵיכָה . . . . 227, c, 389, 420
15. Sentences expressing Oath and Asseveration 477
16. Desiderative Sentence . . . . . 227, b; 235—237, 239, 478

www.ingramcontent.com/pod-product-compliance
Lightning Source LLC
Chambersburg PA
CBHW071428150426
43191CB00008B/1072
9781606083482